1895

Edinburgh Critical Studies in Victorian Culture

Series Editor: Julian Wolfreys

Volumes available in the series:

In Lady Audley's Shadow: Mary Elizabeth Braddon and Victorian Literary Genres
Saverio Tomaiuolo
978 0 7486 4115 4   Hbk

Blasted Literature: Victorian Political Fiction and the Shock of Modernism
Deaglán Ó Donghaile
978 0 7486 4067 6   Hbk

William Morris and the Idea of Community: Romance, History and Propaganda, 1880–1914
Anna Vaninskaya
978 0 7486 4149 9   Hbk

1895: Drama, Disaster and Disgrace in Late Victorian Britain
Nicholas Freeman
978 0 7486 4056 0   Hbk

Visit the Edinburgh Critical Studies in Victorian Culture web page at www.euppublishing.com/series/ecve

Also available:
Victoriographies – A Journal of Nineteenth-Century Writing, 1790–1914, edited by Julian Wolfreys
ISSN: 2044–2416

www.eupjournals.com/vic

1895

Drama, Disaster and Disgrace in Late Victorian Britain

Nicholas Freeman

Edinburgh University Press

© Nicholas Freeman, 2011

Transferred to digital print 2012

Edinburgh University Press Ltd
22 George Square, Edinburgh

www.euppublishing.com

Typeset in 10.5/13 Sabon
by Servis Filmsetting Ltd, Stockport, Cheshire, and
printed and bound in Great Britain by
CPI Group (UK) Ltd, Croydon, CR0 4YY

A CIP record for this book is available from the British Library

ISBN 978 0 7486 4056 0 (hardback)

The right of Nicholas Freeman
to be identified as author of this work
has been asserted in accordance with
the Copyright, Designs and Patents Act 1988.

Contents

Illustrations   vii

Series Editor's Preface   ix

Acknowledgements   xi

Abbreviations   xiii

Into the Past: A Brief Foreword   1

Winter: 15 September 1894 – 28 February 1895   7
  Changes in the Weather   7
  Punching the Pimp   11
  Artificial Flowers and Strange Perfumes   13
  On the Prowl   20
  Death in Kensington   24
  Christmas Lists and Resolutions   29
  Decorative Salaciousness   36
  A Man's Game   42
  First (K)nights   44
  Changes for the Worse   54
  Renewing Hostilities   58
  Women Who Did   63
  Trivial Comedy, Serious People   69
  Notes   73

Spring: 1 March 1895 – 30 May 1895   75
  Degenerate Days, Lugubrious Psychologists   76
  The Tooting Tragedy   83
  Freezing Footballs   85

Blazing Bibles   87
Irish Affairs   92
A Wretched Band of Youths   97
Panic in Vigo Street   102
Up Against It   106
A Grand Day Out   110
Wilde on Trial   112
Problem Pictures   118
Jabez and Oscar   124
Rosebery Returns   133
Notes   136

Summer: 1 June 1895 – 31 August 1895   137
Dandy in the Underworld   137
Elevation and Excoriation   141
Flaming June   146
Rosebery Resigns   147
The Noble Game   151
A Dreadful Business   156
En Vacances   164
Summer Gleanings   171
Notes   174

Autumn into Winter: 1 September 1895 – 31 December 1895   175
Revolting Ladies   176
Welling Up   179
Silver and Rubies   181
Trilbymania   185
Ave Satani!   189
Far From Dear Father   196
Exit Jabez   199
Jude the Obscene   200
An Epidemic of Indecency   205
Endings   207
Notes   214

Bibliography   215

Index   228

Illustrations

1. 'Decadent Guys' Lord Raggie Tattersall and Fustian Flitters ponder the dandyism of Guy Fawkes. *Punch*, 10 November 1894.   17

2. Mrs Prowlina Pry hopes she doesn't intrude; *Punch*'s acerbic view of Laura Ormiston Chant's campaign against immorality in music halls, 27 October 1894.   23

3. Guy Domville (George Alexander) and Mrs Peverel (Marion Terry) share an intimate moment in Henry James's lavishly staged drama. *Illustrated London News*, 12 January 1895.   51

4. The fierce winter brought Arctic conditions to Liverpool, with the Mersey having to be kept open by icebreakers. *Illustrated London News*, 23 February 1895.   62

5. The notorious Agnes Ebbsmith (Mrs Patrick Campbell) pleads with the Duke of St Olpherts (John Hare), dressed in what Shaw called 'a horrifying confection apparently made of Japanese bronze wallpaper'. *Illustrated London News*, 6 April 1895.   90

6. A dramatic moment in the Cup Final vividly captured by H.M. Paget, as WBA's Tom Higgins (foreground) and Villa's John Devey collide. *Graphic*, 27 April 1895.   111

7. The *Illustrated Police News*'s memorable image of the finale of Wilde's first trial, 4 May 1895.   119

8. W.F. Yeames's unsolved riddle, the enigmatic *Defendant and Counsel*.   123

9. The defeated Rosebery beside the bonfire of his hopes, *Punch* 3 August 1895.   152

10. The *Illustrated Police News* treated the Plaistow Murder with characteristic insensitivity, 27 July 1895.   159

11. The bare-footed Trilby O' Ferrall (Dorothea Baird) serenades
    Svengali (Herbert Beerbohm Tree) with 'Don't
    you remember sweet Alice, Ben Bolt?' *Illustrated London
    News* 21 September.   186
12. The 'picturesque' but defiant Edith Lanchester.   197

Series Editor's Preface

'Victorian' is a term, at once indicative of a strongly determined concept and, simultaneously, an often notoriously vague notion, emptied of all meaningful content by the many journalistic misconceptions that persist about the inhabitants and cultures of the British Isles and Victoria's Empire in the nineteenth-century. As such, it has become a by-word for the assumption of various, often contradictory habits of thought, belief, behaviour and perceptions. Victorian studies and studies in nineteenth-century literature and culture have, from their institutional inception, questioned narrowness of presumption, pushed at the limits of the nominal definition, and have sought to question the very grounds on which the unreflective perception of the so-called Victorian has been built; and so they continue to do. Victorian and nineteenth-century studies of literature and culture maintain a breadth and diversity of interest, of focus and inquiry, in an interrogative and intellectually open-minded and challenging manner, which are equal to the exploration and inquisitiveness of its subjects. Many of the questions asked by scholars and researchers of the innumerable productions of nineteenth-century society actively put into suspension the clichés and stereotypes of 'Victorianism', whether the approach has been sustained by historical, scientific, philosophical, empirical, ideological or theoretical concerns; indeed, it would be incorrect to assume that each of these approaches to the idea of the Victorian has been, or has remained, in the main exclusive, sealed off from the interests and engagements of other approaches. A vital interdisciplinarity has been pursued and embraced, for the most part, even as there has been contest and debate amongst Victorianists, pursued with as much fervour as the affirmative exploration between different disciplines and differing epistemologies put to work in the service of reading the nineteenth century.

Edinburgh Critical Studies in Victorian Culture aims to take up both the debates and the inventive approaches and departures from convention that studies in the nineteenth century have witnessed for the last half century at least. Aiming to maintain a 'Victorian' (in the most positive sense of that motif) spirit of inquiry, the series' purpose is to continue and augment the cross-fertilization of interdisciplinary approaches, and to offer, in addition, a number of timely and untimely revisions of Victorian literature, culture, history and identity. At the same time, the series will ask questions concerning what has been missed or improperly received, misread, or not read at all, in order to present a multi-faceted and heterogeneous kaleidoscope of representations. Drawing on the most provocative, thoughtful and original research, the series will seek to prod at the notion of the 'Victorian', and in so doing, principally through theoretically and epistemologically sophisticated close readings of the historicity of literature and culture in the nineteenth century, to offer the reader provocative insights into a world that is at once overly familiar, and irreducibly different, other and strange. Working from original sources, primary documents and recent interdisciplinary theoretical models, Edinburgh Critical Studies in Victorian Culture seeks not simply to push at the boundaries of research in the nineteenth century, but also to inaugurate the persistent erasure and provisional, strategic redrawing of those borders.

Julian Wolfreys

Acknowledgements

I have incurred a number of debts in the writing of this study and would like to record my thanks to the following people and organisations. Julian Wolfreys, the editor of this series, encouraged my original idea and provided much appreciated support throughout. At Edinburgh University Press, Jackie Jones showed why academics hold her in such esteem – I am particularly grateful for her patience concerning word counts and picture rights. Loughborough University's Research Leave Scheme provided a semester of vital teaching relief, without which the book would not have been finished. The Department of English and Drama at Loughborough made a much appreciated contribution to image reproduction expenses; Phil Wilson and Jagjit Samra of the university's Design and Print Services worked wonders with my mouldy old magazines. The university's library staff provided invaluable support in tracking down errant volumes.

Outside the East Midlands, I would like to thank Stephen Homer and Frances Pond, the archivists at Birmingham City University, for their help in guiding me through John Lane's papers. Julia Carver, Collections Officer of Bristol City Museums and Art Gallery, was far more helpful and courteous than the barristers in W.F. Yeames' *Defendant and Counsel*. Further gratitude is due to librarians at the British Library, Birmingham University, Bristol City Reference Library, Bristol University, Bath Spa University, the Brotherton Library Leeds University, and the University of the West of England.

For permission to quote from the Lane papers, I would like to thank the Harry Ransom Center, Texas. Images from the *Illustrated London News* are reproduced courtesy of the Mary Evans Picture Library – many thanks to Tess Hines for her help in locating these. H.M. Paget's sketch of the 1895 FA Cup Final is courtesy of Getty Images. Yeames's painting is reproduced courtesy of Bristol City Museums and Art Gallery. The front pages of the *Illustrated Police News* were supplied by the British Library, and the photograph of Edith Lanchester is included by kind permission of Linda Edwards.

In May 1992, Miroslav Holub told the *TLS* that an author is only an author when actually creating 'his small artistic performance'. The rest of the time, he added, 'he only pretends to be an artist, or displays certain associated artistic characteristics such as restlessness, hypochondria, sloppy dress, unbridled temperament, clumsiness and sentimentality.' I have been guilty of all of these and more, and so am especially grateful to the friends, colleagues, family and students who put up with me during the project. They include: Alan Bairner, Anne-Marie Beller, Abi Bendall, Carol Bolton, Borka (the Featherless Goose), Bob Brocklehurst, Roger Clarke, Lucy Dawkins, Gowan Dawson, Jan Elliot, Kerry Featherstone, Duncan Ferguson, Caroline Flynn-Ryan, Anne and Norman Freeman, Holly Furneaux, Lisa Gledhill, Bill Greenslade, Michelle Greet, Elaine Hall, Tom Hibbert, Elaine Hobby, William Hughes, Rachel Jackson, Neil Jagger, Stephen James, Brian Jarvis, Sally Ledger, Catherine Maxwell, Lina Minou, Deborah Murden, Peter Rawlings, Catherine Rees, Kelly Reid, Helen Relf, Carrie Rhys-Davies, Ruth Robbins, Ruth Salt, Carolyn Scott-Jeffs, Kerri Sharp, Marion Shaw, Gillian Spraggs, Victoria Stewart, John Stokes, Lizzie White, Janet Walwyn, Dan Watt, Nigel Wood, and Helen Wright. Thank you all.

Abbreviations

The following abbreviations are used in this book.

A	*Athenaeum*
BDP	*Birmingham Daily Post*
CLAA	Criminal Law Amendment Act 1885
DN	*Daily News*
DT	*Daily Telegraph*
FR	*Fortnightly Review*
GH	*Glasgow Herald*
ILN	*Illustrated London News*
ILP	Independent Labour Party
IPB	*Illustrated Police Budget*
IPN	*Illustrated Police News, Law Courts and Weekly Record*
JLA	John Lane Archive
LCC	London County Council
LWN	*Lloyd's Weekly Newspaper*
MCC	Marylebone Cricket Club
MP	*Morning Post*
NVA	National Vigilance Association
NYT	*New York Times*
OT	George Bernard Shaw, *Our Theatre in the 'Nineties*, Volume I
PMG	*Pall Mall Gazette*
RA	Royal Academy
RN	*Reynolds's Newspaper*
SDF	Social Democratic Foundation
SR	*Saturday Review*
T	*Times* (London)
WBA	West Bromich Albion
WCL	Wilde, *Complete Letters*
WCW	Wilde, *Complete Works*
YB	*Yellow Book*

Into the Past: A Brief Foreword

It is pleasant to think what a splendid time the historians of the 21st century will have when they take to writing monographs.
Rudyard Kipling to Charles Eliot Norton, [8] February 1895
(Kipling 1990: 173–4)

I can never forget 1895. To lie awake night after night, staring wide awake, hopeless of sleep, tormented in nerves, like a disembodied spirit, to watch one's own corpse, as it were, day after day, is an experience which no sane man with a conscience would wish to repeat.
Lord Rosebery, 30 September 1903 (McKinstry 2005: 347)

వై

In Lewis Carroll's *Sylvie and Bruno, Concluded* (1893), the mysterious 'Mein Herr' tells how, in his country, maps are no longer drawn to scale: each mile on a map is a mile long. Jorge Luis Borges's parable, 'On Exactitude in Science' (1960) relates a similar story, explaining how the Cartographers Guilds of an ancient civilisation surveyed their empire in such detail that the map they produced was the same size as the terrain it covered. The fate of these hapless geographers is a salutary one, and I was mindful of it throughout my work on this book. During the 1890s, the British Isles had around thirty million inhabitants, each of whom lived through a different version of their period. This is not to say that there were no moments of shared experience – the ferocious winter of 1894–5, for example – but a Dundee sailor hunting whales off Greenland, a Cardiff alderman mired in committee meetings, the female proprietor of a Norfolk lodging house, and an Irish Nationalist newspaper editor covering the General Election and its aftermath lived through significantly different 1895s. All are equally worthy of record, and in what follows I am not suggesting that the famous (and infamous) are any more deserving of examination than their fellow citizens. However, with so many stories to be told, and so many voices to be heard, a chronicler has to make editorial as well as intellectual decisions about the most convincing ways to engage with historical realities. Henry James memorably observed that 'The historian, essentially, wants more documents than he can really use; the dramatist only wants more liberties than he can really take' (H. James 1934: 161–2), but while this is a neat polarisation, it ignores the historian who desires liberties just as much as she or he needs source data. There are as many histories as there are historians, and the relationship between them is symbiotic. While this book's core is the front page news of the day, its margins reflect my particular interests in literature and culture, from the theatre reviews of George Bernard Shaw to the advertising column of the *Illustrated Police News* and the football reports of the *Birmingham Daily Post*. I have not taken liberties with verifiable detail, but each scholar who reviews the year will construct a different version of it, adding to the list of 'lived' 1895s an infinite plurality of reinterpretations.

This book is therefore a subjective composite of a year that took millions of subtly distinct forms even as clocks and calendars divided it into the shared units of hours, weeks and months. In some ways, it is a Venn diagram, with vast numbers of individual sets (or lives) intersecting at moments of national significance; in others it is more akin to the notion of the multiverse advanced by William James in *The Will to Believe* (1895). Seventy years later, Michel Foucault coined the term 'heterotopia' to describe the simultaneous juxtaposition of apparently incompatible events in the same space. Juxtaposition is a crucial structural, dramatic and analytical principle in what follows, not least because it also reflects the miscellaneous content of a late-Victorian newspaper, with its important lead story and editorial rubbing up against the 'Gleanings' column and the racing results. I am far from the first scholar to trace Wilde's trajectory from theatrical success to solitary confinement, Lord Rosebery's calamitous final year as Prime Minister, or the critical reception of *Jude the Obscure*, but when revisiting these events, I hope to show how they overlap other, less familiar happenings and circumstances and thus reveal something of the year's multifarious unfoldings. The details of sport and meteorology are therefore no less important than those of literature and politics. The result oscillates between the public record and more private sources such as letters and diaries, as well as identifying those moments when the private was made public in court and in the media. I have tried to let the people of 1895 speak for themselves as much as possible, without overlaying them with material from more recent critical or historical works. This is, after all, a study of a year rather than a detailed consideration of *The Importance of Being Earnest* or the intricacies of life in 10 Downing Street.

A single frame of film can be memorable or revealing, but it remains only a part of something larger. By the same token, it would be disingenuous to claim that the events of 1895 always speak for the *fin de siècle* as a whole. What this book tries to show instead is how certain events were unique while others belong to currents that flow through the era. Certain aspects of British life were unchanged from much earlier in the century, but elsewhere, daily existence was altering at an increasingly rapid pace, with new technology unsettling those who favoured the horse over the bicycle, the fountain pen over the typewriter or the needle over the sewing machine. Debates about the sexual content of fiction, or the question of whether children are corrupted by what they read (or see), are clearly not confined to the late-Victorian period, but they are significant aspects of 1895. Similarly, the complex interconnection of 'high' and more popular art, or the discussions of the likely consequences of professionalising sport are characteristic of both the 1890s and a more general 'modernity'. Detaching a year from those around it does permit concentration on its detail, but it rarely allows narrative or argumentative closure.

It is all too easy to examine the past with a teleological conclusion in mind, a tendency that mars a number of otherwise valuable studies of Wilde. Even a subtle and politicised sexual campaigner such as George Ives did not, in 1895 at least, see Wilde's conviction as significant in the formation of later conceptions of homosexual identity: he wished to kill himself in despair. Moments of change are rarely recognised as such immediately and their significance may only become clear much later. We may now read Wilde's downfall as a collision between the dissident modern and the brutally reactionary, and as a contribution to a wider debate about the policing (in all senses) of private life. However, we should not co-opt Virginia Woolf's rash claims about December 1910 and argue that 'on or about May 1895, understandings of human sexuality changed'. Wilde's trials, and the media furore that surrounded them, are extraordinarily revealing, but quite what they reveal varies according to the perspective from which they are viewed. The ways in which the newspapers of the day discussed Wilde and 'vice' are a case in point, for here Wilde's conviction quickly became part of a much broader discussion about the ways in which criminal(ised) sexualities were formed by the very culture that condemned them. The letters pages of *Reynolds's Newspaper* ally 'immorality' with the 'unnatural' conditions of public schools, suggesting that class and education are more significant in nurturing same-sex desire than any inbuilt tendency: the working class homosexual, rather than the male prostitute whose behaviour is motivated by material need (or greed), is almost a contradiction in terms. The *Daily Telegraph* meanwhile wields the blunt instrument of popular prejudice in caricaturing Wilde as a cancerous social menace. In its reading of the case, it is not the public school but radical literature and art, and the unapologetic intellectual iconoclasm that accompanies them which endanger the public at large, a public who could hardly be at risk when the *Yellow Book* was selling only 5,000 copies an issue. An Irishman informed by contemporary French thought and the pagan teachings of the classics, Wilde represented a rootless contagion instead of a set of acceptable and fixed attitudes. For the *Telegraph*, his 'deviant' sexuality clothed 'deviant' thought and taste, but papers across the social and educational spectrum, from the *Telegraph* to the *Illustrated Police News* thought Wilde needed cutting down to size long before any hint of his sexual transgressions became public knowledge. Few analysts of the 1890s have considered the ways in which an ever-growing reading public treated newspaper accounts of his trials as lurid entertainment that titillated and evoked mild *schadenfreude* before being relegated to use as kindling and lavatory paper. Inconvenient as it may be for those who would see Wilde's fate as a decisive moment in sexual taxonomy, millions of Britons cared little about him or his nocturnal adventures. Few outside London had seen his plays, none of his books had come close to rivalling the sales of Rider Haggard, Marie Corelli or Hall Caine, and though one of his plays could fill the Theatre Royal, such popularity was dwarfed by Everton Football Club's ability to sell 16,000 tickets a week to people who would stand for a couple of hours in rain, sleet and snow for unpredictable and on occasion minimal reward.

Hindsight is a wonderful thing. We can now see that the Labour party was going to displace the Liberals as the primary opposition to the Conservatives in the twentieth century, even if *Punch* was sure Keir Hardie was a spent force after the 1895 Election. It is clear that pensions are a more humane and socially productive measure of alleviating poverty among the elderly than the workhouse ever was; that agitation for Irish independence or reform of the House of Lords did not end with Rosebery's electoral defeat; that cycling was not a mere fad; that Arnold Bennett and Joseph Conrad were going to become major figures in early twentieth-century literature whatever their initial struggles. *Punch* may have felt that the New Woman was a thing of the past by the end of 1895, but that was because her 'newness' was becoming ever more socially assimilated; the term 'New Woman', coined by Sarah Grand in March 1894, post-dated the realities of socio-political change. Although it became a useful means of self-identification as well as pejorative dismissal, its use and life-span were limited. Talk of the 'New Woman' soon began to give way to that of suffrage agitation, while other campaigners for women's rights (or sexual equality in general) started to be described as 'feminist', a term the *OED* records as first appearing in the *Daily News* of 12 October 1894. Another French import, 'feminism', quickly joined it in the lexicon of 'advanced' opinion, cropping up in the *Athenaeum* of 27 April 1895. That young women can still provoke debate about the 'decency' of their dress, or that a woman writer can turn heads with a sexually explicit novel, demonstrates continuity with our late-Victorian forebears, but only the most optimistic, pessimistic or visionary predicted the endurance of such things a century ago. In 1895, few Britons imagined that 'skirmishes' on the North-West frontier would ever be anything but a distraction for the Great Powers, though the military and economic rise of Japan was being studied in Whitehall and elsewhere. I have tried to resist the seductions of hindsight, but I have not always managed to stop my ears to the equally beguiling sirens of retrospective irony.

Parallels between ages and historical figures can be analogous to the 'false friends' that traditionally bedevil the lives of language students. For instance, Laura Ormiston Chant's attempts to 'clean up' music hall entertainment are in some ways suggestive of the efforts of Mary Whitehouse to do the same to theatre, film and television during the 1960s and 1970s, but despite superficial similarities, Chant emerged from more specifically Victorian concerns with 'purity' and moral vigilance, belonged to a much more widespread and significant reforming constituency, and also performed a great deal of valuable work in the causes of sexual equality and humanitarianism. Nevertheless, readers of this book will notice that a great deal of 1895 is familiar to them today. Consciously or otherwise, the historian often reshapes the past in the light of the present's preoccupations, but even allowing for this, it is notable that the 1895 budget struck some now very familiar chords concerning public spending and taxation. The role of the House of Lords continues to be debated. Politicians and reformers tussle with the brewing industry over the regulation and pricing of alcohol. Britain is little better at coping with snow or drought or outbreaks of disease than it was a century ago. People still queue to view London from a giant Ferris wheel; literary critics struggle to explain the overwhelming popular success of certain novels, whether they are by George Du Maurier or Dan Brown. In the twenty-first century, the government of London remains a controversial topic. Debates about juvenile crime and social inequality are as agonised as ever. An increasingly intrusive and hypocritically moralistic tabloid press delights in dramatising (rather than simply reporting) high profile cases of sexual scandal. In an undeclared war in Afghanistan, mounting British losses in no way presage ultimate victory. Conservative commentators worry that women are becoming less 'lady-like' and all-too-willing to claim the 'traditionally' masculine right of promiscuity without reputational taint. Popular entertainment (chiefly singing), and professional sport (chiefly football and boxing) remain recurrent foci of working class aspiration and achievement. Pornography is still advertised in newspapers which excoriate its appearances elsewhere. Writing this book from 2009 to 2011, I saw football results that were eerily similar to those found in the sports pages of the 1890s. The First Division was now the Premier League, but the same teams played each other: Aston Villa, Blackburn, Bolton, Burnley, Everton, Liverpool, Newcastle, Sunderland, West Bromich Albion, Wolves and others pursued their ancient rivalries, even if my preferred team failed to recapture the successes of yore. In 1894–5, an English cricket team captained by the Middlesex batsman Andrew Stoddart defeated the Australians 3–2 in a five match series; in 2010–11, an English team led by the Middlesex batsman Andrew Strauss led England to a 3–1 win. While the relation between 'Gentlemen' and 'Players' has changed, and the composition of the modern team represents shifts in the post-imperial landscape, the sporting struggle remains equally keen, though after Gallipoli and Bodyline, the Australian crowds no longer cheer the victorious English from the field. In 1895, men rushed to telegraph offices for updates on the match scores. Today, fans consult websites, but the principle remains.

Pondering his failure to produce an encyclopaedic account of city life in *London: A Pilgrimage* (1872) Douglas Jerrold quoted Emerson's 'we touch and go, and sip the foam of many lives.' 'Ours is a touch and go chronicle,' he said (Doré 1872: 16). The phrase now has unwelcome associations of the unconvincing and tenuous, but the notion of the 'touch and go chronicle' remains a useful one and certainly more empowering than the fate of Borges's map-makers.

Winter: 15 September 1894 – 28 February 1895

Thunder in November indicates a fertile year to come.

Illustrated Police News, 1 December 1894

How strange to live in a land where the worship of beauty and the passion of love are considered infamous. I hate England; it is only bearable to me because you are here.

Oscar Wilde to Lord Alfred Douglas, 9 November 1894

Everything is a pose now, especially genius [. . .] I believe that he merely poses; but do those who imitate him merely pose?

Anon. [Robert Hichens], *The Green Carnation*, September 1894

This book is so terribly actual and up to date that in six months it will be old-fashioned.

Glasgow Herald on *The Green Carnation*, 20 September 1894

And you, young shaver, what is it you bring?
Razor and soap, like shavers young and old –
The soap to soothe, razor to cut and sting?
Will wedding-bell be heard, and death-knell toll'd?
You see, my lad, we're anxious as to what you have in store,
For there's still some things to put to rights bequeathed by 'Ninety-Four.

Punch greets the New Year, 5 January 1895

To give an accurate and exhaustive account of the period would need a far less brilliant pen than mine.

Max Beerbohm, '1880' in *The Yellow Book*, Volume IV, January 1895

☙◆❧

Changes in the Weather

Late 1894 was unseasonably warm, with raspberries picked in Essex the week before Christmas. The high temperatures prompted thunder-storms, with the south-west seeing its heaviest rain since 1882. On 14

November, George Gissing noted the 'Newspapers are full of floods and wrecks' (Gissing 1978: 353), and a deluge in the Thames Valley meant 'Eton was flooded out, and the school had to be broken up' (Hamilton 1986: 190). Oscar Wilde received an intimation of changes in the moral climate a few days earlier. The first night of Haddon Chambers's *John O'Dreams*, starring Herbert Beerbohm Tree and Mrs Patrick Campbell (Beatrice Stella Tanner), attracted an 'exceedingly brilliant audience' of 'well known "first-nighters"' (*Leeds Mercury* 9/11/94), but 'the lower orders who thronged the stalls' (*WCL* 622) were less starstruck than they might have been, and Wilde was coldly received. He retired to a box with the Home Secretary, Herbert Asquith. The incident was minor in itself, but Wilde's relationship with senior government figures would soon become controversial.

While Asquith did his best to enjoy a play Wilde felt was 'not bad, but oh! so badly written,' Lord Rosebery's Liberal government tottered from crisis to crisis. Gladstone had won the 1892 election with a majority of only forty, one that left little room for manoeuvre and was dependent on support from Irish Nationalists. Taking office for the fourth time, Gladstone was, at the age of eighty-two, the oldest PM in electoral history and his increasingly poor health led to his resignation in the spring of 1894. The 'Grand Old Man' had been the undisputed Liberal leader since the late 1860s, but Rosebery was a vexed successor. The office of Premier was but one of many he initially declined during a frustrating career 'rooted in a genuine fear of inadequacy and of failure' (J. Davis *ODNB*). Exemplifying William James's belief that 'there is no more miserable human being than one in whom nothing is habitual but indecision' (W. James 1890: 122), the vacillating Rosebery was politically and personally besieged, and was, said the *Times*, 'a reed painted to look like iron' (29/10/94). The Liberals had become notably factionalised since Gladstone embraced Home Rule in 1880, and the internecine warfare accompanying this and a movement towards social radicalism intensified after he retired.

The new PM was twenty years younger than his Chancellor, Sir William Harcourt, and the latter, reinforced by his venomous son, Lewis (known as 'Loulou'), felt he was far more suited to high office than a peer who had never been a constituency MP, a charge Rosebery countered by pointing out Harcourt's inexperience of international diplomacy. The two fought over the 1894 Budget, which alarmed Rosebery by introducing death duties and an increase in income tax that hit the party's wealthy supporters, but even when they lacked an obvious bone of contention, their incompatible personalities made it difficult for them to work together for the common good. Rosebery showed political intelligence and diplomatic skill as Foreign Secretary and the Chairman of the newly formed LCC, but he lacked Harcourt's parliamentary ring-craft and his aristocratic politesse could be overwhelmed by the older man's 'blustering manner and hectoring insensitivity' (McKinstry 2005: 213). Rosebery's personal charm won him widespread (and cross-party) popularity, but Harcourt had a firmer grasp of everyday affairs and procedure, and considered Rosebery's persistent attempts to reform the House of Lords an electoral irrelevance. Even his friends struggled to grasp his schemes for constitutional change, and his cause was weakened further by strong opposition from the Queen, who could not understand why an aristocrat should seek to undermine the traditional order. The *Times* found his radicalism repugnant too. 'It is a reproduction of the evil traditions of Jacobinism [. . .] a fanatical folly,' it said of the mooted Lords abolition (29/10/94).

John Morley, the Chief Secretary for Ireland, was a further complication. Rosebery, Harcourt and Morley should have been a formidable triumvirate, but their differences of policy and focus were emblematic of the fission within Liberal ranks: the parodist Owen Seaman called them 'Allies in Blunderland' (Seaman 1895: 28). Cabinet meetings were fiery and frosty affairs, not helped by further divisions between Asquith, Joseph Chamberlain, Edward Grey and R.B. Haldane. Rosebery was not a militant imperialist or 'Jingoist' like Chamberlain, but he was more enthusiastic about Empire than Harcourt or Morley. Rosebery and Morley supported Home Rule; Harcourt opposed it. The best part of fifty Liberal Unionists, notably Chamberlain, added to the confusion. Harcourt balanced increases in income tax with a corresponding rise in tax allowances, which appealed to the party's bourgeois supporters as well as those at the upper end of the working class who might otherwise flirt with socialism, but Rosebery disliked his targeting of the aristocracy. Indeed, death duties proved a serious matter for his own heirs when he died in 1929.[1] Rosebery's enthusiasm for the turf upset Nonconformists, a major constituency of the Liberals' support. Harcourt antagonised brewing (and Irish) interests by raising duty on beer and spirits, and by suggesting local controls on the sale and distribution of liquor. Morley sided with Rosebery on the issue of 'ending or mending' the Lords, but disagreed with Harcourt over women's suffrage, which Morley favoured, and over the introduction of an eight hour working day, which Harcourt saw as against the national interest. Morley had been a journalist and newspaper editor, and his experience of the world beyond Parliament gave him useful electoral insights, but 'his fondness for intrigue sometimes got the better of him' (Hamer *ODNB*). Regarding Harcourt as an opportunist, Morley supported Rosebery's claim for the

Liberal leadership. That Harcourt blamed Rosebery for popularising his unflattering nickname, 'Jumbo', based on his apparent resemblance to a celebrated circus elephant, made relations between them increasingly fraught. In late January 1895, the *PMG* wryly observed of a brief Cabinet concord, 'this unanimity is touching, especially because it is so rare nowadays' (31/1/95). The formation of the National Old Age Pensions League in November 1894, an occasion on which the sociologist, Charles Booth, suggested that 9 per cent of Londoners died in the workhouse, helped intensify a division between the left and right wings of the party, with Chamberlain criticising government policy on 6 December at a pensions conference in Birmingham, a city where 39 per cent of the elderly were paupers (*IPN* 3/11/94). Rosebery's leadership problems were well nigh insurmountable, particularly for a man of his temperament.

In October, the *Spectator* suggested Rosebery was 'a bundle of seven aliases' rather than a creature of flesh and blood: the Home Ruler, the Unionist, the Democratic Socialist, the Political Boss, the Man above Party, the Sphinx and the Man of the Turf (McKinstry 2005: 4). Riven by self-contradictions, Rosebery's oratorical flair, his greatest political asset, began to evaporate. On 30 October, he unveiled a statue of Edmund Burke in Bristol and received the freedom of the city, but his flippant address upset local worthies. The following month, the *SR* noted his speeches' 'remarkable poverty of ideas' and condemned his 'vulgar love of jocularity and colloquial style [. . .] even when dealing with the most serious affairs of State.' His behaviour, it went on, 'scarcely approximates to the ideal of a First Minister of the British Empire' (17/11/94: 523), a view *Punch* supported in 'The Perils of a Jesting Premier' (22/12/94: 298). Such comments drew attention to Rosebery's masculinity, his aristocratic high-handedness, humour's place in parliamentary discourse, and the relationship between public and private selves. The no-nonsense editorial was astute. Rosebery's 'place in the Cabinet is anything but a bed of roses,' it continued, 'and his position in the country is still worse.' He was 'riding for a fall', and the Liberals had little chance of avoiding electoral disaster.

Rosebery's personal life was equally troubled. The death of his wife, the heiress Hannah de Rothschild, in November 1890 left him inconsolable. His hair began greying; he lost much of his conversational sparkle and from then on, wrote only on black-bordered notepaper. Harcourt's one-upmanship was an occupational hazard, but since Hannah's death Rosebery had made a still more dangerous foe, a man with a limitless capacity for personal grievance. If Rosebery was, in the words of the Foreign Office's Esme Howard, a 'highly polished eighteenth-century snuff-box [. . .] filled with perfumed snuff, which would be opened on special occasions' (McKinstry 2005: 188), his antagonist was a rabid bulldog whose jaws frothed and slavered as they clamped upon their victim. John Sholto Douglas, the eighth Marquess of Queensberry, was a menace. 'Impetuous, reckless, combative and temperamental,' mountaineer, pugilist, equestrian, gambler, philanderer and eccentric secularist, he had four sons, and was more or less estranged from all of them (Roberts 1981: 25). 'His principal preoccupations were sport and atheism,' says Montgomery Hyde, 'and he knew much more about his horses and dogs than about the human members of his family' (Hyde 1948: 21). His volcanic temper led Wilde to nickname him 'the Scarlet Marquis' (*WCL* 632).

Punching the Pimp

In 1894, Queensberry briefly allowed familial concerns to override sporting ones, though in many respects, he simply swapped foxes for lions. He was especially concerned about his eldest and youngest children, Francis, Viscount Drumlanrig and Lord Alfred, known to all but his father as Bosie, a variant on 'Boysie', his mother's childhood pet name for him. Rosebery made Drumlanrig his assistant private secretary when he left the LCC for the Foreign Office in 1892, despite his lack of experience, and deemed him successful enough in his new role to persuade Gladstone to promote him to one of the Queen's Lords-in-Waiting. This in turn led him to be made an English peer, an honour denied to Queensberry who had been a Scottish elective peer but who had not been re-elected to the Lords in 1880, ostensibly because of his secularist sympathies.

Drumlanrig became Lord Kelhead in June 1893. Initially acquiescent, Queensberry soon objected to the honour, complaining to Victoria about Rosebery's 'bad influence' on his son and writing repeatedly to Gladstone criticising the appointment. Rosebery ignored this provocation, even when an abusive letter was read out at a Cabinet meeting, but he had a frightening experience in August 1893 when, having gone to Homburg at his doctor's suggestion, he was followed by Queensberry, armed with a dog-whip. Rosebery received threatening mail before leaving for Germany, but Queensberry's anti-Semitic and homophobic aggression reached new depths in his message of 6 August. 'Cher fat boy,' it began:

Oh fat boy, keep yourself fit. Use a skipping rope mightily, man of valour. You will find it good for your fat carcass. I have a punching ball here on which I am having inscribed in black letters, 'The Jew Pimp'. I shall daily punch it to keep my hand in until we meet once more. (McKinstry 2005: 359)

Rosebery joked about the Marquess in a letter to the Queen, observing that one of his more onerous duties as Foreign Secretary was 'to be pursued by a pugilist of unsound mind' (R. James 1995: 287), but the German authorities took Queensberry's threats very seriously, and forced him to leave the country.

Queensberry denounced Rosebery in the foreign press where he was beyond the reach of British libel laws, but his fury was chiefly reserved for Wilde, whom he saw as leading Bosie ever deeper into the moral mire. Like Rosebery, Wilde underestimated the Marquess, but by the winter of 1894 he had realised that while Queensberry had given his name to the rules of boxing, he disdained all forms of etiquette and social regulation. Earlier that year, Bosie had been in Florence, being 'taken up by a coterie of expatriate homosexuals' and, as the art historian Bernard Berenson recalled in 1949, becoming 'dissipated, batty, a fucked out whore' (Cadden and Jensen 1995: 64). During his absence, Wilde faced an intimidating visit from the Marquess, who burst into his house in Tite Street, Chelsea, and threatened to thrash him and Bosie if he caught them together in public. 'I don't know what the Queensberry rules are, but the Oscar Wilde rule is to shoot at sight,' Wilde purportedly replied, characterising his uninvited guest as 'the most infamous brute in London' (Roberts 1981: 197). Queensberry hoped to provoke Wilde into suing him for libel, and almost managed to do so, since Wilde's solicitors wrote to him on 11 July demanding he retract his allegations. Queensberry refused, but his plan to lure Wilde into the courtroom was stymied by Sybil Montgomery, Bosie's mother, who helped by her cousin, the Conservative MP George Wyndham, talked Wilde out of legal action. The situation remained tense, not least because Queensberry was convinced Wilde was a 'damned cur and coward of the Rosebery type' who was causing a 'hideous scandal' (Roberts 1981: 199).

Queensberry changed tack in October. Drumlanrig was to marry Alix Ellis, the daughter of one of the Prince of Wales's equerries, and the couple, her parents and brother, went to Somerset to stay with the Conservative MP for Bridgewater, Edward Stanley. During a shooting party on 18 October, Drumlanrig was found dead in a bramble patch with a gunshot wound to the forehead. What Brian Roberts terms a 'perfunctory inquest' (1981: 183) – the *Times* gave it less than a column on 22 October – delivered a verdict of Accidental Death, positing he was killed while unwisely clambering over a hedge with a loaded gun in search of a winged pheasant. The swift if not wholly convincing verdict limited but did not quash the rumours circulating in the wake of the tragedy that Drumlanrig had shot himself because he feared the exposure of a relationship with Rosebery, or because he was torn between the PM and Alix. Queensberry lashed out in a letter to Alfred Montgomery, his former father-in-law. 'Now the first flush of this catastrophe and grief is passed,' he wrote on 1 November, 'I write to tell you that this is a *judgement* on the whole *lot of you*. Montgomerys, The Snob Queers like Rosebery [. . .] I smell a Tragedy behind all this and have already *got Wind* of a more *startling one*' (Ellmann 1987: 402). Queensberry had begun to fear that a monstrous conspiracy was destroying his clan, and he redoubled his attacks on Rosebery and his attempts to reclaim Bosie. In Ellmann's words, 'he had begun to see homosexuals everywhere' (381).

Rosebery's sexuality was a topic of scurrilous interest for society gossips. However, it might be observed that while homosexuality had yet to be articulated in the bourgeois consciousness, and late-Victorian perceptions of it had not crystallised into the fatally neat syllogism, 'he is not "manly" therefore he may be an "invert"', Rosebery's departure from conventionally understood signifiers of aristocratic masculinity was significant enough to be commented on by friend and foe alike. He was clean-shaven, an accomplished linguist who read French literature for pleasure, a former pupil of the notorious Eton master William Johnson and a close friend of Johnson's acolyte, 'Regy' Brett (M. Kaplan 2005: 113–65). He shrouded himself with an 'air of mystery and reserve' that 'provok[ed] others to think he was permanently engaged in dubious activities' (McKinstry 2005: 152), and insisted on opening his own mail despite the many calls upon his time. A preening wit, a widower whose pose of perpetual mourning – sanctioned by regal example – served as an impenetrable disguise, it was muttered, for all manner of deviant activities, a misogynist: all of these encouraged wagging tongues. Queensberry was hardly a rational judge of sexual questions, but he was not alone in harbouring suspicions concerning Rosebery's appearance, behaviour and character.

Artificial Flowers and Strange Perfumes

Queensberry's view of his son's relationship with Wilde was not improved by the appearance of a satire, published anonymously on 15 September. Filled with 'smartly written impertinences' (*GH* 20/9/94) and 'smartly-perverted aphorisms' (*MP* 20/9/94), and taking its title from the dyed flower Wilde wore in his buttonhole to demonstrate the superiority of art over nature, *The Green Carnation* depicted the relationship between Lord Reggie Hastings, whose 'pale gilt hair', blue eyes and 'mouth like the mouth of Narcissus' (Hichens [1894] 1949: 2), made him an all-too-recognisable caricature of Bosie, and his mentor, Esmé Amarinth, turner of paradoxes, admirer of Walter Pater and smoker of gold-tipped cigarettes. 'Let us sin while we may,' he says, asking 'Why, why do the young neglect their passionate pulsating opportunities?' (106). In the conclusion to *The Renaissance* (1873) Pater maintained that the secret of life was devotion to 'art and song' and 'getting as many pulsations as possible into the given time' (Pater [1893] 1986: 153), but fearful that it 'might possibly mislead some of those young men into whose hands it might fall,' he withdrew the essay until 1888. On the evidence of *The Green Carnation*, his fears were well-founded. Dying on 30 July, Pater was spared further controversy, but Wilde encouraged it even as he sought to distance himself from the novel. 'I invented that magnificent flower,' he told the *PMG*, 'But with the middle-class and mediocre book that usurps its strangely beautiful name I have, I need hardly say, nothing whatsoever to do. The Flower is a work of art. The book is not' (*WCL* 617). Such correspondence only stimulated public interest in the novel, and encouraged speculation about its authorship (Kingston 2008: 138–47). By late October, the perpetrator of the skit was unmasked as Robert Hichens, a friend and travelling companion of Bosie, but not before such unlikely suspects as Alfred Austin, Marie Corelli and even the manufacturers of Bovril had been considered. Wilde himself initially suspected Ada Leverson, though he later told her that the book was 'the false gospel' of a 'doubting disciple' whose talent was 'unrelieved by any flashes of physical beauty' (*WCL* 615).

The Green Carnation 'pretended to be a parody, but was more like a documentary' (Ellmann 1987: 400), its satire 'tripped up by Hichens's obvious fascination, even admiration, for his subject' (Danson 1989: 49) as it shimmered between ridicule and homage. Wilde hovered over proceedings, alluded to but unseen. 'I am dining out with Oscar Wilde,' says Esmé, 'and that is only to be done with prayer and fasting' (Hichens [1894] 1949: 27). Comments such as 'People teach in order to conceal their ignorance' (167) or 'To know how to be disobedient is to know how to live' (168) surely owe much to Hichens's encounters with Wilde and Bosie. The exceptionally close relationship between the book's content and real life troubled reviewers, with the *SR* arguing:

> It goes without saying that allusions, thinly veiled, to various disgusting sins are freely scattered throughout the book [. . .]. There is no use in spreading

unpleasantness by holding it up to reprobation; otherwise it might almost be thought that some of these remarks on living people exceed even the bounds of extreme bad taste, and render the book [. . .] open to an action for libel. (10/11/94: 517)

Hichens's novel forges damaging associations between certain types of self-presentation, humour, attitude and sexuality, and sailed close to the wind when depicting Reggie and Esmé preaching their gospel of pleasure and sin to the village choirboys, and offering a green carnation to a nine-year-old child. Neil McKenna sums up the pair as 'proselytising, politicised sodomites', adding that if this was not 'damaging and dangerous enough', portraying Reggie as a 'predatory pederast' was an 'appalling indictment' of Bosie's behaviour ([2003] 2004: 411). Fearing legal action, not least because the book reprinted as Reggie's a telegram sent by Bosie to his father, William Heinemann had the manuscript of the novel read by Wilde's solicitor, Sir George Lewis. Reviews were mixed, but the *Bookman* reported it was selling well across the country by mid-November, alongside Hall Caine's *The Manxman*, Anthony Hope's *The Prisoner of Zenda*, and Robert Louis Stevenson's *The Ebb Tide* (11/94: 41).

The most perceptive response came from Max Beerbohm in the *ILN*. Wit, dandy and caricaturist *par excellence*, Beerbohm was a friend of all concerned (Hall 2002: 34–40), and ideally placed to review the book as a literary critic and social insider: he had apparently 'been through it carefully' with Hichens (Cecil [1964] 1985: 108). Fifteen years younger than Wilde, Beerbohm was, like his friend and contemporary Aubrey Beardsley, his senior by all of three days, keen to break with earlier aestheticism. 'Mr Wilde, had he not always been received with titters, would perhaps not have been tolerated here,' he wrote, suggesting he 'would have had to fly the country, like Byron and many another who has been ecstatic in life and thought.' 'The portrait drawn of him is certainly offensive,' Beerbohm continued, depicting a man with Wilde's walk and smile, 'a man of genius, who lacks the formal capacity for production, whose mind has become as a garden of rank and tropical luxuriance.' Wilde once claimed that 'it is only the Philistine who seeks to estimate a personality by the vulgar test of production' (*WCW* 1095). Now Beerbohm paraphrased his 'Pen, Pencil and Poison' (1889) in a shrewd assessment. 'The caricature is capital,' he wrote, before anticipating the refrain of Wilde's last major work, *The Ballad of Reading Gaol* (1898), 'And surely the highest kind of satire is that which is done with a loving hand. You cannot betray but with a kiss'. As far as Beerbohm was concerned, Hichens's satire was 'full of fun and humour' despite its offensiveness (Beerbohm 1894: 406). It was therefore destined for popular success, even if it ventured into unwholesome territory.

Like the *SR*'s assessment of Rosebery's speeches, the piece raises fascinating questions about the cultural and sexual currents of the time. Hichens elides endorsement and derision; the 800 word review praises Hichens and faintly praises Wilde while yet consigning 'Flamboyant Oscar!' to history. Beerbohm implies Wilde's sexual unconventionality, and underscores his own modernity and detachment in passing judgement on the novel, its author, its subject, and its representation of decadence. The review fuses analysis with self-advertisement. To link Wilde to Byron was a provocative move, clearly not made on the basis of shared heterosexual promiscuity, the writing of regularly anthologised love poems or self-sacrifice in the cause of Greek independence. Beerbohm's parallel slyly evoked the 'bad' Lord Byron, the reckless libertine around whose name gathered all manner of unsavoury rumours. That the details of Byron's sexual life were not widely known and certainly not discussed by the average reader of the *ILN* made the allusion all the craftier. At the same time, the notion of 'ecstasy' recalled Pater's dangerous counsel, 'To burn always with this hard, gem-like flame, to maintain this ecstasy, is success in life' (Pater [1893] 1986: 152). And was the allusion to Byron prophetic, a coded warning that Wilde's life of romantic and sexual transgression would lead to exile and an evil reputation?

The Green Carnation traded on its topicality, Arthur Symons telling readers of the *Athenaeum* it was a book, like Iota's *A Yellow Aster* 'which glitter[s] in the buttonhole for an evening with painful conspicuousness, and [is] forgotten before [it is] thrown away' (5/1/95: 10). *Punch* depicted 'Lord Raggie Tattersall' and his friend 'Fustian Flitters' as 'The Decadent Guys', subtitled 'A Colour-Study in Green Carnations'. Earnestly discussing their preparations for Bonfire Night, the scruffy yet dandified duo, whose buttonholes are adorned with purple cabbages, reprise several key jokes and incidents. Alluding to Wilde's habit of reheating his wittiest asides, Fustian quips 'The true *impromptu* is invariably premeditated' and observes, 'Does not consistency solely consist in contradicting oneself?' (10/11/94: 225). With parodies of parodies in circulation, it was difficult to tell whether Wilde or Amarinth was responsible for 'A Few Maxims for the Instruction of the Over-Educated', an unsigned collection of epigrams published in the *SR* on 17 November. 'Our proverbs want re-writing,' said Lord Henry in *Dorian Gray*, and his creator set about his mission with gusto. 'Education is an admirable thing,' the list began, 'but it is well to remember from time to time that nothing that is worth knowing can be taught.'

" My dear Raggie, you are looking very well this afternoon."

Figure 1. 'Decadent Guys' Lord Raggie Tattersall and Fustian Flitters ponder the dandyism of Guy Fawkes. *Punch*, 10 November 1894.

Another maxim advanced the claim 'The criminal classes are so close to us that even the policeman can see them. They are so far away from us that only the poet can understand them' (17/11/94: 533–4).

By late 1894, Wilde had almost abandoned poetry but his knowledge of crime increased by the day. He was well aware of the risks of 'feasting with panthers' (*WCL* 758), but they were reiterated in a news report of 24 November. Major William Parkinson, aged forty-five, committed suicide in Holloway Prison while on remand charged with 'indecently assaulting and attempting to procure for illegal purposes two boys on Tower-hill.' In a letter to his housemate, a retired major named Aylmer, Parkinson pleaded with him to come to Southwark police court bringing 'a smart solicitor'. 'I am accused of indecent behaviour to two boys,' Parkinson wrote. 'I need not say that it is a regular case of blackmail.' Before the case came to trial, Parkinson slit his throat with a broken mirror in his cell, the Coroner recording a verdict of 'suicide while temporarily insane' (*IPN* 24/11/94). Whether Parkinson assaulted the boys, or whether he was the victim of a blackmail plot – the criminalising of consenting homosexual acts, even in private, by Henry Labouchere's Amendment to the Section 11 of the CLAA 1885 led to the act being termed the 'blackmailer's charter' – his position was a desperate one, with the humiliation of a trial looming and a possibly severe sentence of two years hard labour and concomitant social ruin if found guilty. He was far from the only man in such an invidious position to resolve it through suicide.

The *SR* was about to enter its golden age under the dynamic editorship of Frank Harris. It would boast drama criticism from George Bernard Shaw, literary criticism by H.G. Wells (who reviewed 285 books between November 1894 and April 1897), and an impressive roster of freelance contributors including Beerbohm, Symons and Ada Leverson. The appearance of Wilde's 'Maxims' attracted little comment, but the same could not be said of a superior selection of them, 'Phrases and Philosophies for the Use of the Young', originally intended for the *SR* but published instead in a new and extremely subversive Oxford University magazine, the *Chameleon*, on 1 December. The editor was John Francis Bloxam, a school friend of Bosie's and an undergraduate at Exeter College whom Wilde said possessed a 'strange beauty' (*WCL* 625). Bloxam perhaps inspired the Bloxham of *The Importance of Being Earnest*, but in 1894 the would-be priest had literary ambitions of his own.

Bloxam's title was apparently suggested by Wilde's eccentric friend, George Ives, criminologist, cricketer and campaigner for penal reform, in the autumn of 1894. It was inspired by an earlier Oxford magazine, the *Spirit Lamp*, edited by Bosie in 1892–3, which in May 1893 printed a French poetic paraphrase by Pierre Louÿs of a letter from Wilde to Bosie, Wilde's vignette, 'The Disciple', and verse by Lionel Johnson. Lord Henry Somerset, an aristocratic writer of sentimental songs, contributed 'T'amo', a lyric whose subject was obvious to those who knew that his wife had left him in the late 1870s because of his homosexual inclinations. Lord Henry now lived in Florence, and Bosie may have met him when visiting the city in early 1894. The most outspoken contribution was, however, the editor's 'Sicilian Love Song', which as Timothy d'Arch Smith remarks, could 'hardly have failed to shock the vulgar and impress the initiate' with its open declaration of same-sex passion (d'Arch Smith 53). The next issue, Bosie's last, was far less 'Uranian' in content, perhaps, as d'Arch Smith suggests, the authorities had warned him about repeating May's performance.

The new magazine sported a green morocco cover (hinting, like the green carnation, at homosexual connotations), and the subtitle, *A Bazaar of Dangerous and Smiling Chances*, a quotation from Stevenson's *More New Arabian Nights: The Dynamiter* (1885). Stevenson's phrase refers to the London streets' rich capacity for prompting adventure, but as McKenna comments, in this setting it suggests 'the eye contact used by men in dangerous street pick-ups' (2004: 432), the more so since the novel involves a character named Somerset and a secret society committing crimes in the capital. The *Chameleon* solicited those able to decipher its allusions; by the time it appeared, the name 'Somerset' had been further linked with homosexuality because of the role played in the so-called Cleveland Street Scandal of 1889–90 by Lord Arthur Somerset. By contrast, those expecting a typical undergraduate journal found it even more alarming than the *Spirit Lamp* had been.

Wilde cancelled one of his more provocative maxims, 'Manliness has become quite effeminate', but his others were nonetheless unsettling. 'The first duty in life is to be as artificial as possible,' he began. 'What the second duty is no one has yet discovered.' Such a claim could have come from *Dorian Gray*: the surprising apothegm, 'No crime is vulgar, but all vulgarity is crime. Vulgarity is the conduct of others,' reused in *An Ideal Husband*, began life there, though it originally claimed 'all crime is vulgar' and that it belonged 'exclusively to the lower orders'. 'The well-bred contradict other people. The wise contradict themselves' was an observation similar to those of *Intentions* (1891) or his early comedies, but elsewhere, Wilde's assertions hinted at more personal revelations. 'If one tells the truth, one is sure, sooner or later, to be found out' followed the glorification of style over sincerity. 'Any preoccupation with ideas of what is right and wrong in conduct shows an arrested intellectual development,' he continued, moving from the defence of artistic freedom in *Dorian Gray*'s preface, 'No artist has ethical sympathies. An ethical sympathy in an artist is an unpardonable mannerism of style' (*WCW* 17), to an altogether amoral position. That this seemingly extended to encouraging prostitution ('If the poor only had profiles there would be no difficulty in solving the problem of poverty') and consequence-free hedonism ('Pleasure is the only thing one should live for'), made his contribution a provocative read. Its subversive impact was enhanced by other contributions, 'Judicial Wit of Recent Times', Bloxam's 'The Priest and the Acolyte' (signed 'X'), which recounted a homosexual suicide with poisoned communion wine, and his pseudonymous poem of boy-love, 'At Dawn' (credited to 'Bertram Lawrence'). Bosie's 'Two Loves' (dedicated to Leverson), and 'In Praise of Shame', appeared unashamedly as the work of 'Lord Alfred Douglas'. The latter's notorious closing line, 'I am the Love that dare not speak its name', would attract particular opprobrium.

While Bloxam worked on the *Chameleon*, Constance Wilde was assembling another collection of her husband's witticisms, printed privately as *Oscariana* in January 1895 (Guy and Small 2000: 178–83). Here Wilde was read on his own terms, but in the *Chameleon*, words and phrases resounded in an echo chamber of esoteric meaning and allusions. Jerome K. Jerome was appalled, using his editorial in *To-day* to draw a distinction between the private 'dirty stories in the club smoking-room' and the public issuing of a magazine which 'any immature youth, or foolish New Young Woman' might buy. The *Chameleon*, he bawled, 'appears to be nothing more nor less than an advocacy for indulgence in the cravings of an unnatural disease', and his conclusion was as sombre as it was denunciatory. 'It can serve no purpose but that of evil [. . .] this is unbridled licence [. . .] garbage and offal' (29/12/94: 241). Perhaps he recalled *The Green Carnation*'s words on colour-changing reptiles. 'Lord Reggie,' wrote Hichens, 'is one of the most utterly vicious young men of the day. Why? Because, like the chameleon, he takes his colour from whatever he rests upon, or is put near. And he has been put near scarlet instead of white' ([1894] 1949: 70).

On the Prowl

Jerome was outraged by the *Chameleon*, but one wonders how he encountered it. With a print run of only 100 copies, and a high price of 15s, the result of paying for it on subscription (three numbers were planned per volume), its influence was limited. Even the controversial *YB* did well to sell more than 5,000 copies an issue after its sensational debut in April 1894. The two publications are seen as agents of what Gissing termed 'sexual anarchy', the dissolution of traditional constructions of masculinity and femininity often regarded as a keynote of the *fin de siècle,* but they were only part of a more complex dispute about sexuality, gender, morals and the relationship between the state and the individual. In late 1894, the press was less preoccupied with the corrupting effects of undergraduate journalism than with a prolonged argument over prostitution in London's music halls, specifically the Empire and Alhambra Theatres in Leicester Square. As E.S. Turner observes, it now seems remarkable that when prostitution was all but unanimously regarded as a social evil, so many commentators defended 'the highly-scented houris and attendant harpies whose only interest was in emptying the pocket books of a raffish male clientele' (Turner [1950] 1966: 229). Young male prostitutes also frequented the theatre (T. Davis 1992: 124). Nevertheless, those who sought to curb the theatres' excesses were subjected to remarkable levels of ridicule and abuse. The Empire was notorious for the revealing costumes of its dancers, its titillating 'living pictures' (which intrigued Shaw, *OT* 79–86) and the expensive prostitutes who congregated in its promenade. They were, said W. MacQueen-Pope, 'wonderful women wonderfully dressed, noiseless on the rich carpet, overwhelmingly alluring in their "known haughtiness,"' who 'floated – none of them seemed to walk' in 'an atmosphere of rich blue cigar smoke, frangipani, patchouli and the heady scent of champagne' as an orchestra played in the background (Turner [1950] 1966: 232–3). The spectacle was recorded in poetry by 'decadent' poets such as Symons and Theodore Wratislaw, and in the naturalist fiction of Hubert Crackanthorpe and others who adopted Wilde's view that 'vice and virtue are to the artist materials for an art' (*WCW* 17) and attempted to represent theatre scenes without passing moral judgement upon them (Stokes 1989: 53–94; Beckson 1992: 110–28). The Empire promenade was a moral anomaly, its clientele permitted to engage in activities which would have risked arrest if pursued outside. When two American tourists visited the Empire to hear, they hoped, the coster songs of Albert Chevalier, they were shocked by the dancers and by the prostitutes thronging the theatre's interior. Their horrified hostess, Laura Ormiston Chant, a temperance and vigilance campaigner who belonged to the NVA, took her friend Lady Henry Somerset (sometime wife of the *Spirit Lamp* lyricist) and went to see for herself.

What resulted from this and subsequent visits was Chant's determination to go before the LCC's Theatres and Music Halls Committee and oppose the renewal of the Empire's licence. When she did so on 19 October her stand led to considerable publicity, with her becoming 'the most popular effigy on Guy Fawkes night' (Turner [1950] 1966: 235). There followed an increasingly ill-tempered correspondence in the *DT* initiated by 'Englishman', whose letter, headed 'Prudes on the Prowl' inspired a music hall song and 'released a riptide of ridicule' against Chant and her supporters (238). 'How long are we patiently to endure the shrill shriek of the emancipated female[?]' 'Englishman' asked:

> How long must we listen to the impudent piety of these provincial pedlars in social purity who come red-hot from their Chicago platforms and tinpot tabernacles [Chant was often mistaken for an American] to tell this London of ours how she is to amuse herself and how she is to dispose of and harass and drive from pillar to post these unfortunate outcasts whom we have always had and always shall have amongst us? (Turner [1950] 1966: 238)

Chant's protests, and the restrictions on the Empire that followed, sparked demonstrations in London halls, protests from cab drivers and theatre employees, and a legal challenge from George Edwardes, the Empire's owner: the embattled Edwardes and his moralistic persecutors were pictured as 'George and the Dragons' in satirical cartoons. *Punch* charged the hawk-nosed, lorgnetted frump, Mrs Prowlina Pry, with 'intruding' upon the theatre and ruining the livelihoods of 3,000 employees (27/10/94: 194).[2] Yet Chant did not seek to close the theatre, only, as she explained in her pamphlet, 'Why We Attacked the Empire' (1895) to prevent it from being 'a haunt of vice' (Ledger and Luckhurst 2000: 70) to which the authorities turned a blind eye. Declaring war on drink, vice and gambling, she argued in person and print that theatres should be venues for legitimate entertainment rather than fleshpots or fronts for the sale of alcohol, yet her views were travestied in the press, with the *IPN*'s 'The Mummer' protesting that 'a few busy bodies' are 'wrecking the amusements' of 'London's pleasure-seeking public' (3/11/94). Radical newspapers such as *RN* supported her up to a point in order to attack the rich for 'the cynical indulgence of their lusts' (Turner [1950] 1966: 246), though their help alienated conservatives. Chant won a partial victory when the LCC forced the Empire to screen off its bars and promenade, but it was short-lived. The flimsy partitions were torn down by a mob, prominent among whom was the young Winston Churchill, then a Sandhurst cadet, who fondly recalled the incident in *My Early Life* (1930). The theatre's licence was renewed unconditionally, after its management protested it had been unfairly singled out by vigilance campaigners. The Empire's promenade remained open until 1916, although theatres which did not have promenades were not allowed to install them. Chant, meanwhile, organised relief for Armenians persecuted in Turkey. In March 1896, she told the *NYT* she had no wish to lead further agitation in London since 'nothing could be worse for a reform movement than for it to be constantly associated with the name of a single person' (14/3/96).

Chant's campaign demonstrated the deep-seated resistance of the establishment to women who 'interfered' in male domains – her mastery of cross examination and legal procedure had taken Edwardes, as well as the Empire's barrister, C.F. Gill, by surprise during the LCC hearing. It showed the continued hypocrisy of the authorities and, as the radical press made clear, foregrounded inequalities between 'toffs' in evening dress, who could seemingly behave as they wished, and London's less privileged citizens, who could not (a private box cost as much as three guineas, while box stalls were 7s 6d). As Barry Faulk shows, Chant also problematised the role and status of the charity worker by visiting the theatre in disguise and by attacking the 'pleasures' of privileged men rather than primarily ministering to their victims (2004: 75–110). Like

MRS. PROWLINA PRY.—"I HOPE I DON'T INTRUDE!"

THOUSANDS OF FELLOW-CREATURES FLUNG FROM WORK   THAN *PUNCH* IMAGINES, OUR NEW BUMBLE-BAND,
AT THE MERE PEN-STROKE OF A HASTY CENSOR!—   IF MISTRESS PRY'S DECISION THEY ABIDE BY;
AN UNCONSIDERED TRIFLE ZEAL MAY SHIRK!   BUT *SHOULD* THEY FAIL US, *PUNCH* THROUGHOUT THE LAND
BUT SENSE MAY NOT, NOR JUSTICE! THEY ARE DENSER   WILL WAKE THE PEOPLE PRUDES AND PRIGS ARE TRIED BY!

Figure 2. Mrs Prowlina Pry hopes she doesn't intrude; *Punch*'s acerbic view of Laura Ormiston Chant's campaign against immorality in music halls, 27 October 1894.

Shaw, who took a lively interest in the controversy, and whose *Mrs Warren's Profession* languished unperformed during it, Chant exposed the interdependence of legitimate business and illegal trade. Finally, the Empire affair showed the might of the press when its firepower was directed at a single issue or person. Those caught in its fusillade were unlikely to emerge unscathed, and it says much for Chant's courage and personal resilience that she managed to brave the broadsides.

Chant's enemies argued that although the Empire was a venue for prostitution, the women involved were better off safe inside the theatre than the Hogarthian derelicts walking Whitechapel's streets. Life beyond the haze of gas-light and cigar smoke was often dangerous.[3] The CLAA had raised the age of consent for girls to sixteen, and had created in its wake the NVA, a group which combined the Society for the Suppression of Vice, the Minors' Protection Society, the Belgian Traffic Committee (which dealt with British girls abducted for the European sex trade), and the Central Vigilance Society. As Trevor Fisher shows, it encouraged a more assertive response to prostitution from the police, and the result was a marked rise in prosecutions against brothel keepers, pimps and dealers in pornographic literature and goods (Fisher 1997: 137). The NVA's efforts increased the number of cases coming to court, which in turn filled the columns of newspapers such as the *IPN*, a penny weekly founded in 1864 whose circulation had blossomed with the increasing literacy brought about by the educational reforms of the 1870s and 1880s, and which grew from four to eight pages in 1895. Hypocritical and sensational in equal measure – a typical headline was 'Terrible Panic Amongst Schoolchildren – Exciting Details' (15/12/94) – and voted 'the worst newspaper in England' by readers of the *PMG* in November 1886, the *IPN* delighted in stories of sexual misconduct and violence (*PMG* 23/11/86). Its success showed the public appetite for such journalism, and gave dramatic glimpses of crime and vice through-out the land.

Death in Kensington

On 10 November, the *IPN* reported the arrest of an 'artist', Walter Schultz, who was charged with 'being a suspected person and loitering in a woman's dress for an unlawful purpose.' Police observed him accosting men in Whitechapel High Street between midnight and one o'clock in the morning wearing 'a black dress, light jacket and cape, black and gold bonnet with large scarlet flowers, a veil, earrings [and] rings'. They soon discovered he wore corsets and 'padding' too. Schultz told them he was 'a man right enough' and a medical examination to prove such was unnecessary. 'A gentleman brought me down from Piccadilly,' he added. 'I have done this since I came over [from Germany].' As Charles van Onselen has shown, sex-trafficking was rife in the East End despite the efforts of the NVA, while the research of H.G. Cocks (98–105) and Matt Cook (42–72) gives some idea of the number of cross-dressed male prostitutes at work in the capital during the 1890s: Schultz lived with a woman who dressed as a man. Two constables testified to having seen Schultz in Whitechapel before, in the company of another 'lady' and with men on either arm. When he asked in court why he had not been arrested, the police replied they thought he was female.

In May 1871, Ernest Boulton and Frederick Park, cross-dressing theatrical artistes known as Fanny and Stella, had been the subject of a remarkable trial when, following a long period of surveillance, they were arrested leaving the Strand Theatre in drag. Suspected of sexual misdemeanours, and charged with conspiring to commit a felony, the pair claimed they were simply playing a high-spirited prank. Found innocent by the jury after less than an hour's deliberation, they disappeared into obscurity (M. Kaplan 2005: 19–101). The case was a nine-days' wonder, 'Experto Crede', a contributor to *RN*, later recalled that though the trial was a 'fiasco', it did reduce the 'swarms' of 'sexless youngsters, painted and powdered, sometimes in male dress and sometimes, in female, accosting passers, and becoming daily more brazen and impudent' (*RN* 26/5/95). A defence of innocent fun was impossible for Schultz. Judge Robert Biron had no doubt the German loitered 'with intent to commit a felony'. He sentenced him to three months hard labour.[4] 'The defendant attempted to speak, but was gently lifted out of the dock by the assistant gaoler,' the report concludes. 'And I, my Lord, may I say nothing?'

Abuse, assault, rape and even murder were daily realities in Whitechapel, but more prosperous districts of the city were not necessarily safer for lone women at night. On 20 November, a woman lost an eye after her face was slashed by a 'female fiend' in Stanhope Gardens, Kensington (*IPN* 8/12/94). Late on the night of 25 November, the body of Augusta Dawes, also known as Margaret Dawes and Gussie Dudley, a 'member of the "unfortunate" class' was found in Holland Park Road outside the house of the artist, Valentine Prinsep (*IPN* 8/12/94). Her throat had been cut, and a sharp knife and a cherry-wood walking stick were found nearby. Herbert Schmaltz, a painter, who, like Prinsep, was working on a picture for the forthcoming RA exhibition, witnessed the crime. He gave chase but lost the attacker in Kensington High Street.

'The Kensington Murder' horrified West London, not simply because it was a brutal crime but because of where it had occurred, the gentrified (if poorly lit) suburb which was home to the likes of Lord Leighton, President of the RA; Schmaltz reported he first saw Dawes and her assailant near Leighton's house (*T* 11 and 17/12/94). Alarm increased when a letter describing the murder in detail arrived at Kensington police station on 28 November. It bore a Dublin postmark and was signed 'On the job. From Jack the Ripper' (*T* 10 and 11/12/94). On 1 December, another woman was attacked in Stanhope Gardens. Kensington police were now on full alert, seeking a veiled woman 'who is expected to turn out to be a lunatic with murderous instincts' (*T* 4/12/94). She was never found, but on 4 December, 'Jack the Ripper' was arrested in Belfast. Four days later, William Hicks was arrested following a chase through Holland Park, having apparently stabbed a woman 'between the eyes' (*PMG* 10/12/94).

Those who suspected the Whitechapel Murderer of being a 'toff' in 1888 may have felt vindicated by the capture of Reginald Treherne Bassett Saunderson, the son of an Irish JP and Lady Rachel Saunderson, a daughter of the Third Earl of Clonmel. Saunderson's uncle was Colonel E.J. Saunderson, the Unionist MP for North Armagh, and one of his sisters was married to another MP, H.L. Mulholland (North Derry). Unfortunately, as Reginald Saunderson only celebrated his twenty-first birthday on 23 November, he could not have been responsible for the earlier killings, even if he had stabbed Augusta Dawes. The knife and stick found near the murder scene were recognised, and his handwriting was identified by Dr Langdon-Down, who had cared for the young man at a private school-cum-asylum in Hampton Wick since December 1888. 'Boyish', 'pallid', and 'fatigued', the chain-smoking Saunderson was brought to London for questioning, charged with wilful murder and taken to Holloway Prison (*IPN* 11/12/94).

Langdon-Down's establishment cared for those who were 'exceptionally backward or addicted to eccentric habits' by offering 'physical, moral, and intellectual training under medical supervision' (*T* 4 and 29/12/94). Security was minimal. Saunderson was not kept under restraint, and absconded on several occasions, even enlisting in the Surrey Militia in August 1892. Discharged when his identity was discovered, he was not considered dangerous. His murderous inclinations were apparently triggered by reading news reports of another sensational crime.

On 1 December 1894, the *IPN* reported nine men were awaiting execution in England. Most had murdered their wives or partners in the course of domestic disputes; one, John William Newell, of Loughborough, had beaten his wife Isabella to death with a coal pick in front of their young son, believing she had been unfaithful (*IPN* 1 and 15/12/94; *Leicester Chronicle* 15/12/94). Such tragedies received only passing mention in the national press, but occasionally, murders seized the public imagination, forming a pantheon of 'classic crimes'. One such case was the murder of the pregnant 23-year-old Florence Dennis, found shot dead in the almost dried-up Prittlewell Brook, near Southend, in June 1894.

What gave Dennis's murder particular interest was the tangled domestic life of the accused, 39-year-old James Canham Read, a cashier at the Royal Albert Dock. Seemingly a model employee and loyal husband who lived in Stepney with his wife and eight children and earned £150 per year, Read was a reckless sexual adventurer who, together with his brother, Harry, exploited the full potential of southeast England's railway network. In a quadrille that made remarkable demands on his stamina, his income and his capacity for deceit, Read was involved with his wife, Florence Dennis, and Beatrice Kempton, a woman in Upper Mitcham with whom he had a child and with whom he lived occasionally as 'Mr and Mrs Edgar Benson', posing as a commercial traveller. He had also pursued an affair with Florence's older sister, Bertha. Utilising aliases, telegrams and post office boxes, Read ran two separate households as well as visiting the Dennis sisters. When Florence became pregnant, Read's house of cards collapsed. Absconding with £160 from the Docks, he killed her and fled to Upper Mitcham, where an alias and a new moustache failed to prevent his arrest in early July. He sent his wife £20; despite her parlous domestic state, she returned it to the dockyard, which awarded her a gratuity of £23 the following year. A police search of Read's home revealed many blank marriage certificate forms.

Read's private life had been uncovered before Southend magistrates in a sensational hearing. Such was the local prejudice against him that November that his trial had to be held in Chelmsford. Large crowds gathered. Robert Coombes, a thirteen-year-old Londoner, was so fascinated by the case that he walked to the trial from Plaistow dressed in his cricket whites. Prosecuted by the Solicitor-General, Sir Frank Lockwood, Read maintained his innocence, but until 1898, the accused was not allowed to testify in their defence in murder trials. Read therefore relied on his brother, who sported a heliotrope tie and a white chrysanthemum buttonhole. His foppish demeanour failed to impress the jury, who swiftly reached a guilty verdict. Despite Harry petitioning the Home Office for clemency, Read was hanged on 4 December. A few days after releasing his brother's final letter, which pleaded his innocence, Harry Read drowned himself in the Thames (*IPN* 8 and 15/12/94).

Quite how Read's case inspired Saunderson to emulate Jack the

Ripper only he knew, since the Stepney Lothario and the Whitechapel murderer shared neither motive nor method. Nevertheless, it was apparently reports of the Southend hearing that caused Saunderson to take a knife, send out a servant to get it sharpened, and embark on his murderous mission. The relationship between crime, sensational literature and journalism was of growing concern.

Before the murder, Saunderson's parents had planned to train him as a gardener and ship him off to Canada. Now they sought to use their wealth and influence to rescue him from the Old Bailey, hiring C.F. Gill, the Belfast-born barrister who had one of the capital's largest practices, as defence counsel. 'Every effort will be made [. . .] to avoid the publicity of a murder trial,' the *Times* reported (7/12/94). At the inquest on 10 December, Saunderson's father proffered an account of his son's mental history, only to be told by the Coroner his sanity was not yet an issue. At the remand hearing on 21 December, Gill argued that trying Saunderson would simply waste public money. The police now had a detailed account of his movements on the night of the killing, and Mrs Langdon-Down admitted that although he had 'never shown any violence, she had heard that he had threatened to put a knife into a lady' (*T* 29/12/94). Saunderson had also attacked an assistant gaoler and attempted to escape from the West London police court. His condition deteriorated in Holloway, and he was placed in a straitjacket and padded cell. His trial was due to open at the Old Bailey on 30 January before Mr Justice Wills, but although the jury was sworn in, Saunderson was deemed unfit to plead by reason of insanity and ordered to be detained at Her Majesty's Pleasure (*T* 31/1/95).[5] He was obviously disturbed, but the murder seemed premeditated, and this merited further investigation. Whether or not family pressure had any bearing on the trial's abandonment, the affair was not well publicised; the *Times* devoted only a brief paragraph to the insanity ruling, and Saunderson was quickly forgotten.

One final crime to make the headlines in 1894 occurred at Wilde's beloved Café Royal in Regent Street. Early on 6 December, the night porter, Marius Martin, was struck with a blunt instrument, dying in Charing Cross hospital without regaining consciousness (*T* 7/12/94). An inquest decided he had probably disturbed burglars tempted by £450 in the restaurant's cash box, and ruled he was murdered by person or persons unknown. The case was never solved.

Christmas Lists and Resolutions

As the police hunted the Kensington Murderer, publishers, theatre managers and music hall performers turned their attentions towards Christmas and the pantomime season. Having treated London audiences to her new song, the 'very saucy' 'He Knows a Good Thing when He Sees It', Marie Lloyd was at Liverpool's Shakespeare theatre in *Pretty Bo-Peep, Little Boy Blue, and the Merry Old Woman who lived in a Shoe*, a role which called for tight breeches, singing, acting and dancing. 'No one else is so clever in suggesting a *sous-entendre*,' said the *SR*. 'No phrase was ever so innocent that she would not pass it on to you as an insinuation' (24/11/94: 557). The cross-dressing Vesta Tilley delighted audiences as Dick Whittington at Birmingham's Prince of Wales theatre. Cross-dressing helped criminalise Walter Schultz; it also played a key role in Brandon Thomas's farce, *Charley's Aunt* (1892), which was enjoying phenomenal popularity at London's Globe – it celebrated the second year of its run on 21 December, eventually clocking up 1,466 performances in the capital, to say nothing of its success in the provinces and abroad. The doyenne of pantomime dames, Dan Leno, returning in November from a residency in Manchester, was not however called upon to don drag this year, since he was Idle Jack in Drury Lane's *Dick Whittington*. Such performers earned considerable sums – though they could not match the great operatic divas such as Nellie Melba, who sang at Covent Garden for £400 a night, and Adelina Patti, who could earn as much as £800 for a single performance in one of the larger provincial cities, the likes of Marie Lloyd and Bessie Bellwood, 'hearty, British, sympathetically vulgar, full of dash and bounce' and capable of silencing the rowdiest heckler, still drew £100 per week (*SR* 24/11/94:557).

With such success came the pressure to demonstrate star status off-stage. In early December, the comedian Charles Bignell was declared bankrupt with liabilities of £909, ruined by ill health, gambling and moneylenders' crippling interest rates. The obligation to act 'swell' devoured his assets, despite an average income of £750 in the years 1892–4 (*IPN* 8/12/94). Life in the halls was physically and emotionally demanding. At the end of October, a 'music hall artiste' playing the Golden Fleece in Grimsby was committed to the Bracebridge asylum after roaming the streets in her nightdress (*IPN* 3/11/94). In November, Ben Fuller, a highboard diver at the London Aquarium, was killed attempting a daredevil leap from Tower Bridge (*IPN* 24/11/94). On Boxing Night, Kittie Tyrell, 'The Rat' ('a rattling demonstrative demon' according to the programme) in the Elephant and Castle theatre's production of *Dick Whittington and His Cat* left the stage feeling faint after singing 'His road to fortune he'll pave o'er my corpse'. Within minutes, she died from heart disease in her dressing room, leaving her husband, who was also in the production and contracted for the entire season, to go on with the show (*IPN 5/1/95*). Even a star of Bellwood's magnitude was worn out by the demands of her profession. Having gone from being a fur dresser in a Bermondsey clothing factory to the darling of the halls, she died in 1896 aged only thirty-nine.

Lloyd may have been the star of *Little Bo Peep*, but its scenic artist 'was called to take a bow three times during the course of the show' (Gillies [1999] 2001: 95). Expensive to stage and with a short seasonal lifespan, pantomimes required financial prudence from theatre managers as well as crowd-pleasing storylines and performers. The same rules applied in the more elevated theatrical world, where productions aspired to higher levels of artistic worth but were equally dependent upon audience approval. In 1894, claimed 'The Mummer', almost 500 new plays debuted in London and the provinces, and such plenitude made it very difficult for any new work to succeed. With one theatre for every 145,000 Londoners, playgoers had plenty of choice, and while provincial cities could not match London in this regard, most had several theatres and halls (*IPN 29/12/94*). Larger venues spent heavily on advertising and gimmicks. Collins' Music Hall had a 4 ft by 3 ft iron-framed sign made of coloured glass illuminated by gas jets: the profusion of such devices led to the London Sky Signs Act 1891 to control their use. Failure in such surroundings was as public as it was costly.

As 1895 drew near, Arthur Wing Pinero, Oscar Wilde and Henry James were looking to have new plays on the London stage, with Wilde's *An Ideal Husband* due to open on 3 January at the Haymarket's Theatre Royal, James's *Guy Domville* opening two days later at the St James's and Pinero's *The Notorious Mrs Ebbsmith*, the follow-up to *The Second Mrs Tanqueray* (1894) due to be performed at the Garrick in March. The supreme actor of the day, Henry Irving was meanwhile rehearsing for the title role in J. Comyns Carr's lavish *King Arthur*, scheduled to open at the Lyceum on 12 January.

Dearly wishing to write for the stage yet eternally unsuccessful, James was anxious about the forthcoming production. His friend Rudyard Kipling in far-away Vermont attempted to calm him by prophesying 'This year is going to bring you luck and you'll have a play that goes' (Kipling 1990: 163), but James still complained of the 'nervousness and the exhaustion' of rehearsals (James 1980: 496). He was, he told one of his many correspondents, '*too* preoccupied, too terrified, too fundamentally distracted, to be fit for human intercourse' (496). As the opening night approached, he told Edmund Gosse 'I am more or less, already under chloroform' (504). In the preface to the second series of *Theatricals*, a collection of his unperformed plays published in late 1894, James wrote, 'There is no room in a play for the play itself until everything (including the play, the distracted neophyte pantingly ascertains) has been completely eliminated. Then the fun, as the vulgar phrase is, begins.' Such beliefs did not bode well for *Guy Domville*, especially when espoused by a man of negligible dramatic pedigree. Although James had written a number of plays and dramatic scenarios, only *The American* had made it to the stage, managing sixty-nine performances at the Opera Comique in 1891. The *NYT* felt James's plays exhibited 'a lack of theatrical "perspective,"' regretting 'there is not a theatre in the whole English-speaking world where such plays can be properly tried for the benefit of the few who would like to see them' (15/12/94).

Wilde had enjoyed notable successes with his society comedies *Lady Windermere's Fan* (1892) and *A Woman of No Importance* (1893). His understanding of theatrical time and space was far superior to James's, but he lacked Pinero's practical experience as an actor and director and became irritating in rehearsals, chain-smoking his way through observations and asides of questionable utility. He caused particular ill feeling by summoning the cast of *An Ideal Husband* to a meeting on Christmas morning, antagonising Charles Brookfield who played Lord Goring's valet. In May 1892, Brookfield had written and starred in *The Poet and the Puppets*, with Charles Hawtrey, Lord Goring in *An Ideal Husband*, playing 'A Poet' in an obvious caricature of Wilde.[6] Brookfield's squib which, as Beerbohm said, depicted Wilde as 'a fat man with a taste for dyed flowers and epigramme' (*ILN* 15/9/94: 406), was an attempt at revenge; according to Ellmann, he had never forgiven Wilde for highlighting his *faux pas* in keeping gloves on at a tea party. Educated at Westminster and Trinity College, Cambridge, where he won the Winchester Reading Prize in 1878, Brookfield came from an illustrious artistic family (his mother was a niece of Henry Hallam and friend of Thackeray) and aspired to be known as a wit. Resenting Wilde's success, he did not appreciate his patronising manner, and their relationship deteriorated quickly. The damaging consequences of their rivalry would soon become obvious.

The Christmas book market was buoyant, not least because 1894 was a decisive year in Britain's shift from being primarily a book-borrowing nation to becoming a book-owning one. Before that June, many novels initially appeared in three volume form, with each volume available from Mudie's or other subscription libraries. Annual membership cost a guinea, allowing members to borrow one volume at a time, a fair bargain when a three-decker cost 31s 6d. Variable levels of subscription up to one hundred guineas allowed for increased borrowing; it was normally months before a 6s edition of a novel appeared. The system encouraged novelists to spin out a story into three volumes – as with mid-Victorian ladies' fashion, the original form became invisible beneath layers of padding. It also allowed libraries to police the content of fiction by refusing to stock works they deemed unsuitable for family reading. Unofficial censorship had angered progressively-minded novelists since the 1870s, but it remained in place despite the growing success of writers such as Stevenson and Rider Haggard who wrote affordable single volume adventure fiction, and publishers such as John Lane who issued single volume collections of controversial short stories; his edition of George Egerton's *Keynotes* (1893) quickly sold over 6,000 copies. Such writers sidestepped the library system altogether, with Lane 'introducing the publishing principle that *all* authors should *always* get a royalty' (Lambert and Ratcliffe 1987: 51), even if his payments to them were often embarrassingly delayed.

On 27 June, Mudie's signed an historic agreement with W.H. Smith, the firm which monopolised railway bookstalls and specialised in single volume reprints of older fiction. Despite selling on their three-deckers once cheap editions had appeared, the libraries were becoming overwhelmed by storage problems, and this finally forced them to take action, reducing the fees paid to publishers for new books in an attempt to slim down the size of individual novels and the numbers of them in circulation. They also sought, less successfully, to retard further the appearance of cheap editions of single volume works. The impact, combined with the declining cost of paper, was immediate. Publication of three-deckers fell from 184 in 1894 to fifty-two in 1895, twenty-five in 1896 and a mere four in 1897 (Keating [1898] 1991: 26). The ending of the libraries' virtual monopoly had important consequences for the content as well as the sales and distribution of novels, since although books were still borrowed from Mudie's, it could no longer easily control their content. Transgressive subject matter and radical technical innovation increased for, as Arthur Morrison lamented, the library system had placed literature under 'irresponsible', 'arbitrary' and 'intolerable censorship' (*A* 27/4/95: 536–7).

Children's books were usually single volumes and tended to bypass the library system. They were an especially popular Christmas present for middle class children, and the market for them was expanding yearly. Kipling's *The Jungle Book*, which Wilde bought for his son Vyvyan, sold 8,000 copies in the weeks before Christmas (*Bookman* 3/95: 167). The veteran G.A. Henty offered *Wulf the Saxon, When London Burned, In Freedom's Cause: A Story of Wallace and Bruce* and *In the*

Heart of the Rockies; his even more prolific female counterpart, L.T. Meade *Betty, a Schoolgirl* and *Red Rose and Tiger Lily* alongside adult novels *A Life for a Love,* the two volume *In an Iron Grip* and the three decker, *A Soldier of Fortune.*[7] E.A. Lemann's illustrated edition of Hans Christian Anderson's *The Snow Queen* was widely commended. Boys' books celebrated British martial triumphs on land and sea, frequently dramatising episodes from the Indian Mutiny or the naval battles of the sixteenth and seventeenth centuries. A typical example, Commander C.N. Robinson and John Leyland's *To the Honour of the Flag: A Story of Our Sea-Fights with the Dutch* was a book 'every boy should read' (*PMG* 15/12/94). That only a fraction of the nation's children were at public school did not prevent tales of public school life being extremely popular. One of the more imaginative examples was Robert Overton's *Lights Out!*, which adapted the narrative structure of the *Decameron* to the dormitory of Dr Audlem's college.

Adults meanwhile shuddered round the fire with Mrs J.H. Riddell's ghost stories, *The Banshee's Warning and Other Tales*, Conan Doyle's *Round the Red Lamp*, a collection that included the horrific tale of sexual jealousy and mutilation, 'The Case of Lady Sannox', and typically sensational offerings from Mary Braddon, *Thou Art the Man,* and Ouida, *Two Offenders and Other Tales.* More serious fiction included Arthur Morrison's vivid sketches of East End life, *Tales of Mean Streets,* George Moore's *Esther Waters,* Gissing's *In the Year of Jubilee,* Hardy's *Life's Little Ironies* and bitter critiques of marital mores such as Egerton's *Discords* and Mona Caird's *The Daughters of Danaus,* all of which were unlikely Christmas gifts. Readers with scholarly inclinations could quibble with Gladstone's translation of Horace's odes: many did. The best-selling new poets were John Davidson, with *Ballads and Songs* and William Watson with *Odes and Other Poems* but in his overview of 1894, Arthur Symons singled out Swinburne's *Astrophel*, 'wonderful in its display of technique' as the year's finest volume. Symons praised work by his friend W.B. Yeats, Yeats' friend 'AE' (George Russell), Ernest Rhys and Laurence Binyon, but castigated Lewis Morris, who had an outside chance of filling the vacant office of Laureate but had 'once more given inadequate expression to nullities'. He felt the *Second Book of the Rhymers' Club* (to which he himself contributed four poems) was very mixed in quality, and dismissed Wilde's *The Sphinx* as 'a "Sphinx" without a secret' (*A* 5/1/95: 9–10). In the *Weekly Sun,* Richard Le Gallienne announced seven new major poets had come to prominence in 1894: Watson, Davidson, Symons, Yeats, Kipling, Francis Thompson and, less convincingly, his Bodley Head stable-mate, Norman Gale. His choice was widely attacked as a 'logrolling' exercise on behalf of John Lane; as Le Gallienne's pseudonym was 'Logroller' he could hardly have been surprised.

Symons was an accomplished critic and one with catholic tastes. His review of the year showed the liveliness and diversity of the literary scene by singling out G.S. Street's satire on decadence, *The Autobiography of a Boy*, the naturalistic short stories of Frederick Wedmore, Israel Zangwill's ethnographic fictions of the Jewish East End, and the Stevensonian adventure fiction of Stanley Weyman. Anthony Hope, by contrast, offered 'brilliant dialogue and [the] inability to construct a story', while Mrs Humphry Ward's *Marcella* had 'every excellence but that of the novel.' Finally, Symons delighted in George Du Maurier's *Trilby*, a novel of 'real charm and liveliness', and Lane's 'quarterly caprice', the *YB*, which he pronounced 'an interesting experiment' though not yet of lasting value.

Symons's survey had its mournful aspect too, for 1894 saw the deaths of several leading literary figures. Pater, Symons's mentor, died in July, and the poets Roden Noel and Augusta Webster, and the art critic P.G. Hamerton also joined the majority. December saw two other significant passings. On 3 December, Robert Louis Stevenson died in Samoa of a cerebral haemorrhage. He had long been in poor health though he continued to write at a hectic pace and was working on the unfinished *Weir of Hermiston* (1896) on the morning he died. 'His death leaves a melancholy blank in the literary world,' said the *Times*. 'We regret Mr Stevenson selfishly as well as sincerely, because in the crowd of successful and rising writers there is no one left who can even approximately fill his place' (18/12/94). The *SR* ran a four column obituary on 22 December. Stevenson received many tributes from friends, with J.M. Barrie's 'Scotland's Lament' in the *Bookman* imagining his weeping homeland:

> Ye sons wha do your little best,
>   Ye writing Scots, put by the pen,
> He's deid, the ane abune the rest,
>   I winna look at write again. (1/95: 108)

Stevenson's death brought a tear to Mr Punch's eye in an 88–line elegy hailing the 'Brave bringer-back of old Romance' (29/12/94: 303), and Andrew Lang was volubly appreciative in the *ILN* (5/1/95: 15). Kipling told Weyman Stevenson's death seemed impossible. 'It must be one of his jests,' he wrote on 3 January, 'and he'll "come up with a song from the sea" while we are mourning over him' (Kipling 1990: 167). Kipling was later disgusted by the publication of Stevenson's letters, picturing Gosse, their editor, as a magpie with carrion in its beak (174). Henry

James told Gosse the 'ghastly extinction of RLS' was 'an absolute desolation. It makes me cold and sick'; he wrote a lengthy and touching letter of sympathy to his friend's widow (James 1980: 495, 497–501).

Debate about Stevenson's lasting place in Victorian letters began almost immediately. Most public commentators felt he had joined the immortals as a novelist and children's poet, but Gissing was less convinced. 'Sincerely sorry' for Stevenson's death, he nonetheless confided to Clare Collet, 'I don't know if he is a great writer; but an exquisite one (in the right sense of the word) certainly.' To his close friend Eduard Bertz, Gissing was blunt. 'I think now, as ever, that his merit is much exaggerated. But he was a most interesting personality' (Gissing 1994: 267, 271).

Despite Kipling's comment, Stevenson's death was hardly unexpected. The same was true of Christina Rossetti's from cancer on 29 December. She 'takes her place among the great poets of our century,' wrote Symons, 'not on suffering as a woman, but by right, as an artist' (*SR* 5/1/95: 6). Her work, said the *Times,* showed 'grace and delicacy combined with a clear and pellucid style and a singular tenderness and sensitiveness of feeling' (1/1/95). Her funeral included her hymns, 'The Porter watches at the gate' and 'Lord, grant us grace to mount by steps of grace.' Swinburne, who had hailed Rossetti as 'the Jael who led our hosts to victory' (Gosse 1917: 137) in the aftermath of *Goblin Market* (1862) and dedicated *A Century of Roundels* (1883) to her, was particularly upset by her death. 'The last words I wrote last night and last year were some lines in memory of her,' he told his mother on New Year's Day. 'I looked out of window [*sic*] and have never seen a more magnificent heavenful of stars' (Swinburne 1962: 78). The elegy, 'A New Year's Eve', appeared in the *Nineteenth Century* in February. Given 'a table-cover hallowed by her use at the very last' (79), Swinburne found he lacked a table of sufficient size and ended up draping the relic over his sofa. He praised Rossetti's 'beautiful nature and its inevitable spiritual attractiveness' (81), though in 1904, he unwisely told her brother, William Michael, that her 'noble and beautiful nature' had been 'spiritually infected and envenomed by the infernal and putrefying virus of the Galilean serpent' (Henderson 1973: 278).

While Symons examined established figures, new voices waited to be heard. Enoch Arnold Bennett, as yet uncertain how to sign himself, was determined to make his mark, paying 2s 6d for two-hourly French conversation classes in a strenuous programme of self-improvement. By late November he had 'sold ten stories to appear in the first quarter of 1895', including 'A Letter Home' to the *YB*. This was the only one of other than 'fiscal' importance, he noted (Bennett 1968: 15), recording that his literary earnings for 1894 were £55 5s 5d (McDonald 1997: 69). H.G. Wells was finalising his divorce in late 1894 and hard at work transforming his *New Review* serial, 'The Time Traveller's Story' into *The Time Machine*. He was also the newly appointed theatre critic for the *PMG*; his first assignment was to review *An Ideal Husband* despite only having previously seen two plays. A third emerging writer, later a close friend of Wells, was the Polish émigré Józef Teodor Konrad Korseniowski, about to make his novelistic debut as Joseph Conrad with *Almayer's Folly*, a story set in the jungles of Borneo. Conrad wished to promote the book as 'a civilised story in savage surroundings' (Conrad 1983: 199). He sold the copyright to T. Fisher Unwin (known to Gissing's son as 'the man who sends our fish') for £20, and spent Christmas Eve studying his proofs. 'I was horrified: absolutely horrified by the thing in print, looking so stupid – worse – senseless,' he told his aunt (193). Already suspecting the reading public would dislike his tragic story and its method, Conrad was encouraged by Edward Garnett to 'follow his own path and disregard the public taste'. 'I won't live in an attic,' Conrad replied, though his financial status was soon to be greatly improved by a £4,000 legacy from his uncle (McDonald 1997: 24).

For many middle class readers of the mid-1890s, however, the most notable new talents were those gathered beneath the umbrella of the Bodley Head's *YB*. While other magazines had a far greater readership – the first issue of the *Windsor* sold out its 100,000 copies in a few days in January 1895 – it achieved immediate notoriety, representing the literary and artistic avant-garde with a brazen contempt for decorum.

Decorative Salaciousness

The *YB* was launched as an 'illustrated quarterly' in June 1894, with Henry Harland its editor and Aubrey Beardsley its art editor and designer-in-chief. Deliberately provocative in its content, marketing and price of 5s, the journal was a hybrid of magazine and book designed to appeal as a material object. *Blackwood's* 'The Looker-On' was unimpressed. 'Apparently, the "Yellow Book" was an attempt at an illustrated magazine of supreme pretensions,' he wrote, 'professing to be wittier, daringer, and wickeder than ever magazine was – and dearer.' It was a haven for:

> the writers of all the nastiest stories and all the sickliest songs; all the dissolute young gentlemen who have tremendous adventures with indescribable women, and all the artists who can make these indescribable women sprawl through the nasty obscenity of a 'process' print. (1/95: 164)

The chief target of such remarks was the notorious Beardsley, who was regularly attacked in the press as well as parodied in *Punch*. The frontispiece to *Punch's Almanack* for 1895, acknowledged his fashionable but unsavoury status with 'Britannia *à la* Beardsley', by 'Our Yellow Decadent' (E.T. Reed), a depiction of a disdainful woman surrounded by 'symbols of emasculated national pride' such as a 'delicate lion' an 'effeminate bull-terrier' (in a ruff) and an 'effete Punch figure'. Such iconography implied, as Colette Colligan says, 'decadence, exoticism, and obscenity' with Beardsley's interests in French and Japanese art much to the fore (Colligan 156). The *PMG* dubbed the *YB* the 'mustard plaster' and its designer, 'the patron saint of the back parlour', a devilish pornographer whose art was a moral menace (9/2/95). Beardsley responded with provocative letters to the newspapers and ever more outrageous images. His dark-haired, thin and sneeringly superior figures challenged prevailing conceptions of female beauty, with Henry Labouchere's *Truth* providing a recipe for their creation in its Christmas number:

> Equal parts of venom take,
>   Slime, and impudicity,
> Belladonna, sewer-gas,
>   Laudanum, and lubricity. (Marks 1990: 168)

Whether or not Beardsley's images were misogynistic seemed less important than their sheer newness; his voraciously syncretic style moved rapidly from imitation to caricature to originality and back again, bewildering those who had inspired him, such as Edward Burne-Jones, and disgusting those who saw his 'art' as no more than a parade of perverse mannerisms. At the same time, when his fragile health permitted, he was a shrewd organiser with a clear idea of his own worth; his list of costings for the *YB*'s October 1894 number shows he was easily the highest paid artistic contributor, commanding a fee of £15 per drawing. His nearest rival, Walter Sickert, received only £7 10s, with Philip Wilson Steer receiving £5 and William Hyde a couple of guineas (JLA). Only Crackanthorpe, who received £20 for 'A Study in Sentimentality', was paid more highly. To put such earnings into context, it is worth noting that Anne Medhurst, engaged by the Gissings as a general servant in February 1895, accepted a salary of £16 per annum.

The fourth *YB* appeared in January. By now its novelty was wearing off, and the formerly outraged were growing blasé, and characterising the journal as the Bodley Head's house magazine. Beardsley continued to challenge conservatives however; his cover design showed a woman receiving a flower from a half-naked androgyne as she moved through a formal stone gateway into a menacingly dark wood. The image primed readers for a similarly disconcerting experience. Henry James, Harland's star contributor, was missing, but in his place were new women poets and short story writers; Graham R. Tomson (Rosamund Marriott Watson), Ménie Muriel Dowie (parodied in *Granta* as 'Melia Mascula Dowdie'), Dolf Wyllard, Olive Custance, E. Nesbit, Ella Hepworth Dixon and Leila Macdonald. There was also a story by Evelyn Sharp, the first of six she would publish in the magazine over the next two years. Alongside these was Beerbohm's tart satire on Wilde, '1880', a mock-historical essay that peered into a time 'mobled in the mists of antiquity' when impressionable young women 'fired by the fervid words of young Oscar, threw their mahogany into the streets' (Beerbohm 1895: 276). Beerbohm's subtly antagonistic relationship with the older writer had informed his review of *The Green Carnation* and made the initial version of '1880', 'A Peep into the Past', 'far too indiscreet and hurtful for publication' (Sturgis 1998: 187). It was not published until 1923.

All but one of January's artists were male, and they constituted a formidable roster of emerging talent. The sole exception was the obscure Margaret L. Sumner who contributed 'Plein Air', an undistinguished landscape, though even this hinted at artistic radicalism, with its title alluding to the practice of outdoor painting associated with Impressionism. Beardsley's friends Sickert, Charles Conder, William Rothenstein and Wilson Steer were all present, and the art editor included four contributions of his own. Most controversial was 'The Mysterious Rose Garden', in which an angel whispers in the ear of a naked and curiously elongated woman. This was, said the artist, 'the first of a series of biblical illustrations' (Sturgis 1999: 233) and should be understood as a vision of the annunciation. His other offerings were less startling, though none escaped comment. 'The Repentance of Mrs ****' showed a woman at prayer leered at by a turbaned dwarf and a dissipated bewigged figure with more than a suggestion of Wilde. A portrait of the actress, Winifred Emery, demonstrated Beardsley's interest in contemporary theatre, being a successor to drawings of Mrs Patrick Campbell and Gabrielle Réjane. Finally, there was a 'Frontispiece for Juvenal', a double page spread in which two liveried monkeys carried the poet in a sedan chair through Georgian London in a veiled allusion to Johnson's Juvenal translation, 'The Vanity of Human Wishes' (1749). The drawing was swiftly parodied in *Punch* by Linley Sambourne, with 'Daubaway Weirdsley' in dress and feathers pulling a cart filled with rouged and masked harlots past a building labelled 'This fine doll's house to let', Sambourne equating a love of Ibsen with the 'rubbish' purveyed by Lane's 'Bogey Head'. The drawing was 'intended as a Puzzle

Picture to preface of Juvenile Poems, or as nothing in particular' (2/2/95: 58). 'Mr Beardsley's designs may not be great art,' said the *Athenaeum*, 'but they always show a very original turn for the decorative expression of the salacious' (26/1/95: 137).

The *Athenaeum* found January's issue provincial and ill-bred, though the heartiest conservative could not have objected to A.S. Hartrick's drawing of a boxing match, 'The Knock-out', or a long essay on the mid-Victorian poet, Alexander Smith by James Ashcroft Noble.[8] Nevertheless, a subversive strain persisted through Beardsley's drawings, '1880', John Davidson's 'Proem' to his forthcoming novel, *The Wonderful Mission of Earl Lavender*, and, most radically of all, 'Theodora. A Fragment' by 'Victoria Cross' (Annie Sophie 'Vivian' Cory), a young woman writer who had chosen her pseudonym 'to make Victoria cross' and because she felt she deserved a gallantry award for writing such daring stories (Knapp 1994: 76). Since Elaine Showalter included 'Theodora' in *Daughters of Decadence* (1993), it has attracted considerable comment, with Sally Ledger judging it the 'most challenging exploration of sexual desire and eroticism' to be found in the magazine (Ledger 2007: 22). 'Theodora' drew the broadsides fired at Beardsley and others in earlier issues, offering a potent hint of the sexual tensions behind the closed doors of the English metropolitan bourgeoisie and showing the *YB*'s female contributors were far more than the decorative caprice of 'Petticoat' Lane.

Davidson's 'Proem' boasted how 'our age-end style perplexes | All our elders time has tamed', and compounded its offence with the lines, 'On our sleeves we wear our sexes, | Our diseases, unashamed' (*YB* 284). Quite what sex 'Theodora' wore was not easily discerned. Inspired in part by the cross-dressing protagonist of Gautier's *Mademoiselle de Maupin* (1835–6), the story stages erotic encounters between a New Woman and an aesthete, Cecil Ray, their relationship being complicated by the ambiguous figure of Ray's friend, Digby. During 1894, *Punch* ran occasional cartoons under the banner 'Our Decadents', one of which depicted two elegantly-suited young men complaining of having had insomnia 'every afternoon for a week!' (27/10/94: 203). Cecil is cut from similar cloth, and the story opens with him in his dressing gown and slippers at 10 a.m. as Digby visits, eager for impressions of Theodora Dudley. She is, it seems, of 'very peculiar' appearance, her body Beardsleyesque in its combination of a Pre-Raphaelite powerful throat and shoulders with a very slim waist – she is 'so like a young fellow of nineteen' (Cross 1895: 157, 167). The friendship between Cecil, who narrates the story, and Digby is ostensibly heterosexual, but Ledger's suspicion that Digby's interest in Theodora is a transference of his interest in his friend is not unreasonable. Cecil's sexual identity is equally conflicted, not least when he sits in his rooms, surrounded by treasures from his Eastern travels and maintains, 'I have heard of men remaining celibates before now, especially men with my tastes' (Cross 157).

Ann Ardis shows how the term 'New Woman' was a convenient but misleading label that identified and therefore managed a diversely disruptive set of attitudes and behaviour (Ardis 1990: 10–28). A catch-all term for everything from opposing vivisection to having short hair and riding a bicycle, and applied to everyone from Laura Ormiston Chant to George Egerton, it nevertheless signalled the increasing visibility of social change and, in the cartoons and lampoons of the press, tapped 'a deep fear of gender transference' (Marks 1990: 206). It is not entirely fair to term Theodora a 'New Woman', for she is an individual as well as a symptom of the changing climate. Nevertheless, for many readers of both sexes in 1895, the classification was uncontroversial and for some at least, not necessarily prejudicial. Theodora lives an independent life on £6,000 a year inherited from a maiden aunt, but she will lose this should she marry. 'A girl like that, if she can't marry, will probably forego nothing but the ceremony' (159), says Cecil, who notes an air of 'fatigue and fashionable dissipation that seemed to cling to her' (161), along with 'a dash of virility [. . .] a suggestion of a certain decorous looseness of morals and fastness of manners' (162). She is less a blushing violet than 'a well-trained hothouse gardenia' (162), and despite his initial reservations, Cecil is powerfully attracted to her.

The story is structured around Cecil's visit to Theodora's rooms, where he finds her unchaperoned and discovers she prefers to lie on the floor when conversing, and Theodora's visit to Cecil's rooms with Helen, her married sister; the bounds of respectability can only be pushed so far, even by her. Theodora is highly intelligent, well read, confident and direct. 'To love or at least to strive to love an object for the object's sake, and not our own sake, to love it in its relation to *its* pleasure and not in its relation to our own pleasure, is to feel the only form of love which it is worth offering to a fellow human being', she tells Cecil (164–5) in words that echo Pater's proposal, 'Not the fruit of experience, but experience itself is the end' and *The Renaissance*'s concluding sentence exalting valuing 'your moments as they pass [. . .] simply for those moments' sake' (Pater [1893] 1986: 152). If Pater had worried about his young male readers, Theodora may have induced panic.

Theodora savours Cecil's collection of oriental curiosities in a scene filled with confusions and ambiguity. Cecil has a drawing of a young

Sikh she mistakes for a girl, and later refuses to allow Theodora to keep his personal sketchbook. His evident friendliness with young Arab men passes without comment, though a discussion of Hindu figurines has an obvious sexual undertone in pairing the goddess of love, the here unnamed Parvati, with her consort Shiva, characterised as the god of 'self-denial' (180). Shiva's restraint is dismissed by Theodora as 'false, absurd, and unnatural'; she, like Wilde, believes the only way to rid oneself of a temptation is to yield to it. Trying on various Eastern outfits, her androgynous body, at once anti-maternal and powerfully erotic, saps the narrator's poise and self-control, culminating in his wish for Theodora to take hashish and opium with him. 'I make it a rule not to get intoxicated in public,' she says knowingly (184), before kissing Cecil in an unsupervised moment of freedom before her departure. The passionate kiss burns his lips, and he retires to his bedroom where, in a concluding deployment of the pathetic fallacy, snow drifts through the open window (188).

'The thing is written in open contempt of good taste and common sense. There is not a phrase which does not disgust by its vulgarity or quicken laughter by its folly', the *PMG* snorted. Even Cross's name 'with its inapposite pun' was, it felt 'an indication of folly': the story typified the worst aspects of a 'movement' in art and letters that was in no way to be tolerated, much less encouraged (9/2/95). For a woman to take a pseudonym profaning the nation's highest award for (male) gallantry, to write as a man, to offer titillating glimpses of a seemingly sexually permissive beauty, and to play out a courtship narrative through veiled allusion to Hindu mythography was beyond the pale. The story was explicitly condemned for its cross-gendered narration by B.A. Crackanthorpe in the *Nineteenth Century* that April, though *Woman* felt it was 'a brilliant and penetrating study of the beginning of a passion' (Knapp 1994: 78). The battle-lines between conservatives and literary radicals were being drawn ever more clearly.

Ada Leverson satirised Beerbohm ('Mereboom') and 'Charing Cross' in *Punch*, with 'Theodora' becoming 'Tooraloora' and getting involved in a drunken fight: 'I make it a rule always to get intoxicated in a public-house,' she says (2/2/95: 58). Adroit though Leverson's travesty was, it illustrated the fundamental ambivalence of her position. She was a friend of Beerbohm, told Lane Cross's story was 'brilliant', and was in the process of writing a tale for the next *YB* that, though very different in style from Cross's, would nonetheless inhabit terrain quite at odds with that approved by *Punch* (Speedie 73). At the same time, the level of detail in her parodies (and in those of Reed and Sambourne) showed that she expected *Punch*'s readers to be more than passingly familiar with 'decadent' art. Cultural boundaries were not impermeable; whether the same applied to moral ones remained to be seen.

A Man's Game

Conservatives felt the radicalism of Rosebery's government, the refusal of many young (and not so young) bourgeois women to accept the social order, and the rise of 'demoralising' literature and art required a response beyond simple condemnation. One approach was to demand a more vigorous and manly national politics, beating the drum for Imperial expansion and 'traditional' moral standards. Another was to exalt older models of beauty, as the SR did in a discussion of William Morris's *The Wood Beyond the World*, published in the elaborate faux-medieval style of his Kelmscott Press. Ignoring Morris's political radicalism, the journal explained his real purpose was 'the presentation of beautiful things in a beautiful way'. In 'these degenerate days when we love ugliness for its own sake,' it concluded, 'for what better, or more uncommon, purpose could we wish'? (26/1/95: 121).

While the SR and *Blackwood's* worried about the morally corrosive effects of reading Victoria Cross, millions were oblivious to such dangers. For many northern working class men, the crisis of masculinity epitomised by Rosebery and Amarinth was a peripheral issue. As 40 per cent of British males did not have the vote, many parliamentary questions, the abolition of the Lords, for instance, were of less than pressing urgency. Such men did not tend to read undergraduate magazines or squander five hard-earned shillings on the YB. What occupied thousands in the winter of 1894–5 was not the forthcoming production of *Guy Domville* but the fate of the English cricket team in Australia and, even more pressingly, the destination of the Football League championship.

When the Football Association legalised professionalism in 1885, it set in motion a collision between sporting and financial interests that reverberates today. Initially, football clubs continued to determine their own fixtures which meant a chaotic calendar of professional, amateur, and regional matches, not to mention uncertain revenue. In an attempt to clarify matters, the Football League was founded in 1888 by William McGregor, chairman of Birmingham's Aston Villa, originally with twelve members drawn from the Midlands and the North. Its impact was immediate, with the wealthy professional clubs determining the future of the English game.[9] With a proper system of meaningful home and away matches in place alongside an ever-expanding sporting press publicising the events and personalities of the day, football was turning from a pastime into a business. By 1895, 14 per cent of the *News of the World* was devoted to sports coverage (Huggins 2004: 154), and the result-prediction competitions, which would soon evolve into the football pools, were well under way.[10] This delighted those who could spend their Saturday afternoons away from the steel mill or shipyard, but more privileged observers who supported the Corinthian code, men such as 'Creston' of the *FR*, spoke out against rising wages for footballers undermining the dignity of work, the growing numbers of foreign (typically Scottish) players in the English game, and the gamesmanship and sharp practice that grew out of football's burgeoning financial importance and rewards (*FR* 1/1/94).

By the 1894–5 season, the Football League had added a second division of sixteen clubs, only one of which, Woolwich Arsenal, came from southern England. The professional game was firmly the preserve of the northern counties; Arsenal's nearest opponents in league matches were Walsall Town Swifts and Leicester Fosse. Other clubs, dissuaded from joining the Football League by the logistical and financial challenges of travel, formed the Southern League, a mixture of professional and amateur sides, in 1894. Football was an important agent of civic pride for the towns and cities transformed by the industrial revolution, a working class complement to grandiose town halls and art galleries stocked with Rossettis and Waterhouses. There were two professional clubs in Nottingham, Sheffield, Liverpool, Birmingham, and Manchester, while the Lancashire conurbation had teams in Bolton, Blackburn, Bury, Preston, and Burnley. In the north east were Sunderland and Newcastle United; Middlesborough Ironopolis folded at the end of the 1893–4 season; a new club, Middlesborough, would be elected to the League in 1899. The northern bias bemused the *IPN*'s 'Our Veteran'. When Everton beat Blackburn 2–1 at Goodison Park on 24 November, he told his readers, 'Down in the south here we can hardly realise the intense interest and excitement of a League game such as this' (8/12/94). Goodison, built in 1892 at a cost of over £8,000 (over £500 was spent on turf alone), was England's first purpose-built football stadium.[11] The Football League did not record attendances until the 1925–6 season, so it is difficult to be certain of crowd sizes and ticket prices. Also, some clubs allowed women to watch games for free, believing their presence curbed the excesses of male supporters, but this practice was disappearing by 1894–5 for the simple reason that too many women were watching football and revenue was being lost. Drawing on Brian Tabner's *Football Through the Turnstiles ... Again* (2002), Richard Sanders suggests Everton's average gate in 1894–5 was around 16,000, with Aston Villa and Sunderland averaging a little over half that figure (R. Sanders 280).

Individual matches, such as local derbies, attracted still larger audiences. Even without firm statistical data however, football's growing popularity was obvious and important matches were highly remunerative for the home side. When Everton drew 2–2 with Sunderland at Goodison on 27 October, the match receipts were almost £700. 'Good business this for Everton,' said 'Our Veteran' (10/11/94).

By December, the title race was a three-way fight between Sunderland, Everton, and Villa, with Villa, the reigning champions, outsiders after a slow start. Everton had won their first eight matches, but on 20 October during a match against Blackburn Rovers, their centre-forward, Jack Southworth, was carried off with a serious leg injury that ended his career. With no substitutes permitted, Everton were reduced to ten men, and having led 2–1, lost 4–3. The loss of Southworth was a blow from which they struggled to recover. In the run-up to Christmas, Sunderland were in imperious form, hammering Small Heath (who became Birmingham in 1905 and Birmingham City in 1943) 7–1. Villa were in London in mid-December, beating the amateurs of Corinthians 5–3 at the Oval cricket ground, with their speedy outside-right, Charlie Athersmith, attracting widespread attention.[12] Putting together an impressive unbeaten run from mid-November onwards, Villa briefly overtook Sunderland when the Wearsiders surprisingly lost to Nottingham Forest and Preston either side of New Year. Having played four games fewer, it was now Everton who had the best chance of winning the title, while Liverpool, their local rivals, were caught in a relegation dogfight with Derby, Wolves and Stoke. Everton however came badly unstuck against The Wednesday on New Year's Day, losing 3–0 in Sheffield, and although Sunderland could only draw at home to Forest on 5 January, Everton lost 1–0 at Wolves, and left the championship wide open.

First (K)nights

Wilde joked football was a game for 'rough girls, and not suitable for delicate boys'. He flirted with 'sporting' dress, a checked tweed suit and bowler hat, in his early Oxford days, attending cricket matches and even contemplating rowing for Magdalen, but by 1895, he had long since decided that 'the only possible exercise is to talk, not to walk' and travelled almost everywhere by hansom (Ellmann 1987: 38). While others crowded into telegraph offices to follow the fortunes of the English cricketers in Australia, he retired to London's Continental hotel for a New Year celebration with George Ives, Jack Bloxam and (perhaps)

Bosie Douglas. Ives acknowledged the official calendar but preferred to live by a more personal measure that began in 338 BC with the slaughter of the Theban Band by Philip II of Macedon at the Battle of Chaeronea. By this reckoning, 1895 was 'the year of the Faith 2233'. A correspondent of Edward Carpenter, Ives apparently 'shaved off his moustache to be more Hellenic' (Rowbotham 2008: 196), but shy and intense, he was outshone by his fellow diners. His diary recorded that 'After going about in that set it is hard to mix in ordinary society, for they have a charm which is rare and wonderful.' At the same time, Ives sensed trouble in the wind. 'I wish they were less extravagant and more real,' he wrote. They were 'so gifted and so nice, yet here is this terrible world [. . .] I see the storm of battle coming' (Stokes 1996: 77).

An Ideal Husband was eagerly awaited by Wilde's supporters and by those who felt he needed cutting down to size. The playwright himself remained perfectly calm, telling Gilbert Burgess of *The Sketch*, 'My nervousness ends at the last dress rehearsal; I know then what effect my play, as presented upon the stage, has produced upon me.' 'My interest in the play ends there,' he continued. 'I feel curiously envious of the public – they have such wonderfully fresh emotions in store for them' (9/1/95).

Wilde's comedy, billed as 'A New and Original Play of Modern Life' saw him once again letting off epigrammatic firecrackers in the drawing rooms of the ruling class. The plot concerns the moral dilemma of Sir Robert Chiltern, Under-Secretary for Foreign Affairs, as he deals with the consequences of a youthful indiscretion. Having sold state information to a Stock Exchange speculator early in his career, a deal netting him £110,000, Chiltern is blackmailed by the cunning Mrs Cheveley into publicly supporting the Argentinean canal scheme in which she has a significant interest. Fortunately, Chiltern's dandified friend Lord Goring, 'the first well-dressed philosopher in the history of thought' (*WCW* 553) is able to confound her knavish tricks, repair the breach in the Chilterns' marriage and win the love of Chiltern's sister, Mabel. Kerry Powell has shown how the play was one of a number of political dramas on the London stage of the mid-1890s, as well as contributing to contemporary debates surrounding marriage (Powell 1990: 89–107), and the critic of the *Morning Advertiser* saw this topicality as a significant weakness. Wilde's play was 'a thing of shreds and patches,' he said, 'a stringing together of a number of inconsequent incidents [that] have been in use for years past' and should consequently be 'borne' like 'the ancient jokes of an elderly, highly respectable, and, above all, wealthy member of one's family' (4/1/95). *The Sketch* carped at the lack of living and believable characters (9/1/95), but *An Ideal Husband*'s originality lay less in its setting, plot, or melding of melodrama with farce, than in its stylised yet seemingly naturalistic dialogue and its deliberate artificiality: though Mrs Cheveley 'prefer[s] to be natural', she finds it 'such a very difficult pose to keep up' (*WCW* 519). Such posing made significant demands on Wilde's cast, who needed perfect timing and control to maintain the play's 'delicate balance' between what Peter Raby terms 'melodramatic action and heightened private emotion, on the one hand, and the appearance of rigid public decorum and polite conversation on the other' (Wilde 1995: xx). The erratic acoustics of the Theatre Royal posed an additional challenge.

That Chiltern is able to advance his political career and even invigorate his marriage despite his dubious dealings with Baron Arnheim, the millionaire speculator, casts ironic light on Wilde's title. At the same time, the play's ingredients of indiscretion, secrets, compromising letters, imperilled marriage, outraged aristocrats and eroticised blackmail were drawn from Wilde's own life, even if its central situation owed much to Disraeli's conduct over the building of the Suez Canal. Wit, in all its senses, is the key to success in such a world; to think quickly and clearly, and to make one's audience laugh, is everything. To imagine however that such ethics could succeed beyond the confines of the stage was, in Wilde's case, wish-fulfilment of an intoxicatingly dangerous kind.

The opening night's audience included the Prince of Wales, Joseph Chamberlain, Asquith, the Conservative politician and philosopher, A.J. Balfour, the drama critics Wells (who had to buy evening dress specially), Shaw and William Archer, and the publisher William Heinemann. Aubrey Beardsley and his actress sister, Mabel, shared Ada Leverson's box. Beerbohm, and Wilde's close friend and former lover, Robbie Ross, were also present, as were many notable Irish political figures (*Belfast News-Letter* 4/1/95). Subsequent performances would be attended by Gosse, and Rosebery's friend, Sir Edward Hamilton, who judged the play 'well written and well acted' (Hamilton 1986: 217). Wilde's comedy was enthusiastically received, especially by the Prince, and the playwright told the audience at the second curtain call he was glad they had enjoyed the play. He thanked the company and admitted he had enjoyed his evening immensely. He then continued his celebrations at a triumphant dinner at the Albemarle Club.

Reviews were ambivalent, partly because Wilde had been denigrating journalists for two decades and could hardly have expected to escape unscathed. *Punch* felt the play was let down by its fourth act though it remained 'an unmistakeable success' and Brookfield's cameo was delightful (2/2/95: 54). Wells pronounced it 'very poor', though he noted the 'applause and emotion' during the Chilterns' final scene together and praised a number of the actors. The play was 'interesting' but spoiled by its melodramatic elements and curious construction – the relationship between Lord Goring and Mabel was superfluous, and other characters were merely decorative (*PMG* 4/1/95). In the *Pall Mall Budget*, Archer found it 'a very able and charming piece of work' though 'there are times when the output of Mr Wilde's epigram-factory threatens to become all trademark and no substance.' He was also dubious about the play's moral stance, and hoped the British electorate would choose men 'of less provisional probity' than Sir Robert Chiltern (10/1/95). The *Athenaeum* was similarly unconvinced by Chiltern's redemption, suggesting lines such as 'only dull people are brilliant at breakfast' were 'impertinent and extravagant' and the play as a whole was 'a vigorously ridden hobby-horse of affectation' (12/1/95: 57). Clement Scott, while noting how Wilde's 'whimsicality of dialogue tickle[d] the public', felt the play owed too much to Sardou's *Dora* and was mechanistic in its humour. Inventing 'Oscar Wildeisms' was, he claimed, 'the easiest thing in the world. All you have to do is to form an obvious untruth into a false epigram' (*ILN* 12/1/95: 35). Finally, A.B. Walkley of the *Speaker*, noted how the play was 'clever with a cleverness so excessive as to be almost monstrous and uncanny'. He went further than Scott in dismissing the 'cheapness' of Wilde's 'inverted commonplaces', concluding that though its 'sheer cleverness keeps one continually amused and interested [. . .], Mr Wilde's work is not only poor and sterile, but essentially vulgar' (12/1/95).

Shaw was more subtle. 'I am the only person in London who cannot sit down and write an Oscar Wilde play at will,' he began, arguing that Wilde made his critics 'dull' since they reacted predictably to epigram-matic prompting rather than thinking about his conception of dramatic art. Wilde, he wrote, 'plays with everything: with wit, with philosophy, with drama, with actors and audience, with the whole theatre' and, as an Irishman, saw the world in ways fundamentally different from those of the English aristocrats he dramatised or the 'scribes' who ventured to interpret and judge him. This, coupled with Wilde's refusal to lay claim to hard work, however long he may have laboured, 'scandalizes the Englishman', 'wit and philosophy' being harder to master than 'a football or cricket bat'. Drawing a damaging parallel between art and sport, Shaw pointed out that the Englishman 'has the consolation, if he cannot make people laugh, of being the best cricketer and footballer in the world', even if his diligence and dedication debar him from aesthetic accomplishment (*OT* 9–12). Such a provocative reading of Wildean dif-ference, coupled with sideswipes at national pastimes, stressed Shaw's credentials as an outsider as well as Wilde's. Like Beerbohm, he under-stood very well the reflexive nature of reviewing.

An Ideal Husband was an immediate financial success, taking over £100 per night. Its writer made around £1,600 from its 124 perform-ances (Guy and Small 2000: 125). Wilde's bankers, creditors, and indeed, family, saw little of this income, for Wilde lived with Neronian extravagance, smoking expensive cigarettes, drinking Veuve Cliquot champagne and spending 10s a day on buttonholes at a time when infantrymen earned a shilling a day and many agricultural workers in the Home Counties 8–11s per week (*IPN* 16/2/95). Henry James was more frugal, not least because his income was steadily declining as his popular appeal waned. Wilde flaunted his vanity. James, though desir-ing of public acclaim and commercial triumph, essayed a pessimistic hauteur. 'I feel more and more that I *may* be made for the Drama,' he told the actress, Elizabeth Robins, 'but am not made for the Theatre!' (James 1980: 503).

Alexander's production of *Guy Domville* spared no expense, replac-ing traditional gaslight with newfangled electricity and delighting in elaborate sets and sumptuous costumes. James was pleased to note £1,500's worth of advance ticket sales, but his tortured nerves would not allow him to sit through its premiere. At first he planned to take shelter in a nearby pub, allowing Gosse to scuttle to and fro with updates on the performance. James and Gosse were unlikely pub-goers at the best of times though, and the plan was quickly abandoned. Instead, James occupied himself by going to see *An Ideal Husband*, despite his dislike of its author, whom he considered an 'unclean beast' and from whom he had endured high-handed put-downs since an uncomfortable meeting in Washington in 1882 (Ellmann 1987: 170).

On the morning of 5 January, two mysterious women, perhaps dis-gruntled actresses, sent Alexander a telegram: 'With hearty wishes for a complete failure'. Alexander concealed this from James, but it was a foretaste of the doom to come. The dramatist spent the afternoon pacing the London streets, then wrote to his brother, William, request-ing 'Psychical intervention' on his behalf before finally heading off to watch Wilde's comedy (James 1980: 507). Preoccupied by events at the St James's, he endured a dismal couple of hours at the Theatre Royal, surrounded by an audience whose hilarity he could neither share nor understand. That Wilde's play gave 'every appearance [. . .] of com-plete success' only intensified his misgivings about the reception of *Guy Domville*. *An Ideal Husband*, he told William:

> seemed to me so helpless, so crude, so bad, so clumsy, feeble and vulgar, that as I walked away across St James's Square to learn my own fate, the prosper-ity of what I had seen seemed to constitute a dreadful presumption of the shipwreck of *G.D.*

Approaching the theatre 'paralyzed by the terror' of failure, he asked himself, 'How *can* my piece do anything with a public with whom *that* is a success?' (512). Adopting the Wildean 'inverted commonplace' he sighed, 'You can't make a sow's ear out of a silk purse' (509).

Whatever its vulgarities and unacknowledged borrowings, *An Ideal Husband* was funny. Even its detractors admitted Wilde's comic flair. What is more, Wilde's pursuit of celebrity and publicity, allied with his recent theatrical successes, made the play a social event; the approbation of the heir to the throne counted for far more than the humourless obloquy of its critics. *An Ideal Husband*'s details were less significant, in many respects, than the fact it was a 'modern comedy' by Oscar Wilde. Wilde's name on the theatre poster guaranteed epigrammatic and paradoxical wit, contemporary aristocratic settings and a refined and deliberate air of triviality. Leverson's *Punch* parodies caught this precisely in short dialogues between characters from Wilde's different plays. In a sense, his first three comedies emerged from a self-contained parallel world, as much an imaginative creation as Dickens's London, Hardy's Wessex or Trollope's Barsetshire, so there was no reason why *A Woman of No Importance*'s Lord Illingworth should not trade witticisms with Lord Goring, or indeed, speak lines from Wilde's other creations. In one brief playlet, Illingworth remarks, 'If one tells the truth, one is sure, sooner or later, to be found out' while Goring objects to his 'atrocious' cigarettes on the grounds that 'they leave me unsatisfied', a reworking of an exchange on the 'perfect pleasure' of smoking in *Dorian Gray* (P 12/1/95: 24; *WCW* 67). Wilde was delighted. As jokes moved from plays to undergraduate magazines, to *Punch* and back to the stage, so their context changed; what was satirical in *Punch* became subversive in the *Chameleon* (Denisoff 2001: 97–119).

Wilde was a celebrity. James was not nearly so well known. Essentially private if sociable, he tended to appear in the press only when his fiction was reviewed, and was certainly not a 'personality' in Wilde's sense of the term. He had no record of theatrical success and though some of his early novels – *Daisy Miller*, *Washington Square*, *The Portrait of a Lady* – enjoyed popularity with discerning readers, recent fiction had proved much less palatable. A dramatic version of *Daisy Miller* complete with a hopefully audience-pleasing happy ending remained unperformed. Wilde told Gilbert Burgess 'There are as many publics as there are personalities' (*Sketch* 9/1/95), but as he watched *An Ideal Husband*, probably unrecognised by his fellow theatre-goers, James was increasingly aware that there were only two publics, a small one capable of appreciating his subtleties, and a much larger one indifferent or even antipathetic to them. James's writing was distinguished by psychological nuance, sophisticated conception of character, and a fascination with its own mechanics, as explained in his theoretical and critical musings such as 'The Art of Fiction' (1884). On stage however, when events happened in theatrical time and were heavily reliant upon dialogue, James struggled to adapt to the immediate needs of the well-made play: a 'Meissonier among novelists' he was 'a complete theatrical fiasco' said the *QR* (10/95: 406). His dialogue was difficult to learn and to enunciate, making demands on an audience in a hot, crowded theatre that it did not make upon a leisurely reader. This would not have mattered if *Guy Domville* had been underpinned by an involving plot, but the agonies of a wealthy Catholic heir of the 1780s torn between the demands of continuing the Domville line and entering the priesthood had little appeal for an overwhelmingly Protestant and tentatively secularised audience, particularly as its treatment of romance did not allow a satisfying finale. Richard Salmon argues that *Guy Domville* is 'fascinating' because of the way that its protagonist 'is seemingly propelled from one extreme to the other without the assistance of plausible meditation' (Salmon 1997: 69), and Michèle Mendelssohn points out that in 'refusing his audience a smooth synthesis of the two opposites he presents them with', James offers 'a privileged insight into a fraught consciousness representative of the dilemmas attendant upon modern selfhood' (Mendelssohn 1997: 174). In 1895 however, few theatre-goers were attuned to such nuances, and fewer still expected them from a night out.

James's play had obvious weaknesses which should have been identified much earlier. Its curtain raiser, Julian Field's *Too Happy by Half*, was a piece of airy froth, 'a farce', said Shaw, which was 'capital fun for the audience' but thoroughly inappropriate (*OT* 9). It was as if the overture to *The Barber of Seville* prefaced *Fidelio*. Then there was the casting of W.G. Elliott, whom James felt too 'stagey' in the crucial role of Lord Devenish. His intuitions were correct: 'He might have come out of Hogarth' but had 'no business' in *Guy Domville*, said Wells (*PMG* 7/1/95). Another difficulty was a consequence of the play's sumptuous production and its general accuracy in matters of eighteenth century costume. Mrs Edward Saker, the dowager Lady Domville, wore a velvet hat more suited to Edward Lear's Quangle Wangle than a serious drama, a view shared by a number of giggling playgoers. Despite his play opening in the pantomime season, James had not countenanced audience participation, and as the stalls succumbed to hilarity and boredom, a drinking scene in which Guy and a deceitful naval lieutenant plied each other with port, only for each man to surreptitiously pour his drinks into flower pots, meant those already restive smirked at the laborious business. Their dissatisfaction unsettled the cast, culminating

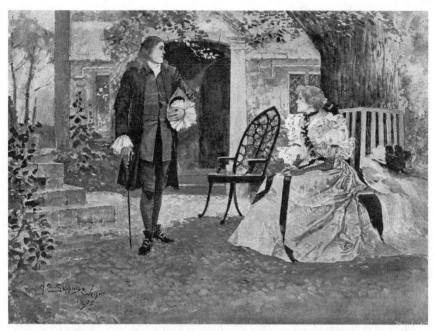

Figure 3. Guy Domville (George Alexander) and Mrs Peverel (Marion Terry) share an intimate moment in Henry James's lavishly staged drama. *Illustrated London News*, 12 January 1895.

in the moment when Guy's 'I'm the *last*, my lord, of the Domvilles!' was met with the derisive heckle, 'It's a bloody good thing you are' (Edel 1996: 420). The most serious defect of the play however was that, as Wells maintained, it was 'too delicate for acting'. 'It would be difficult to select among modern writers a man whose method had less that lends itself to stage treatment,' the *Athenaeum* concurred (12/1/95: 57). 'Delicate, but unhappily obscure,' said the *ILN* (23/2/95: 227). These weaknesses combined to disastrous effect as James made his way back from the Theatre Royal, bewildered and jealous of Wilde's comic triumph.

Guy Domville did not have the royal patronage enjoyed by *An Ideal Husband*, but it still drew Lord Leighton, John Singer Sargent, Edward and Philip Burne-Jones, Gosse, G.F. Watts, Mrs Humphry Ward, and George Du Maurier. Enoch Arnold Bennett, as yet unknown to James, watched too. Henry Harland saw the play twice, but Pinero, behind schedule with *The Notorious Mrs Ebbsmith*, was forced to decline his invitation. James's guests were, however, in the minority, for most playgoers had come to see Alexander and knew little of the novelist. Alexander was generously applauded at the play's conclusion and insisted James join him. Ignorant of earlier mishaps, James did so, only to be exposed to hisses and abuse. His allies fought back with renewed cheers, and arguments and shouting broke out. James was left to face the horror, a poor review nothing beside prolonged public humiliation.

At this point, Philip Burne-Jones 'stood up and began sarcastically to applaud the demonstrators in the gallery,' a declaration of faith that only worsened James's plight (Fitzgerald [1975] 2003: 265). Trapped in the footlights' glare, the failed dramatist was painfully conspicuous. Alexander stepped forward to appeal for calm, pleading that his cast had done their best and would resolve to do better in future. 'T'ain't your fault, guv'nor, it's a rotten play' shouted someone in the gallery (Edel 1996: 421). When order was at last restored, the traumatised James was already rushing back to his flat at De Vere Gardens. Though he attended the second night, and heard the actors cheered, he was deeply disturbed by his encounter with the many-headed monster of the pit. His 'cruel ordeal' left him 'weary, bruised, sickened, disgusted', since it had pitted 'all the forces of civilisation' against the 'hoots and jeers and catcalls of the roughs, whose *roars* [were] like those of a cage of beasts at some infernal "zoo"' (James 1980: 508). The Morlocks of Wells's *Time Machine* had ventured above ground, and the delicate Eloi had been devoured. James sought the solace of his friends, one of whom, Edward White Benson, the Archbishop of Canterbury, entertained him at his Episcopal residence on 10 January and told him the anecdote that became *The Turn of the Screw* (1898).

The ignominy of *Guy Domville* lingered though, and was reinforced by critics, even if they deplored the audience's misbehaviour. Ungovernable energies were breaking out everywhere, it seemed, from West End theatres to football grounds. When, on 26 January, a late penalty allowed Burton Wanderers to equalise against Woolwich Arsenal at Plumstead, disorder erupted. The referee, was attacked by 'a gang of roughs' and the Burton players were jostled (*IPN 2/2/95*; *DN 28/1/95*). The Football Association suspended Arsenal from playing home matches for six weeks. It would be wrong to draw too close a parallel between the two events, but they suggest, in their different ways, that 'decorum' represented an uneasy and fragile truce between social expectation and the dangerous undercurrents flowing beneath it. The press and popular writers were fascinated both by French anarchists and by the thought that their dangerous gospel was spreading across the Channel, a fear intensified by a number of mysterious explosions in the capital. Throughout October and November 1894, the *IPN* carried Paul Martin's exposé, 'Among the Anarchists', a series given added impact by the events of the night of 4 November when a bomb went off on the doorstep of 2 Tilney Street, Mayfair, the home of Rosebery's close friend, Regy Brett. No one was hurt, but Brett's wife, who was in the hall at the time of the blast having arrived home only minutes before, narrowly escaped injury when the explosion blew open the front door and smashed all the windows in the house (*T* 5/11/94). Tilney Street had only seven dwellings, housing Brett, Horace West, Secretary to Herbert Asquith, Lord Montagu, Earl Manvers and Mr Justice Hawkins, who was probably the bomb's intended target (*T* 6/11//94). No one was arrested. Arthur Morrison satirised a misguided attempt to introduce anarchist ideas to London's working class and 'blow up the bleed'n gas-works' in 'The Red Cow Group' (Morrison 114), but the anarchists at large in his 'The Case of the Lost Foreigner' (*Windsor Magazine* 6/95) could only be stopped by the brilliant detective, Martin Hewitt.

Football hooligans and continental anarchists are obviously different from those who tittered at Lady Domville's hat, but all three refused to abide by law and custom. Reviewers were clearly shocked by the eruption of disorderly behaviour at the St James's; rowdiness in music halls was one thing, but humiliating an important literary figure quite another. George Meredith felt 'the treatment of Henry James at the close of his play will prove to Americans that the Old Country retains a fund of the cowardly part of barbarism' (Meredith 1912: 473–4). The 'admirable and delightful' play, wrote Clement Scott, 'was treated with unwonted severity – nay, with a hardness and cruelty alike discourteous and reprehensible' (*ILN* 21/1/95: 35). The business, said the *Athenaeum*, was 'deplorable', the 'outrage' indefensible, though it questioned the conduct of Alexander and James in getting involved with curtain calls and addresses to the audience (12/1/95: 57). By naming his hero Guy, *Punch* quipped, James had asked to be 'guy'd', shrewdly adding that 'if he knew as much about play-writing as he does about novel-writing' he 'would probably be in the first flight of dramatists' (19/1/95: 25). Shaw meanwhile praised James's dialogue, explaining the play's failure on the grounds of its being unfashionable. Siding with 'the cultivated majority' who applauded James rather than 'the handful of rowdies who brawled at him', Shaw insisted that 'it is the business of the dramatic critic to educate [. . .] dunces, not to echo them' (*OT* 7).

The third major play of the new season, *King Arthur*, was far less con-troversial, and its success – it ran for 105 performances despite lasting four hours, and only closed because of its stars' other commitments – demonstrated the enduring popularity of Arthurian legends. With Henry Irving as Arthur and Ellen Terry as Guinevere, the production had two of the most accomplished and popular late-Victorian actors in its lead roles. It could also boast sets by Burne-Jones and music by

Arthur Sullivan. Comyns Carr opted for a mixture of rhymed and blank verse, and concentrated on the Grail, the adulterous love of Guinevere and Lancelot, and the treachery of Mordred. With first class performers, designers, scene painters, costumiers, armourers, music and lighting, plus the 'combined weight of Malory and Tennyson and many another', Comyns Carr had, in Shaw's words, 'put his hand cleverly on a ready-made success, and tasted the joy of victory without the terror of battle' (*OT* 14). Arthur Machen found the play 'very dreadful indeed' (Gawsworth 2005: 132), but it was warmly received, with even the *IPN*, which ignored Wilde and James, praising the 'lovely' music and the 'masterpieces' of its scenery. It was, said 'The Mummer', 'a lovely show', reporting that there was a queue outside the Lyceum from lunchtime on 12 January (19/1/95). Distance lent enchantment, it seemed, for as the *Athenaeum* pointed out, 'very far from ideal is the love depicted: the stories are rooted in incest, and marriage here, as in modern French fiction, appears more of a whet to appetite than a restraint upon advance' (19/1/95: 93). Only Shaw developed the implications of this parallel in lamenting how the play turned an actress of Terry's stature into 'a mere artist's model [. . .] a heartless waste of an exquisite talent' (*OT* 17). How he longed to see her tackle Ibsen!

Changes for the Worse

With many Liberals resigned to electoral defeat, the New Year Honours represented a final opportunity for Rosebery to reward his supporters, though the *Times* felt the list of recipients was more 'remarkable' for 'what it does not contain' (*T* 1/1/95). Rosebery refused to add to the House of Lords, instead conferring his largesse on Cecil Rhodes, who was elevated to the Privy Council, perhaps as a replacement for the Canadian Prime Minister, Sir John Thompson, who had died at Windsor Castle after attending a meeting of it on 12 December, or, more cynically, as a reward for generous donations to Liberal funds. The publisher and Liberal MP, Sir George Newnes, creator of *Tit-Bits* and the *Strand*, was made a baronet, but having decided to snub the Lords, Rosebery's appointments were generally to reward merit in medicine and the arts. Dr J. Russell Reynolds, President of the Royal College of Physicians received a Baronetcy, as did John Erichsen, former President of the Royal College of Surgeons. There was a knighthood for the composer, Alexander Campbell Mackenzie, the Principal of the Royal Academy of Music who had conducted the London premiere of Tchaikovsky's *Pathétique* symphony on 28 February 1894, and Richard Garnett, Keeper of Printed

Books at the British Museum, was made a CB. There were also a number of recognitions of colonial service, the overall impression being of merit rewarded, and hard work and dedication approved.

Rosebery's Honours were overshadowed by the final illness of Randolph Churchill, the Conservative MP whose lengthy battle with syphilis was widely reported though without disclosing the nature of his complaint. A friend of Rosebery's since Eton – they had both belonged to the notorious Bullingdon Club at Oxford in the 1860s – his death on 26 January shortly before his forty-sixth birthday added to the PM's woes, even though the two men had seen little of each other for several years. The loss of his old friend, coupled with the death of George, his nephew, upset Rosebery considerably. The mercurial Churchill had not achieved the political success his talent merited but was nevertheless widely mourned, Rosebery publishing a biography of him in 1906. His absence from the Commons and committee rooms would however make Lord Salisbury's leadership easier in an election year.

Newspaper coverage of politics was sandwiched between reports of worsening weather. On 22 December, high winds at Chelford, near Macclesfield, blew a railway wagon down a gradient, where it collided with others and blocked the track as the Manchester to Crewe express was approaching. In the resulting collision, fourteen passengers were killed and forty-eight injured. A few days later, a ferocious gale ravaged the Welsh coast, causing serious damage in Rhyl and driving the *Osseo*, a Londonderry coal barque, onto rocks off Holyhead. The ship sank with the loss of twenty-six crew. Many other ships were reported missing, with the trawler fleets of Hull and Grimsby particularly badly hit: the *BDP* speculated that there had been as many as 120 deaths on land and sea, not including the Chelford accident (31/12/94). Temperatures plummeted. At Box Hill, near Dorking, George Meredith complained on 8 January 'I can hardly feel the pen in my hand, the chalet is a refrigerator' (1912: 473). Epsom, where Gissing and his family had a miserable Christmas, shivered under frost, snow and sleet for weeks, though Gissing at least had the satisfaction of recording that his literary earnings in 1894 were £453 12s 5d, a profit of c. £200. 'Bravo!' he wrote, in a rare moment of happiness (Gissing 1978: 358). A month later, the weather had still not improved, and he was struggling to write with frozen hands, managing only a page of prose on a day of especially joyless toil (362).

As householders struggled to keep winter at bay, the human cost of their coal fires became horribly apparent. At Audley, near Newcastle-under-Lyme, a combination of heavy snow – drifts of up to eight feet were reported – and incessant rain led to flooding and to rising water

levels in long abandoned mine workings. These now formed a huge subterranean reservoir, one dangerously swollen by the recent downpours.
A new pit, Diglake, had thrived alongside its exhausted predecessor for
twenty-five years, but no accurate records were kept of the thickness of
any natural barrier between the two. On the morning of Monday 14
January, William Sproson (sometimes given as Sproston), the 'shot firer'
detonated dynamite in an extension to the East 10 Foot Seam. It was
probably this that caused the reservoir to burst through into Diglake as
around 240 miners, a significant number of them aged between thirteen
and nineteen and working alongside their fathers, hacked at the coal
seam deep underground.

The Diglake flood was a catastrophe. The colliery's pumps were all but
overwhelmed by freezing water and sludge, and although there were acts
of great individual and communal heroism – William Dodd, an under-
manager whose prompt action saved forty men, received the Albert
Medal (Gold Class) from the Queen, and the Royal Humane Society
awarded eleven bronze and two silver medals for acts of gallantry (*T*
11 and 23/3/95) – seventy-seven were drowned. Sproson and his son
Enoch were two of them, though his second son, William, escaped and
testified at the inquest into the disaster which began four days later. The
last survivor, Aaron Mayer, was brought out at five o' clock on Monday
evening. Those who did not escape quickly stood almost no chance; on
18 January, two ponies which had somehow survived over three days
in the mine were fished out, 'none the worse for their imprisonment,
though decidedly hungry', but the bodies of seventy-two miners were
left unrecovered (*ILN* 26/1/95: 99). Four days later, twenty tonnes of
water was still rushing through the pit every minute.

Death and injury were common in British mines; as recently as July
1893, 135 men had been killed in an explosion at Thornhill Colliery,
Dewsbury. Such accidents were, however, largely invisible in literature of the time: there was no English novel that could match Zola's
Germinal (1885). What emerged from the Diglake disaster was folk art,
ballads and dialect poems that were occasionally sold to raise money for
the disaster fund. Wells later claimed that 'the coal-mine and its inevitable explosion' had been 'worn to tatters' in 'penny reciters', exposing the
absence of more enduring artistic representations of such disasters (*SR*
20/6/96: 627). A typical work, William Baron's powerful 'Vanquished
Heroes, An Appeal for t'sufferers o' th' Audley Mining Disaster, 1895'
included the stanza:

> Scoffers at unskilled labour – Lord mayors, or what yo be –
> Pluck's still a place in t'toilers breast – sooa he's humanity;

These men 'at risked their lives to get their comrades eawt o' th' pit,
Belonging to t'classes at which yo throw yor insults an' coarse wit.
To-day ther's families desolate i' th' Audley district yon;
Ther's close on eighty corpses stretched – as yet unseen bi mon;
If yo'd atone for t'wrongs yo've done, lessen these poor folks' grief
Bi plankin' deawn, an' handsomely, to fund for their relief.[13]

Baron was from Blackburn and wrote many dialect poems of everyday life; the Diglake tragedy struck a chord with working people throughout the north, who contributed generously to the relief fund despite their sorely-limited means. Official compensation was correspondingly meagre. The North Staffordshire Permanent Relief Society paid the families of the bereaved £20 compensation per man and £10 for boys under the age of sixteen, adding funeral expenses of 5s. Widows were to receive 4s a week for five years and 2s a week for the five years after. Children who lost their fathers received a weekly payment of 2s until the age of thirteen. A variety of charitable activities raised money for the stricken community, with memorial football matches, circuses and a performance by the D'Oyley Carte opera company of *HMS Pinafore* amassing £17,000 for thirty-seven widows and eighty-eight children by the end of the year. Admirable as this was, some trade unionists felt charity was a poor substitute for workers' safeguards. The inquest into the disaster however noted that 'the colliery appeared to be carefully managed, and no blame attached to anybody', except perhaps those who had abandoned the original pit in 1850 and left only sketchy maps of their excavations (*T* 14/6/95). It was six months before it ruled that the deaths were the result of an accident, since proceedings were continually adjourned to accommodate the search for bodies and the source of the breach.

The terrible weather was accompanied by disease. There had been signs of an influenza epidemic in October, when Wilde contracted 'a sort of malarial fever' from Bosie (*WCL* 620), which left him bedridden and enfeebled and ruined a holiday in Brighton. Douglas promptly deserted him, sending him a letter on 16 October (Wilde's fortieth birthday) that finished, 'When you are not on your pedestal you are not interesting. Next time you are ill I will go away at once' (*WCL* 700). Wilde swore that Bosie's selfish cruelty had ended their relationship, but on his return to London on 19 October he read the newspaper reports of Drumlanrig's death and re-established contact. Whether the influenza epidemic that began in January was a recurrence or a virulent new strain, Wilde succumbed. On 8 January he was confined to bed, his chief comfort a bouquet from Leverson. 'Your flowers are so lovely that they have made me well again,' he told her by telegram. 'You are the most wonderful Sphinx in the world' (*WCL* 628). Revived, he gave an interview to the *St James's Gazette*, perhaps pocketing the £20 fee he had told Robert Sherard he would charge for such favours (*WCL* 624), and then, ignoring the rehearsals for his forthcoming play, left for a holiday with Bosie in Algiers on 15 January. The climate would certainly be of benefit to his health, but the trip was unwise and had unpleasant repercussions.

Renewing Hostilities

The weather affected the country in diverse ways. Food and fuel prices rose in major cities, consumption of rum increased (though beer drinking declined), rail services were ravaged by heavy snow and frozen points, canal traffic was impeded by icy waterways and ocean-going vessels faced serious storms. On the night of 30 January, the German trans-atlantic liner, *Elbe*, collided with the steamship *Crathie* off Lowestoft. All but one of her lifeboats were glued to the deck by frozen ropes, and 300 passengers drowned, despite the gallant efforts of the *Wildflower*, a Lowestoft fishing smack which saved twenty more. The *Crathie* had not stopped to pick up survivors, her captain fearing she would be overwhelmed by mountainous seas. The weather was no better in Europe. Hard at work on a series of 'Brigadier Gerard' stories in Davos, Switzerland, Arthur Conan Doyle complained on 24 January that the snow was very bad and that 'Everybody has sore throats, coughs, &c.' (Lellenberg 347). Ironically, he was in Switzerland with his tubercular wife, Louisa, because the Swiss air suited her. Next year, he vowed, he would winter in Egypt instead.

In such awful conditions, amateur football in southern England ceased for most of February. In the north however, postponing matches was a last resort, and the pitches at professional clubs were heaped with straw to protect them as the league and FA Cup moved towards their climax. The FA Cup, the world's oldest such competition, was devised by C.W. Alcock, who modelled it on the Cock House knock-out tourna-ment at Harrow, and was first contested in 1872. It was initially domi-nated by public school old boys, but when Blackburn Olympic defeated Old Etonians 2–1 in the 1882–3 final, the *Eton College Chronicle* was horrified to report that 'So great was their ambition to wrest the Cup away from the holders that they introduced into football a practice which has excited the greatest disapprobation in the South.' Blackburn's secret weapon was a course of training in Blackpool before the final; the *Chronicle* was surprised working men were granted such time off (and as

Richard Sanders shows, exaggerated the length of their training), though in a sign of things to come, it acknowledged the money and prestige football attracted in Lancashire (Money 122; J. Wilson 20; R. Sanders 104). By 1894–5, the Old Etonians' captain, Lord Arthur Kinnaird, a 'muscular Christian' who played in eleven FA Cup finals for the Old Etonians and Wanderers, and championed the practice of 'hacking', the deliberate kicking of an opponent's shins as a crucial aspect of football's manly ethos, was Vice-President of the NVA and poised to replace Alcock at the FA. However, any hope that his presence would improve football's sportsmanship was misplaced. Intense local rivalries made for volatile occasions, especially when large sums of money were involved.

After four qualifying rounds, the Cup's first round proper, played on 2 February, saw all the southern clubs eliminated. Woolwich Arsenal, the south's best hope, lost 1–0 at Bolton, while the amateurs of Fairfield were mauled 11–1 by league leaders Sunderland. Southampton St Mary's lost 4–1 at home to Nottingham Forest, in front of around 7,000 supporters. Such was the money at stake that the match was played despite there being 3 inches of snow on the ground. In the midlands, Villa overcame Derby 2–1, and WBA edged a hotly contested match against Small Heath by the same score. 'We have no further interest in the Cup down here,' mourned 'Our Veteran' (*IPN 9/2/95*), as fans elsewhere waited to see whether the league's dominant teams would prove equally successful in the knock-out competition.

A knock-out contest of a very different kind began on 5 February, with the re-opening of Parliament. It was one of Rosebery's many quirks that he enjoyed football, often kicking a ball about with his servants and attending a number of FA Cup Finals, notably the 1897 Villa Everton match that saw the Birmingham side complete the League and Cup double. He was also the Honorary President of the Scottish FA and Edinburgh's Heart of Midlothian, Scottish champions in 1894–5. His English football allegiances are not known; he probably deemed it diplomatic to remain neutral. Perhaps though, the second round ties of 16 February offered him momentary distraction, with Villa disposing of Newcastle 7–1, Wolves beating Stoke, Forest beating Liverpool and Sunderland overcoming Preston. Several days later, WBA beat Sheffield United, and Everton Blackburn, following draws in the Saturday matches. The two matches between Everton and Blackburn generated just over £1,000 in gate receipts, and even Villa Newcastle, where there were far fewer away fans, took £260 (*IPN 2/3/95*).

Rosebery's Liberals were as ragged and demoralised as Newcastle's defence. On 23 January, a by-election at Evesham saw the Conservatives double their majority despite polling being disrupted by serious floods and a Liberal campaign attacking the Tory candidate as an overly-severe magistrate. The Liberal majority was now down to fourteen, and though Rosebery and Harcourt gave defiant speeches in Cardiff and Derby, the cracks in the government were visible to all. 'Rot has set in,' wrote Richard Haldane, a Fabian Socialist, telling Beatrice Webb that 'none of the Ministers are doing any work'. Rosebery 'sees no one but Eddy Hamilton, a flashy Treasury clerk, his stud-groom and various non-political fashionables', while Harcourt and Asquith were doing little to shore up his position (McKinstry 338). The government, remarked *Blackwood's*, resembles 'the ass in the lion's skin', not least because it set out 'with the object of making root-and-branch work of the British Constitution, Church and State' despite having a majority 'which would not, at one time of day, been thought their retaining office to pass even a Turnpike Road Bill' (3/95: 490). On 11 February, the Government just survived a Unionist motion for the immediate dissolution of Parliament. A week later, Rosebery was attacked in the Commons by the radical Liberals Sir Charles Dilke and Henry Labouchere, without any of the Cabinet coming to his aid. As the Colchester by-election approached, Rosebery called a Cabinet meeting and announced his resignation.

Rosebery's Cabinet address drew attention to the ways in which, as a Peer, he was 'kept secluded in the House of Lords while his policy, his character, and his speeches' were criticised in the Commons. The vote of No Confidence, he said, was addressed primarily at him; that no Liberal had offered their support meant 'no man with a vestige of self respect' could continue to hold office (McKinstry 2005: 340). There was shock and protestation from the Cabinet, and the PM agreed to defer his decision for a week. Loulou Harcourt saw that though Rosebery's resignation might make his father Liberal leader, the Government was in such desperate straits that he would have no chance of winning the election. A year earlier, he confided in his diary, 'we should have had a run for our money and gone down fighting like a hell-cat.' Now though, 'we shall go down like a cat with a brick tied round its neck.' The vacillating premier was 'behaving like a spoilt child and wants slapping' (McKinstry 341–2).

Rosebery did not resign, and the Liberals somehow managed to win at Colchester, perhaps because the seat was fought on local and personality issues rather than party political ones. On 22 February, Rosebery told the Cabinet the supportive messages he received after his threat had convinced him to soldier on. Senior Liberals were relieved to be spared the poisoned chalice of leadership but were scornful of what they saw as a fit of pique. Years before, William Johnson, Rosebery's Eton tutor, had remarked that his charge was 'one of those who like the palm without the dust' (McKinstry 2005: 20; R. James 1995: 31). Such a comment fails to encompass the enormous pressure Rosebery was under as his administration headed inexorably towards collapse. It was no wonder that the day after he had vowed to continue as Liberal leader, he was taken seriously ill.

Weakened by insomnia and the strain of vicious Liberal in-fighting, Rosebery was no match for the virulent influenza sweeping the nation. Temperatures reached record lows. Gissing's hands were 'frozen and felt like stones' on 7 February, though he continued to write, warming himself by reading Zangwill's *Children of the Ghetto* (1892) (Gissing 1978: 383). Four days later, Braemar in Grampian logged a temperature of 16.96°F (–27.2°C), still the lowest recorded in Britain. On 14 February, London experienced a serious snowstorm. That same week, workers at the Prince's End ironworks in Tipton in the heart of the Black Country were locked out after the works froze. Similar incidents occurred nationwide. In Brampton in Cumberland, snow drifts twenty feet deep were reported after weeks of frost were topped off with ten hours of continuous snowfall. The *IPN* drew attention to the over-stretched charitable organisations attempting to cope with the freak weather, and to the suffering endured in London's East End. It noted a wide range of other conditions and accidents: deaths from exposure, cold-induced heart failure, skating, tobogganing and exploding boilers. At Brampton Castle in County Durham, James Glendenning, a Glasgow footballer returning from an unsuccessful trial in Lancashire, was killed by a train when attempting to walk home – he had taken to the railway line after heavy snow left roads impassable (*IPN* 16/2/95). Soldiers alarmed onlookers by drilling on London's frozen Serpentine. The Mersey and Thames required icebreakers to keep river traffic moving, while in Oxford, coaching, and an exhibition of ice skating by the university's star athlete, C.B. Fry, took place on the frozen Isis and Cherwell. Animals at London Zoo were kept indoors. Frozen waterways had a catastrophic effect on the kingfisher population. It was the severest winter for over a decade.

In early January, there had been fears diphtheria would take hold in London, but by the end of February it was flu that was causing widespread debilitation in all major cities. The Metropolitan Police was decimated by illness, and such was the prevalence of the disease, a doctor in Poplar, East London, saw 250 cases in six days (*T* 28/2/95). Schools were closed and railways left short-staffed. London's Local Government Board issued a memorandum with advice for halting the spread of the virus. The sick were to be separated from the well, and sputa put into disinfected vessels. 'Unnecessary assemblages' were to be avoided, and

Figure 4. The fierce winter brought Arctic conditions to Liverpool, with the Mersey having to be kept open by icebreakers. *Illustrated London News*, 23 February 1895.

rooms should be disinfected regularly. Those suffering contagion should beware of relapses, keep warm and get medical attention (*IPN* 16/3/95). Jeyes Fluid was heavily advertised as a disinfectant. Newspapers' public health columns tracked the mounting death toll. By 9 March, the day the *ILN*'s Mrs Fenwick-Miller announced 'sable is the fur of the hour' (362), the *SR* was reporting 38.5 flu deaths per thousand in London while in Liverpool, deaths reached 'the astonishing point of 55.5, which sounds like a report from some plague-stricken town of the Orient, rather than a great self-governing English city.' The situation was little better in Nottingham (49.2), Halifax (43.3) or Plymouth (39.2). In the final week of February, 1,120 Londoners died from respiratory diseases, with the toll rising in the first week of March to 1,449, 768 of whom were over the age of sixty (*SR* 9/3/95: 305). 'London is so full of microbes. Do microbes go to parties?' asked *The Green Carnation* (Hichens 48). No respecter of status, the flu numbered among its victims Balfour, Lord Aberdare, Walter Besant, Coningsby Disraeli, the Conservative MP, Sir Walter Wilkin, the Lord Mayor of London, Sir John Everett Millais, the actress and writer Elizabeth Robins, the poet, Lord De Tabley, Julia Stephen, the mother of Virginia Woolf, W.B. Yeats and T.H. Huxley.

Women Who Did

In early March, Mrs Fenwick-Miller noted how 'One by one, those who helped "the New Woman" in her beginnings are passing from the stage of life.' The suffrage campaigner Barbara Bodichon died in June 1891, and the women's education pioneer, Frances M. Buss, 'who received probably the largest salary ever paid to a woman teacher', died on 23 December 1894. On 16 February, they were followed by Dowager Lady Stanley of Alderney, who had helped to establish both the Girls' Public Day School Company in 1872 and Girton College, Cambridge in 1869. A determined advocate of women's education, 'she was a true *grande dame*,' said the *ILN*, 'absolutely independent of the small prejudices and sneers which often pass for public opinion' (2/3/95: 270). Her daughters, it noted, were similarly committed to the cause.

Whether or not Lady Stanley was able to read the slighting depiction of Girton in Grant Allen's *The Woman Who Did*, published on 2 February as part of John Lane's 'Keynotes' series, the novel had an immediate impact, tapping in to ongoing popular debates concerning the 'sex problem': Sidney Grundy's satirical comedy, *The New Woman*, finished a 173 performance run at the Comedy Theatre in the same week. Allen's heroine, the strong-willed Herminia Barton, whose 'face and form' possess 'every element' of 'physical, intellectual, emotional, [and] moral loveliness', forms a 'free union' with Alan Merrick, a barrister and 'firebrand' some years her senior (Allen 2004: 57). Stifled by England, they decamp to Perugia where Merrick soon dies from typhoid and their daughter, Dolores ('Dolly') is born, Herminia scorning the idea of a death-bed wedding. Years later, back in England, Dolly becomes engaged, for she shares none of her mother's views about the evils of marriage and has no desire to assault bourgeois sensibilities. When her fiancé discovers her unconventional background, the outraged girl confronts Herminia, hating 'her ideas, and her friends, and her faction' (161). She plans to leave home and live with her grandfather, though she cannot marry while Herminia lives since she 'couldn't think of burdening an honest man with such a mother-in-law' (163). The broken-hearted Herminia retires to her bedroom, writes a brief letter of self-justification and 'a more formal one' for the coroner's inquest (164). She then kills herself with a phial of prussic acid.

Allen's novel was far from the first late-Victorian study of the 'marriage question', 'woman question' or 'sex problem', and should be seen as contributing to, rather than initiating, discussion. It was not even the first such fiction by a male novelist, and in no way compares with Hardy's *Tess* (1891) or Gissing's *The Odd Women* (1893), though

Hardy himself liked the novel and reassured Allen that although he would be 'condemned in some quarters', he would be spared the treatment *Tess* had received. 'We have moved on since then', Hardy said, erroneously, later advising Allen on the book's foreign rights (Hardy 1980: 68, 74–5). While *The Woman Who Did* was not the first such novel, its brevity and strident polemics made it widely discussed. Lane's shrewd appetite for publicity, which extended to reprinting even negative reviews, also helped to propel it into the *Bookman*'s bestseller lists, and it sold especially well in London, appealing to the capital's many 'advanced' readers. It was 'a tract for the times', though it was a world away from Cardinal Newman and made its heroine 'an automaton used for an object lesson'. 'An 'entirely unconvincing but honest book,' *The Woman Who Did* glorified 'the mere brute instinct of mating' and was thus 'calculated to do not a little harm' (*Bookman* 3/95: 184).

After years of hackwork – his 'sins of commission' joked Hichens ([1894] 1949: 157) – Allen claimed his new novel (one of several he published in 1895) was written 'wholly and solely to satisfy my own taste and my own conscience' (53), but his motives were less transparent than such a claim suggests. 'If it fails to boom, I go under,' he told his nephew, implying a commercial imperative Wells seized upon in the *SR* and in his scepticism towards Allen's 'ostentatious sincerity' in the *PMG* (20/2/95) – Wells later told Allen that he admired his work in popular science but abhorred his treatment of 'sexual sentiment' (Wells 1998: 245). The novel was, Allen claimed 'the first shot fired in the war against' prostitution, a questionable claim unless one read the novel in terms of free-thinkers' critiques of marriage as legalised whoredom (Clodd 1900: 165), and even here, George Egerton's 'Virgin Soil' in *Discords* (1894) had been much more courageous in attacking 'a legal prostitution, a nightly degradation' (Egerton 1894: 155). At the same time, the novel offered a softened version of the argument Allen had put forward in 'The Girl of the Future' (1890), namely that, as Brooke Cameron summarises, 'monogamous marriage looks only to secure one man's monopoly over his wife and thus distorts natural selection' and inhibits 'women's inherent reproductive instincts' (Cameron 2008: 288–89). This may have appealed to 'advanced' readers of the *Universal Review*, but it was unlikely to find a warm welcome in traditional homes.

Reviewers attacked Allen on several fronts. Some addressed stylistic solecisms, flaws in plot and characterisation. The strength of the 'free union' was not tested because of Merrick's early death, the *Bookman* pointed out, while the *Athenaeum* thought it unlikely Dolly

would learn her history from a third party rather than her proselytising mother (2/3/95: 277). *Punch* ridiculed Allen's botanical asides,
picturing 'Pseudonymia' as a recognisably 'Beardsley woman' in an
accompanying illustration of 'The Woman Who Wouldn't Do' by E.T.
Reed (30/3/95: 153). Even W.T. Stead, who made the novel the book
of the month in his *Review of Reviews* suggested Herminia was 'much
more a woman who preached than a woman who did' and claimed the
book sought to reduce 'the woman's standard of morality to that of the
man's' (*RR* 2/95: 190, 177). Other readers, such as the *Academy*'s Percy
Addleshaw, were goaded by Allen's sub-Shavian provocations into rash
overstatement. '[A] married woman at the present time in England is
freer than any other person, male or female, has ever been since English
history began,' he spluttered (2/3/95: 187). Shaw himself found the book
'amusingly boyish' (Shaw 1965: 493), but there was a general sense that
Allen's dedicating the book to his wife was hypocritical, and Edward
Clodd's memoir of his friend included the tale of an interview with him
that 'closed with the words, "he is happily married"'. Apparently, 'the
compositor soothed his doubts by thus punctuating it: "he is, happily,
married"' (Clodd 1900: 162).

Whatever the book's faults, Wells felt 'it may not merit praise, but it
merits reading' (*SR* 9/3/95: 320). Allen, like Wilde and Beardsley, helped
boost his sales by arguing with reviewers in the correspondence columns
of influential weeklies. What became increasingly obvious over the next
few months however was that a growing faction of the British press
was politically radical, not in the sense of parliamentary radicalism but
in terms of its engagement with questions of personal ideology. Shaw's
review of *King Arthur* had shown how a socialist and (problematic)
feminist could bring fresh insights to even an apparently uncontroversial pageant, but a polemical and topical work such as Allen's brought
such approaches into yet clearer focus. When Millicent Garrett Fawcett
turned to the book in the *Contemporary Review* in May, her barbed
critique drew attention to its plentiful ideological falsehoods. Allen, she
pointed out:

> has never given help by tongue or pen to any practical effort to improve the
> legal or social status of women, and it is as an enemy that he endeavours
> to link together the claim of women to citizenship and social and industrial
> independence, with attacks upon marriage and the family. (Allen 2004: 221)

Fawcett recognised the novel's 'melodramatic absurdities' but argued
they were less important than its iniquitous political message. Fraser
Harrison terms the novel 'deviously realistic', since in creating a woman
who won the (radical) reader's admiration while yet revealing 'her

essential femininity', Allen was able to reaffirm gender stereotypes and 'demonstrate that the price of absolute liberation was self-destruction' (Harrison [1977] 1979: 119–20). Other reviewers however picked up on the recurrence of the 'woman with a past', a stock character in sensation fiction, and now a familiar figure on the 1890s' stage in Pinero's *The Second Mrs Tanqueray* (which also concluded with a suicide), *An Ideal Husband*, and Henry Arthur Jones's comedy, *The Case of Rebellious Susan* (1894). So prevalent was she that *Punch* was able to announce *The New Heroine*, a play in which the female lead, 'brought up from early infancy by a mother of unblemished reputation' does not have 'a past'. 'Must there be one law for women and another for dramatic authors?' she laments, peeping coquettishly over her fan (22/12/94: 293). In the years when purity campaigning was at its height, and attacks on the double standard increasingly outspoken, authors and playwrights fused topical debate with mid-Victorian staples in order to garb themselves with 'advanced' views while continuing to extract dramatic mileage from proven ingredients. Tellingly, the same tactics were employed by many of the New Woman's champions as well as her opponents. So firmly was the convention established by the mid-1890s that those who departed from it, as Mrs Comyns Carr did in *A Model Wife and Other Stories*, found their work adjudged graceful, charming, but somewhat thin (*A* 16/2/95: 215).

The Woman Who Did was a major success for Allen (who received an initial royal of 9d a copy) and his publisher, but it was as much a conversation piece as a literary work. Its notoriety overshadowed a subtler and more accomplished novel, Ménie Muriel Dowie's *Gallia*, published a fortnight later and advertised in the same issue of the *PMG* that saw Wells ridiculing Allen's impossible heroine. Allen was a well-known figure, a populariser of Darwin and Herbert Spencer, a prolific essayist as well as churner-out of potboilers. Dowie by contrast was making her debut as a novelist at the age of twenty-seven, having previously published little beyond an anthology of women's travel writing, a short story in the *YB* and a successful volume of travel sketches, *A Girl in the Karpathians* (1891). As yet uncontroversial, she was nevertheless eye-catching, having spent her honeymoon on a fishing holiday in Scotland. 'The figure of Mrs Norman issuing to the chase in a smart Tauntz knickerbocker suit, with a cigarette between her lips, and a salmon rod in her hand' was a 'charmingly unconventional' vision, said *The Woman's Herald* (Dowie xxix). When the fly-fishing heroine of Egerton's 'A Cross Line' appeared two years later, the inner life of such women as well as their dress attracted controversy: *Gallia* placed its author in the vanguard of the 'new fiction'.

Gallia's omniscient narrator is often reminiscent of Gissing, whose fiction Dowie greatly admired. She bought all his novels in their three-volume form, much to his astonishment (Gissing 1994: 301), and told him she ranked him 'as one of the *three* first novelists' (Gissing 1978: 364). Her style was less radical than Egerton's, but her ideas were equally shocking and hardly softened by Dowie's dedicating the novel to her husband. Gallia Hamesthwaite is a wealthy and privileged young woman, highly intelligent, educated and politically aware. She finds herself caught between two men, the handsome and vain Dark Essex, the black sheep of Balliol, and the altogether more conventional Mark Gurdon, 'born to be a successful, honourable, gentlemanly, "decent" kind of fellow' (Dowie [1895] 1995: 20). Dowie departed from formulaic romance by making her heroine a woman who is deeply subversive in two ways. First, she feels and admits to, powerful sexual desire for Essex. Second, she weighs this desire against her maternal ambitions quite calculatingly. 'I certainly hope to bring up a child,' she tells Essex during a tryst in the cloisters of Westminster Abbey. 'I think it is all I do want' (126). Although she is passionately drawn to her lover, she finds him poor breeding stock due to his hereditary heart condition and 'small, sallow hands' (178). As Angelique Richardson shows, Sarah Grand's fiction had caused disquiet with its espousal of eugenic principles and 'fitness', and Egerton had hymned the glories of motherhood, but Dowie went further in that her heroine chooses Gurdon for a husband despite not feeling for him the love she does for his rival (Richardson 95–131).

John Davidson's satirical novel, *The Wonderful Mission of Earl Lavender* may have been 'a stupid book that makes valiant, but unsuccessful efforts to be funny' (*A* 9/3/95: 310) or 'a plagiarised absurdity tempered by beastliness' (*PMG* 19/2/95), but it had a keen eye for the preoccupations of its day and appearing in the same month as *Gallia*, offered a revealing counterpart to it: Earl Lavender, a devotee of natural selection, plans to choose as his bride 'the fittest among women' (Davidson [1895] 2008: 113). His views are countered by The Lady of the Veil, an elegant dominatrix who inhabits an 'Underworld' beneath a London hotel. Acknowledging the growing freedoms of middle class women, she points out that 'Doctoring, travelling, journalising' are but 'antique things that men have been doing for centuries, and can do much better, and always will do much better than women. There is only one thing that women can do better than men – a thing men can't do at all' (130–31). *Gallia*'s creator may have tried travelling and journalising, but she is less sceptical than Davidson about the political force of reproduction. Gallia cares little for Gurdon's sexual history, and in a remarkable conversation with Essex, sums up her reasons for choosing him:

> 'He's got virility, alertness [. . .] He is keen and gamey and lifey. Then he's got iron self-control, a princely obstinacy, an Imperial power of faithfulness [. . .] Added to which, he is a handsome fellow, with all the bone and muscle and blood and fibre that a man ought to have – not wasted by athletics, nor injured by slothfulness.'
>   'My dearest girl,' Essex said, when the list of Gurdon's virtues was full, 'he's the very man for you. Marry him. Marry him by all means!' (Dowie [1895] 1995: 178)

That Gallia's reasoning would have been acceptable in a man – Henry Maudsley's *The Pathology of Mind* (1895) advised men to examine prospective wives for the 'outward defects' that were 'the visible signs of inward and invisible faults which will have their influence in breeding' (Greenslade 1994: 102) – only compounded the novel's offensiveness. Frankness was welcomed by some – Gissing bought a copy of *Gallia* on 13 March and felt it was 'not at all a bad book' (Gissing 1978: 366) – but it unsettled others. 'A lady has stepped in where even a Grant Allen has dared not to tread,' said the *SR*. Dowie:

> has gone further in sheer audacity of treatment of the sexual relations and sexual feelings of men and women than any woman before. *Gallia* is remarkable for extraordinary plainness of speech on subjects which it has been customary to touch lightly or to avoid, and the anatomy of emotion shows a coolness and daring, and the analysis of character an uncompromising thoroughness, for which the ordinary male reader finds himself unprepared. (23/3/95: 383)

Wells shows no hesitation in attributing to Dowie qualities which Victorian culture typically classified as 'masculine'; as he says, few male readers would have been prepared for a woman writer who writes frankly about sex but with 'coolness', 'daring' and analytical rigour. The *Athenaeum* was more cautious, praising the book as being 'distinctly above the average of novels written about the eccentric and rather outrageous young woman' but admitting there were 'some scabrous scenes' (13/4/95: 470). 'A book for the study rather than the drawing room,' Wells concluded, apparently gendering the book's readership. Praised by *The Queen* and the *Daily Chronicle*, *Gallia* was denounced by the *DT*, no friend to the New Woman, which felt its heroine was 'monstrously eccentric' (8/3/95).

Despite its literary merits and considerable press coverage, *Gallia* was not a commercial success. After an initial flurry of sales, it was reprinted only once in Britain and ran to just an initial edition in America. By the time Henry Harland was praising it in the *YB* in October, it was already fading from view (Harland 1895: 138–40). *The Woman Who Did* meanwhile was reprinted nineteen times in its first year, helped by Stead's endorsement, its memorable title, which became proverbial, and Lane's aggressive advertising campaign. *Punch* offered an astute imitation of this in its cartoon, 'The "Sexo-Mania"', in which a woman novelist complains to her publisher about negative press notices in adverts for her novel, *Gone Astray*. 'We've paid you a large price for your book, and brought it out at great expense – and we naturally wish to sell it!' he replies (23/3/95: 138). The more sober Methuen could not compete with such tactics, and fell back on lamely stressing the success of Dowie's Carpathian travelogue rather than foregrounding her novel's daring.

Trivial Comedy, Serious People

Wilde and Bosie arrived in Algiers on 17 January. The Wilde home in Tite Street had a Moorish smoking room, but this paled beside Algerian realities. A letter to Ross told how hashish was 'quite exquisite: three puffs of smoke and then peace and love.' 'The beggars here have profiles, so the problem of poverty is easily solved,' Wilde added, reprising the sentiments of 'Phrases and Philosophies' (*WCL* 629) and oblivious to the political ironies of his position. Accompanied by André Gide, he initially enjoyed his break from the London fog, but even in the midst of sexual and narcotic abandon, his relations with Bosie were fraught. The latter's toxic combination of sexual voracity and petulance made him an unpleasant companion. When Wilde left Algiers on 31 January, Douglas stayed behind, 'held fast by the lasso of desire to a sugar-lipped lad. He is of extraordinary personal beauty, and is aged fourteen,' he told Ross in a letter of 11 February (McKenna [2003] 2004: 443).

Wilde returned from Algiers with more than a sun-tan. One of his first acts in London was to see Dr Lanphier Vernon Jones, a specialist in the treatment of gonorrhoea. His usual doctor was Charles de Lacy of Grosvenor Street; McKenna observes that Wilde was still seeing Vernon Jones three months later, running up a large bill in the process (447). Having already had a serious case of influenza, Wilde may now have exposed himself to dangerous doses of emetics and 'curative' poisons, as well as the opiates countering their side-effects. Dosed with powerful drugs, drinking heavily, dismissive of exercise, and chain-smoking opium-tainted cigarettes as well as breathing the poisonous London fog, Wilde was increasingly unhealthy. Nevertheless, he looked forward with some confidence to the opening of his new play, a romantic comedy due to open on Valentine's Day.

The play was the subject of considerable gossip. 'The Mummer' disliked the 'feeble impertinence' of Wilde's recent interviews and asked 'When are we going to hear the last of this self-advertising gentleman?' (*IPN* 2/2/95). *The Era* was worried a 'common pun' lay at the heart of the play, though it conceded that 'the author of *Lady Windermere's Fan* is a law unto himself, and we must hear even his puns before striking them – or him – off the rolls of the serious drama' (2/2/95). The *DN* reported Wilde's next play would be 'The Advantage of Being Earnest' (*sic*), 'a more mirthful and extravagant' offering than his previous efforts. It was due to open on 12 February. Inaccurate with regard to title (as was *The Era*) and dates, the report was correct in announcing the play would replace *Guy Domville* at the St James's, with Alexander swapping his Georgian finery for Jack Worthing's modern dress. 'Those who would see Mr Henry James's *Guy Domville*, which, in spite of its faults, is a work of many beauties, acted throughout with exquisite charm and finish, have therefore now but little time to lose' (28/1/95), it added, words James probably did not appreciate. The play had netted him around £750, a poor return on the best part of five years' work.

Earnest's rehearsals were well advanced and had led to considerable changes to the play when Wilde returned from North Africa. Having been persuaded to drop the fourth act, he was unimpressed by the dress rehearsal since a number of the cast were struggling with colds. Another concern was Queensberry, who had recommenced his harassment campaign and planned to sabotage the opening night. Fortunately, Wilde learned of his intentions and got Alexander to cancel his ticket and place twenty policemen around the theatre. In his place would be Arthur Humphreys, manager of Wilde's favourite bookshop, Hatchard's of Piccadilly, and the publisher of *Oscariana*, and the translator Teixeira de Mattos. Leverson, who again shared a box with the Beardsleys, recalled in 1926 how the play opened on the night of a fearsome snowstorm but that crowds still turned out in force, some to watch the play, others because they were 'Wilde fanatics who appeared to regard the arrivals as part of the performance and cheered the best known people' as they appeared. Men wore lily-of-the-valley in their buttonholes as a tribute to an 'absent friend' who was still in Algiers. Wilde, dressed with 'florid sobriety', was at his most charming whatever his anxieties about Queensberry's next move (Mikhail II 1979: 267). The Beardsleys enjoyed the play, Aubrey's mood being further improved by the controversy he had provoked with a frontispiece to *Earl Lavender* that illustrated a flagellatory scene.

The day *Earnest* opened, James reflected in his notebook on 'the whole tragic experience' of his theatrical adventure, and pondered the relationship between 'the narrative and the dramatic': perhaps 'his infinite little loss' would yet lead to 'an almost infinite little gain' (Moore 1974: 77). Wilde however had no need for morbid self analysis, for *Earnest*, 'A Trivial Comedy for Serious People', was to be his greatest theatrical success. The play has attracted a great deal of critical comment in the last twenty years, much of it concerned with its gender and sexual politics and its engagement with Victorian theatrical tradition. Three couples perform an elaborate romantic *passepied* under the acerbic eye of Lady Bracknell, but the exchanges between the young lovers Jack and Gwendolen, Algernon and Cecily, and their older counterparts Miss Prism and Canon Chasuble are underscored by subversion. Wilde realised like no writer of his day the intense personal pleasure of dramatising one's secrets without confessing them, and the play is filled with parallels between his private life and opinions – engraved cigarette cases, claims that 'Fathers are not popular at present' – and those of his characters (Craft 118–28). More disconcertingly still, as Ruth Robbins argues in an insightful discussion, Wilde makes the case throughout *Earnest* that language 'distorts rather than mimetically represent[ing] the real', being 'non-referential and transitive' (Robbins 2003: 109). Wilde detaches words from things, punning on the Victorian virtue of earnestness, destabilising notions of identity and overturning theatrical and social convention by making words lose their intended meaning 'between utterance and reception' (116). The mechanics of theatrical farce – though in the sedentary Wilde these come from plot and dialogue, not from physical exertion – cloak a refusal of moral orthodoxy. 'The good [end] happily, and the bad unhappily. That is what Fiction means,' says Miss Prism (*WCW* 376), adhering to the outdated moral rubric of the three decker and the expectations of many theatregoers. In *Earnest* though, 'good' and 'bad' are difficult to define, much less calibrate. Perhaps drawing on Socratic dialogues that rebuke Athenians for failing to differentiate between an example and an abstract definition, Wilde's comedy presents 'an amoral world where competent lying is presented as the route to romantic success' (Robbins 2003: 106).

The play garnered excellent reviews. H. Chance Newton, 'Carados' of *The Referee*, felt 'It is time to take Oscarissimus seriously now he has written a farce,' an assessment which shows how some at least were becoming more willing to read Wilde on his own terms (Goodman 1988: 24). In the *PMG*, Wells praised Wilde's 'excellent fooling', noting how one member of the audience, one of the 'serious people' that

Carlyle had regarded as the majority of the population, felt the play had been robbed of 'convincingness' by its far-fetched incidents (15/2/95). Positive responses appeared in *The World, Truth, The Speaker*, where Walkley felt Wilde had at last 'found himself' as a dramatist (23/2/95), and the *ILN*. Leverson delighted her friend with her new *Punch* skit, 'The Advisability of Not Being Brought Up in a Handbag' on 2 March. Some were less impressed however, with the *Athenaeum* one of several journals to see Wilde as an inferior Gilbert, 'frivolous, saucy, and impertinent' (23/2/95: 260). 'The Captious Critic' felt he struggled to individuate characters and noted that by 9 March, the 'better seats' were filled though 'pit and gallery were the reverse of crowded' (Goodman 1988: 33). Shaw meanwhile felt 'amused' but not 'touched' by Wilde's comic vision, feeling the play was already dated in its mechanical plotting and compromised by its nakedly commercial ambitions (*OT* 42). Almost everyone found themselves smiling at some point though, the sole exception being Queensberry, who, denied entrance to the show, prowled around 'chattering like a monstrous ape' before leaving a bouquet of vegetables at the stage door (*WCL* 632).

Wilde had not wished Bosie to know of his father's plot, but Percy Douglas summoned him by telegram from Algiers, telling him something was afoot. He returned to London on 20 February and joined Wilde in the Avondale Hotel – Wilde was *persona non grata* at the Albemarle Hotel because of an unpaid bill – where they ran up expenses of £140 in ten days. At some point, Alexander sent Wilde a cheque for £300, though this was not enough to cover his outstanding debts or to allow him to leave the 'loathsome' Avondale. 'I am sorry my life is so maimed and marred by extravagance', Wilde told him, 'But I cannot live otherwise' (*WCL* 633). As Wilde attempted to devise a stratagem for dealing with the 'monstrous ape', Bosie insisted he be taken to court and punished by due process of law. Not content with offering unwise counsel, he also brought a young man, probably a prostitute, back to the hotel.

On 18 February, the Marquess came to the Albemarle Club in search of Wilde, who was elsewhere. Scribbling something on his card, he handed it to the porter, Sydney Wright, who placed it in an unsealed envelope in Wilde's pigeonhole with his other mail. For ten days, Wilde savoured the acclaim of the press, spent his royalties, argued with Douglas, took Dr Vernon Jones's medicine, dined with friends, read reviews of new books such as Balfour's *The Foundations of Belief* and Bram Stoker's *The Watter's Mou'*, worried about how best to respond to the Marquess's harassment, and avoided contacting his wife and family. He even planned to leave for France, but was forced to remain in London when the manager of the Avondale refused to release his luggage until he had settled his account.

It was not until five o'clock on 28 February that he arrived at the Albemarle and consulted his post.

Notes

1. Rosebery's annual income during 1894–5 was c. £140,000. His will left £1,554,339, a figure which does not include the substantial properties he made over to his heirs before his death. Queen Victoria's household expenses in 1894 were c. £172,000 (*IPN* 19/1/95).
2. The accompanying poem argued 'petticoat-government' would be unable to solve social ills, and that puritanical zeal was unwelcome and unwise. 'Prowlina Pry' was an allusion to the eponymous busybody of John Poole's *Paul Pry* (1825), still being staged as late as the 1870s and given an opportunistic forty-one performance run at Toole's Theatre, London, from 26 December 1894. Midge Gillies notes how the music hall performer Herbert Chapman satirised Chant's 'stridently mannish *modus operandi*' by singing 'let her chant in her backyard' while wearing 'a lady's short tweed coat, with collar and tie, skirt hitched up, boots, gaiters, and a Homburg' (Gillies 89). For further discussion of the cartoon, see Faulk (87–90).
3. The Metropolitan Police's annual reports showed the average number of prostitutes arrested in London between 1893 and 1896 was 3,352, with average conviction and discharge rates 585 and 139. Numbers increased significantly in 1897 due to more aggressive policing and the revelry surrounding the Diamond Jubilee (Petrow 132). The figures do not include male prostitutes, since they were usually charged with offences such as indecency, conspiracy to commit a felony, and demanding money with menaces.
4. Biron's son, Chartres, at this time a London QC, later became the judge who ordered the destruction of Radclyffe Hall's *The Well of Loneliness* as obscene, ruling on 16 November 1928 that 'in the present case there was not one word that suggested that anyone with the horrible tendencies described was in the least degree blameworthy. All the characters were presented as attractive people and put forward with admiration. What was even more serious was that certain acts were described in the most alluring terms' (*T* 17/11/1928).
5. A lengthier report in the liberal *DN* noted how the jury requested further details of Saunderson's mental state before reaching its decision. On the same day, Gill prosecuted twenty-year-old Henry Turner for demanding money with menaces from Walter Hugh Silver, his former employer. Turner sent letters threatening 'a false accusation of a serious nature', probably one of sexual misconduct. Justice Wills showed his disgust by 'remarking on the atrociousness of the crime' and sentencing Turner to seven years in jail (*DN* 31/1/95).
6. The cast included Harley Granville-Barker. The play had forty performances at the Comedy Theatre, 19 May–2 July 1892. Brookfield retired from

performance in 1898 after being diagnosed with tuberculosis. He worked as a writer and critic, and despite scandalised responses to his *Dear Old Charley* (1908), became the Lord Chamberlain's Examiner of Plays in 1911. Hawtrey, whose father taught at Eton, was educated at Rugby and Pembroke College, Oxford. He shared Brookfield's distaste for Wilde.

7. Henty published over 100 historical novels for children between 1870 and 1902, in addition to magazine fiction and (unsuccessful) adult works. He averaged 6,000 words a day. Meade published 250 books and was 'the most industrious of Victorian authors', often turning out six per year during the 1890s. She also edited the girls' magazine, *Atalanta* from 1887–93 (Sutherland 294, 432).

8. It is surprising to see Beardsley include this drawing at a time when, as the *SR* argued in 'The Barbarity of Glove-Fighting' (19/1/95: 86–8), boxing was regarded in 'advanced' circles as a cruel pastime on a par with bull-baiting. Had Queensberry not been pursuing Wilde, he may have tackled Frank Harris on this issue. Shaw however was an enthusiast and sometime practitioner; his *Cashel Byron's Profession* (1886) praises boxing at the expense of prize-fights.

9. The League's founder members were: Accrington, Aston Villa, Blackburn Rovers, Bolton Wanderers, Burnley, Derby County, Everton, Notts County, Preston North End, Stoke (who became Stoke City in 1928), WBA and Wolverhampton Wanderers ('Wolves').

10. Cigarette cards would become an important means of disseminating sporting images, not least because they were in colour. Wills issued its first set, 'Ships and Soldiers' in 1895, its second, 'Cricketers' the following year. 1896 also saw the first set of football cards, 'Footballers and Club Colours', by Manchester's Marcus and Company.

11. Goodison's initial capacity was c. 12,000, but there was little attention to safety or crowd control and 37,000 packed in to see Notts County beat Bolton 4–1 in the 1893–4 FA Cup Final. Nearly 30,000 saw Everton defeat Liverpool in the semi-final of the Lancashire Cup in March 1895. The first football stadium built in Britain was Ibrox, home of Glasgow Rangers, inaugurated in 1887.

12. In 1901, Villa played Sheffield United in appalling sleet. A number of players suffered mild frostbite, but football folklore maintains that Athersmith (1872–1910) borrowed an umbrella from a spectator and played on, even scoring a goal. The widening gulf between professionals and amateurs was illustrated by Villa's 11–0 victory over Cambridge University on 19 January 1895. The inspirational captain of Villa's 1887 FA Cup winning side, Archie Hunter (b.1859), died from consumption on 29 November 1894. He received a generous obituary notice in the *BDP* (30/11/94).

13. Two days before the disaster, *Punch* asserted that 'many a spouting member of the "Independent Labour Party" is a "party" who wishes to be independent of labour' (12/1/95: 21). My account of the Diglake tragedy owes much to the research of Susan Bradley, whose website, warrinersprimaries.com/topic/diglake.htm (accessed 21 May 2010) contains many press reports and images, along with details of the colliery's subsequent history. Some of William Baron's work appeared in George Hull's anthology, *The Poets and Poetry of Blackburn* (1902).

Spring: 1 March 1895 – 30 May 1895

Spring came out of the woodland chase,
With her violet eyes and her primrose face,
With an iris scarf for her sole apparel,
And a voice as blithe as a blackbird's carol.

> Alfred Austin, 'The Coming of Spring', *Blackwood's*, March 1895

Let us talk about *Moral Indignation, its Cause and Cure*, a subject on which I think of writing.

> Oscar Wilde, *The Critic as Artist* (1889)

Nowadays, with our modern mania for morality, everyone has to pose as a paragon of purity, incorruptibility, and all the other seven deadly virtues. – and what is the result? You all go over like ninepins – one after the other. Not a year passes in England without somebody disappearing. Scandals used to add charm, or at least interest, to a man – now they crush him. And yours is a very nasty scandal.

> Mrs Cheveley in *An Ideal Husband*, Act I

City Editor (philosophically): People never gain anything by leading double lives.
New Reporter: Er, what about the Siamese twins?

> 'Funny Wheezes', *Illustrated Police News*, 2 February 1895

Some people may term the abnormal nerve state 'degeneracy', but I don't know where the world would now be without it.

> George Ives, Diary, 16 March 1895

It is very painful for me to be forced to speak the truth. It is the first time in my life that I have been reduced to such a painful position, and I am really quite inexperienced in doing anything of the kind.

> Jack Worthing in *The Importance of Being Earnest*, Act III

Does the Crown aver, that if Apollo were still alive and were to visit this country, Scotland Yard would run him in?

> 'I. Playfair', 'Some Gentle Criticisms of British Justice' (1895)

దీయం

Degenerate Days, Lugubrious Psychologists

'Should golf be encouraged at public schools?' Golf was perfectly acceptable in itself, said *Blackwood's*, but it should not join cricket and rugby on the educational curriculum. 'Except in rare cases, we should instinctively condemn the boy who devoted his play-time to a more or less solitary and selfish game,' it announced, characterising golf as a pastime in which 'bad temper towards adversaries, and mutual recrimination between partners' replaced the cricket eleven's *esprit de corps*. Cricketers recognised and applauded their opponents' successes, but golf had no moral compass. Indeed, its presence in schools risked swelling the numbers of 'malingerers or boy-hypochondriacs'. Warming to his theme, the writer attacked 'victims' of 'modern humanitarianism', the 'hothouse plants [. . .] whom a cold in the head drives straight to the sanatorium.' 'We do not send our boys to Eton and Harrow' merely to 'read the classics,' he concluded, 'but that by rubbing up against other boys in their play-hours they may smooth down the rough corners and get rid of the cranks in their characters.' Those unable to 'rub along' become set in a groove forever, and, in an unconscious paralleling of Pater's claim, 'our failure is to form habits' (Pater 152), the writer observed, 'Grooviness in adult life is often a vice' (3/95: 417–23).

Only a tiny percentage of the nation's youth was educated at Eton and Harrow, but this article demonstrates the model of masculinity inculcated by team sports, implying a moral hierarchy with cricket at the top and golf somewhere near the bottom. Amateur football came somewhere between the two extremes – a varsity match had been established in 1884, and Oxford would win the 1895 tussle 3–0, helped by a match-winning performance from C.B. Fry. Golf however encapsulated the vices of solitariness, crankiness and an inability to 'rub along'. Academic studies encouraged these even more damagingly than a day on the links, and by *Blackwood's* estimations, Rosebery, Douglas and Wilde were equally wanting. Rosebery had played cricket at Eton, but his professed boredom with it was, in some eyes, evidence of a furtively deviant character unsuited for high office.[1] After initial bullying Bosie became popular at Winchester, but apart from the occasional round of golf, his only notable sporting prowess was in running; he might have gained a half-blue at Magdalen but for a knee injury. Wilde scorned all sporting endeavours, though he did confess to playing dominoes outside French cafes. To reject cricket was to reject a wider set of masculine virtues gathered under the umbrella term 'sportsmanship': courage, determination, selflessness, good humour, team spirit, obedience to one's captain, masculine indomitability and dedication to the cause. At one time, members of the amateur I Zingari club were even forbidden to rub their wound if hit by the ball.

On 1 March, England's cricketers began the fifth test of the Ashes series against Australia. They had won the opening game at Sydney in December by the narrowest of margins. Forced to follow on, they managed to set a target of 176, a total easily within the Australians' reach when they finished the fourth day on 113–2. However, conditions then favoured England, and Yorkshire's Bobby Peel and Lancashire's Johnny Briggs bowled them to victory by ten runs. It was the first time a test match had been won by a side made to bat again, a feat not repeated until another remarkable English victory against Australia at Leeds in 1981.

The second test, played in Melbourne over New Year, saw another England win, with their captain, Middlesex's Andrew Stoddart, scoring 173. Stoddart epitomised *Blackwood's* ideas of sporting and moral excellence. A member of I Zingari, he was a rugby international, a fine batsman and fielder, a useful bowler, and a natural leader whose magnificent moustache and military bearing commanded respect on and off the field.[2] Nevertheless, he was unable to prevent an aggressive Australian fight back. On 15 January, England mustered only 143 in their second innings having been set over 500, Australia winning by the huge margin of 382 runs. Worse was to follow. At Sydney in the first week of February, England suffered an even more humiliating defeat. Responding to Australia's 284, they were bowled out twice in a day, mustering 65 and 72. With Nottinghamshire's Bill Lockwood unable to bat after a soda water bottle exploded in his hand, England were battered, bruised and homesick when they arrived in Melbourne for the deciding test.

Initially, the match went Australia's way as they posted a first innings score of 414. England replied with 385, 120 of them from Lancashire's Old Harrovian captain, Archie MacLaren. In the second innings, the Australians made 267, pegged back by the fearsome fast bowling of Surrey's Tom Richardson. This left England needing 297 runs for victory, and though in trouble at 28–2, they were seen home by Yorkshire's Jack Brown, who scored 140 (the first 50 runs in less than half an hour), and Lancashire's Albert Ward, who made a watchful 93. England won by six wickets in front of 23,000 spectators.

Commenting on this success, the *Times* drew attention to the ways in which 'all the resources of civilisation are called into play' to keep English supporters in touch with the progress of the game (7/3/95). On 24 November 1894, the *IPN* reported a telegraph message could be sent from Manchester to Victoria, British Columbia and back in only

90 seconds. The telegraph allowed a detailed report of the Melbourne test to appear in English newspapers the day after the game had finished, cause for technological as well as sporting pride. The Australians' good-humoured cheering was seen as evidence of strong imperial bonds, while the victorious blend of north and south, professional and amateur, spoke well for national unity and the long-established class system. Mr Punch was delighted by it all (16/3/95: 122–3), though left unmentioned the fact that Players did not stay in the same hotels as Gentlemen, and were not always invited to official functions. The divide was deep-rooted. At Lord's, professionals took to the field by side gates, while amateurs strode out from the pavilion. Scorecards signified class and status by the inclusion of titles and reversals of name order. In 1896, professionals threatened a strike after a refusal to increase appearance fees for tests and Gentlemen versus Players matches agreed in 1871. The fee in question was £10.

Perhaps the most notable aspect of the cricketers' success was its moral message. 'We may, like other races and other times, have our decadents and degenerates,' wrote the *Times*, 'but the capacity for strenuous sport may be regarded as a fairly satisfactory reply to the lugubrious predictions of certain psychologists' (7/3/95). Cricket epitomised virtues perceived as quintessentially English (at least by the English themselves), but for *Blackwood's* and the *Times* it assumed additional significance as a bulwark against tendencies that would ruin the individual and corrode the moral, spiritual, and military force of the Empire. While the NVA explained 'immoral' behaviour as a consequence of biological essentialism (the 'natural' urges of men being a frequent topic of condemnation) and the undermining of Christian belief by 'progressive' socio-political forces, psychologists ranged over science, sociology and art in issuing jeremiads on national decline.

The *fin de siècle*, says William Greenslade, saw 'a lack of synchrony between the rhetoric of progress' and 'the evidence in front of people's eyes, of poverty and degradation at the heart of ever richer empires.' Politicians, churchmen, journalists and novelists all addressed the matter, some blaming the waning of Christian values, others identifying the iniquities of the class system or those who objected to them. Alongside these voices ran another line of seemingly more objective investigation, which drew its ideas from biological and racial science and transformed a theory of 'degeneration' into a 'fully fledged explanatory myth' (Greenslade 1994: 15).

Darwinism suggested evolution carried forward the adaptable and, in its social application, the forward-looking, while making marginal or extinct those unwilling or unable to cope with new conditions.

Degeneration endorsed such ideas but argued organisms could also regress to older forms of brutality, and physical grossness because of race, heredity, habit and the condition of modern life. When such reasoning was applied to animals, it led the Oxford scientist Edwin Lankester to the erroneous belief that the barnacle was a degenerate crustacean rather than a creature suited to a specialised existence. When applied to people however, the atavistic threat of degeneration had genuinely alarming implications, especially when it seemed to be supported by a battery of photographic and statistical 'evidence'. Lankester worried that 'the white races of Europe' were 'drifting' and 'tending to the condition of intellectual Barnacles' (Lankester 1880: 59–60). Researchers such as Cesare Lombroso bolstered their claims with contemporary scientific terminology and methods, yet uprooted language from its rationalising context and replanted it in the fertile soil of Carroll's Wonderland, Wilde's comedies, or the debating chambers of parliaments and courtrooms. In such environments, the meaning and purpose of words is determined almost entirely by their user, allowing 'modern' and similar terms to acquire a spectrum of idiosyncratic and often contradictory meanings. 'Degeneration' was itself a suggestive example of semantic legerdemain, with the British scientist Henry Maudsley pointing out that despite its popularity, it remained imprecise and unrevealing rather than being the conclusive diagnostic label its advocates desired (Bourne Taylor 2007: 16).

Degeneration theory had grown in popularity since the 1870s, explaining everything from falling birth rates to French military humiliation. However, the appearance of Max Nordau's *Entartung* in 1892, and its translation into English as *Degeneration* in 1895, made the German its most well-known advocate. A hotchpotch of ideas going back to the 1850s, Nordau's book was a ferocious attack on the citadel of European high culture, with its author insisting the work of Baudelaire, Nietzsche, Wagner, Zola, Ibsen and Tolstoy exhibited every sign of mental and moral decay. Degenerate art emerged from a degenerating culture, feeding back into it to intensify the rate of moral decomposition and inspire ever more pernicious literature, painting and music. 'We stand now in the midst of a severe mental epidemic,' Nordau shrieked, 'a sort of black death of degeneration and hysteria' (Nordau 1895: 537).

Dedicated to Lombroso, *Degeneration* 'constituted one of the most extraordinary examples of a book which was at once intellectually risible and strangely compelling, methodologically absurd and yet a logical extension of positivistic thought' (Greenslade 1994: 121). Running through seven reprints in six months, it offered a pungent vocabulary with which to attack the radical aesthetics of the gallery and stage. Though confining himself mainly to European writers and artists, Nordau also flayed the theories of Ruskin and the painting of Rossetti and Burne-Jones. With the first two safely dead, and the third a pillar of the establishment designing sets for Henry Irving, attention turned instead to Nordau's other British target, the flamboyant and egotistical Wilde, whose work apparently exemplified the worst excesses of undisciplined and morbid subjectivity. Women, weak-willed, emotional and irrational were particularly at risk; in June 1894, Nordau told the *New Review* they should receive 'physiological teaching' to help them resist the evil influences of 'wild fictions based upon morbid art, detestable literature, suggestive plays and inconsidered drawing-room and table-talk' (Greenslade 1994: 172). Wilde later joked that he agreed with Nordau's view that 'all men of genius are insane', qualifying it by observing, 'Dr Nordau forgets that all sane people are idiots' (Mikhail II 1979: 384).

Like *The Woman Who Did*, *Degeneration* did not merit praise but did merit reading, with several critics using the book's own argument to diagnose its author as everything he deplored. Devoting 40,000 words to Ibsen, whom he claimed was obsessed by 'the restless repetition of one and the same strain of thought' seemed to make Nordau as much a 'graphomaniac' as Ibsen himself, wrote B.A. Crackanthorpe (*Nineteenth Century* 4/95: 611). George Saintsbury, soon to be elected Professor of rhetoric and English literature at Edinburgh University, took a similar line. 'The book is a very amusing one,' he wrote. 'Somehow or other books of lamentation and mourning and woe of this kind generally are.' After airy dismissal of Nordau's argument, and a passing reference to 'the excellent Mr Oscar Wilde', Saintsbury concluded 'we fear that by his own showing Herr Nordau is an undoubted "degenerate"' (*Bookman* 4/95: 13–14). William James found *Degeneration* 'a pathological book on a pathological subject', though he approved the breadth of Nordau's reading. Shaw replied to Nordau at length in the anarchist newspaper *Liberty*, recognising the commercial boldness of *Degeneration* as a counter to growing enthusiasm for Wagner and Ibsen but lambasting its 'general staleness and occasional putrescence'. Nordau was, he maintained, 'a born theorist, reasoner and busybody' who exemplified every neurosis he diagnosed in others, was immune to the perils of self-contradiction, and utterly without humour. Gissing read *Degeneration* in early March, later deciding that while there was 'much truth in it', Nordau was prone 'to see madness where there is only affectation' (Hick 1973: 25). Edward Hake meanwhile felt affronted by the book on patriotic grounds, and cried out 'not for leaders, but for more light'. 'We want a higher philosophy,' he insisted, 'nobler arts, a loftier literature, sounder principles of legislation, a purer religion.' It was up to England to lead other nations to a higher plain (Ledger and Luckhurst 2000: 18–22).

Whether or not Queensberry waded through Nordau's diatribe, its argument, and Hake's response, would have appealed to him. His own commentary on Wilde was more succinct. The card he left at the Albemarle may have been 'unfit for publication', 'imperfectly spelt' and 'objectionable' (*RN* 3/3/95), but it was brutally direct, bearing 'an opprobrious epithet which can be more easily grasped than written' (Hamilton 1986: 225). When Wilde saw the scrawled salutation, 'For Oscar Wilde posing somdomite' or, as Ellmann has it 'ponce and Somdomite' (1987: 412), he was deeply distressed by the 'hideous words,' and wrote to Ross at once. 'My whole life seems ruined by this man,' he wailed. 'The tower of ivory is assailed by the foul thing. On the sand is my life spilt.' Amid the histrionic flourishes was a sober admission of exhaustion. 'I don't see anything now but a criminal prosecution' (*WCL* 634).

Relations between Queensberry and his family worsened daily. He told Percy and his wife that Alfred needed 'the shit kicked out of him', and that Wilde was 'a cock sucker' (Murray 2000: 73–4). Bosie longed to see his father in the dock, but cooler heads felt a libel prosecution unwise. A restraining order might have kept Queensberry at bay, but Alexander and his theatre's staff, unwilling to risk harassment, refused to support one. Wilde was also denied the wise counsel of his friend Sir George Lewis, who had helped Bosie hush up a blackmail case in May 1892, since he was already engaged by Queensberry. On 1 March, Wilde met with Ross's solicitor, Charles Humphreys, and, after denying there was any truth in Queensberry's allegations, and hearing Bosie guarantee his family would fund a prosecution, went to Great Marlborough Street's magistrate's court to apply for a warrant. Queensberry was arrested on 2 March at Carter's Hotel in Albemarle Street. He seemed pleased, telling the arresting officer, 'This thing has been going on for about two years' (Hyde 1948: 31). After a brief hearing, the magistrate adjourned the case for a week, whereupon Lewis withdrew, compromised by having known Wilde for almost twenty years. His replacement was Charles Russell, an ambitious young advocate whose father was the Lord Chief Justice. As Queensberry's case seemed founded on personal antipathy and rumour, Russell may have questioned its strength, though 'posing' represented a useful means of avoiding definite proof of sexual misdemeanour. Ruthless and resourceful, Russell bolstered Queensberry's defence by engaging Edward Carson, a barrister with a growing reputation who had been at Trinity College, Dublin, with Wilde. He also advised the Marquess to hire a private detective to dig more deeply into the prosecutor's private life. He recruited John Littlechild, a former detective chief inspector who had been Adolphus Williamson's deputy in the Metropolitan Police's Special Irish Branch in 1888. Littlechild had become a private enquiry agent since leaving the force in 1893, and was well used to surveillance of Irish dissidents. On this occasion though, the focus of his investigation was sexual rather than political, and here he had less experience. Luckily for him, he made contact with the disgruntled actors, Brookfield and Hawtrey, who put him on the trail of a story every bit as explosive as the Fenian dynamiters.

While Queensberry's team got to work, Wilde's legal costs were mounting. With Bosie contributing only £360, Wilde was helped by the prompt action of Ada Leverson's husband, the appropriately named Ernest, who immediately lent £500. Constance Wilde supplemented this with a £150 loan from Edward Burne-Jones, £200 from various relatives and £50 from her £800 annual allowance (Bentley 1983: 111). It represented a useful fighting fund, one reinforced by Wilde's royalties, but if he were to lose, it would vanish into the ever-deepening chasm of his debts. The stakes were growing higher. On 7 March, when Wilde, Constance and Bosie braved the gossips at a performance of *Earnest*, some thought Constance was weeping (Ellmann 1987: 414).

On 9 March, Wilde arrived at Great Marlborough Street accompanied by Bosie and Percy Douglas. About thirty journalists were present. Bosie soon withdrew from the court on the magistrate's instructions, and Wilde watched as lawyers sparred with the bench about the admissibility of questions and evidence. Their exchanges introduced the suggestion that 'exalted persons' were referred to in Wilde's letters and that they therefore could not be read out in open court. The journalists' reaction to this is easily guessed, and Rosebery's name was mooted. It was also decided Wilde could not be cross-examined by Carson at the hearing, and the tussle between them was therefore postponed. Queensberry, annoyed by his family's support for Wilde, told the court he 'wrote that card simply with the intention of bringing matters to a head, having been unable to meet Mr Wilde otherwise, and to save my son.' He was committed for trial, but not before Carson had dropped an ominous hint about the witnesses he would call. His lack of specificity was especially troubling.

It was three weeks before the trial was due to open. Wilde allowed Bosie, who had told Percy that it would be a 'walk over' (M. Holland xxiv), to persuade him into another serious (and expensive) misjudgement, a holiday in Monte Carlo. They were away for a week from 12 March. Wilde told Leverson he would return 'to fight with panthers'

(*WCL* 635), but his bravado was founded on utter ignorance of the defence's knowledge of his private life.

The Tooting Tragedy

Wilde's Monaco trip at least rescued him from the still-ferocious winter. As ever, it was Britain's poor who suffered most severely, none more so than thirty-nine-year-old Frank Taylor, a plasterer from Tooting. Industrious, teetotal, and unlucky, Taylor lost his job when the weather brought building work throughout London to a standstill. He and his family – he and his wife had seven children – survived on penny dinners at the Tooting Parish Church. They sold food from their allotment, but were soon caught between supplying others and feeding themselves; their rent was badly in arrears. On 12 February, Taylor sought relief at the Tooting workhouse, but after being shown the stone-breaking yard, did not return. On 4 March, he at last started a new job, only to be taken ill with flu. He dragged himself into work after a couple of days, ill and despairing. Finally, in the early hours of 7 March, Taylor's oldest child, fourteen-year-old Frank, fled the house and raised the alarm. Bleeding from cuts to the throat, the boy told neighbours his father had gone berserk with a razor.

Even the *Times*' sober report conveys the horror of the event, but the *IPN* excelled itself in a luridly-illustrated account of how Taylor killed not only his wife, Martha, but also six of their children, the eldest thirteen years old, the youngest eighteen months, before cutting his throat over his wife's body. Such were the scenes in the Taylors' home that two policemen fainted, for 'it had more the appearance of a slaughterhouse than a human habitation': Martha had put up a ferocious struggle (*IPN* 16/3/95). A note left by Taylor read, in part, 'I love my wife and children too dearly to allow people to jeer them. They are all pure.' The note was accompanied by copies of Psalms 23 and 25, and a hymn, 'Shall we all meet at home in the morning?' (*T* 11/3/95). An inquest recorded a verdict of suicide and killing while of unsound mind, adding that the latter was perhaps aggravated by illness. The event shocked the local community, not least because the family was eminently respectable despite their hardships. Huge crowds attended their funeral on 19 March, along with sixty volunteer pallbearers. Fourteen pickpockets were arrested (*IPN* 23/3/95).

The 'Tooting Tragedy' demonstrated how the winter exposed shortcomings in charitable provision; that Taylor's best hope seemed the stone-breaking yard disgusted those unaware of the realities of London life. At the other end of the social scale, meanwhile, Rosebery remained dangerously ill, ravaged by flu and insomnia. Hamilton noted how difficult it was to find two nurses for him, such was the shortage of medical personnel (Hamilton 1986: 220). On 22 February his temperature was 101°F and his pulse barely perceptible. He was first given bromide, then morphine injections. On 25 February the sleepless PM was 'very seedy'. Hamilton noted his 'very slow progress towards convalescence' on 4 March, as well as detailing a reaction against 'Progressives' in the LCC elections that made painful reading for Liberal supporters. Although the Progressives hung on through having a majority of aldermen, the actual election was a tie, and 'The Mummer' was one of many delighted to see 'the Paul Prys and ultra-purists of the Chant faction' driven out by 'sober and decent citizens' (*IPN* 16/3/95). Calls for the dissolution of Parliament grew louder, with *Blackwood's* clamouring for 'an end to all suspense, not only about Home Rule but about many other questions as well' (3/95: 494). On 9 March, the *Times* announced the impending resignation of the Speaker, Arthur Peel, which prompted a fresh round of internecine squabbling as the government sought his replacement. The first contested speakership election since 1839 saw William Gully, Liberal MP for Carlisle, best Matthew White Ridley by eleven votes on 10 April after an aggressive speech by Harcourt. On 11 March, an exhausted Rosebery almost passed out during an audience with the Queen. His doctor, Sir William Broadbent, now suspected his insomnia was due to a distended stomach which put pressure on his heart, an affliction caused by solitary reading after meals rather than exercise. Nothing improved his plight, with 'Turkish baths, massages, glasses of porter during the night, political business during the day' all ineffectual (McKinstry 2005: 345). A worried Broadbent told Regy Brett he feared 'a fatal termination' (344). Parliamentary work only made matters worse, with Harcourt noticeably unsympathetic and Loulou positively glorying in a vision of the insomniac tormented by his errors of the previous decade (346). Depressed and finding morphine useless, Rosebery took Sulfonel, a powerful sedative. This allowed some respite, but left him unable to cope with ministerial paperwork. He told Brett he was intensely lonely, which led Brett to observe on 14 March that 'the P. Minister cannot in these days have a mistress. Certainly he requires intimate friends, or he will die' (M. Kaplan 2005: 250). The *Times* had now discovered the extent of his illness, and journalistic curiosity concerning his likely resignation intensified. Was the war between Queensberry and Wilde at the root of his anxiety?

Freezing Footballs

The terrible weather continued to have economic repercussions. Dundee's whalers and sealers were hampered by frozen seas, killing only 13,400 seals, a marked decline from the 36,000 killed in the winter of 1893–4, and a mere three whales, down from fifteen the previous year (*IPN* 30/11/95). In Birmingham, it was estimated that the winter had cost outdoor workers around £50,000 in lost wages, with parish councils spending £10,000 on relief. Thousands of water pipes burst, with daily repairs costing around £1,000. In some areas, water carts had been the only means of supplying drinking water (*IPN* 16/3/95; *P* 30/3/95: 150).

Football offered some a distraction from these privations, and spirits were lifted in parts of Birmingham by Aston Villa's run in the FA Cup. A 1–1 draw with Burnley in late February may have impaired their championship hopes but their cup form was excellent and they began March by sweeping aside Nottingham Forest 6–2 in front of 20,000 fans. Their neighbours WBA were also through to the semi-finals after squeezing past Wolves, 1–0. Sunderland stayed on course for a league and cup double after a 2–1 victory over Bolton, but Everton's hopes were dashed when they went down 2–0 to The Wednesday. Matches continued to be played in awful conditions, but it was the behaviour of spectators, rather than Mother Nature, occupying sporting journalists. Intense local rivalries inspired crowd trouble even in amateur fixtures. On 23 February, a match between Darlington and Middlesborough that must have been played on a frozen pitch saw the referee require police protection after his decisions incensed home fans. In Chesterfield, footballers John and Charles Gee attacked officials after a game and were sentenced to 14 days hard labour. In London, a Reading fan was hit by a stone during a match against the Old Westminsters. The sporting paper *Grasshopper* criticised Birmingham's football supporters for their 'narrow-minded and prejudiced views' 'blind partisanship' and 'adulatory sycophancy' (Huggins 2004: 245). While cricket was held to promote sportsmanship, football encouraged anti-social behaviour on and off the field. Similarly, if test cricket allowed a comforting illusion of national unity, international football revealed continuing regional and class tensions.

On 9 March, an England XI thrashed Ireland 9–0 in the Home International Championship at Derby's Racecourse Ground, their thirteenth victory over the Irish in fourteen encounters. Derbyshire newspapers gave more detailed coverage to the traditional Shrovetide football match in Ashbourne, but gate receipts of £228 suggested the growing importance of internationals in the sporting calendar. Had the match been played in a city with a large Irish immigrant population, such as Liverpool or Birmingham, attendance would surely have been even higher.

Football demonstrated a social inclusivity not always evident in other areas of late-Victorian life, though it was dependent on individual merit and often short-lived. In the England Ireland match, one of the scorers was Sheffield United's 'Raby' Howell, the only Romani to play for the national team. Born in a caravan outside Sheffield, Howell twice represented England. On 23 February, the Sheffield team that lost 2–0 at Sunderland included him alongside Arthur 'Darkie' Wharton, the mixed race goalkeeper signed from Rotherham Town the season before. Wharton, born in Ghana of mixed Scottish-Ghanaian parentage, had played for Billy Sudell's successful Preston North End, but his form was inconsistent and he was unable to displace Sheffield's regular keeper, William 'Fatty' Foulke. He soon returned to Rotherham, enjoying considerable celebrity in South Yorkshire in the 1880s and 1890s as an athlete, cricketer and footballer: he was the first mixed race professional player in British football. Neither he nor Howell enjoyed lasting success however, with Wharton disappearing into poverty and obscurity after retiring, and Howell's career being mired in controversy. Following suggestions that he was bribed to help throw a vital match against Sunderland, he was sold to Liverpool in April 1898.

England's next game on 18 March saw an entirely different team draw 1–1 with Wales at the only international played at London's Queen's Club. 6,000 spectators watched English amateurs from Oxford and Cambridge universities and the southern clubs Corinthians, Old Carthusians, Casuals, Old Etonians and Old Westminsters. The Welsh, meanwhile, whose star player was the Manchester City winger, Billy Meredith, a twenty-year-old ex-miner who had only turned professional in January, were largely drawn from the ranks of English professional sides. On the same day, the Staffordshire Cup saw Wolves defeat Villa, while WBA beat Small Heath in the Birmingham Cup, suggesting national and club commitments were as much at odds in 1895 as they are today. Once again, superficial unity masked all manner of contradictions and divided loyalties. The Welsh FA was prepared to select Welshmen who played in England (so long as their English clubs were prepared to let them play – Manchester City often debarred Meredith from internationals), but the Scottish FA insisted on a wholly Scottish team. The Irish too picked from their home league, partly for nationalistic reasons, partly because fewer Irish players yet played for top English teams.

As the home international competition unfolded, Preston North End, the greatest English team of the late 1880s and early 1890s, was rocked by scandal. On 20 March, their autocratic chairman, Billy Sudell, who had dominated the club since 1874, was arrested on charges of embezzlement and false accounting. Sudell had spent the previous nine years managing the Goodair family's mills, and his financial acumen won him a salary of £500. However, he was far more interested in football than in cotton, and since 1890 had defrauded the Goodairs out of £5,326, money which had been diverted in the club's coffers. Preston's star had waned with the rise of Villa, Sunderland, and Everton, and Sudell had used the Goodairs' wealth to furtively bankroll signings and player payments, as well as for what would now be termed 'corporate hospitality'. As Richard Sanders shows, Sudell was a major force in the football's professionalisation, and the first chairman 'to abandon all pretence of creating a local side' by signing players from outside the Lancashire conurbation. 'Visionary, tactician, businessman and fraudster', he was sentenced to three years in jail. Denied his stewardship, Preston's decline intensified (2009: 147–50).

England emerged victorious from the home international tournament, Ireland and Wales drew 2–2 in Belfast on 16 March, Wales and Scotland drew 2–2 in Wrexham on 23 March, Scotland beat Ireland 3–1 in Glasgow on 30 March before England overcame Scotland 3–0 at Goodison on 6 April, this time with their professional team. Meanwhile, the title race continued. On 23 March, Bolton defeated Villa 4–3, ending their challenge. Sunderland beat The Wednesday 8–1 and though Everton remained hard on their heels, the Wearsiders were favourites to secure their third title in four seasons. They would not win the Double though. Two league games with Villa had seen a 4–4 draw at Sunderland's Newcastle Road and a narrow win for Sunderland in Birmingham, but on 16 March they lost a thrilling cup semi-final at Blackburn's Ewood Park, 2–1. The defeat also cost the team the £20 per man bonus they had been promised if they secured the Double. The final would now be an all-Midlands affair, for in the other game, WBA beat The Wednesday 2–0, the match one of the last important fixtures played at Derby's Racecourse Ground.

Blazing Bibles

Back in London, theatregoers eagerly awaited Pinero's *The Notorious Mrs Ebbsmith*, hoping it would have the same impact as *The Second Mrs Tanqueray*, his coruscating examination of the sexual double standard. Its star was Mrs Patrick Campbell who, turning thirty on 9 February, was one of the most commanding actresses of the day. Her performance as Paula Tanqueray had been hugely acclaimed, disguising weaknesses in supporting characterisation and motivation; when the play was revived with Evelyn Millard as Paula in June 1895, it had only thirteen performances.

Joel Kaplan terms Pinero's 'sex problem' plays, 'curious amalgams of drawing-room melodrama, well-made play, and Ibsen accommo-dated to Mayfair sensibilities' (J. Kaplan 1992: 38). As Penny Griffin points out, these 'serious' dramas – Pinero also wrote farces and romantic comedies – must be read against a background of 'demands for women's rights, both legal and social' (Griffin 1991: 212). As such, *Ebbsmith*, which opened at the Garrick on 13 March, can be seen in the company of *The Woman Who Did*, *Gallia*, and the fiction of Egerton and Caird reviewed alongside it. Egerton's *Discords* displayed 'want of reticence' and a 'plentiful lack of good taste', said the *Athenaeum*, whose reviewer spoke for conservatives alarmed by fiction's growing willingness to discuss sexual matters (23/3/95: 375). Wells had said in reviewing *Gallia*, 'woman with her own hands has pulled down the curtain which a conspiracy of silence had kept in its place' (*SR* 23/3/95: 383), but though female interventions in the cultural debate prompted disquiet, writers of both sexes were pushing the boundaries of permis-siveness. Some, such as Hardy, Egerton and Moore saw artistic opportu-nities in the movement away from Victorian propriety, but others were more cynical (Keating [1989] 1991: 241–84). In April's *Contemporary Review*, James Noble, dismayed by 'the fiction of sexual sensualism' which placed 'sexual passion' at the heart of human experience, pointed out that 'a number of books' were not 'the outcome of any spontaneous impulse [. . .] either healthy or diseased,' but came instead from 'a delib-erate intention to win notoriety and its cash accompaniment' through 'an appeal to the sensual or vulgar portion of the reading public'. He was especially appalled by Egerton, whose 'sickening' stories portrayed men and women as little more than 'conduits of sexual emotion' (4/95: 490–8). A *Punch* cartoon saw a New Woman say of so-called 'problem plays' that 'If there's a demand for these plays, it must be supplied' only to be answered by a 'Woman not New', 'Precisely! Just as with the bull-fights in Spain' (5/1/95: 6). Later in the year the magazine published 'The Problem Playwright's Vade Mecum', which placed the woman with a past at the heart of any drama (26/10/95: 201). Richard Le Gallienne toured the country giving a lecture called 'The Revolt of the Daughters', one which was well received by young women but less so by their elders. The piece was an opportunistic extension of B.A. Crackanthorpe's essay of the same title published in the *Nineteenth Century* in January 1894. This advocated greater social freedoms for unmarried girls and stressed the importance of education for roles other than marriage and mother-hood. The article found itself on many drawing-room tables, but while its author was sympathetic to the New Woman, the term 'revolting daughters' quickly acquired negative connotations (C. Nelson 2001: 261). Reviewing reactions to Crackanthorpe a year later, Le Gallienne asked a Birmingham audience if the revolt existed, answering:

> Some pooh-poohed it, others denied it, whilst all [. . .] got into a temper over it. Meanwhile one girl here, and another there, quietly joined the cult of the cigarette, shamelessly invested in divided skirts, rode in hansoms and on the top of omnibuses, even attended meetings of secret cycling societies, where they took dreadful oaths to wear the rational costume, and, worst of all (so it was thought a short time ago), courageously earned their own livings. (Whittington-Egan 1960: 265)

The *BDP* hoped the council would 'take measures to prevent a repetition of the impropriety', while another midlands newspaper criticised Le Gallienne's 'axnt' ('To adopt the speaker's pronunciation of "accent"') and dismissed his 'callow wit', 'intellectual trifling' and 'sickly affectation'. Such behaviour was all very well in 'a Chancery Lane saloon where sirens administer to the male unshorn', but Birmingham expected something nobler from its speakers than 'esoteric views on connubiality'. Le Gallienne, one correspondent felt, showed a wilful 'disregard' for 'the most sacred traditions of our lives' (Whittington-Egan 1960: 280). He seemed more flirt than prophet, and another lecture, 'The World, the Flesh, and – the Puritan', given at the Playgoers' Club on the evening of Sunday 9 December reinforced this impression (Townsend 1961: 155–7).

Situating Pinero within the wider arguments about the New Woman and 'reticence' is not easy, for unlike his novelist contemporaries, he was bound by formal stage censorship rather than the unwritten laws of publishers and subscription libraries. As *Ebbsmith* was in rehearsal, the double standards of stage and page were thrown into relief by the death of E.F. Smyth Pigott on 24 February. Examiner of plays for the Lord Chamberlain's department for two decades, Pigott had banned Ibsen's *Ghosts* and was a determined opponent of progressive theatre. In a lengthy and damning *SR* article of 2 March, Shaw addressed the many anomalies of his position, cursing him as 'a walking compendium of vulgar insular prejudice', and protesting against theatrical censorship. Shaw was especially annoyed by the inequality whereby novels such as *The Woman Who Did* or Grand's *The Heavenly Twins* could be published as fiction but were highly unlikely to be licensed for the stage (*OT* 49, 52). Working within artificial constraints, Pinero was caught

Figure 5. The notorious Agnes Ebbsmith (Mrs Patrick Campbell) pleads with the Duke of St Olpherts (John Hare), dressed in what Shaw called 'a horrifying confection apparently made of Japanese bronze wallpaper'. *Illustrated London News*, 6 April 1895.

between the censor and pandering to 'popular' or 'advanced' taste. He consequently fell foul of Shaw even as he impressed critics such as Archer and Clement Scott – the latter was disgusted by Shaw's attack on Pigott, 'the most abusive article ever written on a recently dead man', as Shaw proudly put it (Shaw 1965: 489).

Pinero accepted the limits of propriety, and *Ebbsmith* was not cut by the Lord Chamberlain (Pinero 1974: 166). It was set in traditionally licentious Venice, where Agnes Ebbsmith, a widow and former politi- cal agitator, lives with Lucas Cleeve, a young Conservative politician estranged from his wife. While Agnes, like Herminia Barton, preaches against marriage and has 'something of the man in [her] nature', Cleeve's relatives, in the form of the Duke of St Olpherts, attempt to engineer his return to his wife for the sake of his career, offering Agnes a cottage and servants if she will remain discreet as his mistress (Pinero 1998: 76). Agnes soon discovers Cleeve's desire for her is stronger than his friendship, not least when he buys her a beautiful gown, 'cut rather lower in the pectoral region than I had expected' said Shaw (*OT* 64), whose 'Rustle of silk, glare of arms and throat' (Pinero 1998: 83) make it obvious that he is drawn to 'the flutter of lace, the purr of pretty women' (93) rather than shared intellectual and political principles. When it seems Cleeve will return to his wife, Agnes dons the dress despite her apparently strongly held convictions and her knowledge that he is 'nervous, bloodless, hysterical' and 'in morals – an epicure' (93). The situation made for passionate drama, with Campbell at her most impressive. Shaw praised her at length as 'a wonderful woman' (*OT* 61). 'She has Eleonora Duse's gift of a naturalness so persuasive that all thought of artistic effort is lost in the achievement of reality,' said the *ILN*, though Mrs Fenwick-Miller found her beautiful gown 'quite out of the present fashion' (6/4/95: 403, 390). Male viewers were less concerned by such niggles, with the 'Captious Critic' enjoying 'a low cut costume which show[ed] more of her charms' and the cartoonist Alfred Bryan picturing her smoking a cigarette and drawling 'How's this for ALL RIGHT?' (J. Kaplan 1992: 54–5).

Shaw felt the end of the third and the whole of the final act were dramatic misjudgements on Pinero's part, as Agnes denounces the Bible and throws it into the fire, only to pluck it out again in her conversion to sentimental religiosity. The rescue of the Bible from the flames was simply 'gross claptrap,' he felt, though the first night audience roared its approval. Shaw's review upbraided Pinero not only for his unconvincing portrayal of political agitation but also for his reliance on stock characters and his tendency to do 'something daring' and '[bring] down the house by running away from the consequences'. Shaw was a keen rival of Pinero's and jealous of his commercial and critical success; his review ended 'My criticism has not, I hope, any other fault than the inevitable one of extreme unfairness' (*OT* 63–5). On 12 March, he told Clement Scott the play should be 'The Obnoxious Mrs Ebbsmith' (Shaw 1965: 497). In a letter to Archer six days later, he also revealed anti-Semitism at odds with his egalitarian outlook, claiming Pinero 'is a Jew, with the Jew's passion for fame and effect and the Jew's indifference to the reality of the means by which they are produced' (501). While such outbursts remained private, he was not the only critic to be frustrated by Pinero's unsatisfactory resolution, with Campbell herself feeling Agnes would never have 'drifted' into 'Bible-reading inertia' (Dawick 1993: 211). She never worked with Pinero again, although they 'maintained a cordial relationship for the next four decades' (J. Kaplan 1992: 58). G.S. Street maintained that *Ebbsmith* 'amply justifies the verdict that Mr Pinero comes near to being, and yet beyond all question is *not*, a writer of great plays' (*PMG* 14/3/95), while the *Sketch* found it 'powerful, painful, unsatisfactory' (20/3/95). The *Athenaeum* was more positive, praising Campbell's star turn and adding that the play, while 'unconventional and in some respects aggressive [. . .] stimulates in a high degree' (16/3/95, 353). *Punch* meanwhile allied Pinero with John Lane's sexually radical writers in retitling the play 'The "Key-Note"-orious Mrs Ebbsmith' and lobbying for a new series of books called 'Wed-lock-and-key note' (30/3/95: 148; 13/4/95: 174). *Ebbsmith* ran until 11 May, but after fifty-eight performances as Agnes, each of which apparently exhausted her to the point of prostration and accentuated what Kaplan calls her 'anorexic exoticism' (47), Campbell was contracted to work with Beerbohm Tree in *Fedora*, an adaptation of Sardou, from 25 May, and replaced by Olga Nethersole, an actress Pinero had considered for the role of Paula Tanqueray, only to decide she was too old. 'Miss Nethersole gave us nothing but the stage fashion of the day in a very accentuated manner' said Shaw (*OT* 127) and audiences dwindled. The play closed a month later. Whereas *Tanqueray* eventually proved in revivals that it can succeed without Campbell at its heart, *Ebbsmith* remains less convincing, perhaps because, as Archer maintained, Agnes's 'spiritual history does not hang together. It is not probably constructed or probably expressed' (*World* 20/3/95). The play was nevertheless a significant commercial coup, the run taking £14,168 11s at the box office with Campbell, an average of £244 5s per performance, and another £3,477 10s 6d at £124 4s with Nethersole (Pinero 1974: 171).

As theatre reviewing was a male-dominated profession, it is difficult to reconstruct a female response to the play, though one might note the *PMG*'s report of 2 April, 'Death of the Real Mrs Ebbsmith: An Extraordinary Coincidence.' This told how Alice, the divorced wife of a solicitor called Joseph Ebb-Smith, had been found drowned in the Thames with two tickets for the play on her person. Her brother told the court she had written to tell him the play 'was a superb work of art'; she felt 'flattered by it' even though it may have 'preyed upon her mind'. Her ex-husband, who had added 'Ebb', apparently his mother's Christian name, to his less distinctive cognomen, was taking steps to 'prevent the name being used on the stage'. An open verdict was recorded.

Irish Affairs

Those unsatisfied by *Ebbsmith* could always watch events in the House of Commons, where Rosebery's beleaguered government was making a final attempt to introduce reform of Irish land ownership. On 4 March, John Morley moved the first reading of the new Land Bill, anticipating Unionist opposition on either side of the house and knowing his sympathies for the Irish Nationalist cause – he had been made a Freeman of

Dublin in 1888 – would make his task yet more difficult. Surprisingly, the Bill went forward without undue controversy to a second reading. Edward Carson, Unionist MP for Dublin University, watched with interest.

English views of Ireland were complex, but often distinguished between an Anglo-Irish Protestant landowning caste and a Catholic peasantry whose lives were caricatured as being of wretched poverty, rural superstition and unthinking popery. Visiting the Lord Lieutenant of Ireland in mid-March, Henry James found 'six days at [Dublin] Castle' a 'Purgatorio'. 'I was not made for viceregal "courts,"' he groaned, 'especially in countries distraught with social hatreds.' 'The English are encamped there as in a foreign country,' he went on. 'Will they ever have imagination to do more?' (James 1984: 8–9). The simplistic views of many English observers were challenged by the increasing pace of nationalist political agitation and accompanying cultural revival, a movement strongly associated with W.B. Yeats, who was dividing his time between Sligo and his father's house in London's Bedford Park, working in a study painted with the signs of the zodiac (Clayton 2005: 67). A profile in the *Acton and Chiswick Gazette* of 27 April described him as 'half-poetic, half masculine', a 'literary dandy' who yet possesses a 'firm and reliant' chin and a mouth 'close set with an air of strong determination'. Yeats was a key figure among nationalists writing in English, studying Irish legend and folklore and conjuring visions in works such as *The Celtic Twilight* (1893) of Ireland as an ancient and magical place with culture, myths, and traditions entirely independent from those of its colonisers. 'For committed nationalists, Yeats' London home, his English and Ascendency friends, his indifference to the Irish language, were evidence that he was an obstacle and an enemy,' writes David Ross (2001: 66), yet in the mid-1890s, his determination to be 'always ransacking Ireland for people to set writing at Irish things' (Yeats 1954: 256) gave nationalism undeniable impetus. On 27 February, his lengthy letter to the editor of Dublin's *Daily Express* listed thirty books Irish people 'should read'. The survey included seven by Standish O'Grady and three by Douglas Hyde, later to be President of the Irish Free State but at this time the editor of works such as the dual language *Love Songs of Connaught / Abhráin Ghrádh Chúige Connacht* (1893) (Yeats 1954: 246). The letter stirred up discussion of the Irish canon, as well as increasing anticipation for Yeats' anthology, *A Book of Irish Songs*, the introduction to which was hailed as 'unusually able, original, and courageous' by the *Athenaeum* (6/4/95: 434) which reviewed it alongside works by O'Grady, A.P. Graves (soon to be the father of Robert) and Jeremiah Curtin. Yeats' selection was not yet as bold as his notorious *Oxford Book of English Verse 1892–1935* (1936) but it nevertheless questioned Anglo-Irish interrelations, including the 'English' Emily Brontë on the grounds of her Irish father, a move that may have disquieted those gathered in Haworth for the opening of the Brontë museum on 18 May.

Yeats' evocation of a Celtic dream-world was precisely judged. Its literary sophistication, shown in its creator's engagements with Blake, Verlaine, and Maeterlinck, demonstrated a modern aesthetic (as well as political) sensibility at work, even as the subject-matter of his poems seemed to repudiate that modernity and retreat into the Irish mist. Yet while he and a loose aggregation of radical Irish writers were demonstrating the power and nobility of ancient traditions, events in contemporary Ireland were demonstrating how the same allegiances to the world of faerie could lead to the very opposite of what the cultural revival sought to encourage.

The death of Bridget Cleary on 15 March in what became known as the 'Clonmel Witch Burning', caused a sensation on both sides of the Irish Sea. Bridget, a twenty-six-year-old dressmaker-milliner, was killed by her husband, aided and abetted by her father, aunt, and four cousins who seem to have believed either that she was possessed or that she was no longer the 'real' Bridget, only a changeling substitute. They attempted to drive out the impostor by holding Bridget over a fire and applying heated irons to her body, before deciding that she was neither possessed nor a changeling but had been seized by the faeries. Even after her badly burned remains were found on 22 March, her family believed she would yet return alive from 'under the hill', but after the coroner's verdict of death by burning, nine people were remanded on a charge of wilful murder. The story bubbled away in the media, even receiving coverage on the east coast of the USA, home to many Irish emigrants, as the public waited to see whether the judiciary would press for a verdict of murder or take a sympathetic position regarding rural beliefs and argue for manslaughter instead.

As Angela Bourke shows, the Cleary case was reported on the same pages of many newspapers as Wilde versus Queensberry, making journalists confront two startling different images of Ireland: the *IPN* of 13 April is one example. In London, Wilde was an intellectual, mixing with aristocrats and over-civilised to the point of decadence. In Tipperary, the Clearys and their associates personified backwardness. The case prompted 'bloodthirsty editorials' in Dublin's unionist press and caused embarrassment for nationalists (Bourke 1999: 178), though, 'with a fine sense of discrimination', Mary Battle, George Pollexfen's housekeeper, told Yeats that 'the tragedy occurred simply because "they are so superstitious in Tipperary"': normal practice would simply have been to 'threaten the fairies out' (Foster 1997: 143; Brennan 1986: 207–15). Such a comment localised the atrocity rather than regarding it as symptomatic of rural Ireland, but it was hardly a convincing rebuttal of the charge made in sections of the Irish press that writers' folkloric enthusiasms might do more harm than good.

Wilde at last returned from Monte Carlo on 19 March. He immediately faced further financial demands from Humphreys, whose services had cost him 150 guineas already (M. Holland 2003: xxv) and who wanted more money before briefing counsel. Such fees were a world away from the small sums demanded by 'renters' and blackmailers, but as in his dealings with criminals, Wilde had little option but to pay up. Humphreys had at least secured representation of the highest class. Sir Edward Clarke was a distinguished barrister and Conservative MP who had been Solicitor-General under Lord Salisbury from 1886–92. Believing Wilde's declarations of innocence, Clarke agreed to represent him without payment little realising that Carson, who had only been called to the English bar in 1893, would prove a ferocious opponent.

As Queensberry's detectives tracked down prostitutes and informants, Wilde sought out Mrs Robinson, a society fortune-teller whom he called 'the Sibyl of Mortimer Street'. Wilde had long been superstitious, dramatising his beliefs in palmistry in 'Lord Arthur Savile's Crime' (1887) and according to Ellmann having his palm read in April 1893 by the Irish palmist Cheiro (William John Warner), who prophesised brilliant success followed by ruin and exile (Ellmann 1987: 360).[3] Fortune-telling was another aspect of British life strongly marked by class inequality, for while the likes of Robinson and Cheiro thrived, and newspapers carried all sorts of adverts regarding divination, Sophia Robson ('Madame Minerva'), a 'professor of palmistry' in Cheapside who charged 2s 6d for readings, found herself in court accused of unlawfully pretending to tell fortunes by reading palms. Despite testimonies from satisfied clients, and the defence's pointing out the palmists of the West End, Robson was found guilty, and told that while reading palms was legal, fraud was not. The Witchcraft Act 1735 and the Vagrancy Act 1824 made fortune-telling a profession that 'always savours of illegality to a lawyer' (Marjoribanks [1929] 1989: 105), and Alderman Green of Mansion House Police Court robustly dismissed the defence's objections. He fined Robson the exorbitant sum of £25 or a month's jail (*IPN* 23/2/95).

Wilde was buoyed by the Sibyl, who 'prophesised complete triumph', he told Leverson on 25 March (*WCL* 636), the day Queensberry submitted his Plea of Justification. Nevertheless, he was in poor physical condition and his critical intelligence and judgement were dulled by years of heavy drinking and the sycophantic (and sometimes financially motivated) adulation of his associates. In late March, obviously under stress, he bought 'a dozen sleeping draughts from Alsop and Quiller, the chemists' (McKenna 2004: 483). Used to dominating social situations and complacent about the worth of his impressive academic record, he underestimated Carson, who had gained only a pass degree. To defeat Queensberry, Wilde would need to be at his most acute and to make a favourable impression on a jury which included a butcher, a boot-maker and a bank messenger. He also required the support of two constituencies, the general public and journalists, which he had denigrated for twenty years. The Ulsterman by contrast was thoroughly prepared, highly skilled in cross examination rather than verbal display, and in possession of damning evidence. 'Without irony, without subtlety,' Tom Paulin writes, Carson 'possessed a peculiarly harsh and negative will which was stoked by huge bunkers of moral self-righteousness' (Paulin 1984: 118). These qualities, the very antitheses of Wilde's, made him a fearsome adversary, one who could claim to represent the moral convictions of many Victorians in defending a father's concern for his son's welfare in the face of deviance and aberration. Wilde's friends feared the worst, and George Alexander asked why he did not withdraw his suit and go abroad. 'I have just been abroad,' Wilde replied, 'and now I have come home again. One can't keep going abroad, unless one is a missionary, or, what comes to the same thing, a commercial traveller' (Hyde 1948: 43–4).

Shortly before the trial began, two articles appeared in the press which may have given the superstitious playwright pause. The first was the *Athenaeum*'s obituary of the classicist, Sir Edward Bunbury, whose surname, shared by *Earnest*'s fictitious invalid, has become the most famous excuse in English literature and more recently, the focus of highly speculative criticism (Craft 114–20). A Whig MP during the 1840s and an Honorary Fellow of Trinity College Cambridge, Bunbury's 'published writings were few', and, refusing to let production be the test of his personality, he 'never let the world know how great was the range of his knowledge' (*A* 16/3/95: 347). If 'Bunburying' was a homosexual euphemism in the play, as some contend, then the death of Bunbury before the libel case opened was potentially a dire omen. Equally disconcerting for Wilde was an essay by 'F.H.', perhaps the jurist and historian Frederic Harrison, on the death of the 'Sacred Band' at Chaeronea in 338 BC. After noting the discovery of 254 bodies in a mass grave in October 1880, F.H. gave a survey of classical accounts of the battle, before deciding the Sacred Band died in a conscious imitation of the Spartans at Thermopylae and not for 'the reason that Plutarch gives' in 'the days of sensual degeneracy' (*SR* 30/3/95: 408). Plutarch maintained that 'a band cemented together by friendship grounded upon love is never to be broken, and invincible, since the lovers, ashamed to be base in the sight of their beloved, willingly rush into danger for one another' (Carpenter [1902]1920: 23). This was certainly George Ives's view, but a reference to the Thebans' destruction only four days before the trial opened was ominous indeed.

A Wretched Band of Youths

If Wilde was not alarmed by literary portents, he may have been by the weather around the spring equinox. Terrible gales on 24 March blew down chimneys at Magdalen, his old college. There was widespread damage elsewhere. In Wolverhampton, four pinnacles on St Peter's church were toppled and a boy was killed when his house collapsed. Peterborough Cathedral lost three turrets; there were ferocious storms across the East Midlands and talk of a hurricane in Leamington Spa. Around 2,000 trees were blown down on the Queen's Sandringham estate, and another 3,000 at Castle Rising (*IPN* 30/3/95, 13/4/95). The national mood remained dark. In Leicester, a strike by increasingly militant boot and shoemakers was soon joined by bricklayers and carpenters. Shoemakers were also on strike in Northampton. The closure of businesses and factories during the cold weather had had adverse effects on industrial relations.

Once the gales blew over, writers became more willing to venture out of doors. Gissing, the habitual pessimist, visited his family in Sheffield, taking a brace of ptarmigan as a gift; having just received £150 for his new novella, *Sleeping Fires*, he was in a better mood than usual (Gissing 1978: 367). John Lane, accompanied by Le Gallienne and Beerbohm, had left England on a promotional trip to New York on the Cunard *Umbria* on 31 March. H.G. Wells resigned from the *PMG* and went on holiday to Sidmouth for a fortnight. Henry Harland went to Paris. Conrad meanwhile was becoming increasingly annoyed by the delay in issuing *Almayer's Folly*. People 'are writing letters full of anxiety and tears to know when – Oh! When! they will be able to get the immortal work', he berated Unwin (Conrad 1983: 206). Scheduled for publication in early March, the novel was finally issued on 29 April to generally positive reviews, though the *World* said it was 'as dull as it well could be', the 'dreary record of the still more dreary existence of a solitary Dutchman doomed to vegetate in a small village in Borneo'. 'The poor old "World" kicks me (in 15 lines) like a vicious donkey,' Conrad told Unwin on 18 May (1983: 219).

Wilde's action against Queensberry opened on 3 April, the day England's morally-upright cricketers finally left the Antipodes after trouncing South Australia by ten wickets. Wilde arrived at the Old Bailey immaculately dressed, clean-shaven and with his hair freshly waved: 'In all important matters, style, not sincerity, is the essential', he had said in 'Phrases and Philosophies'. Arriving in style was however, expensive, for his hired carriage and pair cost him £2 5s 6d (M. Holland xxvi). The less stylish Carson had a heavy cold, while Queensberry donned his Cambridge-blue hunting stock. A packed courtroom (women were conspicuous by their absence) heard jokes about 'the importance of being early' before battle commenced, presided over by Mr Justice Henn Collins. Queensberry pleaded not guilty, confident that his approach, while unorthodox, had been the only way to rescue his son from a moral abyss. Clarke, whose opening speech painted an impressively innocent picture of the friendship between Wilde and Bosie, defended the content of works such as *Dorian Gray* with calm authority and branded Bloxam's 'The Priest and the Acolyte' 'a disgrace to literature' (Hyde 1948: 115). Wilde's high-flown letters to Douglas should not be judged by the standards of 'commercial correspondence' (112), Clarke argued, but by those of poets.

Trusting in Wilde's innocence, Clarke was under-prepared in key respects. He was ignorant of the defence's research into Wilde's sexual history and even believed Wilde's claim to be thirty-eight years old. In *The Green Carnation*, Amarinth had asked why 'we should take infinite trouble to find out how old we are' when 'Age is a question of temperament' (Hichens [1894] 1949: 110), but Amarinth was not Edward Carson.

Carson's cross-examination of Wilde is regarded as one of the greatest duels ever seen in a British court. It began badly for Wilde with the exposure of his actual age – he was forty, not thirty-eight or thirty-nine – but then turned into the type of literary and philosophical debate he must have hoped for. Wilde's repartee was sparkling, but throughout the afternoon of 3 April, Carson took the role of the canny slow bowler, who may get hit for boundaries by a flamboyant batsman but who plugs away, knowing that should the batsman make a mistake, his dismissal is certain. In some respects, Carson's argument that an author's literary production reveals his actual character seems naive, for he would surely not have expected Conan Doyle to have been a criminal just because he wrote about crime. Wilde had attacked such assumptions in 1890 when, replying to the *Scots Observer*'s review of *Dorian Gray* in a letter

Clarke later read to the court, he suggested it was 'an unpardonable sin' to 'confuse the artist with his subject matter' (Hyde 1948: 158). In fact though, Carson used the discussion of *Dorian Gray* and 'Phrases and Philosophies' less to discover whether those works were 'immoral' – no move had ever been made to prosecute Wilde's novel as obscene in the four years the volume had been available – than to prompt a wider discussion of immorality, one in which Wilde, lulled into a false sense of security by his literary prowess, would hopefully let slip unpalatable extra-literary opinions. In this respect, it did not particularly matter that Wilde was questioned about fiction he had not written, such as J.-K. Huysmans' *A rebours* (1884) or contributions to the *Chameleon* for it was his wider views that were at issue. How much of this the jury understood is open to question – as *A rebours*, a novel Carson termed 'sodomitical' – was not available in English translation, it probably bewildered them. Nevertheless, Carson's masterly use of insinuation and his understanding of popular prejudice meant he could influence the jury regardless of Wilde's answers to his questions. Simply to initiate a discussion of French culture, classical paganism or 'advanced' opinions was enough to leave Wilde on the wrong side of the debate. As Alison Hennegan says, this approach meant 'Wilde was being forced to conduct his case within the framework of an external imposed moral universe whose authority and value he utterly repudiated':

> The key words – beauty, morality, art, goodness – which Carson hammers home time and again, menacingly, sneeringly, incredulously, mean utterly different things to the two men and, despite brilliant parries as dramatic as anything the London stage could offer, Wilde was slowly and relentlessly cornered in a setting where only Carson's reading of those words was permitted. (Hennegan 1990: 188)

With Wilde stressing the independence of art from morality, refusing to class Bloxam's story as blasphemous, admitting that although most people were Philistines and illiterates he 'had found wonderful exceptions' (Hyde 1948: 124), and claiming 'Everything I write is extraordinary. I do not pose as being ordinary' (134), significant damage had been done to the prosecution even as Wilde amused the gallery.

Whatever the jury made of an argument about literary works they may not even have heard of, they sided against Wilde. More wounding revelations followed as Carson began to imply Wilde's persona was more than a 'pose'. Here both parties had to tread carefully, with neither wishing to involve Bosie, and Carson reluctant to mention Wilde's friend Maurice Schwabe, a nephew of the Solicitor-General's wife. Clarke's slip-of-the-tongue in mentioning Rosebery during his opening speech when he meant Queensberry added another layer of caution to the proceedings. With these restraints in place, it became almost impossible for Wilde to repel Carson's insinuations without incriminating his friend, and as the afternoon wore on, the roles of defendant and prosecutor became reversed.

Littlechild had done his work well, tracking down male prostitutes, blackmailers and witnesses to Wilde's behaviour in restaurants, theatres, and hotels. The men in question were nearly all twenty or more years younger than Wilde (several were younger even than Bosie), generally working class, unemployed or engaged in relatively menial professions and all too willing to reveal how Wilde had feasted them, plied them with iced champagne and given them presents – silver cigarette cases, walking sticks, clothes, books and so on. Wilde's counsel did not know that some of these witnesses, 'a wretched band of youths' (Hyde 1948: 47) were being paid or pressured by Queensberry, and so was often unable to challenge their evidence effectively. As their accounts stacked up, it seemed Wilde had transgressed in class as well as sexual terms, for what could a respectable man of letters known in many of the great houses of England possibly want with a youth such as Alfonso Conway, who sometimes sold newspapers on Worthing pier? 'It is the first I have heard of his connection with literature,' Wilde joked, before Carson disclosed they had stayed in a hotel in Brighton, their adjoining rooms linked by a green baize door (139). By now, Carson was focusing on the ways in which Wilde 'gave unstintingly of himself and his material resources to young men who were beneath him in age, station, and position', receiving in return 'only the joy of their company and the philanthropic joy' that came from their material assistance (Foldy 1997: 114). As Kaplan observes, this meant portraying Wilde as a corruptor of youth 'not only through sexual misconduct and literary subversion but also through exploitation of the working classes' (M. Kaplan 2005: 242).

Carson's relentless questions, his list of dates and places, and his reading out of affectionate inscriptions in books and cigarette cases left Wilde floundering. Equally serious was Wilde's connection with Alfred Waterhouse Somerset Taylor, a Marlborough-educated friend of Schwabe's in his early thirties, whom he had met in the autumn of 1892. Taylor was charming and thoroughly disreputable: McKenna claims he was expelled from school 'after being caught, quite literally, with his pants down in the school lavatories with a much younger boy' (2004: 278). He had run through an inheritance of £45,000 in eight years, later admitting in court that since he came of age in 1883, he had 'no occupation' and 'lived a life of pleasure' (Hyde 1948: 242) in extravagantly decorated rooms above a disused bakery in Westminster, where the blinds were always drawn and scented pastilles burned. Any association with Taylor could only harm Wilde's case, and by now the jury must have been well aware that Queensberry's fears about Wilde's influence were justified, even if it was not revealed that Bosie had instigated many of their escapades. Wilde's admissions became cumulative evidence of depravity, however insignificant they were in themselves: how many of the men in the courtroom on 4 April would have admitted to burning perfumes in their rooms as he did? With the momentum now firmly with Carson, Wilde was asked about his relationship with Walter Grainger, a sixteen-year-old whom he had once employed as an under-butler. 'Did you ever kiss him?' asked Carson. 'Oh, dear no,' Wilde replied, insouciantly. 'He was a peculiarly plain boy. He was, unfortunately, extremely ugly' (Hyde 1948: 150). That Wilde was being true to his own valuation of aesthetics above morals here only showed the pernicious nature of his credo, Carson felt, and the relentless harrying continued.

Wilde had probably lost his suit long before he made his unwise comment about Grainger's ugliness, but once he had, there was nothing Clarke could do to repair the damage. Reading out some of Queensberry's letters gave a strong sense of the Marquess's confrontational personality, but it did not alter the court's mood. When Wilde was late back from luncheon on 4 April, there was speculation he had fled for France, though his tardiness was only the result of a slow restaurant clock. He then sat through the beginnings of Carson's speech for the defence, which made it clear that none of his attempts to distinguish between the artist and his subject matter had had the slightest effect. Carson's address was, said the *Evening News*, 'a horrid nocturne of terrible suggestions, a thing of blackness, only half defined, but wholly horrible' (5/4/95). When proceedings finished for the day, Wilde and Clarke attempted to formulate a means of securing peace with honour, but their position was hopeless.

Wilde was absent from the courtroom on the morning of 5 April. As Carson pressed home his considerable advantages, Clarke touched his sleeve, and whispered consultation ensued. At length, Clarke announced his client's withdrawal from the case, and proposed a Not Guilty verdict. Queensberry's claims could be upheld, he admitted, if some of Wilde's work was read in a particular way. However, as the judge made clear, it was for neither side to set conditions on the proposed verdict. After a brief discussion, the jury found Queensberry Not Guilty without even withdrawing. There was cheering and applause in court. It was about 11.15 a.m. Later, the judge wrote to Carson, telling him 'I never heard a more powerful speech nor a more searching crossXam. I congratulate you on having escaped most of the filth' (Schroeder 2002: 165).

Wilde was liable for sizeable costs. He was also to face criminal proceedings. After Queensberry's acquittal, he went to the Holborn Viaduct Hotel, followed by Littlechild, and wrote to the *Evening News*, explaining he had withdrawn his prosecution because he had decided not to put Lord Alfred Douglas into the witness box. If Carson could provoke Wilde into rash admissions, he would surely have enraged the irascible Bosie, but aside from this, evidence of family feuding was largely irrelevant to the terms of the case. It was probably now that Wilde sent an urgent note to Constance. 'Allow no one to enter my bedroom or sitting-room' and 'see no one but your friends', it commanded. It was signed, 'Ever yours, Oscar', an unconvincing valediction in view of recent evidence (*WCL* 637).

There was still time for Wilde to escape to the continent, but he made his way instead to the Cadogan Hotel, accompanied by Bosie, Percy and Robbie Ross, and was trailed not only by Littlechild but also by a number of reporters. Bosie left for Parliament, to seek help from his cousin, George Wyndham, who told him Wilde's prosecution was certain and his own liberty by no means secure. Meanwhile, the Director of Public Prosecutions chaired a hastily-arranged meeting with Asquith, the Attorney-General Sir Robert Reid, and Sir Frank Lockwood, the Solicitor-General. Ross was dispatched to Tite Street, to brief Constance before she shut up the house and left for her aunt's. Wilde was then joined by his friend, Reggie Turner, who urged him to flee. Wilde did not. As the afternoon wore on, he seemed incapable of decision, and sat drinking either brandy and soda or hock and selzer. At 5pm, Thomas Marlowe, a reporter from the *Star*, informed him a warrant had been issued for his arrest. This galvanised him into half-packing a suitcase, but he remained at the Cadogan. At just after six o' clock, two policemen arrived. A little drunk but quietly courteous, Wilde was taken by hansom to Bow Street Police Court and formally charged with various counts of indecency. As he left, journalists noted he was carrying 'a yellow book'. It was probably a French novel, but the link between Wilde and John Lane's radical magazine was now assured.

Panic in Vigo Street

The ripples from Wilde's arrest spread quickly. Beardsley and Brandon Thomas abandoned work on a short satirical play, for which Beardsley would also design the costumes. Its working title was *Attitude* and its characters were to be 'posers' (Sturgis 1999: 237). George Alexander refused to stand bail for Wilde. Journalists muttered about the speed of the prosecution, hinting at a connection between Queensberry and the PM. On 8 April, James told Gosse the Queensberry trial was 'hideously, atrociously dramatic, and really interesting – so far as one can say that of a thing which the interest is qualified by such a sickening horribility' (James 1984: 9). On 9 April, Symons wrote to Paul Verlaine, saying 'We can think of nothing here but the Oscar Wilde case' (Symons 1989: 110), and Edward Carpenter, depressed by the exultation that met Queensberry's victory, told a friend, 'Oscar W. has been very foolish (and naughty)' (Rowbotham 2008: 193). In New York, John Lane saw a headline, 'Arrest of Oscar Wilde, *Yellow Book* under his arm'. Worse still, Edward Shelley, a Bodley Head clerk, was one of the youths involved in the case. Lane had published a number of Wilde's works, including *Salomé* and *The Sphinx*, which had been selling reasonably well, earning Wilde royalties of £47 so far that year (JLA), but he supported Beardsley's wish to exclude him from the *YB*. Wilde professed to dislike the quarterly and made no effort to appear in it. The cautious Lane telegraphed his office manager, Herbert Chapman, telling him to withdraw Wilde's works, but he little realised the tumult at the Bodley Head's offices outside which, on the night of 5 April, a mob had gathered. Windows were smashed. With Harland in France and the *YB* about to go to press for publication on 15 April, William Watson, encouraged by Mrs Humphry Ward, cabled Lane demanding the withdrawal of Wilde's books and the dismissal of Beardsley or risk losing him to another publisher. He castigated Lane and Harland for printing 'such filth as disgraces' the *YB*'s 'every number' – fearing the 'hideous possibility' of being 'tarred with *The Yellow Book* brush' (J.M. Wilson 1981: 125). Rosebery's government had awarded Watson an annual pension of £100 in March, backdating it to July 1894, and this helped bolster his self-appointed position as the Bodley Head's moral guardian.

Watson and Wilfrid Meynell, editor of the Catholic journal *Merrie England*, visited Vigo Street and presented an ultimatum to Chapman, demanding Wilde's removal from Lane's lists. Two days later, they added the sacking of Beardsley as the price for their continued loyalty, using the works of Meynell's wife, Alice, another possible contender for the Laureateship, as a further bargaining tool. 'Chapman was a little man and he didn't like Beardsley,' recalled Ella D'Arcy, *YB* contributor and unofficial sub-editor (Mix 1960: 145). He therefore acquiesced to Watson's demands and neglected to tell Lane he had, even as Lane pondered Watson's telegram 'Withdraw all Beardsley's designs or I withdraw all my books.' For *Punch*, 'art' was 'the jargon of an epicene disgrace', a throwback to 'debased Petronian ways'. 'If such be "artists" then may Philistines | Arise, plain sturdy Britons as of yore,' it concluded in an appeal Carson and Watson certainly understood (13/4/95: 177). The Bodley Head struggled to counter such charges despite the unexceptionable nature of many of its authors.

Hard at work selecting pictures for the New English Art Club's spring exhibition, Beardsley was unaware of these clandestine dealings. However, when Chapman summoned Harland from Paris and explained the situation, doubtless misleadingly, the art editor's fate was sealed. Lane considered it unjust to punish Beardsley for the sins of Wilde, but 'he let Chapman take command and watched him toss overboard the first mate, an unwilling Jonah, to the whale of public opinion' (Mix 146). Like Marie Lloyd, Beardsley thrived on teasing innuendo, a trait which exasperated Lane even though he usually forgave it. Chapman was less indulgent, and Beardsley's latest cover design, which Chapman hinted was his most subtly obscene, was the first casualty of the new editorial policy. A satyr reading to a girl amidst a subtly eroticised landscape where water-lilies and tree-trunks each suggested parts of the female body was being replaced at very short notice by F.H. Townsend's less provocative image. Such was the haste and panic that Beardsley's spinal decoration and back cover were left intact, but even Townsend's apparently anodyne drawing invited speculation in its depiction of a young woman reading while a 'lion clipped' poodle lies on the floor nearby. The first *YB* had opened with James's 'The Death of the Lion' – was the magazine to change from lion to poodle? Was James to replace Beardsley as the magazine's guiding spirit? Harland, who revered James, still thought he could combine the two, telling Gosse that 'his absence from the *YB* is deplorable: but what is one to do with a capricious boy whose ruling passion is to astonish the public? He'll be in the July number, I hope, larger than ever' (Beckson 1978: 81). Ironically enough, by then what *RN* called 'A Magpie Season' was well under way, with black and white the favoured attire of 'leading lights in the world of fashion'. 'The ever-fresh and lady-like combination' was especially popular for evening gowns (2/6/95).

The new edition finally appeared on 30 April. It opened with Watson's 'Hymn to the Sea', but if the poet had hoped to set a high moral tone for the post-Beardsley era, he was undercut by the tediousness of his verse, his self-characterisation as 'a tarrying minstrel, who finds, not fashions his numbers' and by stories by D'Arcy and Leverson. Mrs Ernest Leverson, as she was billed on the title page and in a portrait by Sickert, offered 'Suggestion', an acidic social comedy that 'might possibly have been expunged, had the timid *YB* vigilance committee read its provocative opening line' (Weintraub 1964: xviii). An earlier Leverson essay, 'In Defence of Snobbishness', had not impressed Harland, but the new story was funny, cynical, and written with all the economy she had honed in her *Punch* sketches. 'If Lady Winthrop had not spoken of me as "that intolerable effeminate boy," she might have had some chance of marrying my father,' 'Suggestion' begins. Its narrator, Cecil, known to his sisters as 'Cissy', is at once camp, gossipy, and a shrewd manipulator of others who engineers romantic attachments like a selfish Cupid. At seventeen, he already has a taste for expensive cigarettes and Pierre Loti, and longs for 'an onyx-paved bath-room, with soft apricot-coloured light shimmering through the blue-lined green curtains' (Leverson 254). Cissy wears lily-of-the-valley in his buttonhole, burns incense, and refers to a society palmist, 'Mrs Wilkinson': he is a teenage Lord Goring but with the worst interests of others at heart. 'Suggestion' displeased *Punch*'s editor, Francis Burnard, who told Leverson it was 'A clever little sketch . . . *but*' (Speedie 81), and though it amused Beerbohm, nothing so overtly Wildean would appear in the magazine again. Leverson's 'The Quest of Sorrow' in Volume VIII, a sequel to 'Suggestion' was witty but less controversial, its 'playful satire on the aesthetic yearning for melancholy' (Kingston 160) unpleasantly ironic in view of Wilde's circumstances.

D'Arcy's 'The Pleasure-Pilgrim' was a psychologically richer study of two Englishmen abroad and their tragic encounter with Lulie Thayer, an American girl who is a dangerous combination of Daisy Miller and Hedda Gabler. Sexually desirable and highly engaging, Lulie may be, says Mayne, the more experienced of the pair:

> the newest development of the New Woman, she who in England preaches and bores you, and in America practises and pleases[.] Yes, I believe she's the American edition, and so new that she hasn't yet found her way into fiction. She's the pioneer of the army coming out of the West, that's going to destroy the existing scheme of things and rebuild it nearer to the heart's desire. (D'Arcy 1895: 46)

The story's depth of characterisation led Osbert Burdett to suggest that Lulie 'leaves us wondering, as real people do' (Burdett 1925: 251) about her true self and motives, while more recently, Anne Windholz has drawn attention to D'Arcy's 'equally masterful' portrait of the 'neurotic, sexually repressed British writer who drives the young girl to her death' (Windholz 1994: 88). D'Arcy could create convincing male characters, and in this story, the interplay between Mayne and his idealistic young friend Campbell shows her to be a highly observant chronicler of sexual mores. The story was singled out for praise when it was collected in D'Arcy's *Monochromes* the following month. Indeed, Wells, who reviewed it alongside James's *Terminations* and Harland's *Gray Roses* found her 'remarkably promising' and the best of the three '*Yellow Book* Storytellers', a writer capable of 'masterly' characterisation who, unlike many of her female contemporaries, valued restraint above hysteria (*SR* 1/6/95: 731).

Lane's other authors were less warmly received. 'Gone Under' and 'Wedlock' in Egerton's *Discords* were adjudged 'simply revolting' (*A* 23/3/95: 375) while M.P. Shiel's *Prince Zaleski*, three elaborately decadent detective stories, was, the worst 'Keynote' yet, 'a veritable frenzy of impure English' that is 'too foolish even to keep one laughing at it' (*SR* 6/4/95: 453). Somehow fusing Poe, Huysmans and Conan Doyle, Shiel's collection celebrated the deductive prowess of Zaleski, a mysterious émigré who has 'renounced the world, over which, lurid and inscrutable as a falling star, he had passed', and puffs a 'gemmed chibouque' stuffed with cannabis while reading 'an old vellum reprint of Anacreon' (Shiel [1895] 1928: 1, 5). Wilde never walked anywhere, but Zaleski took indolence to new levels, rarely leaving his 'darksome sanctuary' (60) and solving cases by virtue of his superior intelligence. Such a book would not have gained (or indeed, sought) the favour of the common reader even before the Wilde case, but in April and May its commercial prospects were even bleaker, reviewers battering the book with Nordau's diagnostic terminology (MacLeod 2006: 128–34).

Dismissed from the *YB* and facing a dearth of advertising commissions, Beardsley was in a difficult spot. After a brief visit to Harland in Paris, he returned to London and an uncertain future, drinking heavily and endangering his fragile health. It was around this time that he became increasingly friendly with a wealthy Russian, André Raffalovich, a minor poet and Catholic proselyte who would play an important role in his conversion to Catholicism in 1897. The extent to which Beardsley blamed Wilde for his troubles is uncertain – in a letter to Leverson, Wilde was a 'Poor dear old thing' but in another, Beardsley quipped that he was looking forward 'eagerly to the first act of Oscar's new Tragedy. But surely the title *Douglas* has been used before?' (Beardsley [1970] 1990: 82).

Up Against It

Wilde's withdrawal of his libel suit and his subsequent arrest prompted a wave of denunciatory editorials. In *The Critic as Artist* (1890), he decried the 'extraordinary prurience of modern Puritans', suggesting that 'By giving us the opinions of the uneducated, [journalism] keeps us in touch with the ignorance of the community' (*WCW* 1145). He now found himself at the mercy of a vengeful press, which, as Foldy has shown, hailed Queensberry's moral rectitude while lashing out at 'the real or imagined violation that Wilde had perpetrated against an unwitting and vulnerable public; a violation that threatened not only the "family values" of the domestic sphere, but the very fabric of society' (Foldy 53). Queensberry's many messages of support included a telegram reading 'Every man in the City is with you. Kill the bugger!': the Marquess threatened to shoot Wilde 'like a dog' if he saw him with his son again. Jerome K. Jerome's *To-Day* demanded Wilde's head, along with 'the heads of the 500 noblemen [. . .] who shared [his] turpitude and so corrupt youth' (Bentley 1983: 114). The *DT* claimed he had 'inflicted upon public patience as much moral damage of the most offensive and repulsive kind as any single individual could well cause'. It went on to denounce his 'spurious brilliancy, inflated egotism, diseased vanity, cultivated affectation and shameless disavowal of all morality,' an attack supported throughout the metropolitan press. Wilde carried, the *DT* said, a 'French and Pagan plague' that would, unless checked, 'insidiously poison our stage, our literature, our drama, and the outskirts of our press' (6/4/95). 'We begin to breathe a purer air,' said the *PMG* (6/4/95). The *National Observer*, a foe of Wilde's since *Dorian Gray*, went further still:

> There is not a man or woman in the English-speaking world possessed of the treasure of a wholesome mind who is not under a deep debt of gratitude to the Marquess of Queensberry for destroying the High Priest of the Decadents. The obscene impostor [. . .] has been exposed. [. . .]. But to the exposure there must be legal and social sequels [. . .] and of the Decadents, of their hideous conceptions of the meaning of Art, of their worse than Eleusinian mysteries, there must be an absolute end. (6/4/95)

Such rants helped to inspire Watson and Meynell's ultimatums. They also encouraged an exodus of men who, privately homosexual or publicly 'artistic,' could not exist in such a climate. Ives contemplated suicide, but other 'decadents' left for their spiritual home, France. 'We were very unpopular,' Symons told Katherine Mix in the 1930s. 'We didn't dare stay' (Mix 160). Ross, Reggie Turner and Maurice Schwabe all crossed the Channel soon after Wilde's case collapsed, though Ross did so only after his mother had promised £500 for Wilde's defence if he left England. Harland told Gosse 600 men had left for Calais on the night ferry when a more usual figure would be sixty (Ellmann 430). Matthew Sturgis is right to call this 'a facetious exaggeration' (Sturgis 1995: 236), but there was widespread alarm, and 'The Short Sea Cross-Channel Routes', an essay in April's *Blackwood's*, became unexpectedly interesting in the context of sexual and political flight. In Guy Boothby's *A Bid for Fortune*, seri-alised throughout the spring and summer, the heroic Dick Hatteras buys a yacht which, until recently, belonged to 'a young nobleman' who has been 'compelled to flee the country' for unexplained reasons (Boothby [1895] 1996: 52). Shiel's Prince Zaleski was exiled from his native land and 'the rest of men', the 'victim of a too importunate, too unfortunate love, which the fulgor of the throne itself could not abash' ([1895] 1928: 1). For Wilde though, there was neither escape nor exile. His plays were still running, but Alexander had hypocritically removed his name from the theatre's exteriors and programmes. Lane was unimpressed. 'I might just as well have ripped out the title-pages and sold the books,' he scoffed (May 1936: 84), as audiences dwindled. *An Ideal Husband* was advertised more openly, having transferred to the Criterion in early April ostensibly because Beerbohm Tree required the Haymarket on his return from America. The Criterion's manager, Charles Wyndham, pointed out that Wilde had yet to be tried and so could not be judged. The play ran for a fortnight from 13 April, before Wyndham at last surrendered to public opinion.

Wilde's predicament was desperate. Held overnight in a Bow Street cell, deprived of cigarettes and sleeping draughts (though able to have a meal of soup, fish and a small bottle of champagne brought in from the nearby Tavistock Hotel), he faced Police Court proceedings on the morning of 6 April, charged before a packed courtroom with offences of indecency and sodomy under Section Eleven of the CLAA 1885. The magistrate, Sir John Bridge, bald and formidably whiskered, was disgusted by the charges and denied bail, dooming Wilde to being held on remand in Holloway where again, he was denied cigarettes though he did receive a daily allowance of half a bottle of wine. It was at this hearing that key witnesses made their first appearance, allowing Wilde to reacquaint himself with Charles Parker and William and Alfred Wood, prostitutes and blackmailers whom he had entertained at the Cafe Royal, the Savoy Hotel and elsewhere since early 1893. Alfred Taylor was also indicted, and though he refused to turn Queen's Evidence, the linking of their cases nevertheless did Wilde considerable harm, not least because Taylor had left a trail of incriminating letters, telegrams and cheques that even the police were able to follow. Clarke was willing to conduct his defence without payment, but Wilde had few other allies. Only Douglas, the Leversons and Robert Sherard, who fruitlessly petitioned Sarah Bernhardt to buy the rights to *Salomé*, were of much assistance during April, with Bosie visiting daily. Intensely lonely, Wilde was cheered by the 'slim thing, golden-haired like an angel' who stood 'always by my side' (*WCL* 641).

One surprising defender of Wilde was the poet and critic Robert Buchanan, whose moralistic denunciation of Rossetti and Swinburne prompted the 'Fleshly School' controversy of 1871–2.[4] On 16 April, he wrote to the *Star* asking whether those 'who are casting these stones' are themselves 'without sin' or 'notoriously corrupt'. Queensberry took this as a reference to himself and retaliated in furious terms. After nine days of exchanges, Queensberry's final letter of 25 April concluded, 'were I the authority that had to mete out [Wilde's] punishment, I would treat him with all possible consideration as a sexual pervert of an utterly diseased mind, and not as a sane criminal. If this is sympathy, Mr Wilde has it from me to that extent.' Such statements were, as Brian Roberts sighs, 'hardly designed to promote fair play' (Roberts 1981: 232) in an ongoing court case.

RN and the *Daily Chronicle* were the only papers to show discernable sympathy for Wilde (Hyde 1948: 64). After initial antipathy towards all concerned, the former began to see his case as both an individual tragedy – despite its radical affiliations, it nonetheless felt 'There is no defence for the vice of which Oscar Wilde is accused' (14/4/95) – and as a symptom of wider sexual confusion in modern life. 'In the era of the "new woman",' it proclaimed, 'the sex-problem is putting on a new face and marking out a new course for itself.' Evidence for this was everywhere; a fortnight later, *Punch*'s 'Angry Old Buffer' worried that 'To-morrow there may be *no* sexes!' (*P* 27/4/95: 203). In the same issue as it reported on Wilde, *RN* devoted generous coverage to Countess Russell's plea for the restitution of her conjugal rights; the feud between the Russells had begun in 1891, with many scandalous disclosures along the way. A heavily-ironic public letter to Mrs Grundy on 14 April saw 'W.M.T.' list a series of works by canonical British writers – Marlowe, Ford, Jonson, Byron, Burns and the still living Swinburne – that might be deemed immoral, and conclude that the New Woman writer was 'the Faustina of literature'. Vice was not defensible, but it was important to punish it fairly and consistently, said *RN*, noting the severe sentence Justice Wills had passed on the blackmailer, Henry Turner, in January. Wilde, it seemed, had been singled out as a representative of 'decadence' when its origins were actually in 'the great public schools of England'. He had also not yet been tried, much less found guilty (14/4/95). In a description of 'B 24's' generally 'comfortable' cell at Holloway, the paper noted there was no tablecloth or mirror and that Wilde was kept 'in close proximity to the cell in which that unfortunate gentleman, Major Parkinson, committed suicide some months ago.' The implications were horribly clear, and drew a mournful reflection from John Davidson, who likened Wilde to Porphyrogene in Poe's poem,

'The Haunted Palace', 'assailed' by 'evil things, in robes of sorrow'. 'Porphyrogene, whom we admired both to his face & behind his back, who had in the greatest measure an unaccountable something which is genius,' he concluded (Davidson 1995: 101). Already, Wilde was spoken of in the past tense. 'I have no books, nothing to smoke, and sleep very badly,' he complained to Ross on 9 April (*WCL* 642).

A Grand Day Out

April saw the conclusion of the English football season, with Sunderland recapturing the crown they surrendered to Villa in 1893–4. Winning twenty-one of their thirty matches, losing only four and scoring eighty goals in the process – they began their campaign with an 8–0 demolition of Derby – they finished five points ahead of Everton and eight clear of Villa, both of whom managed eighty-two goals for the season. Sunderland however conceded only thirty-eight, helped by their ever-present Scottish goalkeeper, Ted Doig, who played in a black skull-cap to conceal his baldness, an item of headgear he even wore in team photographs. With five wins in their last six matches, they needed only a draw to take the title from Everton, who in turn had to win their final two games. The Sunderland Everton match was therefore a title decider, one the home team won 2–1. The late winner sparked delirious celebration from the Sunderland fans; some estimates suggest 20,000 people had crowded into the stadium.

On the same day, 20 April, Mr Punch hailed the arrival of the much-delayed Spring and an army of Midlanders descended on London for the FA Cup Final. 'Every hour saw its load of excursionists emptied upon the metropolitan platforms,' the *BDP* reported (22/4/95), with special trains running from Birmingham's New Street and Snow Hill stations. Previous finals had been played at Kennington Oval and Goodison Park, but now the FA moved the event to the Crystal Palace, allowing fans to watch the match, stroll about on the pitch before kick-off, and enjoy the Crystal Palace's diverse entertainments. Basic admission was a shilling, but as even the most expensive seats cost only 5s, a big crowd was forecast, with southerners treated to 'football of a species which they seldom have the fortune to witness' (*BDP* 22/4/95). 42,650 people saw Villa defeat WBA 1–0, though far fewer saw the winning goal, scored by Bob Chatt, their outside-left, within a minute of kick-off.[5] The game was tense, with Villa missing many chances – they could not 'look back on their form as shown in the goalmouth with anything like complacency,' said the *BDP* – and WBA constantly menacing with lightning

Figure 6. A dramatic moment in the Cup Final vividly captured by H.M. Paget, as WBA's Tom Higgins (foreground) and Villa's John Devey collide. Note the Crystal Palace's Switchback in the background. *Graphic*, 27 April 1895.

fast counter-attacks, the so-called 'Albion rushes' for which the team was famous. These were led by the nimble Billy Bassett, one of the stars of England's Home International winning side, who had helped Albion to a 3–0 victory the last time the two teams had met in the cup final in 1892. This time though, the Villa defence had his measure. 'From a scientific point-of-view the play was inferior' (*BDP* 22/4/95) to that seen in the Villa Sunderland semi-final, but the game was nevertheless exciting, with Villa's Charlie Athersmith and Steve Smith, a former miner who signed for Villa at the 'the coalface of the Cannock and Rugeley colliery' (Morris 1974: 10) in sublime form, and the crowd cheering Albion's centre-half, Tom Higgins, who played with a bandaged head following a collision with John Devey shortly before half time, and their courageous goalkeeper, Joe Reader. After the poor behaviour of football fans earlier in the season, it was a relief to the clubs and the sport's governing bodies when the match passed without incident. The crowd was 'one of the most orderly and sensible that could be wished for at such an encounter' (*BDP* 22/4/95). Indeed, the paper concluded, the whole event represented 'a brilliant spectacle'.

The victorious Villa players, like those of Sunderland's championship-winning team, were paid a win bonus of £10 per man, with WBA's gallant losers receiving £5; at this time, a top professional such as Athersmith earned £2–3 per week. When Villa's special train returned to Snow Hill on Easter Monday at 12.42 p.m., it was met by char-á-bancs adorned with the club colours of claret and blue. The first contained a band playing 'See the Conquering Hero Comes,' the second took the players and the trophy to the team clubhouse in Albert Road. This was not perhaps the type of civic spectacle Joseph Chamberlain had envisaged when redeveloping and reforming the city as its Mayor in the 1870s (T. Hunt 2004: 232–84), but it was widely reported, and enhanced the reputation and prestige of England's fourth largest city. The last match of the league season was a damp squib however, with only 5,000 watching a 2–2 draw at home to Everton.

WBA gained a measure of revenge on 29 April, defeating Villa 1–0 in the final of the Birmingham Senior Cup, a match watched by 15,000, but there was more interest in the 'test matches' which decided promotion and relegation to and from the First Division. In these, Bury beat Liverpool 1–0 to go up, but the other Second Division teams foundered against higher level opposition and were forced to stay put. Stoke easily overcame Newton Heath, later to become Manchester United, 3–0, while two goals in the last four minutes saw Derby beat Notts County 2–1 to retain their status in the top flight.

Wilde on Trial

Wilde attended further hearings at Bow Street on 11 and 19 April. A fracas developed at the former when a stationer attempted to sell photographs of him, forcing police to step in and stop the sale (Ellmann 1987: 431). As Wilde paced his cell in Holloway, life went on in ways which cast ironic light on his predicament. Amid the verbal mud-slinging, literal mud-slinging brought a premature end to The Wednesday's match with Stoke on 6 April when the referee was hit by mud thrown by the crowd and abandoned the game after only fifteen minutes. The motif of the noble beast at bay came to prominence when Albert Hartwell, an elephant trainer in a Burnley circus, kicked his charge's trunk and was promptly trampled to death (*IPN* 13/4/95). Denied access to the *Athenaeum*, Wilde would not have known that Thomas Fowler's *Progressive Morality: An Essay in Ethics* (1884) had been reissued in an expanded and corrected edition in which the section comparing 'different kinds of pleasure' was rewritten (13/4/95: 477). Neither would he have read the *Bookman*'s report of the national success of Balfour's *The Foundations of Belief* and its carping at Pater's *Greek Studies*, a critical work which displayed 'a distinct absence of knowledge' and in which 'too much is evolved from the inner consciousness, and too little comes from the direct interpretation of the actual works of art' (4/95: 18). In 13 April's *Speaker*, 'Mr Wilde's fancy' was blamed for 'the revolutionary and anarchist school which has forced itself into such prominence in every domain of art.' It is as well that Wilde did not see E.T. Reed's cartoon in *Punch* the same day, which mocked up the cover of 'le "Yellow Book,"' subtitled 'romans pour les anglophobes'. Ostensibly a response to news of the French issuing a 'yellow book' to conclude recent discussions with Britain over the two countries' West African colonies, its wider meaning was easily deciphered. John Bull recoils in alarm from an effeminate figure in cape and slippers who stalks off into the desert carrying a suitcase marked 'Destination inconnue' (178). Across the Atlantic, *Earnest* managed only a brief run at New York's Empire Theatre in front of what the *New York Herald* called, 'a fairly appreciative audience but not a large one' (Tanitch 1999: 260).

Elsewhere, Wells was finishing his new novel, *The Island of Dr Moreau* and sending the manuscript to his agent, A.P. Watt. Conrad was again in poor health and contemplating going to Champel for a course of hydrotherapy (Conrad 1983: 211). Grant Allen's new novel, a pot-boiler about Russian anarchism called *Under Sealed Orders* had failed to build on the success of *The Woman Who Did*. A.E. Housman, Professor of Latin at London's University College was 'unexpectedly seized by an intense excitement, which evoked some fifty poems in the space of a few weeks' (Housman 1971: 35). These would become *A Shropshire Lad*, which Housman published at his own expense the following year. George Chesney, whose *The Battle of Dorking*, the startling story of England's invasion by Prussian forces had caused a sensation in 1871, died on 31 March. A special charitable night at the Empire raised £1,250 for underprivileged Londoners. 'When we hear of Mrs Ormiston Chant and others of the "purity gang" doing something like this, we may perhaps look at their actions in a more charitable light,' said 'The Mummer,' oblivious to Chant's humanitarian work with Armenian refugees (*IPN* 13/4/95).

When Wilde arrived at Bow Street on 19 April, the police carriage had to fight its way through an aggressive crowd. Wilde had been ill and lost weight. 'His face looked almost bloodless, and his eyes heavy and weary,' said the *IPN*, though Alfred Taylor 'was looking as fresh and happy as ever' (20/4/95).[6] Both were committed for trial on 26 April, a plea for a delay based on public prejudice against the defendants being dismissed. They were to be charged under a single indictment. This combined twenty-five counts and alleged they had committed acts of gross indecency, and that Wilde had conspired to procure the commission of such acts. Taylor was also charged with procuring for Wilde. After the detailed and explicit evidence given at Bow Street, much of which was too sordid to appear in the newspapers, there seemed little doubt that the two men would be found guilty despite their pleas of innocence. Bosie wrote to the *Star* after the hearing, depicting the public and press as 'Judge Lynch,' a 'cowardly and brutal mob' which had accepted 'everything connected with this case at Mr Carson's valuation' (19/4/95). Edward Carpenter, writing under the *nom-de-plume* 'Helvellyn', pointed out how Wilde's accusers were hypocritical representatives of 'a society which is continually and habitually sacrificing women to the pleasure of men' and assumes 'women are always man's lawful prey' (*Star* 22/4/95; Rowbotham 193). In another letter, Carpenter protested against the hypocrisy of removing Wilde's name from playbills and theatres, but such dissident voices were rare. The press's treatment of Wilde made that of Chant seem positively merciful by comparison.

Wilde's prosecution had financial as well as moral and legal repercussions. With dwindling attendances at *Earnest*, the only one of his plays still running, and sales of his books minimal, he was unable to pay his creditors and, after writs for around £400 were served on him, in addition to the £600 costs he owed Queensberry, his belongings were sold at auction by order of the Sheriff. The sale, held at Tite Street, began at 1p.m. on 24 April.

Constance Wilde, who had spoken at length about her beautiful house in *To-Day* back in November now found herself rushing there before the sale to snatch up clothing for herself and her sons, along with a few favourite volumes and the visitors' book the Wildes' had received as a wedding present in 1884 (Bentley 105–8, 116). She was forced to leave much behind however, and, as Thomas Wright has shown, the supposed 'sale' became little more than a legalised looting of the property. Constance, Cyril and Vyvyan left London to stay with relatives in Devon, and so did not witness the appalling scenes. The front door was left open throughout, and many of Wilde's possessions were stolen before ever reaching the auction table. Book and antique dealers gobbled up inscribed *editions de luxe*, paintings, furniture, and ornaments. Though the public sale of private letters and manuscripts was officially illegal, Wilde's study, bedroom, and writing desk were ransacked (Wright 2008: 2). Various typewritten manuscripts were bundled together and sold as job lots: one comprising 'The Happy Prince', 'The Sphinx' and *Lady Windermere's Fan* went for £8 5s but *Dorian Gray* fetched only three guineas (*IPN 4/5/95*). A gloating account of the sale in *The Morning* suggested Wilde's books – one of which was *The Green Carnation* – were 'a miscellaneous lot' and 'fetched more than they were worth' (25/4/95), but as Wright shows, at a time when a three-decker cost 31s 6d, a bundle of twenty-five expensively bound volumes of the classics for the same price represented a major bargain (2008: 3). Wilde's library of around 2,000 volumes, manuscripts, photograph albums, magazines and periodicals fetched £130, a sum that by 1894, he was spending each week on food, drink, hansoms and hotels, not to mention sex (Wright 2008: 3). Thirteen volumes of the findings of the Parnell Commission raised just 8s. In January, a memorial fund had been set up to buy Thomas Carlyle's house in Cheyne Walk for the nation – the National Trust had been founded the same week. Now there was a chance to purchase Carlyle's mahogany writing desk, 'a singularly uncomfortable table' according to the *IPN* (4/5/95), which eventually fetched £14. Although friends such as Ernest Leverson managed to buy a few items, notably Will Rothenstein's pastel of Bosie, books and pictures were seized with rapacity. Women snaffled china and porcelain at bargain prices, and such was the air of bazaar and rummage that 'buyers were as often as not in the position of boys dipping into a lucky bag' (*IPN 4/5/95*). Lot 237 of 246 was 'A large quantity of toys' which 'realised thirty shillings'; for months afterwards, Cyril and Vyvyan, who knew nothing of the sale, unwittingly upset their mother by 'asking for our soldiers, our trains, and other toys' (V. Holland [1954] 1999: 62). Even the rabbit hutch was sold. The sacking of Tite Street left Wilde distraught, especially as Bosie had left England for Calais that morning after giving £50 to Taylor's solicitor to help fund his defence (Croft-Cooke 1963: 125). It was cold comfort that he would at least be spared the presence of Queensberry, the Marquess being distracted by reports that his fourth son, Sholto, had been arrested in California 'and was under close confinement in the county gaol on a charge of insanity' (Roberts 1981: 233). He would also not have to face Edward Carson again, though C.F. Gill was a scarcely less able substitute.

On 26 April, one of *fin de siècle* London's most extraordinary characters died from cirrhosis, Count Stanislaus Eric Stenbock, a homosexual Estonian nobleman who lived in what Symons later called 'a bizarre, fantastic, feverish, eccentric, extravagant, morbid and perverse fashion' (Adlard 1969: 89) and who was, according to Yeats, 'scholar, connoisseur, drunkard, poet, pervert, most charming of men' (Yeats 1936: ix-x). Educated at Balliol, Stenbock contributed a short story to *The Spirit Lamp* in June 1893, and had written a number of poems and tales that eroticised death and adolescence, notably in *Studies of Death: Romantic Tales* (1894). Whether Stenbock and Wilde ever met is debatable despite the claims of Ernest Rhys in *Everyman Remembers* (1931), but they had mutual friends – Stenbock left his jewellery to Robbie Ross and More Adey – and his death, like that of Bunbury before the Queensberry trial, can be read as an ominous portent, as can the bizarre case of Crawford Vincent (a reporter's error for 'Vincent Crawford'?), an attempted suicide whose case was reported by the *IPN* on 27 April. Vincent, a twenty-eight-year-old labourer from Pimlico, threw himself out of a bedroom window after 'repeating that he had letters from Oscar Wilde threatening to give him a hiding'. Wilde's unlikely accomplice was to be Frank Craig, 'The Coffee Cooler,' a black boxer who gave pugilistic exhibitions in London music halls. Vincent was remanded for medical reports.

The trial lasted until 1 May, the day of Stenbock's funeral in Brighton's Catholic cemetery, and the day on which the Scottish socialist Bruce Glasier addressed a May Day rally of 12–16,000 in Glasgow. It revealed little that had not been made public at Bow Street. The activities of Wilde and Taylor were examined in great detail, but Clarke conducted a clever defence, discrediting some of the Crown's witnesses by exposing their involvement in blackmail, succeeding in getting the conspiracy charges dropped and speaking out against the prejudicial treatment of Wilde in the press. In some respects, Wilde's behaviour with the 'panthers' was little different from his behaviour with any of his friends. 'We always had a lot of wine,' Charles Parker told the court. 'Wilde would talk of poetry and art during dinner, and of the old Roman days' (Hyde 1948: 194). The difference was such dinners were invariably the prelude to unsanctioned excesses, with Gill arguing it was the jury's duty, whatever sorrow they may have felt at 'the moral downfall of an eminent man' to 'protect society from such scandals by removing from its heart a sore which cannot fail in time to corrupt and taint it all' (253).

References to Maurice Schwabe and Alfred Douglas left the court in no doubt that Wilde had not acted in isolation, and notes being passed between counsels and the judge led some to wonder whether a wider scandal was brewing. The link between Wilde and Bosie was strengthened by Gill's revisiting the *Chameleon* in his cross-examination of 30 April. Wilde was now more guarded, suggesting 'Shame' in Douglas's poems meant 'a sense of modesty' (235). When Gill suggested 'such verses as these would not be acceptable to the reader with an ordinarily balanced mind,' Wilde joked that 'one man's poetry is another man's poison' (235) before rebutting the claim that the 'Love that dare not speak its name' was 'unnatural love'. It was instead 'that deep, spiritual affection that is as pure as it is perfect.' In a sudden flight of oratory quite unlike anything else he said in court, Wilde suggested this love 'dictates and pervades' the great works of Shakespeare and Michelangelo. 'It is in this century misunderstood,' he continued, 'and on account of it I am placed where I am now.' Defending the relationship between an older and a younger man as 'beautiful,' 'fine' and 'the noblest form of affection,' Wilde concluded 'The world mocks at it and sometimes puts one in the pillory for it' (236). The speech was received with 'loud applause, mingled with some hisses,' but though it greatly impressed Beerbohm and led Ives to place Wilde 'among the great of the earth' (Stokes 1996: 78), it hardly applied to Wilde's relations with Parker or the Wood brothers. It was also not entirely truthful, since, as Neil Bartlett points out, 'At the moment of extreme emotion, with all the attendant mannerisms of honesty, he was quoting himself [in] combining from memory, two unconnected passages from *Dorian Gray*' (Bartlett 1988: 204).

The mixture of applause and hissing suggested fundamental divisions in the courtroom, but the jury's verdict was nevertheless surprising. Frank Harris later wrote that 'Wilde had no more chance of a fair trial than if he had been an Irish "Invincible"' (Harris 167), but Mr Justice Charles was certainly less openly biased than Wilde's other judges. Unlike Bridge, he remained largely fair in his summing up, and thoroughly sensible in his literary attitudes. 'If an imaginative writer puts into his novel some consummate villain' who issues 'sentiments revolting to humanity, it must not be supposed that he shares them,' said Charles, who described 'Phrases and Philosophies' as 'amusing,' 'cynical,' 'silly,' but 'not wicked' (Hyde 1948: 257). After a detailed survey of the non-literary evidence, he finished by telling of his confidence that 'you will do justice to yourselves on one hand and to the two defendants on the other'. Wilde was, after all, 'a man of highly intellectual gifts, a person whom people would suppose to be incapable of such acts as are alleged,' while Taylor 'has been well brought up' and 'belongs to a class of people in whom it is difficult to imagine such an offence' (264). When the jury emerged, the foreman told the Court they found both men innocent on nine of the twenty-five counts they faced, but they could not reach an overall verdict. They were discharged, Beerbohm claiming that nine of the twelve had supported Wilde (Schroeder 2002: 170).

A new trial was ordered, for it was clear an already unpopular government with a very small majority could not be seen to favour Wilde. Whether or not Queensberry had any hold over Rosebery at this point remains a matter for conjecture, but he was not the only one with unwholesome suspicions concerning the PM; Frank Lockwood told the Irish nationalist MP, T.M. Healy, that 'the abominable rumours against _____', surely Rosebery, left him no choice but to continue the case (Schroeder 2002: 170). In the meantime, the *IPN* reported the arrest of George Morris who, having failed to sell copies of a broadside, 'The Life of Oscar Wilde' in The Strand, drunkenly abused passers-by. He was fined 7s or seven days in jail (*IPN 4/5/95*).

Problem Pictures

The Royal Academy's Summer Exhibition at Burlington House, which opened to the public on 7 May, traditionally signalled the start of the London 'season'. The previous week saw the Royal Private View, Press Days, a Private View Day and finally, on the Saturday night before the public opening, the RA Banquet, an all-male affair usually attended by the Prince of Wales. Leighton, the RA's President, was absent through illness and replaced by Millais, who, if *Punch* is to be believed, caused confusion by mistaking one attendant Archbishop for another. The Prince of Wales and Rosebery gave brief speeches, with Rosebery's 'entertaining', perhaps signifying a return to form (*P* 13/4: 221). Other guests included Conan Doyle, and Pinero, who proposed a toast, 'Music and the Drama', and announced that the playwright's 'finest task' to be 'giving back to the multitude their own thoughts and conceptions illuminated, enlarged, and, if needful, purged, perfected, transfigured' (Dawick 1993: 215). Whether his plays, or indeed, the works of that year's Academicians fulfilled such an aim was a matter for some debate.

Private View Day invitations were highly prized, and the event was attended by a cross section of artists, writers, politicians and aristocrats, together with wealthy representatives from industry and commerce. W.P. Frith's *A Private View at the Royal Academy, 1881* (1881), conveys

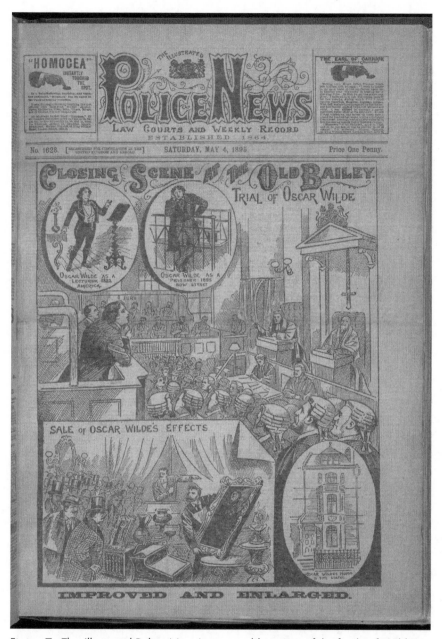

Figure 7. The *Illustrated Police News*'s memorable image of the finale of Wilde's first trial, 4 May 1895.

something of this audience, prominent among whom that year was the young Wilde, the self-styled 'Professor of Aesthetics' reinforcing his credentials as *arbiter elegantiae*. Less elevated visitors paid an entrance fee of 1s, with a catalogue costing a further shilling. With 2,000 or so works on display, the latter was a vital purchase, and for many, a season ticket (5s) was a sound investment. The exhibition was popular, with Pamela Fletcher reporting that the average attendance from 1897–1914 was 'over 280,000' (P. Fletcher 2003: 23). The catalogue of exhibits, a cloth-bound volume costing 7s 6d also sold well, the *Bookman* noting its popularity in far-flung corners of the land such as Aberdeen.

The 127th annual exhibition showcased the current state of British academic art and received lengthy press coverage which praised and quibbled with striking inconsistency. In the *Magazine of Art*'s Academy supplement, M.H. Spielmann felt the show was 'one of the best of recent years' and 'certainly the most interesting' (Spielmann ii), but uniformly positive estimations were uncommon. The *Athenaeum* admired Leighton's *Flaming June* but remarked that 'the legs of the sleeper are somewhat larger than they should be' (4/5/95: 576), a point echoed by the *FR* which found it 'curiously forced and elongated' (Jan–June 932) and by *Punch*'s cartoonist (13/4: 220). Fraser Harrison, who sees the picture as 'perfectly proportioned', implies a political subtext at work, pointing out how the 'statuesque and impotent' sleeper is nameless, 'beautiful and powerless, the epitome, by Leighton's criteria, of woman as she ought to be' (Harrison 119). Leighton's *Lachrymae*, open to similar charges, was considered beautiful and moving despite its overly statuesque female figure. Burne-Jones's portrait of Dorothy Drew, Gladstone's granddaughter impressed, but his grand Biblical work, *The Fall of Lucifer* was judged too obviously derivative of his *The Golden Stairs* (1880). In this case, the *SR* went further, suggesting it 'lends itself to ridicule rather than to appreciation' (4/5/95: 577), while the *FR* felt the rebel angels were too decorative to put up much of a fight (Jan–June 937). Millais's *Time the Reaper* and *The Empty Cage* received only lukewarm praise, while J.W. Waterhouse's *The Shrine* was 'excellent' despite 'extremely mannered colour' (615). His *St Cecilia* however was 'a strumous [thyroidal] young lady of no high breeding; her virginal contours are commonplace' and her angelic companions were scarcely 'celestial personages' (A 18/5/95: 647). Thomas Cooper Gotch's *Death the Bride* which had secured a coveted hanging 'on the line' was even worse, 'the greatest mistake [he] has ever made', with its female subject 'commonplace' and its painting 'crude' and 'slovenly' (A 18/5/95: 646) though other reviewers found its symbolism 'haunting and enigmatic', 'subtle and eerie' (Lomax 2004: 106) and the *FR* thought it 'one of the most complete pictures of the year'

(Jan–June 937). Many paintings on mythological or classical themes failed to impress, with William Blake Richmond's *Aphrodite Between Eros and Himeros* 'graceful' and 'charming' but with the serious flaw that 'Aphrodite is not like a woman and does not come up to our idea of a goddess' (*A* 1/6/95: 712). At the Old Bailey, espousals of pagan interests were most unwise, but on the walls of the RA they were neutralised by their classical settings, becoming what Sheila Rowbotham calls 'the Hellenic stalking-horse' (201). Arthur Hacker's *Daphne* was found to be insufficiently Greek, 'a naked English model of indifferent health and imperfect physique' (*A* 1/6/95: 711), though Spielmann defended it as 'a pictorial and decorative design' rather than a 'subject picture' (Spielmann vi). Herbert Schmaltz, who had been distracted from his work by the unsuccessful pursuit of Reginald Saunderson in December, exhibited *The First Offering*, in which a young girl places a wreath on a shrine. 'Will grass and daisies go far towards softening the heart of a statuette?' asked *Punch* (11/5/95: 227). Philip Calderon, Keeper of the RA, gave the more dramatic *Ariadne*, with Minos's daughter, abandoned by Theseus, wading into the sea in 'distress' and 'despair' (Spielmann viii). H.G. Riviere's *Sanctuary* envisaged a temple to Juno, while Briton Riviere's *Phoebus Apollo* depicted the majesty of the sun god in his chariot drawn by lions. Valentine Prinsep meanwhile opted for the orient rather than the classics in his popular illustration from the *Arabian Nights, The Fisherman and the Jin.*

There was little obvious consistency of critical judgement and approach in the exhibition's reviews, though most had some common features. The *SR*'s view that Holman Hunt paraded 'ridiculous affectations' (4/5/95: 577) was generally shared, while Walter Crane's vigorous depiction of St George and the Dragon, *England's Emblem,* Singer Sargent's portrait of Coventry Patmore, and Edward Stott's *Noonday,* an image of naked boys bathing commended for its 'admirable flesh tones' (*A,* 11/5/95: 615) all proved popular. Hubert von Herkomer's portraits of Cecil Rhodes and Leander Starr Jameson were approved too, but there was a sense that the 'elder painters of today, who have shown themselves so easily satisfied with the repetition [. . .] of past achievements' had either to adapt or face the consequences. 'So apt to resent the intrusion of new ideals, or of progressive movement in a direction to which they are opposed,' said the *FR*, established artists faced a challenge from the likes of Ernest Waterlow's *Golden Autumn,* paintings which offered a 'definitive breach with the popular art, half photographic, half spectacular' of the previous generation (Jan–June 939). Despite these claims, the influence of radical continental art, chiefly impressionism and symbolism, was muted, extending little further than the *plein aire* experiments of the Newlyn School. Painters who were open to European influences were not always approved of. George Clausen's *Harvest*, for instance, saw him praised for casting off the influence of Bastien-Lepage – whether this applied to style or method was unclear – but criticised for his 'easy-going audacities' and 'pretentious style' (*A* 18/5/95: 647). As its name suggested, the RA was the home of 'academic' painting and those seeking work by the likes of Sickert and Wilson Steer needed to attend the exhibitions of the New English Art Club, founded in 1885 as an alternative to the older institution. However, the politics of the late-Victorian art world were far more elaborate than this neat distinction suggests, and the line between the NEAC and the RA was sometimes faint. The former's founders had included Gotch, Singer Sargent and Clausen, all of whom were now showing at Burlington House. It was however most unlikely that Beardsley would ever appear on an RA committee.

Victorian painting frequently allowed viewers gaze on sights and forms that in other contexts would be judged at best tasteless and at worst illegal, drawing painter, spectators and subjects into what Richard Jenkyns terms 'a disagreeable triangular conspiracy of lust' (Jenkyns 118). The smoked glass of mythology, legend and literary allusion allowed male visitors to savour Robert Walker Macbeth's *Unenvied, Unmolested*, which applied a quasi-legitimating line from Goldsmith to 'a buxom beauty of gipsy blood, with all the fire of her race in her sultry-looking black eyes' (*A* 4/5/95: 578). H.A. Olivier's '*Not Juno's Heartless Fowls*' deployed Virgil in showcasing a naked nymph surrounded by peacocks, while Ernest Normand's luxurious *Bondage* showed naked Jewish maidens enduring Egyptian captivity in a scene anticipating Cecil B. De Mille. George S. Watson turned to the *Song of Solomon* for his *The Rose of Sharon*, a semi-nude woman whose looks and surroundings suggested the aesthetic interiors of the 1880s rather than the Old Testament. She had 'more to do with a life school than the Bible' said one critic (*Athenaeum* 18/5/95: 646). Did all those who admired *Noonday* or Henry Scott Tuke's *Swimmer's Pool*, a painting the *FR* felt had 'a delightful bracing freshness' (Jan–June 937), see them as emblematic of youthful innocence, or aestheticise their naked bodies as a technical accomplishment? As Germaine Greer points out, while the 'ostensible subject of images of naked boys on beaches was healthy, innocent, open-air exercise' many of those who painted such pictures (as well as those who collected them) had 'their own homoerotic agenda' (Greer 2003: 144). Tuke told the *Studio* that his art sought to capture 'the truth and beauty of flesh in sunlight by the sea,' but his 'comparative lack of interest in the Uranian statements he seemed so clearly to be

Figure 8. W.F. Yeames's unsolved riddle, the enigmatic *Defendant and Counsel* (1895: Oil on Canvas, 52x78 inches, Bristol City Museum and Art Gallery).

making in his paintings did not deter admirers, writers and artists from making his acquaintance' (d'Arch Smith1970: 61).

The painting which prompted most interest was, on first glance, unexceptional. William Frederick Yeames had achieved great popular success in 1878 with his dramatic Civil War scene, *And When Did You Last See Your Father?*, but his historical and narrative paintings had since failed to attract much critical attention. *Defendant and Counsel* changed this overnight.

Consciously or otherwise, Yeames's painting was highly topical. Exhibited at a time when court reports were front page in every national newspaper, and in a year when the behaviour of 'modern' middle-class women was being widely discussed and interrogated throughout British culture and society, the image of a fresh faced young woman surrounded by intimidating legal personnel could scarcely fail to be noticed. At the same time, it offered mystery as well as sensation. Who was the figure whose gaze met the viewer's so disconcertingly? What had she done or suffered? Was she a Paula Tanqueray or Agnes Ebbsmith, a Herminia Barton living with the consequences of a free union or a Countess Russell whose private life was becoming public property? If so, where did (or should) the beholder's sympathies lie? In prompting yet refusing to answer such questions, *Defendant and Counsel* was an early example of what became known as the 'problem picture', works which, as Pamela Fletcher says, showed modern life in 'ambiguous, and often slightly risqué' ways. '[B]ased on the conventions of Victorian narrative painting', these works 'omit the necessary clues, stock characters and textual titles that made such paintings and their moral messages legible' (P. Fletcher 2003: 1). The result of this is that problem pictures 'violate those conventions of narrative by rendering unreadable the clues that they depict' (13). Hence in Yeames's work, there was no explanatory material in the RA catalogue and the legal papers on the woman's lap are illegible. The result is that the painting extends but does not keep 'the promise of narrative closure' (16). What emerges instead is an open-ended scene which, like the ending of D'Arcy's 'The Pleasure-Pilgrim', leaves its core opaque. Three years later, Gissing would observe there is 'Nothing so abhorred by the multitude as a lack of finality in stories, a vagueness of conclusion which gives them the trouble of forming surmises' (Gissing 1898: 93). While this may have been true as a general principle, it has never prevented speculation about the Mona Lisa's smile and Yeames's wife later recalled that he was 'besieged with inquiries' (P. Fletcher 2003: 33) about his picture's meaning. After all, the picture's title does not necessarily mean that the woman has committed whatever crime she may be accused of; her wedding ring does not rule out her involvement in a divorce case while, as Fletcher notes, her attractive and fashionable appearance might convey 'either her class status or her sexual availability' (32). Noting the woman's 'modernity', the intrigued *Athenaeum* reviewer asked 'if the legal gentlemen are her counsel, why do they treat the fair in so severe a manner?' (1/6/95: 711). The discussion continued until the following autumn, when the *Golden Penny* held a competition to resolve the conundrum. The solution proposed by Miss Alice Fletcher of Malvern Wells found favour with the artist himself, who adopted it as the 'official' explanation. Nevertheless, to claim the scene is a dramatic moment in a 'great Will case' did not actually solve anything, and the work continues to puzzle visitors to Bristol City Art Gallery where it hangs today (P. Fletcher 2003: 34).

Jabez and Oscar

Wilde's trials had dominated the media since March, but as the playwright commuted between Holloway and the Old Bailey, another celebrity was coming ever closer to the courtroom. This was the disgraced financier Jabez Balfour, who 'wrought more woe and misery in English households than anything that has happened since the South Sea Bubble' (McKie 2005: 9). For over two decades, writes Edward Marjoribanks, Balfour 'with his specious puritanism and marvellous genius for financial conjuring tricks' had deceived small investors and financial experts alike (Marjoribanks [1929] 1989: 83). Croydon's first mayor, a one-time chairman of Burnley FC and former Liberal MP, Balfour was also the founder of the Liberator Building Society, the collapse of which in late 1892 alongside the rest of his companies, cost thousands their life savings and led to a number of suicides among the ruined (*IPN* 18/5/95). Balfour fled to Argentina, where he posed as 'a retired civil servant of independent means, named Samuel Butler' (Marjoribanks [1929] 1989: 87). Resisting all attempts at extradition, he was at last kidnapped by a Scotland Yard detective, Frank Froest and placed aboard the *Tartar Prince* en route for Southampton. On arrival in England, the wily Froest smuggled Balfour past the waiting crowd of 'predatory pressmen and vengeful creditors' (McKie 2005: 178) and onto a London train. A heavy police presence misled crowds into thinking Balfour would disembark at Waterloo, but his train made an unannounced stop at Vauxhall, from whence the corpulent prisoner was taken by carriage to Bow Street to explain himself to Sir John Bridge. Other hearings followed, with the enormity of Balfour's frauds astonishing the nation. His defence raised prolonged objection to the legality of his extradition, but Bridge paid no heed. Balfour was committed for trial and conveyed to Holloway jail. The Reverend J. Stockwell Watts, a London clergyman, secretary of the relief fund for Balfour's victims, appealed at once to the public for £50,000 to help the 'hundreds of aged people, widows and invalids' deprived of their savings (*IPN* 25/5/95), and Lord Kinnaird of the NVA proposed 7 July should be 'Liberator Sunday', on which church collections would be donated to the fund (*T* 13/6/95).

When Balfour arrived at Holloway, Wilde had at last managed to escape. Following the jury's failure to reach a verdict in the first trial, he was allowed bail, though he could not leave Holloway until surety came through. £5,000 was a formidable sum, but Wilde somehow managed to offer personal security for half of it. The remainder was provided by Percy Douglas and the Reverend Stewart Headlam, a radical London cleric whom Wilde dubbed 'the heresiarch' (Ellmann 1987: 438). Headlam and Wilde had met only in passing, but the priest objected to Wilde's treatment by the press and defended him even when a mob threatened to stone him outside his Bloomsbury house.

Headlam and Buchanan maintained a man was innocent until proven guilty, but for many other observers, Wilde's conviction seemed inevitable. Frank Harris felt the unfairness of the prosecution made the case 'like trying an Irish Secretary before a jury of Fenians' (Harris [1938] 1965: 184). Even the nominally sympathetic felt the case against Wilde was overwhelming. William Archer told his brother, Charles, on 1 May that 'the luck is against the poor British drama' since 'the man who has more brains in his little finger than all the rest of them in their whole body goes and commits worse than suicide in this way.' Unlike those who saw Wilde as a justly punished deviant, Archer appreciated his conviction would be a serious loss to late-Victorian culture. 'However,' he went on, the progress of the trial 'shows that what I hoped for in Oscar could never have come about – I thought he might get rid of his tomfoolery and affectation and do something really fine' (Archer 1931: 215–16). Archer's comments were private, but two days later, the novelist E.W. Hornung, one of Ives's cricketing friends, registered his son's name as Arthur Oscar Hornung, an act which, as his biographer says, was 'magnificent' as 'a vote of confidence' but hardly prudent (Rowland 1999: 76).[7] It was certainly bold, though softened a little by the choice of Conan Doyle as the boy's godfather. Robert Hichens and William Heninemann withdrew *The Green Carnation*, feeling it harmed Wilde's case, but as Sturgis points out, the less scrupulous Ward Lock & Bowden brought out a second edition of *Dorian Gray*, seeing its discussion during the trials as excellent free publicity (Sturgis 1995: 240). Arthur Humphreys privately reprinted fifty copies of *The Soul of Man Under Socialism* in book form as *The Soul of Man* on 30 May, sending copies to Wilde's friends and supporters.

With Wilde's plays withdrawn from the stage, their actors took new roles. Brookfield and Hawtrey were not long idle. Brookfield appeared in R.C. Carton's *The Home Secretary* at the Criterion as soon as 5 May, while Hawtrey worked on an adaptation of Gustav von Moser's *Der Bibliothekar*, retitled *The Private Secretary*, due to open at the Avenue Theatre in early September. Julia Neilson, who played Lady Chiltern, appeared with Brookfield, making, as Shaw put it, 'the best of an indifferent [part]' (*OT* 122), while Alexander was Sir Valentine Fellowes, the lead in Henry Arthur Jones's *The Triumph of the Philistines*, which replaced *Earnest* at the St James's on 11 May.

After *Guy Domville*, Alexander could be forgiven a sense of *déjà vu* when Jones appeared before the audience on the first night. 'Every play which is a criticism of contemporary life, must, if it is an honest play, involve a certain struggle with the public,' wrote Shaw, one of *Triumph*'s few champions. On this occasion, the actors were cheered, the playwright, jeered, and 'several persons howled piteously, like dogs who had been purposely run over' (*OT* 123). 'Morality is what compels people to conduct themselves properly for fear of being found out' was the only line to receive praise from G.S. Street, who found the play boring and forgettable (*PMG* 13/5/95). The *DN* felt its satire was disfigured by 'cheap and common caricature' (13/5/95), though Archer in *The New Budget* found it 'a profoundly melancholy drama, filling us with an awe-stricken sense of the mystery that enwraps the moral government of the universe' (Jones 169). *Triumph* featured an apparently risqué painting of a Bacchante unseen by the audience, a saucy artist's model, and a withering attack on the hypocritical inhabitants of middle England, in exploring the moral relativism of daily life. Most found it an unpalatable mixture and it managed only thirty-nine performances, taking £4,500 (Jones 1930: 169). It fared better on a provincial tour later in the year, but never achieved wide popularity.

Despite (or because of) being one of London's best-known personalities, Wilde was not always welcome in the capital's literary circles. W. Graham Robertson, who designed the costumes for the banned production of *Salomé* in 1892, recalled in 1931 that 'Among the workers he was never welcomed wholeheartedly as one of themselves. The painters [. . .] would have none of him as a critic, literary men regarded him with suspicion, first as a desultory amateur, then as an incurable plagiarist' (Mikhail 1979: I: 213). It is certainly unlikely Henry James would have invited him to the dinner given to honour Alphonse Daudet at the Reform Club on 6 May, although this may have been a blessing. Daudet, syphilitic and partially paralysed, caused James considerable anxieties with his incontinence, and while Leon Edel maintains that the dinner 'seems to have gone well' (Edel 1996: 441), Edward Burne-Jones endured a miserable evening. Seated between James and George Du Maurier, he endured a conversation 'about friends who were ill, dead or blind' (Fitzgerald [1975] 2003: 268) and found French very difficult to follow. James nevertheless enjoyed Daudet's visit despite its organisational difficulties, though once the Frenchman left England, he was stricken with gout, complaining his foot resembled 'the Dome of St Paul's' (Edel 1996: 443).

Free from Holloway on 7 May, Wilde could hardly return to the ravaged Tite Street. He had no money for a hotel, even if hoteliers had not been intimidated by Queensberry's thugs into refusing him. Some of his friends were abroad, some were unwilling to risk their reputations by associating with him, or, like Harris, encouraged him to flee. After a few fraught days on a camp-bed at his mother's home in Oakley Street, Chelsea, Wilde was rescued by the Leversons, who invited him to dinner and then offered him their house as a refuge. It was in Violet Leverson's nursery that Wilde met with his wife and solicitor, his hairdresser, who called daily, and a delivery man from the nearby florists who brought his buttonhole each morning. He remained upstairs throughout the day to avoid causing embarrassment to his hosts' visitors, though he dined with Ernest and Ada each night, amusing them with a stream of stories and observations and laughing over Ada's new *Punch* serial, 'The Scarlet Parasol', the title of which homaged Beardsley's drawing *The Scarlet Pastorale*. The looming trial was never mentioned.

On 19 May, Yeats visited Oakley Street, not knowing Wilde had left, and gave his mother messages of support from Dublin's men of letters; 'Speranza' was adamant her son, an Irish gentleman, would stand his ground. The same day saw the public momentarily diverted from the Wilde case by a postscript to an older *cause celebre*. The *People* began a six-part series, 'The Confessions of the Tichborne Claimant', in which the man who had posed as Charles Tichborne, long-lost scion of an aristocratic Hampshire family finally revealed that he was Arthur Orton, a London butcher. The case had gripped the nation during the 1870s, ending with 'The Claimant' as he was known, receiving fourteen years for perjury. 'The novelty of telling the truth for once in his lifetime will have a certain charm for him,' said James Payn, though many of The Claimant's supporters felt he had still to tell the whole story of the affair (*ILN* 1/6/95: 666). Enormously fat, Orton inspired the nickname of Harry Relph, the diminutive music hall performer known as 'Little Tich'. The money earned from his confessions allowed the purchase of a tobacconist's shop in Islington; when this was robbed and the thief captured after a hue and cry, The Claimant 'had the unique experience of being believed in a court of law' (Woodruff 1957: 439) as the man was prosecuted and jailed.[8]

Honouring his bail terms, Wilde returned to his mother's on 20 May, though he lodged with the Leversons during the trial itself. This began two days later, with Lockwood leading the prosecution despite a possible conflict of interests concerning Maurice Schwabe. Mr Justice Wills, whose contempt for Wilde was obvious throughout, presided. As the conspiracy charges were dealt with at the earlier trial, Clarke argued the defendants should be tried separately, but though the judge granted his plea, he also decreed the prosecution could determine the order of the trials. Unsurprisingly, Lockwood chose to prosecute Taylor, against whom there was overwhelming evidence, knowing that although separate juries would try the two men, press coverage and gossip would elide their cases. Taylor was duly found guilty on 21 May, much to the delight of Queensberry, who was in court for the drama's final act.

The Marquess was now at war with most of his family, whom he believed to be sheltering Bosie and possibly even Wilde. At one point, he sent Minnie, Lady Percy, a picture of an Iguanadon torn from the *ILN*, scrawling across it 'a possible ancestor of Oscar Wilde' (Roberts 1981: 252). The drawing, in the 18 May issue, was captioned 'The ponderous tail no doubt gave support to the animal when in an erect position' (614). After Taylor's trial, Queensberry sent another insulting missive to Minnie, and then, as he made his way to his Piccadilly hotel, encountered Percy in Albemarle Street. On the corner of Old Bond Street, the Marquess blew a raspberry at his son and a fight broke out. As the two aristocrats traded blows, a crowd gathered and the police had to intervene, though not before Percy sustained a black eye. Queensberry therefore missed the opening of Wilde's trial as he and his son were at a crowded Marlborough Street Court the following morning on a charge of disorderly conduct. After conflicting accounts of the brawl, the magistrate bound them over to keep the peace for six months in their own sureties of £500.

R.J. Tucknor's *In the Shadows of Crime*, a serial running in the *IPN* from March, offered a memorable evocation of the Old Bailey. 'When a prisoner is tried,' one episode began, 'he passes along a narrow passage connecting the ancient prison of Newgate with the modern courts of judicature. No sunshine ever penetrates within these sombre and massive barriers, and the sky can only be discerned when the atmosphere of the great city is clear and free from fog' (*IPN* 2/3/95). Echoing James Thomson's *The City of Dreadful Night* (1880), Tucknor's description summed up the claustrophobia and oppression Wilde now endured. He was very different from the confident dandy of his early sparring with Carson; subdued, drawn and ill, his face was, as the *IPB* remarked 'as white as a miller's apron' (1/6/95). He had lost more weight, his voice was husky, and his morale further eroded by his being served with a bankruptcy notice as he arrived at court on 21 May: the sale of his effects had wrecked his house but not settled his debts.

Little new evidence was produced at the trial, and Clarke made a valiant attempt to discredit key prosecution witnesses on the grounds that they were self-confessed blackmailers. There were, after all, many similar gangs working in London, and even as Clarke attacked Parker and Wood, the press reported the arrest of John Shepherd, George Mooney and George Wilton, who haunted a public lavatory in Oxford Street and threatened to make dangerous allegations against the men who used it. One of these, a hairdresser named Westley Francis, was grabbed and told 'Now I've got you, you scamp.' A 'notorious case', probably Wilde's, was mentioned by way of explanation (*IPN* 18/5/95). Apparently, the criminals posed as detectives and threatened to take Francis to the nearest police station unless he paid them off. He however called their bluff and, during the resulting struggle, the police arrested them: they had had the gang under surveillance for some time. Francis was commended by the magistrate, who said, 'If other people would only be as bold and plucky as you have been it would put an end to a great deal of mischief and wickedness' (*PMG* 11/5/95; H.G. Cocks 130–5).

Clarke's efforts were in vain, not least because Lockwood claimed the Solicitor-General's rarely used right of having the last word with the jury – one Clarke had never exercised during his own tenure in the post – and proceeded to offer 'a damning recitation of [Wilde's] delinquencies' (Hyde 1948: 90). Wilde later recalled being 'sickened with horror' as he heard this but thinking 'how splendid it would be if I were saying this about myself' (*WCL* 769). The case concluded on 25 May, the Queen's birthday, the jury returning their verdict at 5.30p.m. following two hours deliberation. Wilde was acquitted of the charges concerning Lane's office boy, Edward Shelley, whose evident psychological disturbance made him an unreliable witness, but he was found guilty of all the others.

Headlam, Percy Douglas and Queensberry were all in court on the final day. There were murmurs when the foreman of the jury asked whether a warrant had ever been issued for Bosie's arrest, and when the judge admitted that he could yet face action; his noble status was not to be considered a defence against the sword of Justice (Hyde 1948: 333–4). Wills did not dwell on the matter though, and returned to other aspects of the evidence. When the verdicts were announced, the court heard a remarkably censorious closing speech from the seventy-seven-year-old, who told the defendants 'the crime of which you have been convicted is so bad' that it prompted unutterable sentiments in 'any man of honour'. He concluded:

> It is no use for me to address you. People who can do these things must be dead to all sense of shame. [. . .] It is the worst case I have ever tried. That you, Taylor, kept a kind of male brothel it is impossible to doubt. And that you, Wilde, have been the centre of a circle of extensive corruption of the most hideous kind among young men, it is equally impossible to doubt. (339)

Wills's sentence was two years imprisonment with hard labour, the maximum permissible but a tariff he still felt to be inadequate: if Wilde had been found guilty of sodomy, he would have received ten years. There were gasps in court and cries of 'Shame', the richly ambiguous word that had been so discussed in the earlier hearings. Wilde managed to utter a few words, usually reported as 'And I? May I say nothing, my lord?' before the judge waved to the warders, and the newly convicted men were removed from the court. This triggered Ada Leverson to post a letter Wilde had written to Bosie from Holloway on 29 April, the envelope of which bore his instruction 'To be sent after the jury's verdict'. 'Our love was always beautiful and noble, and if I have been the butt of a terrible tragedy, it is because the nature of that love has not been understood,' Wilde wrote (*WCL* 646–7). A second letter, written on 20 May, assured Bosie that he was 'the supreme, the perfect love of my life' and that 'I am going to see if I cannot make the bitter waters sweet by the intensity of the love I bear you' (*WCL* 651–2). The strength of these words was severely tested in the months that followed.

After the trials came the inevitable post-mortems. Ballad-sheets recorded Wilde's fate and future suffering in doggerel verse. 'You've been "An Ideal Husband" in your tin pot way no doubt, | Though "A Woman of No Importance" was your wife when you were out' joked one (Stokes 1989: 4). 'Any man who had long hair or wore an eyeglass or dressed too well or spoke in a refined manner or carried a noticeable bunch of flowers was liable to have "Oscar" yelled at him,' records Hesketh Pearson ([1946] 1985: 294). Some writers, such as *RN*'s 'Experto Crede' argued that coverage of sex scandals provoked rather than deterred immorality (26/5/95), but the newspapers themselves did not share this view. Michael Foldy observes that by the time he was sentenced, there was little new to say about Wilde's case. 'The harsh sentence seemed to satisfy the public's need for retribution,' he argues, 'and this, along with the public's loss of interest in the case due to its overexposure in the Press for two long months, reasonably explains the muted public reaction to Wilde's sentencing and imprisonment' (Foldy 1997: 66). Yet the situation was a little more complicated than this suggests, for though Queensberry enjoyed a victory dinner with Brookfield and Hawtrey, and the *News of the World* felt 'Society is well rid of these ghouls and their hideous practices,' (26/5/95), there was widespread ambivalence. 'That the sentence was deserved I have not the slightest doubt,' said the *IPB*, 'yet I cannot help feeling a kind of sorrow that a man I have admired for his cleverness has, so to speak, gone down to the grave' (1/6/95).

The radical press contained considerable discussion of establishment hypocrisy, with *RN* openly critical of the Labouchere Amendment and printing many accounts of 'immorality' in public schools. Christopher Sclater Millard, who later compiled a bibliography of Wilde's work under the pseudonym 'Stuart Mason', wrote with especial vehemence as 'C.S.M.', pointing out that Wilde had been jailed for 'daring to find another form of satisfying his natural passion' since he would not have been jailed for adultery or sex with a female prostitute. 'Why does not the Crown prosecute every boy at a public or private school or half the men in the Universities?' he asked (*RN 2/6/95*). Stead's *Review of Reviews* June issue took a similar line, commenting that 'if all persons guilty of Oscar Wilde's offences' were jailed, 'there would be a very remarkable exodus' from leading public schools to 'Pentonville and Holloway' (Hyde 1964: 142). John Stokes has shown how James Wilson, a supporter of Wilde and contributor to *RN*'s lively correspondence concerning him, wrote a damning pamphlet, *Some Gentle Criticisms of British Justice* under the pseudonym 'I. Playfair', which exposed serious flaws in the prosecution's case. Such was the moral climate however that this document seems never to have been openly available (Stokes 1996: 39–64). Edward Carpenter's essay, *Homogenic Love in a Free Society* also struggled to find a publisher, being denied coverage in the *Review of Reviews* by its nominally sympathetic editor and turned down by Fisher Unwin (who also dropped Carpenter's long poem, *Towards Democracy* from his list). Carpenter circulated copies as a privately-printed pamphlet, but it was not officially available until 1906 (Rowbotham 2008: 194–5).

The most revealing comments on the Wilde case are often in letters and diaries. 'I am more glad than I can say about the verdict,' recorded Edward Hamilton. Acknowledging a 'prevalent suspicion' that 'the Government were trying to hush up the case in order to screen certain people of higher rank,' he concluded, 'I never had a shadow of a doubt about the guilt of the two beasts' (Hamilton 1986: 250). A panicked Gosse told Ross that 'in calmer times' he and his wife 'shall both rejoice to see you and give you any support we can' despite Ross's 'quixotic and silly but honourable' conduct during the affair (Thwaite 1984: 359). Burne-Jones told Mary Drew he would 'speak up for [Wilde] whenever I hear him abused' (Fitzgerald [1975] 2003: 267), but though he lent Constance £150, his price was the return of all his letters. He burned Wilde's to him. Beardsley told his new-found mentor, Raffalovich that 'two years hard' would 'kill' Wilde (Beardsley [1970] 1990: 88). Wilde's elder son, Cyril, staying with relatives in Dublin, was asking embarrassing question about the city's news hoardings (Bentley 1983: 121), and the family was upset to hear that Arthur, their devoted servant, had killed himself (124). Writing to Lane on the day of Wilde's conviction, John Davidson was 'sorry at the sentence', feeling Wilde's 'crime, so called' had nothing to do with the law. 'Two years hard labour!' he sighed, 'will surely purge him even in the sight of unintelligent England' (Sloan 1995: 139). Davidson's friend Gissing had an ingenious explanation for the 'awful catastrophe'. 'I have a theory,' he told Morley Roberts, 'that he got into this, not through natural tendency, but simply in deliberate imitation of the old Greek vice. [. . .] No doubt he justified himself both to himself and to others, by classic precedent.' It was in all a 'frightfully depressing' business, and Gissing, and many others, 'trie[d] not to think of it overmuch' (Gissing 1994: 339).

Rosebery Returns

One of the ballad-sheets circulated in the wake of Wilde's conviction ended 'the papers say that Lord knows who, they'll have before so long' (Stokes 1989: 4). Some may have read this as an allusion to Rosebery, whose tentative return to public life coincided with the final stage of the Queensberry-Wilde hearings. The Premier was still feeble and depressed. Despite a surprise victory in the East Leeds bye-election, largely attributable to the Liberal candidate being the city's popular mayor, the Government was in its final weeks, and suffered defeats in Oxford City, mid-Norfolk, Warwick and Leamington, West Dorset and West Edinburgh. On 26 April, Rosebery told Haldane political leadership reminded him of 'one of the darker portions of Frederick the Great's campaigns' (R. James 1995: 373): after the rows over the choice and election of the Speaker, the Irish Land Bill, and the suggestion to Disestablish the Welsh church, it was clear the Liberal Party was more divided than ever. Harcourt's Budget, delivered on 2 May, was in some respects academic, for few believed the Liberals would be in power to implement it.

Filled with quirky statistics, Harcourt's typewritten speech was meticulously prepared, the Chancellor knowing it would be in all likelihood a farewell performance. Speaking to a sparsely attended House for two hours, he congratulated himself on revenue raised by death duties and income tax revisions. Hicks-Beach, the Shadow-Chancellor, drew grim chuckles by pointing out how the flu epidemic had boosted income from the former, but Harcourt remained upbeat, pointing out how Government securities were thriving. He noted that tobacco consumption was increasing at three times the rate of the population, and the average Briton now consumed 119 pounds of meat per year as opposed to 108 in the early 1880s. Tea drinking was increasing too, but spirit drinking was declining, even allowing for the 'rush to rum' prompted by the ferocious winter. He warned that the nation had 'already reached the limits of tolerable taxation', and reminded the opposition that 'in public administration, you have to make your taxation keep pace with your profusion. Everyone grumbles if money is not spent on his favourite fancy, but he grumbles still more when he is called upon to find the means of paying for it' (Mallet 1919: 99–100).

Two aspects of the Budget were widely noted. For the first time, naval expenditure outstripped other military spending; the launch of vessels such as the *Magnificent*, at 15,000 tons the navy's largest warship, signalled growing naval rivalry between Britain and France. Also discussed was the rise in beer duty; Irish opposition ensured there would be no increased spirits tax. Higher barley costs were leading, some argued, to the increasing adulteration of noble British ales, though 1894's bumper hop harvest contradicted this to some degree. Harcourt responded by raising duty on beers not made from barley or hops. He could however do little about the growing sophistication of brewers' chemical use. A lengthy list of additives, concluding with caramelose-sucrosan and 'a "stuff" called aphrodite' was, said the *PMG*, a 'golden list of musical names' that when read aloud surpassed 'the Homeric catalogue of ships' or anything in Milton (11/5/95). Only Temperance campaigners showed any enthusiasm for Harcourt's plans to restrict or even prohibit alcohol sales, though Rosebery argued during the Election that 'if the State does not soon control the liquor traffic, the liquor traffic will control the State' (Petrow 1994: 181). The Finance Bill received Royal assent on 30 May.

Rosebery's health was fitful but improving. He spoke well at the RA banquet but a short speech at the National Liberal Club on 8 May saw him lose his train of thought before a plucky recovery (Hamilton 1986: 247). His feud with the Harcourts continued, and he increased his isolation by falling out with John Morley. On 13 May, he joined Lord Spencer aboard the Admiralty yacht *Enchantress* for a cruise round the Scilly Isles, and a week at sea proved remarkably reviving. On 25 May, the *SR* reported he was 'very much bronzed and appears to be in better health' (681), while *Punch* fabricated a spoof diary in which Rosebery reminded himself to 'get ozone and sleep' and found he was 'at sea – politically' (25/5/95: 246).

Michael Foldy argues that the 'comparative chronology between the events surrounding [Wilde's] three trials and Rosebery's "breakdown" is close enough to be suggestive' (Foldy 1997: 161), pointing out how after 28 May, Hamilton makes no further references to Rosebery's health. This, Foldy maintains, 'certainly suggests [. . .] that the (hypothetical) threat of exposure which had privately haunted and publicly paralyzed Rosebery for the previous three months had been lifted,' granting him 'a psychological reprieve' (Foldy 1997: 28). McKinstry stoutly rebuts this view, pointing out how most of the 'evidence' for Rosebery's supposed homosexuality is circumstantial and/or highly speculative. His argument is generally convincing, but he says little about Queensberry's behaviour during this period. Could a 'pugilist of unsound mind' really have sought to bring down the government? While Lockwood and Hamilton knew they must quash rumours of possible favouritism towards Wilde, they largely avoided commenting on Wilde's friendships with Asquith and other leading Liberals. An already unpopular government could hardly save itself by cutting Wilde adrift, yet when the Home Secretary had been seen at the theatre with him only a few months before the libel trial opened, it had no choice but to insist it was acting impartially in trying him. Just as Lane dropped Beardsley in the interests of public relations, so the Liberals were forced to act against Wilde: they were silencing rumours of conspiracy rather than an actual plot. As McKinstry says, 'There was no state conspiracy against Wilde, because there was no need for one. [. . .] he had brought himself down by his reckless and self-destructive behaviour' (McKinstry 2005: 367). Besides, a monomaniac of Queensberry's scarlet hue would surely not have abandoned his attacks on Rosebery, whom he blamed for Drumlanrig's death, if Rosebery had been his primary target.

Back on *terra firma*, Rosebery attended the Derby on 29 May, the day Heinemann published Wells' *The Time Machine: An Invention*. His horse *Ladas* had won it in 1894, but he had no hopes for *Sir Visto* whose 'very consistency stamps him as a moderate performer' (*IPN* 1/6/95). *Punch* depicted the PM as a jockey riding *Majority* who though not much of a mount, would be ridden 'for all he's worth' (1/6/95: 259). Gissing took the train to Bookham, and went for a 'grand walk' to Box Hill to avoid the 'blackguardism' (Gissing 1978: 374), 'brutes', 'fools' and 'verminous vagabonds' associated with the race (Gissing 1994: 341). Thousands travelled in the opposite direction, among them Birt Acres, a cameraman who shot twenty-eight seconds of the race and later screened his film in music halls.

Several weeks of hot weather made the Epsom course very hard, upsetting the highly fancied *Raconteur* and causing a number of runners to be withdrawn. In the event, Rosebery's horse, ridden by Sam Loates, narrowly defeated *Curzon*, the day's surprise package. Rosebery was often a poor judge of horses and believed *Sir Visto* was inferior to *Ladas*, though timings show he was actually a second faster. The photograph of him in the *ILN* (8/6/95) suggests a magnificent animal; that he went on to win the St Ledger on 11 September only re-emphasises Rosebery's error. Gissing thought the PM was 'the disgrace of his country'; his involvement in racing showed him to be 'sparingly endowed with brains, and in moral perception totally lacking' (1994: 341). Hamilton, who watched the race with Rosebery, felt victory was 'a reward for all the pluck he has shown during the last four months' (1986: 252) though he could not ignore a general lack of rejoicing at the Premier's success. This was mainly, he felt, because few had backed *Sir Visto* at 100/8, but

Rosebery's waning popularity could not be disguised (Hamilton 1986: 252). Earlier in the year, Wilde and Douglas had preferred foreign holidays to planning battles. Now, with the Liberals in terminal disarray, Rosebery and Hamilton went yachting from 1–11 June. Rosebery may or may not have shared Wilde's sexual predilections, but he could be just as irresponsible.

Notes

1. Rosebery's Eton tutor, William Johnson, wrote the 'Eton Boating Song', set to music by Algernon Drummond in 1863, and Rosebery was a keen sculler during his schooldays. His son, Harry, also a Liberal politician, captained Surrey's cricket team (1905–7) and was its president (1947–9). His friendship with the Prince of Wales meant Surrey were allowed to use the Prince of Wales feathers as the county crest. Harry received a lengthy obituary in *The Cricketer* (July 1974).

2. Stoddart was unable to cope with his declining powers or the complexities of business, and shot himself in 1915 at the age of fifty-two.

3. This account is challenged by the sceptical Schroeder (135, 208–10) who claims it is a 'preposterous fraud' by the palmist. A reading of Shaw's palm, taken from a cast, appeared in *The Palmist* magazine in July 1895. The playwright called the result 'an amusing study of my character' (Shaw 1965: 553).

4. Wilde had sent Buchanan a copy of *Dorian Gray* in 1891. Buchanan had affectionately parodied him in *The Charlatan*, a play co-written with Henry Murray in 1894 and novelised by the pair in 1895 (Kingston 148–53).

5. Chatt always claimed the goal was scored by John Devey, but in a goalmouth melee, nothing was certain. There is no official timing for the goal, scored somewhere between 30 and 39 seconds, but it was the fastest in cup finals until Louis Saha scored after 25 seconds for Everton against Chelsea in 2009. Football's growing popularity, and the excellence of Crystal Palace as a venue, is shown by the increased attendance for the 1895 final despite it being in essence a local derby. When Villa and WBA met in the final in 1892 at Kennington Oval, the crowd numbered 32,810. The Easter weekend may have contributed to the high attendance in 1895; there were apparently 68,000 visitors to the Palace on Easter Monday, and 30,000 at Madame Tussaud's.

6. Arthur Machen met Wilde at the Bodley Head before the libel action and was shocked to find him 'a great mass of rosy fat. His body seemed made of rolls of fat. He was pendulous. He was like nothing but an obese old Frenchwoman, dressed up in man's clothes. He horrified me' (Gawsworth 139).

7. Arthur Oscar Hornung signed himself 'Oscar' from the age of 12 onwards. He was killed at Ypres on 6 July 1915.

8. Later in the year, Orton was robbed of his watch and chain (worth £3) by William Wells, a Spitalfields coster. Wells was sentenced to six months hard labour (*IPN* 2/11//95).

Summer: 1 June 1895 – 31 August 1895

[M]any another epigram, too well known to quote, rings out like the voice of Lear's fool over a mad age.

W.B. Yeats on *A Woman of No Importance*, *Bookman*, March 1895

A witty paradoxical writer, who nevertheless, *meo judicio*, will do nothing permanent because he is earnest about nothing.

Francis Thompson on Wilde, July 1890

To a man of refinement the sudden association, on terms of equality, for the first time in his life with the noisy and ribald dregs of criminal London is an experience calculated to beget despair even in the most sanguine mind.

Jabez Balfour, *My Prison Life* (1907)

Unsexed, factitious, foolish, coarse, inhuman!
She's not the New, she's but the 'Novel' Woman!

New Name for the 'New Woman', *Punch* (31 August 1895)

Oh who is that young sinner with the handcuffs on his wrists?
And what has he been after that they groan and shake their fists?
And wherefore is he wearing such a conscience-stricken air?
Oh they're taking him to prison for the colour of his hair.

A.E. Housman, 'Oh who is that young sinner?', Summer 1895

Dandy in the Underworld

On the day Wilde was sentenced to two years in prison, Conan Doyle wrote to his mother to tell how, on the advice of Grant Allen, he had decided to spend £3,500 on having a new house built in Hindhead, 'the most improving part of England' (Lellenberg 2007: 353). Had this been public knowledge, a newspaper editor may well have contrasted the two events to illustrate how Vice and dissidence had been punished, and Virtue and conformity rewarded

Justice Wills had passed sentence on a Saturday afternoon, so Wilde and Taylor were held in cells at Newgate until the morning of Monday 27 May. Then, a horse-drawn 'Black Maria' took them, handcuffed, to Pentonville. 'Thus has ended a brilliant life,' announced the *IPB*, 'a life that might [. . .] have become as great as a Shakespeare [. . .] yet a life ruined by the evil indulgence in a sphere of immorality' (1/6/95). Many papers gave detailed accounts of the arduous punishment and brutal regime Wilde – Taylor was soon forgotten – would endure. He avoided the treadmill after the first few days, but the monotonous and painful task of picking oakum was scarcely a sinecure, especially as it confined him to his cell for over twenty-two hours a day. When he did see other prisoners during his hour's open air exercise of circling the prison yard in 'Indian file', or at the daily chapel service, conversation was expressly forbidden. He was to sleep on a plank bed and subsist on cocoa, brown bread, soup, gruel, brown flour suet puddings, potatoes and cold meat, typically Australian mutton. He was denied any reading matter except for a Bible, a hymn book and a prayer book, and though in due course limited access to other texts was permitted, no writing materials were allowed. 'Solitary confinement is calculated, doctors state, to produce melancholia, suicidal mania, and a loss of reason,' said the *IPN*, adding that nine months of it 'are almost certain to result in the mental ruin of the convict' (15/12/94). A 'soul-degrading routine for that amiable, joyous, eloquent, pampered Sybarite,' said Frank Harris. 'An ordeal as by fire' (Harris [1938] 1965: 192).

At Pentonville Wilde was weighed and measured – he was 6 feet tall and weighed 14 stone, suggesting he had lost a lot of weight since the winter – and his hair was cropped 'to so fine a point that even a man with long nails could not get hold of it' (*IPB* 1/6/95), a spectacle newspaper artists found irresistible. He now resembled 'a well-to-do butcher who has served a sentence for fraud' (*IPB* 1/6/95). Given a brief medical examination and pronounced fit for light labour, Wilde was forced into what he described as 'some filthy water they called a bath', drying himself 'with a damp brown rag'. His uniform, 'this livery of shame', was grey with black arrows (Hyde 1963: 5). New arrivals were given a daily dose of potassium bromide to subdue their 'urges', but this intensified Wilde's melancholia, the so-called 'prison head', and was soon discontinued (*RN* 9/6/95).

Wilde's cell was 13 feet long, 7 feet wide, 9 feet high and admitted almost no natural light. It was poorly ventilated and, when illness and the prison diet inevitably produced diarrhoea, almost unendurable. No personal possessions or pictures were allowed. Prisoners were watched through a spy hole in the cell door and subject to unannounced inspection. Cells were to be kept clean and tidy at all times (Hyde 1963: 6–7). Wilde's condition deteriorated quickly as sickness, hunger, insomnia and the harsh regime took their toll. On 7 June, a number of papers carried an official rebuttal by the prison governor of 'cruel fabrications' concerning his ill-health: Wilde was, apparently, 'very well' (*PMG* 7/6/95), a claim few believed.

Prison removed Wilde from the world and rationed the letters he received to one a month, but he was not forgotten by his friends, his admirers, or, indeed, his enemies, though the legal personnel involved in the trials soon moved on to fresh cases. Sir Edward Clarke's next assignment was representing the Gaiety Girl, Birdie Sutherland (Anne Louise Watkins) in a breach of promise suit against the son of Lord Tweedsmouth, his Lordship having intervened to prevent the marriage. Miss Watkins was presently 'ill in the country', perhaps a euphemism for a discreet pregnancy (*IPN* 25/5/95). Bosie Douglas sent a stream of letters to the English and French press defending Wilde and criticising his prosecution. He petitioned the Queen for Wilde's early release, though she never saw his plea (Hyde 1963: 15, 203–4) and hoped his brother would be able to bribe warders to get Wilde special privileges (McKenna 542). On 9 June, a strongly worded note to Henry Labouchere told the formulator of the 'Blackmailer's Charter', 'I maintain that these tastes are perfectly natural congenital tendencies in certain people (a very large minority) and that the law has no right to interfere with these people provided they do not harm other people' (Wintermans 71). Labouchere responded in *Truth* by snidely terming Bosie 'this exceptional moralist' and regretting he was not pondering such attitudes in Pentonville (Croft-Cooke 133). Discussions with W.T. Stead also came to naught (Hyde 1948: 360–3). At London's Oxford music hall, Dan Leno fed off the public fascination with courtroom drama in his satirical treatment of aggressive barristers, 'Not Guilty'. Bram Stoker, husband of Wilde's former love, Florence Balcombe, began work on what would become *Dracula*, a novel heavily inflected by homoeroticism (Schaffer 1994: 381–425). June's *Free Review* contained Ernest Newman's 'Oscar Wilde: A Literary Appreciation', which praised Wilde's mastery of paradox. The same month, Arthur Machen identified 'a severe attack of virtue abroad', telling Lane that Parliament might bring literature 'within the purview of the Criminal Law Amendment Act' (MacLeod 143). Soon afterwards, the *SR* dismissed the 'rubbishy' '*Old Q*', a memoir of the fourth duke of Queensberry by John Robert Robinson (6/7/95, 15), perhaps a muted retaliatory gesture by Harris. A miserable George Ives wrote in his diary on 2 July that Wilde's enemies 'do not know how brutal they can be'. 'If we could show them the truth,' he added, 'I believe they would be both sorry and ashamed' (Stokes 1996: 78–9). On 18 July, Brookfield was Tom Twist in a matinee performance of *She Stoops to Conquer* at the Comedy Theatre. 'His zeal in hunting out homosexuals did not stop when Wilde and Taylor went to prison,' notes Hyde, who points out that it eventually 'became an embarrassment to the authorities' (Hyde 1970: 173).

Hichens and Heinemann may have withdrawn *The Green Carnation*, but books in production before or during the trials revealed Wilde's influence in subtler ways. His epigrammatic wit defied incarceration, surfacing in the phrases and philosophies of Kenneth Grahame's *The Golden Age*, a collection of children's stories the *Bookman* felt was distinguished by 'its refinement, its artistic sense, and the charm of its style' (10/95: 30). 'Grown-up people are fairly correct in matters of fact,' Grahame's narrator observes. 'It is in the higher gift of imagination that they are so sadly to seek' (Grahame 1983: 23). Another story features Rosa, whose character 'was of the blameless order of those who have not yet been found out' (25).

Playful asides were not welcome at the annual meeting of the NVA on 6 June, which heard a denunciation of the growing tendency among 'illustrated papers' to introduce 'pictures of a demoralising and dangerous' kind (*T* 7/6/95). Laura Chant praised the Association's medical endeavours, though the *PMG* was sarcastic about the continued campaign against music hall immorality, pointing out the Empire now had 'handsome brass rails to lean against' while engaging in 'friendly conversation' (7/6/95). Lord Kinnaird, the chairman, received warm applause when suggesting revision of the CLAA. 'The time has come', he argued, 'when public opinion will demand something further in the way of repression' (Winner 29).

R.B. Haldane, a member of the Home Office committee monitoring prison conditions, did not share Kinnaird's views, and visited Wilde on 12 June, probably at Asquith's suggestion. Initially withdrawn, Wilde gradually responded to Haldane's estimation of his career – he had yet to produce the great work that would immortalise him – and when Haldane promised to obtain books other than *The Pilgrim's Progress* inflicted by the prison chaplain, he burst into tears. He even managed to laugh when Haldane suggested Flaubert's fiction was unlikely to be approved by the prison authorities. Cardinal Newman, St Augustine and Pascal were more agreeable suggestions, though the final list also included *The Renaissance*. Wilde was not yet allowed pen and paper, but Haldane did agree to pass news of him to his wife and family.

Any reviving influence was transient. Nine days later, Wilde had a second visitor, a clerk from Queensberry's solicitors who served him with a bankruptcy notice in connection with the £677 costs incurred during his doomed libel suit. As Wilde had believed Percy and Bosie would settle these, the writ's consequences extended far beyond those of reinforcing his bitter and impotent despair. Percy T. Ingram's poem, 'The Democratic World' offered compassion in its closing lines, 'Ungrateful England blights her rising star I And thrusts her brilliant poet where felons are' (*RN* 30/6/95), but a more widely-held view was that of Hugh Stutfield in *Blackwood's*:

> Whence, then, sprang the foolish fear of being natural, the craving to atti-tudinise in everything? It was Oscar Wilde who infected us with our dread of the conventional, with the silly straining after originality characteristic of a society that desires above all things to be thought intellectually smart. (6/95: 846)

Elevation and Excoriation

Rosebery's interest in the arts, another cause for whispering in Whitehall corridors, played a significant role in the birthday honours announced on 25 May. Knighthoods were conferred on Henry Irving, the novelist and founder of the Society of Authors, Walter Besant, and the poet, Lewis Morris. Most welcomed the first of these, though the *SR* carped that though the award was deserved, Irving had 'forced' the PM to knight him by repeatedly giving public lectures stressing acting as the equal of literature, music, and art. 'The Mummer' felt the public were 'the sole judges of his artistic merits' (*IPN* 22/6/95), and that govern-mental approval made no difference to his reputation. The news of Irving's knighthood arrived while he was appearing in a version of *Don Quixote* at the Lyceum. The line 'Knighthood sits like a halo round my head' won 'cheers of approval from the audience' (Richards 2005: 30). He received an MA from Oxford University on 21 June, while Pinero, who had belonged to his company during the 1870s, wrote a celebra-tory address to his friend, got it signed by over 4,000 thespians, and presented it to him in a gold and silver casket on stage at the Lyceum on 19 July. The triumphant Irving embarked on a ten month American tour shortly afterwards.

Rosebery had awarded a civil list pension to William Watson, and he now gave an annual pension of £100 to the widow of the art critic, P.G. Hamerton. Knighthoods for Besant and Morris were much more con-troversial, with the *SR* saying it was 'blind and fatuous' to knight Besant before Swinburne or Meredith. Morris was derided by his peers as the 'poet of the middle class mind' (*SR* 1/6/95: 718); in Owen Seaman's

The Battle of the Bays (1896), his verse is 'blank, I Distinctly blank, and might be measured by the kilomètre' (Seaman 1896: 14). Ifor Evans later described Morris as 'Tennyson-made-easy', pointing out how a 'wide public, not poetically sensitive' mistook his complacent musings for literary greatness (Evans 1966: 329–30). Knighting Morris, the *SR* felt, devalued the institution of knighthood. Kipling agreed. In a congratulatory letter to Besant, he enclosed a facetious coat of arms for the poet, 'a back stairs, bendy, wavy and improper' (Kipling 1990: 188–9). The College of Heralds created something grander for Irving, a sable shield, four swans argent (a tribute to his love of the Swan of Avon) and a laurel wreath or (*IPN* 5/10/95).

Besant was a different matter, since his artistic flaws were counterbalanced by valuable work for fellow authors and the establishing of the People's Palace in the Mile End Road, described by Queen Victoria as a place of 'rational and instructive entertainment, and of artistic enjoyment' (Besant [1882]1997: x). What piqued the *SR* was seeing Besant recognised for services to literature when his novels were undeserving of that term, and when literature itself was ideally independent of political recognition. Conrad was puzzled by the whole business. Irving's knighthood was, he thought, 'weird and unreal', while the Honours in general were 'the fairy tale of the most misty and elusive administration of this practical country'. Rosebery was simply 'astonishing' (Conrad 1983: 224–5). The Society of Authors held a banquet in Besant's honour on 18 July, at which Meredith provided a generous address.

The relationship between literature, politics, and commerce was scrutinised in depth. Nigel Cross maintains that the 'great cultural debate' of the 1890s 'was not about Beardsley's decorative phalli, Dowson's absinthe-soaked verse, Hubert Crackanthorpe's tremendously slight short stories or even Oscar Wilde's homosexuality; it was about art in the marketplace' (Cross 1985: 215). The monetary value of art was one thing, but the definition of art in the first place remained vexed. Reviewing James's collection, *Terminations*, Wells felt its 'singular distaste for the obvious is a thing to be regretted' (*SR* 1/6/95: 731), a view shared by the *YB*'s Lena Milman, who felt his 'unremitting warfare against the Obvious' occasionally 'misled him into artificiality' (Milman 1895: 75). The *Athenaeum* however relished a 'half-perverse air of subtlety and remoteness' which distanced James 'from the heartier and more robust forms of human motive and desire' (15/6/95: 769). 'Robust desire' caused particular unease when Egerton and others combined it with technical innovation. Hugh Stutfield boiled over in 'Tommyrotics', ostensibly a review of Nordau that degenerated into an attack on 'the neurotic and repulsive fiction' he associated with decadence and the

New Woman. Madness, morbidity and erotomania were the keynotes of such writing, he insisted, denouncing *Gallia* as 'garbage pure and simple' and claiming 'effeminacy and artificiality of manner' were 'so common that they have almost ceased to appear ridiculous' (*Blackwood's* 6/95: 833–46). On 6 June, the New Vagabonds Club hosted a guest dinner for women writers, attracting Sarah Grand, Marie Corelli, Muriel Dowie, Violet Hunt, and Ella Hepworth Dixon. The *PMG's* report of the event is frustratingly vague, but one wonders if there was argument about rising levels of permissiveness, or indeed, the absence of women writers from the Honours List (*PMG* 7/6/95). The *Cork Constitution* demanded 'a Baroness be conferred upon the author of *Lady Audley's Secret*', leading *Punch's* pedants to ask, 'What would Miss Braddon do with a Baroness when she got her? Work her up into her next plot?' (15/6/95: 285).

The sales of the 6s edition of Du Maurier's *Trilby*, published on 13 June, demonstrated how 'unwholesome' material could be forgiven if it was complemented by humour, deft characterisation and, most importantly, a memorable and emotionally involving story. It was easy to read Du Maurier's romantic Gothic without speculating on the particularities of relationships between Parisian artists and their models, while the monstrousness of Svengali allowed the audience to take refuge in melodrama (and anti-Semitism) rather than pondering the wider implications of his powers. By setting the novel in the Paris of his student days, Du Maurier also dodged direct engagement with the contemporary world, allowing *Trilby* to be escapist instead of courting controversy. Reading more salacious offerings did incalculable harm, conservatives believed, with *Punch* satirising a 'modern' family, in which the wife, 'an emotional icicle, I rode a bicycle' and her son read Nordau and Lombroso 'till his brain went shaky' and he thought he had turned into a mustard pot (20/7/95: 34).

Edmund Gosse caused disquiet at the Booksellers' Dinner on 26 April by claiming that 'great authors' (and their agents) were 'killing the goose' by making exorbitant demands for royalties (*MP* 17/5/95). Du Maurier had rejected a royalty scheme for *Trilby*, selling the copyright for £2,000, but younger writers and their agents were more aware of the implications of contracts linked to sales (Ormond 1969: 442). Attending Edward Clodd's house party in early June, Gissing had a chance to gauge his fellow writers' views about the current state of English literature. He responded favourably to Grant Allen, even when Allen told him he was 'drawing £25 a week from *The Woman Who Did*, and will soon have had £1,000' (Gissing 1978: 375), but found anecdotes concerning William Watson's mental aberrations less pleasing. Watson had claimed 'the Almighty had declared to him he was to be Laureate', and divine sanction meant he would 'never talk about anything but his own poetry' (376). In all, Clodd's guests made a better impression on Gissing than the members of the Authors' Club had done back in November. Then, Besant, Robert Sherard and Anthony Hope left him unmoved; the meeting was 'a mere gathering of tradesmen, and commonplace tradesmen at that' (354). *New Grub Street* (1891) offered a brilliant dissection of writing as a trade, but four years later, its author remained on the lower slopes of Parnassus, producing not imperishable art but a string of short stories for the *Minster,* the *Strand* and the *English Illustrated Magazine.* Gissing refused to lower himself to journalism during the 1880s, but his rapid production of vignettes from 1892 onwards was motivated in part by their disproportionately generous financial rewards. As Pierre Coustillas points out, 'shorter pieces were less incompatible with a disorderly domestic life than protracted novels,' and Gissing was prepared to compose vignettes for Shorter and Jerome if it did not entail 'lowering of his artistic standards' (Gissing 1993: xvi-xvii). Serialising a novella such as *Eve's Ransom* in the *ILN* proved remunerative – it brought in £150 for 25 days work – but the *PMG* troubled Gissing by suggesting he was '"beating out too thin" for serial purposes' (Gissing 1978: 373). His diary shows how he struggled to maintain his artistic ideals in the face of his daily labours and their commercial obligations or prospects, and he condemned some of stories he sold as 'literary trash' (Halperin 1982: 231). The pragmatic Arnold Bennett was less inclined to agonise, telling George Sturt, 'Am I to sit still & [. . .] see other fellows pocketing two guineas apiece for stories which I can do better myself? Not me! If anyone imagines my sole aim is art for art's sake, they are cruelly deceived' (Bennett 1968: 19).

While Bennett counted his coppers, Vernon Lee (Violet Paget) gave weekly lectures at the South Kensington Museum from 11–25 June. Her topic was 'Art and Life, the Relation of Aesthetic and Moral Development'. Conrad was wrestling with his new novel, *An Outcast of the Islands*, telling Edward Garnett on 7 June that 'the world [. . .] is one big grey shadow and I am one immense yawn' (Conrad 224). Considering sending a story to the *YB*, he told his friend Edward Noble, 'Those people are very aest[h]etic very advanced and think no end of themselves. They are all certainly writers of talent – some of very great talent' (231). One of these writers, Henry James, had returned to the Bodley Head as the dust settled on the Beardsley debacle, and in early June was putting the final touches to the lead story for the forthcoming *YB*. 'The Next Time', a laconic fable of popular neglect, was inspired by 'one's own frustrated ambition' and begun in the aftermath of *Guy*

Domville on 26 January (James 1987: 109). Set in 'the age of flour-
ishing rubbish' (James 1895: 13) – James later changed this to 'trash
triumphant' – in which artistic and commercial success are mutually
exclusive, the story dramatises the struggles of the 'exquisite failure'
(12) Ralph Limbert, a writer who, like Reardon in *New Grub Street*,
attempts to exploit his talent for financial gain. Limbert's ambition
is to produce a bestseller, but he can write only 'shameless, merciless
masterpiece[s]' (41) that never reach a second edition. A man who 'when
he went abroad to gather garlic [. . .] came home with heliotrope' (55),
Limbert dies without ever achieving his aim, a telling comment on the
ever more clamorous dialogue between art and money that dismayed
and yet stimulated his creator.

The death of the elderly Frederick Locker-Lampson, the accomplished writer of society verse, on 30 May renewed discussion about the
nature and purpose of poetry just as John Lane at last issued Francis
Thompson's *Sister-Songs*. Publication had been delayed by difficulties
over Thompson's contract (Thompson 1969: 126) and by Lane's anxieties over Lawrence Housman's illustrations, one of which depicted, said
the artist in a letter of 23 May, 'a human soul, bound among thorns and
roses to the doorway of life' (JLA). Fearful of playing hunt-the-symbol
as he had with Beardsley, Lane vetoed the drawing and excluded it
from the *YB*. Now the volume was out, but the poet's reputation was
waning and he was harshly dealt with by Symons in the *Athenaeum* and
the *SR* as wordy, vague and derivative. Thompson remarked in August
that Symons was 'the only critic of mine I think downright unfair'
(Thompson 1969: 130), but he was not the only one to find *Sister-Songs*
wanting. The unimpressed *Leeds Mercury* commented that Thompson
'revels not only in incomprehensible sentiments, but in unknown words'
(19/8/95). 'A Reformate Wordsworthian' joined the fray, rewriting
Wordsworth's 'Lucy' in Thompsonian style in the letters page of the *SR*:

> By fonts of Dove, ways incalcable,
>   Did habitate
> A virgin largely inamable
>   And illaudate. (13/7/95: 47)

Thompson's obscurity had no place in modern poetry, maintained
Symons, especially at a time when, as Andrew Lang noted, recent
neologisms were not archaic coinages but 'useful' words such as 'mai-
sonnette', 'serialised' and 'typist' (*ILN* 1/6/95: 679). Symons was deter-
minedly modern by comparison, but his own collection, *London Nights*
published in late June and dedicated to Verlaine, would fare still worse
with reviewers.

Flaming June

After the ferocious winter, few expected an equally extreme summer, yet the *IPN* reported deaths from sunstroke as early as May. Morals relaxed as temperatures rose. On 14 May, Charles Henry de Rivez, a forty-year-old stockbroker, was the leader of a group of drunken business-men who misbehaved aboard the steam launch *Trocadero* near Staines, using foul language and swimming naked in the Thames. The judge was appalled, fining them £4–6 each, and regretting he could not impose custodial sentences (*IPN* 22/6/95). On 30 May, Gissing noted it was 70°F (21°C) at 10 a.m. (Gissing 1978: 374). Three weeks later, south-ern England was gripped by drought. The hot weather closed many music halls, and left racehorse owners reluctant to risk their animals on baked courses. Prisons were sweltering. Two balloonists from the Royal Engineers Balloon School at Aldershot narrowly escaped crashing into the Channel near Bexhill after their balloon ascended to 5,000 feet on a hot afternoon and they were forced to deploy their escape valve (*IPN* 6/7/95). On 1 July, sixteen-year-old Robert Sullivan drowned in the Serpentine during an unwise post-prandial swim; police estimated there were 2,000 people in the lake that evening. The Thames was a magnet for over-heated Londoners, and at Chelsea Embankment, police were stoned by a crowd after trying to prevent them from bathing in the busy river. The East End suffered water shortages and sewage prob-lems; in late July, five men died after being overcome by noxious gas at the East Ham sewage plant (*IPN* 20/7/95). Spectacular thunderstorms brought death and devastation. Two miners were killed by lightning in Normanton, West Yorkshire. Further north, two more men died when lightning struck the ash tree they were sheltering under at Darlington's Royal Agricultural Show. Chester and Aylesbury were flooded after violent hailstorms, and there were serious floods after thunderstorms in Burton-on-Trent, Sheffield, Wakefield and Hull. In Liverpool, there were unofficial reports of temperatures as high as 110°F (43°C) before a storm made the sky so dark that the city's gas was lit at 4 p.m. (*IPN* 6/7/95). Forked lightning hit a telephone wire, throwing a chimney over forty feet, and a downpour led to floods and sewage failures across the city (*Liverpool Mercury* 2/7/95).[1] After intense hailstorms and even snow in Kent in early May, there were fears for the strawberry crop, but these proved largely groundless, the *IPN* reporting that on one morning, 90 two-horse vans were needed to transport the fruit from Waterloo Station to the capital's markets (6/7/95). The grain harvest was excellent too, though some noted shortage in the straw. The heat at last revived Millais, who had struggled with flu all winter, but it could not help Julia Stephen, who died on 5 May – James sent a letter of sympathy to her husband, Leslie (James 1984: 13) – nor the naturalist T.H. Huxley. Refusing to rest while working on a response to Balfour's *The Foundations of Belief*, (*A* 6/7/95: 33), 'Darwin's Bulldog' was overcome by the combined forces of bronchitis, heart disease and 'lung and kidney complaints' (*T* 29/6/95).

Rosebery Resigns

By late June, Rosebery's government could go no further, having 'drifted dismally towards inevitable disaster, its councils acrimonious, its leaders divided, its supporters dispirited or violently disillusioned, its stature at home and abroad visibly disintegrating' (R. James 1975: 159). Rosebery's moral authority was undermined by the creation of four Liberal peers in the Honours List, elevations which coincided with donations to Liberal funds totalling £100,000. He protested he was in part honouring a promise made by Gladstone (*T* 13/7/95), but his hypocrisy roundly condemned. A disastrous election defeat in Invernesshire, following controversy over Scottish land reform and the rights of crofters, added to his woes. Seaman amused readers of the *World* with a timely verse:

A Government, dear Editor,
    That drew so scant a breath
Would seem to be intended for
    A rather early death. (Seaman 1895: 110)

Matters came to a head in the week beginning 17 June. A proposal to erect a statue of Oliver Cromwell outside the Palace of Westminster caused prolonged argument, first about a suitable site and then about the £500 the Commons would have to pay for it. Irish Nationalists were outraged by any commemoration of a man they considered tyrannical, and the vote on funding the statue was withdrawn, seemingly without Rosebery's knowledge.[2] This was the first in a series of reverses, with the Government beaten in a Standing Committee on an amendment to the Factory Bill and then scraping home in a substantial amendment to the Welsh Disestablishment Bill the day after (R. James 1995: 382). When Campbell-Bannerman bungled questions about the army's cordite reserves, the Opposition called for a £100 reduction in the War Secretary's salary and the Liberals lost a snap division by seven votes. The following day, 22 June, the Cabinet opted to resign and Rosebery met with the Queen to tell her of the decision. She presented him with a marble bust of herself (Gladstone had received two halfpenny photographs of her), and Salisbury's coalition of Conservatives and Unionists took charge (McKinstry 2005: 380). Parliament was dissolved on 8 July and an election began five days later. Rosebery's administration 'had no more right to their present position than Arthur Orton had to the Tichborne Estates,' *Blackwood's* jibed (7/95: 153). An electorate of 6,332,454 pondered its choices as political parties wooed it with approximately £300,000's worth of advertising. In all, the election was estimated to have cost in the region of a million pounds (*IPN* 24/8/95), though the *Times* found campaigning 'languid' (13/7/95), with many results foregone conclusions and many Conservatives and Unionists unopposed.

As predicted, the Liberals were soundly beaten, Salisbury securing a majority of 152 though the profusion of uncontested seats meant that his party polled only 123,000 more votes than the Liberals. The Unionists now had 411 seats, their opponents 259, giving the new PM enviable freedom of action and sparing him the fragile alliances that hobbled his predecessor. *Blackwood's* explained the Liberal defeat was because radicalism had threatened 'the practical destruction of the most splendid, most kindly, and most highly cultivated social system which the world has ever seen' (7/95: 307). By seeking to destroy the Lords, the landed aristocracy, the Church of England, abandoning the Empire, emasculating industry 'by the discouragement of individual energy' and passing laws instead of compelling self-discipline, Rosebery meant to undermine 'all that is dignified and graceful, all that is vigorous and manly, in the national life' (307). 'We have been praying two or three times daily for the last one year and a half that God would cleanse and defend his church,' said a Bideford rector who held a service of thanksgiving for Rosebery's fall (*IPN* 10/8/95).

The final election results, Orkney and Shetland, were not available until 10 August, but they made no difference. The *QR*'s analysis brought home the full scale of the Liberal disaster, the worst electoral reverse since 1833, when the Liberal majority that followed the 1832 Reform Act was 314. Fifty-four of London's sixty-two seats were now Conservative Unionist, with the Tories surprisingly successful in the East: Lambeth, Bethnal Green, Shoreditch (where they won by a mere forty votes after a recount), and Tower Hamlets were among their gains. John Burns held Battersea for the ILP, but as a man who commanded great local respect and popularity regardless of his political allegiances, this was less significant than it at first seemed. Lambeth North's defeated MP, Francis Coldwells, a long-time business partner of Jabez Balfour, was facing trial for fraud due to his involvement with the Liberator group, but the precise extent of his culpability was concealed by his death on 29 July. Found dead in his Bournemouth summer house, it seemed his heart had given way under the strain of the case, though many suspected he had killed himself to avoid jail (McKie 2005: 212).

The *Times* termed the Liberals' exodus from London, 'the Radical Rout in the East-End' (20/7/95), and *Punch*'s Cockney spokesman, 'Arry, addressed the matter at length (27/7/95: 39). Plymouth was now the sole Liberal stronghold, for the Tories dominated Bradford, Bristol, Cardiff, Coventry, Derby, Glasgow, Hull, Liverpool, Manchester, Newcastle, Northampton, Nottingham, Rochdale, Salford, Stockport, Stoke, Sunderland and Swansea. Only ten Liberals were elected unopposed. The Unionists were popular with urban working class voters and in the counties – seventy Liberal Unionists were elected – but many felt the true cause of Rosebery's downfall was Home Rule. In-fighting among Nationalists made those on the mainland increasingly opposed to self-government, the *QR* argued, pointing out that Ireland had twice as many seats as London despite having only half its population. This was surely a case for electoral reform (10/95: 538–67). The 'unopposed election of the convict James Daly as a Parnellite in Limerick city' upset the *SR* (20/7/95: 66) and the *Times*, who called him 'Dynamiter Daly' (16/8/95). *Punch* commented on how the Irish harp had grown tuneless, for 'The Paddies quarrel, gird, and carp, | Blend petty squeak with mad mock-thunder' (24/8/95: 94).

The Nationalist cause was not helped by coverage of the trial of Bridget Cleary's killers, though in an article in the *Nineteenth Century* in June, E.F. Benson, son of the Archbishop of Canterbury, described the killing as a being 'in accordance with a primitive and savage superstition' rather than being the 'cruel and unnatural murder' which it first appeared. 'Far from wishing to murder her,' Benson argued, 'they wished to bring her back into the land of the living.' Bridget was, they thought, possessed by a malign spirit, and after her apparent death they hoped she would return on a white horse. The whole business was 'appalling', but Benson argued that 'the remedy is not to be found in the hangman's noose' (Benson [1895] 2001: 618–23). Whether the article influenced the judiciary is uncertain, but when the trial opened on 4 July, plea-bargaining saw Michael Cleary found guilty of manslaughter rather than murder, while seven other defendants, including Bridget's father, were guilty of wounding. Justice O'Brien told the court, 'This most extraordinary case demonstrated a degree of darkness in the mind, not of one person, but of several, a moral darkness, even religious darkness, the disclosure of which had come with surprise on many persons' (Bourke 1999: 186), words that unconsciously echoed reaction to Carson's speech against

Wilde, the 'thing of blackness', the 'horrid nocturne of terrible suggestions'. It would be misleading to suggest that readers across the Irish
Sea uniformly regarded Ireland as a barbarous backwater, but the case
helped reaffirm certain stereotypical assumptions.

Back at Westminster, a number of notable parliamentarians were
absent from the new session. Harcourt, the Derby loser to Rosebery's
Derby winner (P 27/7/95: 39), surrendered his seat to the Unionist
and old age pensions activist Geoffrey Drage, by 7,076 to 6,785 votes,
his enthusiasm for Temperance Reform prompting Punch's 'How the
Topers Came Down to the Polls' (27/7/95: 46). Drage's The Problem
of the Aged Poor appeared later in the year and garnered widespread
appreciation (BDP 23/12/95), showing that the Liberals did not have a
monopoly on ideas of social justice. Derby's results were available on
the first day of polling, and the early loss of the Chancellor, who was
seen as stuck in the past, left the Liberals reeling. Morley and Newnes
lost their seats too, though they were back in Parliament within five
years, as was Harcourt. Keir Hardie, the ILP's first MP was also ousted,
losing by 775 votes despite having had a majority of 1,232 in 1892.
Punch depicted him as an extinct museum specimen (3/8/95: 58), but a
fiery letter from Amy Morant of the ILP's Hammersmith branch made
it clear that the party's male and female activists were destined to sup-
plant the Liberals as the voice of Parliamentary radicalism (T 8/8/95):
in a straight fight between the Liberals and the ILP in Bristol in March,
the Liberals had scraped home by only 132 votes, and David Brooks
suggests that ILP candidates split the opposition vote in a number of
Lancashire constituencies, allowing Conservative successes (Hamilton
105). Morant, a highly educated 'New Woman' who had studied eco-
nomics and moral and political philosophy at Bedford and Newnham
Colleges (Shaw 1965: 574) was right, for although the ILP polled only
1 per cent of the vote in 1895, losing all twenty-eight of the seats it contested, Hardie was back in the Commons in 1900.

At a time of overwhelming Conservative and Unionist success, it was
notable that Rider Haggard failed to capture East Norfolk, a constituency hard-hit by agricultural decline. The ILN was most amused. '[B]
esieged by a disgraceful mob in a Norfolk hotel [. . .] Did he follow the
glorious example of Eric Brighteyes or Bulalia the Slaughterer?' it asked.
'He did none of these things; but like a law-abiding citizen, awaited
the police. How are the imaginatively lawless fallen!' (27/7/95: 103).
Haggard's autobiography records only that he was followed throughout
the campaign by a man who bleated like a sheep throughout his speeches
(Haggard 1926: 113), but the disorder had been serious. Women were
'stoned by cowardly ruffians' and Mr Punch wished he had been there

'with a few of his young men and a few revolvers' (3/8/95: 54). Joseph Chamberlain meanwhile joined the Cabinet as a Liberal Unionist in the role of Colonial Secretary, leading *Punch* to depict him as 'the climbing boy' in a circus act (6/7/95: 7) and later as 'The Political Ugly Ducking' (10/8/95: 65).[3] Chamberlain's move angered his former comrades, especially when he attended the opening of the new Parliament with a red orchid in his buttonhole. He has 'opened his mouth pretty widely and [. . .] had it handsomely filled,' sneered Hamilton on 3 July (Hamilton 1986: 265). Others welcomed his appointment though, with the *Times* hoping Britain would now look to her Empire once more, and that the cause of Home Rule was at last finished (*T* 15/8/95). With eighty-two Nationalists in the Commons however, this seemed unlikely.

Punch joked that although MPs claimed honourable motives, they were actually drawn to the prestige of office, pleading 'if the honour ultimately culminates in a baronetcy or a knighthood the distinction will be gratifying to my wife' (6/7/95: 3). Taking their seats in the new Parliament on 12 August were 28 journalists, 25 newspaper proprietors (11 of whom were Nationalists), 6 printers and publishers, and 22 authors (Lee 1976: 294–6). There were some remarkably young MPs, with Benjamin Bathurst, the well-connected member for Cirencester, just twenty-three years old. The national mood was, in most quarters, one of enthusiasm for a fresh start, though Nationalists had little hope of favour from Salisbury's administration. 'The Liberal party is simply annihilated for the time being,' Hamilton mourned (1986: 271), though Rosebery remained its leader, *Punch* depicting him as Napoleon before the bonfire of his hopes for Home Rule (3/8/95: 50). The smouldering ashes were an apt metaphor. In a letter of 21 August, Rosebery himself confessed that the Liberals had been 'purged as with fire'. 'I do not need consolation with regard to this general election', he said. 'It was inevitable, and it can scarcely fail to do good' (McKinstry 2005: 382).

The Noble Game

The hot summer was ideal for sport and open air pursuits of all kinds. The *ILN* pronounced croquet 'almost extinct' (2/2/95: 130), but cycling continued to grow in popularity. In January, Edward Bradford, the Chief Commissioner of the Metropolitan Police, reported a rapidly-rising number of cycling accidents, with nearly as many in 1893 as there had been in the whole of the 1880s. In Cardiganshire, policemen were increasingly using bicycles; 'Peelers' had become 'Wheelers', quipped *Punch* (31/8/95: 97). Although it liked to portray cyclists as

Figure 9. The defeated Rosebery beside the bonfire of his hopes, *Punch* 3 August 1895.

cranks, vulgarians, or subversives undermining the nation's equestrian traditions, many devotees were as respectable as the magazine could wish: the *IPN* reported that recent converts included the Duchess of Portland, the elderly Lady Ashburton and even an unnamed Anglican bishop (16/2/95). It also noted the case of James Greenwood, the veteran investigative journalist and writer of *LWN*'s summer serial, *The Bunbury Twins: A Tale of Tender Entanglement*, who was fined a shilling for riding his tricycle on the pavement (19/10/95). When John Ruck and R.E. Wicker cycled across the Channel on a specially-constructed tandem on 16 May, newspapers were torn between hailing their achievement and questioning its purpose.

The main target of *Punch*'s cycling-related scorn was the New Woman; July opened with Mr Punch pedalling a 'quandem' with three young women in knickerbockers (6/7/95: 1). 'The woman who put on divided skirts and took to the roads on her "safety" not only gained independence but also a measure of health and a sense of well-being that her neurasthenic sister of earlier decades might have envied' says Patricia Marks (1990: 174), adding that the bicycle 'changed patterns of courtship, marriage, and work' (184). H.G. Wells was alive to these possibilities and, having learned to ride a bicycle in June, he made cycling an important aspect of fiction such *The Wheels of Chance* (1896) and *The History of Mr Polly* (1910). Conservative commentators however lost few opportunities to ridicule cycling in general and women cyclists in particular. The *IPN* enjoyed the spectacle of a fight between rival New Women Mrs Alice Wackerbarth and Miss Florence Blyth, a tussle that began with a cycling collision and the abuse of Wackerbarth as 'a devil in trousers' by an on-looker, and ended with the intervention of the Home Secretary. Wackerbarth was fined £3 3s for unprovoked assault, but the fight dragged in PC Peter Eaton, who was charged with assault after apparently pushing Wackerbarth from her machine. Found guilty of technical assault and fined a shilling, Eaton was suspended from his post and only restored to it after Matthew Ridley, Asquith's successor, took a personal interest in the case (*IPN* 20/7, 17/8/95). *RN*'s politics may have been more radical than those of *Punch* or the *IPN*, but its views of female cyclists were no more enlightened when it jeered the 'Wobblers' who thronged Battersea Park, 'damsels in various stages of wobblement [. . .] more or less ridiculously striving to maintain a balance on the slippery steel steed' (9/6/95). The increasing visibility of the cyclist in Britain was symbolised by the 308 feet high Ferris Wheel, a precursor of the London Eye, which opened at Earl's Court on 6 July as part of the Empire of India exhibition. By the time it closed for the winter on 26 October, it had carried over 430,000 people and taken £23,410. 'I don't see what they want to build a great Wheel like that for,' says the bewildered Mr Wheeler in a *Punch* cartoon, only for his wife to reply, 'No. Why couldn't they have had a safety, and geared it up to any height they liked!' (5/10/95: 157).

Another new sport was lawn tennis, which had become popular in the 1880s. The Wimbledon championships were blessed with sunshine throughout late June and early July, with Wilfred Baddeley, a London solicitor, winning the men's title for the third time, and Charlotte Cooper being crowned ladies champion. Tennis, like the increasingly widespread Bridge, was largely a middle and upper class pastime and Wimbledon the preserve of amateurs. Cricket however had far greater social appeal, and throughout the summer, players with bats of varying sophistication stood before wooden or chalked stumps all over Britain. Lady Augusta Gregory got her servants to 'knock in' a new bat for her son, Robert, before taking it to Harrow for him; the less privileged improvised.

Hard and true pitches initially made it a batsman's summer, and bowlers toiled in the heat. Mr Punch was in Tennysonian mood. 'Centuries to the right of us, | Centuries to the left of us,' he crowed

(29/6/95: iv). Cricket's organisation was not yet as clear as football's, with the County Championship, which began on 6 May, only one part of a programme of matches between the north and the south, numerous professional and amateur elevens and, in the summer's social highlight, the Gentlemen versus Players contests at Lord's. There were no test matches, but the County Championship did have some new teams, with Derbyshire, Essex, Hampshire, Leicestershire, and Warwickshire making their debuts and the competition being formally recognised by the MCC for the first time. It was a curious enterprise, with the eventual champions, Surrey, and third placed Yorkshire playing twenty-six matches while most of their rivals played sixteen or eighteen.

Cricket's morally regenerative influence had been hailed even before the Wilde trials, but now the sport seemed to be a means of clearing the air after them. 'They are fond of cricket, and loathe reading poetry. That is what Englishmen consider goodness in boys,' mourns Esmé Amarinth (Hichens [1894] 1949: 156). The implication that cricket represented a regenerating force was strengthened by the *Star*'s front page juxtaposition of Wilde's conviction with a report on the Surrey batsman W.W. Reed's Testimonial Match at Kennington Oval (26/5/95). *Punch* meanwhile celebrated W.G. Grace's 'century of centuries', the 288 he scored for Gloucestershire against Somerset on 17 May being the hundredth time he had reached three figures (25/5/95: 241). David Cecil archly remarks that in the aftermath of Wilde's conviction, 'large numbers of unathletic males joined cricket clubs' to safeguard their moral reputations, apparently 'labour[ing] under the strange and mistaken impression that cricket and homosexuality were incompatible' (Cecil 120). Wilde himself had joked that he never played cricket because it required him to assume 'such indecent postures', but his friend Ives was a lifelong aficionado of the sport, belonging to J.M. Barrie's team, the Allahakberries, where he played alongside Jerome K. Jerome and Conan Doyle. The club's surprising name stemmed from a misunderstanding of the Arabic phrase, 'Allahu akbar', which Barrie thought meant 'heaven help us' instead of 'God is great'.

Gloucestershire's unimpeachably heterosexual W.G. Grace had not been part of the English triumph over Australia, but he remained the world's most famous cricketer, and his season got off to a rousing start on 9 May in a match for the MCC against Sussex. The MCC won a thrilling contest by nineteen runs, but what was most notable was the friendly rivalry between Grace, bear-like, bearded and, at almost forty-seven, the elder statesman of the English game, and Kumar Shri Ranjitsinhji, the Indian batsman making his debut for Sussex after attracting much attention at Cambridge as a cricketer and tennis player. The excellence of their performances in a showpiece encounter set the tone for the rest of the summer. The twenty-two-year-old Indian was a remarkable figure, with his exotic if somewhat vague origins – he was widely believed to be a prince (S. Wilde 1999: 61) – and his dazzling array of leg-side shots, late cuts and glances. Defying the technical orthodoxies of the day, Ranji dismantled attacks across England, though he was at his most danger-ous at Hove, where the small boundaries and batsman-friendly pitches made bowling a costly and frustrating business. Such was his impact that *Punch* hailed him alongside Grace and Archie MacLaren as 'men of one skill, though varying in race' (14/9/95: 130).

Bowlers received some coverage in the press, such as when Leicestershire's Arthur Woodcock humbled Surrey in early May, Essex's terrifyingly quick Charles Kortright, a rare example of an amateur bowler, frightened even the most accomplished players, or the hard-drinking England and Surrey paceman Tom Richardson topped the national averages with 239 wickets at 13.78, but it was batsmen, brave, upstanding and armed with only a slim willow-wand who were lionised. On 14 May, Surrey's Bobby Abel, a professional, scored 217 against Kortright's Essex, while three days later, Nottinghamshire piled up 726 against Sussex at Trent Bridge, defeating them by an innings and 378 runs. Three Nottinghamshire batsmen scored centuries, with England's Billy Gunn, who also played football for Notts County, contributing 219. Sussex's bowling remained weak throughout the season, but when C.B. Fry, fresh from his footballing and athletic heroics at Oxford, joined forces with Ranji, their batting often thrilled, notably in a victory against Middlesex at Lord's, where, in their first game together, the two men scored 117 in little over an hour (S. Wilde 1999: 60). MacLaren, one of England's Ashes heroes and captain of Lancashire, amassed 424 in Lancashire's 801 against Somerset at Taunton on 17–18 July. Beating Grace's 344 against Kent in 1876, and doing so on Grace's forty-seventh birthday, it remained the highest innings in first class cricket until the Australian, Bill Ponsford, scored 429 playing for Victoria against Tasmania in 1922–3 and has only once been surpassed on English soil.[4]

Despite these achievements, Grace dominated the headlines just as he did bowlers. When he made 288 against Somerset, his nearest rival, Nottinghamshire's Arthur Shrewsbury, had reached three figures only 41 times. The *Times* felt he deserved a knighthood, as did *Punch*, who saw him on a par with Irving (8/6/95: 274) and suggested he be made CB ('Companion of the Bat') (15/6/95: 282). His next feat was scoring 1,000 runs between 9–27 May, receiving a congratulatory letter from the Prince of Wales and determining the *DT* and the MCC to establish testimonial funds in his honour: these eventually realised £9,000 (Rae 1998: 396). The music-hall songwriter J. Harcourt-Smith composed 'Cricket' as a tribute (*IPN* 24/8/95). As the summer progressed, Grace scored 'a hundred in each innings of a match three times and on five occasions scored hundreds in three successive innings' (Rae 1998: 498). He topped the national batting averages with 2346 runs at 51; Ranji was fourth with 1775 at 49.30. Notionally an amateur, Grace certainly did not rely on his earnings as a Bristol doctor, for, as well as being rumoured to accept appearance fees and other inducements, he also signed a contract with Colman's Mustard, who used him as the embodiment of British beef in a successful advertising campaign: 'Colman's Mustard, Like Grace, Heads the Field'. Their picture of Grace emphasised his youthful vigour, for contrary to their illustration, his beard was now greying and somewhat straggly. Four hundred guests attended a banquet in his honour at Clifton's Victoria Rooms (only a stroll away from his house in Victoria Square) on 24 June. He was, as Simon Rae notes, 'a wholesome role-model in the year of Oscar Wilde's disgrace', his successes 'lift[ing] the spirits of every right-thinking paterfamilias up and down the country' (Rae 1999: 387).

Cricket seemed, therefore, to be one way of countering the predictions of those 'lugubrious psychologists' who had worried the *Times* in April. It was even one of 'healthy' pastimes recommended by Laura Chant in her lecture, 'Public Amusements: Their Use and Abuse', along with cycling, golf, and tennis (*Women's Signal Budget* 2/95: 59). However, there was one cricket enthusiast who went against the grain. In late 1894, Robert Coombes had walked to James Read's trial in his cricket whites. He was about to follow him into the dock.

A Dreadful Business

On 8 July, the week the Henley Regatta opened, the Gentlemen versus Players match at Lord's saw the Players dismissed for 231 before Grace and the England captain, Andrew Stoddart, replied with an impressive first wicket partnership. Stoddart was out for 71 shortly before the close of play, but Grace stood firm for 79, and left the field to prolonged applause; he was dismissed the following morning for 113. Two of his admirers were Robert (aged thirteen) and Nathaniel Coombes (aged twelve), who had come for the afternoon's play after murdering their mother, Harriet, and stealing £10 and their father's gold watch. 'Many of us doubtless saw them there,' wrote James Payn, 'applauding the proceedings with all the enthusiasm of youth' (*ILN* 3/8/95: 130). The boys spent their haul on 'jam tarts, sausage rolls, some new clothes and riding around the West End in hansom cabs' (*IPN* 27/7/95), though 10s was prudently kept to pay their rent. After the cricket, they went to the theatre before returning to home to 35 Cave Road, Plaistow. They continued to lead 'a somewhat fast life' (*IPN* 27/7/95) for nearly a week, aided by thirty-nine-year-old John Fox, a ship's steward who pawned their father's watch for them. He was 'a simple sort of man' said witnesses, and very much under Robert's control (*DN* 30/7/95).

When Mrs Coombes' sister-in-law went to Cave Road to see Harriet, Robert claimed she had gone to Liverpool to collect a legacy. Fox and the two boys were playing cards in the kitchen, a vile smell masked by their cigarettes. Mrs Burridge was unconvinced by their story, and told at last that Harriet was upstairs, burst open the bedroom door. There she found a horribly decomposed body, along with a dagger and blood-stained clothing, and called the police (*DN* 19/7/95). It appeared Robert killed his mother in revenge after she had beaten Nathaniel; the boys bought a knife and several days later, stabbed her in her bed, a scene illustrated in all its horror by the *IPN* (27/7/95).

The boys' father was a ship's steward and frequently abroad – he received news of his wife's death by telegram while in New York – and the brothers became known as 'very rude [. . .] but very intelligent' (*DN* 30/7/95). Robert was an excellent mandolin player and cricket fanatic who 'always wore something approaching cricketing costume' (*IPN* 3/8/95). According to his former headmaster, he was 'a very clever lad for his age' (*T* 18/9/95), but suffered from headaches and while on remand claimed to hear voices telling him to 'kill her and run away'. Teachers were told 'he must never be chastised on his head' (*T* 18/9/95); a medical examination revealed cranial scarring perhaps caused by birth instruments. He left school in December 1894 and was a labourer at the Thames Ironworks. Neighbours felt his mother had spoiled him.

The case was a shocking one, and between the discovery of Harriet Coombes' body and the trial of Robert and Fox in September – Nathaniel was a prosecution witness – two aspects of it were widely discussed. The first was the supposed insanity of Robert, who showed little sign of remorse or even awareness of the severity of his actions. On remand, he behaved excitably and was placed in a padded cell, where he confessed to missing his mandolin and his pet cats. A letter from prison depicted him leaping from the scaffold saying 'Goodbye, here goes nothing', and contained a will that bequeathed £60,000 to his father and £300 to every warder in Holloway. 'I think I will get hung,' he told a clergyman in a letter that granted him £5,000, 'but I don't care as long as they will give me a good breakfast before they hang me' (*IPN* 28/9/95).

Prosecuted by C.F. Gill, Robert was swiftly found guilty of murder, but was adjudged to have committed the crime in one of his intermittent periods of insanity. He was sentenced to be detained in Holloway at Her Majesty's Pleasure. Fox was found not guilty of any involvement in the killing, though it seemed unlikely he could have spent a week in a small terraced house at the height of summer without becoming aware of a rotting body.

For many commentators however, the case's significance lay in Robert's preferred reading matter, which reawakened debates about cheap, working class literature that went back to the 'Newgate novels' controversy of the 1830s. According to the *DN*, he had been reading a 'dreadful' called *The Last Shot* before committing the murder (30/7/95). 'How far madness was the impelling cause, and how far his act was due to the vile, sensational books which seem to have been his favourite study, may perhaps be in some doubt,' said the *Times* (18/9/95), a view pondered at length. The Wilde case had dwelled on the corrupting influence of J.-K. Huysmans, *Dorian Gray* and the *Chameleon*. Reviewing works by Pater and J.A. Symonds under the title 'Latter-Day Pagans', the *QR* commented that humanism and pagan sympathies rarely led to happiness. '[I]t is melancholy to remember how many have followed [these authors] along slippery paths [. . .] towards the great deep' (7/95: 58), it observed, noting the sinister sway of works such as *The Renaissance* and *Greek Studies* on those susceptible to their teachings. What Andrew Lang termed 'the unmentionable Messalinas of "the New Fiction"' were also seen as eroding public morals (*ILN* 3/8/95: 141), as were problem plays. Machen was impatient with the whole discussion, sending a sarcastic letter to the *Westminster Gazette* on 9 March that identified *Hamlet* and *King Lear* as 'demoralising' and pointed out the 'morbid and revolting' habits of Samuel Pickwick (Gawsworth 2005: 131). Blind to the ironies of its position – it had depicted the murder with ghoulish zeal and had spent much of the year advertising the fifty penny numbers of *Charles Peace; or, The Adventures of a Notorious Burglar*, offering a portrait of Peace and 'a splendid coloured plate' with issues one and two – the *IPN* raged against 'the demoralising influence of pernicious literature' (27/7/95) at regular intervals. The content and role of fiction received further analysis in the *Bookman*, which in a review of George Moore's *Celibates* commented, 'there are no restrictive laws [. . .] against a book that tortures every sensitive mind, that wounds, that brings no opiate at all, and but little promise of future relief' (7/95: 114). Reviewing Richard Marsh's *Mrs Musgrave – and her Husband*, the *Athenaeum* felt 'hereditary homicidal mania is not a promising field for romance': the novel was 'one of the books better

Figure 10. The *Illustrated Police News* treated the Plaistow Murder with characteristic insensitivity, 27 July 1895.

left unwritten' (27/7/95: 124). At least the sixth *YB* had largely avoided controversy, Bennett's 'A Letter Home' receiving praise for its tactful use of naturalist techniques. The delirious gynophobia of R. Murray Gilchrist's 'The Crimson Weaver', which took to extremes *Dorian Gray*'s 'scarlet threads of life' and 'sanguine labyrinth of passion' may however have turned heads (or stomachs) had it been set somewhere other than a nightmarish fairyland. Gilchrist utilised Poe's elaborate, poetically-inflected vocabulary and defiant anti-realism in a pastiche of the medieval quest romance that literalised *King Lear*'s 'But to the girdle do the Gods inherit, | Beneath is all the fiends''. However, its fantastic setting and the obscurity of its author limited any offence it may have caused.

It was against this background that the public read about the Coombes brothers' library of penny dreadfuls, books with titles such as *The Witch of Fermoyle*, *The Bogus Brokers* and *The Crimson Cloak* (*DN* 30/7/95). John Springhall points out the collection was largely 'harmless stage-Irish, Gothic and supernatural stor[ies]' (Springhall 1998: 91), but those unfamiliar with such material identified a simplistic causal relationship between dreadfuls and crime. Anxiety regarding dreadfuls was but one aspect of a wider concern with the effect of literature (in its widest sense) upon the nation's morals, but most commentators examined the problem as if readerships were neatly stratified rather than pointing out that the questions being asked of literature and crime were essentially the same whether they were applied to penny dreadfuls or Pater. In March, *Blackwood's* noted the children of the poor were increasingly 'prone to acts of wanton mischief', their speech and behaviour being characterised by 'rudeness, incivility, indecency and profanity' (3/95: 483–9). Now their reading habits were blamed, with Hugh Chisholm in full cry in the *FR*. 'Coming so soon after the exposure of the abominable immoralities of an accomplished producer of non-moral literature for the upper circles of the reading world,' he began, 'it is not surprising that there should be an outcry against such publications as these, which incite a less cultivated section of the public to ever more dangerous crimes' (7–12/95: 765). The Home Secretary, was powerless to intervene, noting on 16 August that since an 1888 Home Office inquiry had found no demonstrable link between penny dreadfuls and crime, books could only be banned under the existing classifications of blasphemy, obscenity and sedition. Chisholm suggested providing children in Board Schools with superior books and increasing the amount of moral training they received. Penny editions of writers who were out of copyright would make the new century a readers' paradise, he felt.

Not all were convinced that reading what Ridley termed 'quasi-criminal

literature' produced actual criminals. Even *Blackwood's* was inconsistent, with 'The Looker-On' confessing his lack of faith in the idea that
'the dreadful little boy [. . .] who killed his mother' was 'moved to that
act by the Bloody Barber or any other production of the cheap literature
of crime' (12/95: 914). James Payn, whose own fiction was 'marked by
a love of sensational plot and excessively melodramatic complication'
(Sutherland 2009: 500), sided in part with Chisholm, arguing that Board
Schools 'should give their attention to inculcating in their pupils kindness to their fellow creatures and dumb animals'; if they did so, they
'need not be afraid of the influence of a few contemptible periodicals'.
More aggressive action was unnecessary, for 'a crusade against "penny
dreadfuls" would be a ludicrous expenditure of force and not very easy
of accomplishment, like pursuing a wasp with horse soldiers' (*ILN*
31/8/95: 258). *Punch* supported him:

> Ah! thousands on Shockers have fed full,
> And yet *not* of crimes got a head-full.
>   Let us put down the vile,
>   Yet endeavour the while,
> To be *just* to the poor 'Penny Dreadful'! (7/9/95: 109)

A few weeks later, Payn agreed with W.T. Stead that reading is always
better than not reading. 'It is not those with morbid imaginations who
commit atrocities,' he argued, 'but those with no imaginations at all'
(28/9/95: 418).

Pornography was a different though related matter. Its nature and
contents received only clandestine discussion, but it was difficult to
avoid. The advertising columns of the *IPN* were a rich source of illicit
material, offering booklets on family planning, abortifacients such as
'Dr Davis's Famous Female Pills – No Irregularity or Obstruction Can
Resist Them' (19/1/95), as well as fiction and pornographic photographs
(100 'photos from life' in 'different positions' cost 1s 3d, 30/3/95).
Confessions of a Lady's Maid (1s 6d) jostled for attention with *Gay
Girls of the Ballet* (1s 2d), the hoary anti-Catholic propaganda of
Maria Monk (1s 3d), and the works of Zola (unpriced) (*IPN* 28/9/95)
Typically, the paper also reported the arrests of those responsible for
the production and sale of goods it advertised. In February, Howard
Hogben, 'a respectable-looking middle-aged man' was sentenced to
twenty-one months hard labour for selling what the judge described as
'abominable articles'; these the paper glossed as 'indecent photographs'
and 'indiarubber goods intended to be used for an immoral purpose'
(*IPN* 19/1/95, 2/2/95). In July, John Jones (age sixty-two) offered what
he termed 'spicy pictures' to a passer-by in St Martin's Lane, London,

who turned out to be a policeman. 'By jingo, it's a fair cop,' said Jones, who received three months hard labour (*IPN* 13/7/95). In August, police began an investigation of Percy & Company, based in the Strand, eventually arresting William Walker after he sold them thirty photographs for £1, eleven of which were judged indecent. Walker denied obscenity, claiming the pictures were 'artists' studies from abroad' sold as aids to painters who increasingly worked from photographs rather than from models. The court conceded the truth of this practice, though was unconvinced by Walker's claim that 'some very bad ones' had got into the batch by mistake (*BDP* 16/10/95). Despite the authorities' efforts, and the constant crusades of the NVA, pornography, contraceptives, aphrodisiacs and abortifacients remained readily available, sometimes sold alongside dreadfuls in the back-street emporia memorably dramatised in Conrad's *The Secret Agent* (1907).

The topic of 'demoralising literature' resurfaced throughout the year, spilling over into wider discussions of the school curriculum and, in a lengthy piece in the *FR* by Thomas Case, Oxford's Waynflete Professor of Moral and Metaphysical Philosophy, women's encounters with the classics. It was one thing for men to study Juvenal and Aristophanes, he argued, but 'disgusting that they should hear and study obscenities' in female company. 'A man may hear and read many things which a woman should not,' he opined, pointing out how mixed classes would horrify 'respectable parents' and prompt the university to 'degenerate' into a 'Middlesex Club'. 'It is a lamentable fact,' he wrote, 'that girls now read books which would make their mothers blush' (July–Dec: 96–9). He seemed oblivious to Mary Wollstonecraft's argument in *A Vindication of the Rights of Woman* (1792) that the right to study the classics was a cornerstone of women's equality.

Arthur Symons's *London Nights* was clearly intended for a male readership, being, as Laurel Brake has said of his later editorial work, 'full of male discourse, masculine constructions of women, and misogyny' (Brake 1994:151). It was however another work to be caught up in debates about the content of literature and the moral standing of authors. The collection had been rejected by Heinemann and Lane, whose readers, Le Gallienne and Davidson, had worried about the poems' sexual content. Davidson recommended publication, but while he found Symons's 'dexterity [. . .] very notable', he was less impressed by the 'mere and sheer libidinous desire' that produced 'the most charming lines in the most cold-blooded inferior mood' (Symons 1989: 109). 'Ten years ago I suppose it would have been to risk a sojourn in Holloway to publish [. . .] "White Heliotrope"', Davidson remarked, a comment which 'may have scared Lane' (Sloan 1995: 115). Le

Gallienne, who had encouraged the publication of Egerton's *Keynotes* and other controversial works, was wary too, though he found aesthetic criteria on which to reject the volume. On 15 January he told Lane in a note accompanying his report, 'I wish it were more favourable, as you know, I have nothing but friendship for him and his work [. . .] but they are not good poems' (JLA).

When Lane declined *London Nights*, or when its author, piqued by the treatment of Beardsley, withdrew it from consideration (Nelson 2000: 63), Symons joined forces with Leonard Smithers, a former solicitor with considerable experience in '*sub-rosa* publishing enterprise[s]' having dealt in pornography, 'gallantiana', and forgeries as well as in legitimate rare books (Mendes 1993: 16). Wilde called him 'the most learned erotomaniac in Europe' (*WCL* 924), while his former business partner, H.S. Nichols, preferred to describe him as 'a lustful, lascivious and shameful satyr' (Mendes 1993: 17). When Nichols and Smithers parted company, Smithers decided to become a publisher, specialising in contemporary literature too daring for mainstream houses. *London Nights*, issued in an edition of 500 copies, was his first venture into contemporary poetry, and such was its reception that he could have been forgiven for returning to the murky underworld of his 'Erotika Biblion Society' imprint.

Reflecting on the book's reception in the preface to its second edition in 1897, Symons recalled it was 'received by the English press with a singular unanimity of abuse', chiefly because journalists had confused artistic and moral considerations and attacked *London Nights* 'not because it is bad art, but because it is bad morality' (Symons 1924: 165). Esmé Amarinth had asked of Symons, 'Why are minor poets so artless and why do they fancy they are so wicked?' (Hichens [1894] 1949: 135). Now the question was put more seriously. Some reviews noted the book only in passing – 'erotic poems of little originality,' said one (*MP* 19/8/95) – but others, such as Symons's regular employer the *SR*, were actively aggressive. The book revealed 'elaborate, artificial, insincere' passion, it began, lashing out at Symons's 'cool, deliberate cult of sensations', his 'morbid sensuality' and his willingness 'to lift the curtain of the *lupanar*', a reference to the most notorious of Pompeii's brothels. 'In lack of reticence, of decency, Mr Symons has nothing to learn from anyone,' the review continued, yet in the last analysis he was 'merely posing, anxious to keep up a much more abandoned sensualist than he is' (10/8/95: 177). 'Posing' was a loaded word in the wake of Wilde's libel case, but its use here suggested a difference of opinion between the poet, who pictured or evoked experiences that were artistic productions, and the critic, who insisted on regarding them as autobiographical.

What the latter saw as an attempt to present 'exceptional depravity' was, for Symons, another variation on Wilde's 'vice and virtue are to the artist materials for an art' (*WCW* 17); he did draw on his tempestuous relationship with Lydia, a dancer at the Empire, but the Bianca of the ten poem sequence in *London Nights* should not be considered a mimetic transcription of the woman with whom he enjoyed passionate trysts beneath the crucifix in his Fountain Court rooms. Smithers's regular customers would have found the poems flaccid fare, but less worldly readers responded to them with disgust.

The review which grieved Symons most appeared in the *PMG* and was headed 'Pah!' 'Mr Arthur Symons is a very dirty-minded man, and his mind is reflected in the puddle of its bad verses,' it began, going on to say that the poet's life resembled a pigsty. 'Every woman he pays to meet him, he tells us, is desirous to kiss his lips; our boots too are desirous, but of quite another part of him, for quite another purpose' (*PMG* 2/9/95). The brief review dismissed and insulted Symons's work and everything it stood for in an unapologetic declaration of pugnacious philistinism; Symons demanded an apology, but lacked the resources necessary to sue the newspaper. The last word went to the *Leeds Mercury* which conceded that though *London Nights* contained 'delightful bits of verse-making', its author's 'decadent sympathies seem out of place' in the language of Milton and Wordsworth (16/11/95). As Symons had realised when he left England in the days following Wilde's conviction and the collapse of his relationship with Lydia, France was far more sympathetic to new forms of art.

En Vacances

Harland was exaggerating when he said 600 men decamped to France following Wilde's trials, but there was nonetheless a significant English-speaking presence there in the summer of 1895. Unkindly described by Malcolm Bradbury as 'natural Parisians who could not quite summon up the cross-channel fare' (Bradbury [1976] 1991:174), male writers and artists such as Symons, Smithers, Beardsley, Sickert, Crackanthorpe, Harland, Dowson and Charles Conder had strong Gallic sympathies; most spoke fluent French and several were well known in French artistic circles. Symons in particular fulfilled a quasi-ambassadorial role, organising Verlaine's visit to England in 1893 and befriending writers and artists such as Mallarmé.

While John Lane holidayed in Padstow, keen to put some distance between himself and the louche figures associated with the *YB*, and

Harland travelled on to Aix-les-Bains to be 'douched and swindled' (Harland 1895: 131), young radicals enjoyed a respite from cricket reports and hostile reviewers. France was by no means an unproblematic oasis, but it offered freedoms Britain did not. The cost of living was also lower, another significant attraction for impecunious bohemians.

There was a fine line between the visitor and the exile, as Bosie Douglas discovered while in Le Havre in late July. Having bought a small sailing-ship, 'something between a yacht and a fishing-smack', he hired 'two young sailors' as crew. Within days, the *Journal de Havre* 'accused him of corrupting the youth of the town', leading Bosie to leave first for Paris, and then for Naples and Sorrento (Croft-Cooke 1963: 134–5). It was here, in August, that he wrote 'Rondeau', a lament for Wilde built around the mournfully reiterated phrase, 'If he were here'. On 15 August the *Mercure de France* had printed a discussion of the Wilde affair, 'Défense d'Oscar Wilde' by Hugues Rebell, an inflammatory article which attacked the Solicitor-General, Queen Victoria and the general Puritanism of the English. It also suggested the only way to free Wilde was to burn down Pentonville: Rebell did not know Wilde had been transferred to Wandsworth on 4 July. The article pleased Douglas, who wrote to More Adey telling him to buy multiple copies and send one to Frank Harris, but it was undeniably extreme and lacked an insider's perspective. Having contacted the *Mercure*'s editor, Bosie began work on an article addressing this, one in which he proposed to reproduce Wilde's letters to him in the wider causes of defending homosexual relationships and settling old scores.

Before embarking for the continent, Beardsley, Symons and Smithers discussed founding a new quarterly magazine to replace the *YB* as the standard-bearer for radical art. Beardsley suggested entitling it *The Savoy*, a name linked in many minds with a luxury hotel and Wildean excesses. The project galvanised him, and once in Dieppe, he worked on an illustrated pornographic fantasy, *Under the Hill*, and composed a poem, 'The Three Musicians', which appeared in *The Savoy*'s first issue. He also spent much of his time gambling on the *Petits Chevaux*, a 'species of horse-racing slot-machine at the Casino' (Colvin 1998: 77), appreciating what Symons termed 'the sense of frivolous things caught at the moment of suspended life' (Symons 1966: 8) and further endangering his fragile health in drunken escapades with Smithers and Conder.

Symons's account of the summer, 'Dieppe: 1895' appeared in the first *Savoy* alongside Beardsley's poem. It begins, 'I went to Dieppe this summer with the intention of staying from Saturday to Monday. Two months afterwards I began to wonder, with a very mild kind of surprise, why I had not yet returned to London' (Symons 1918: 227). A letter to his friend and fellow poet Herbert Horne in early September summarised his activities neatly, though without mentioning the proposed magazine. 'As for England, I have almost forgotten that it exists,' he said proudly. The summer had been spent writing verse, having his portrait painted by Jacques-Emile Blanche (who also painted Beardsley), meeting minor nobles, 'lounging about the Casino, and altogether having the most amusing and irresponsible holiday I have had for a long time' (Symons 1989: 111). The letter and essay show Symons 'flaunting his independence in the most elementary way,' says John Stokes, 'insisting upon his freedom to linger, to ignore regulated time' (Stokes 1996: 134). For once Symons was able to play the leisured connoisseur, 'turning the map of Dieppe into a personal menu' (134–5) and taking a break from journalistic commissions. His bibliographers list only ten items, mostly brief reviews, between 6 July and 21 September, though he did find time to squash Edwin Arnold's new book, *The Tenth Muse*, which celebrated Ephemera or 'the modern press'. 'There is nothing in [his] new book of verse which could easily be mistaken for poetry,' Symons said (*A* 3/8/95: 151), a mild rebuke beside the *SR*'s, which judged Arnold's verse 'the plaintive bleating of a toy lamb. He is a past master of claptrap, of the turgid, the bombastic, and the rhetorical' (28/9/95: 417). The message was clear if casuistical: Symons's work was in the service of Art rather than Mammon, and when he wrote for the press it was as a poet, not a hack. *The Savoy* would be built upon similar principles.

The Dieppe sojourn had its raucous moments. According to Conder, Smithers was accompanied 'by a harlot or two – big, florid, noisy creatures' (Weintraub 1967: 144) who caused uproar in the Casino. The most surprising event however was the arrival of Sanger's travelling circus. Hubert Crackanthorpe, holidaying after the publication of the generally well-received *Sentimental Studies* in July, a book he dedicated to Harland (who felt he 'strain[ed] a little too hard, a little too visibly, for the *mot juste*' (Harland 1895:141)), stepped in as the circus's interpreter. According to J. Lewis May, he rode off on an elephant at five o' clock one morning and did not return for four days (May 1936: 82–3). During this time, he drove wagons through the night, and slept alongside the elephant-keepers and their beasts, an adventure he recollected in his fictionalised diary 'Bread and the Circus' in October's *YB*.

While Beardsley played the slot-machines, other writers and artists spent the summer in varied ways. Conrad went yachting off the Dutch coast, telling a friend in a letter of 24 August, 'We lived mainly in oilskins and all our various guests [. . .] were very seasick' (Conrad 1983: 239). Conan Doyle was in Maloja, Switzerland, writing *Rodney Stone* at the rate of 1–2,000 words per day (Lellenberg 2007: 356). Henry James had gone to Torquay, where he remained until early November working on stories that became 'Glasses', 'The Figure in the Carpet'(1896) and *The Spoils of Poynton* (1898). At the end of August, he received £100 from Ellen Terry as an option on a one-act play, 'Mrs Gracedew', she had invited him to write for her in the aftermath of the *Domville* fiasco. James was flattered, but the play was never produced. Shaw wrote a long causerie about the year's theatre in the *SR* (27/7/95) in which he again attacked Pinero and praised *Guy Domville*, though he suggested James had more in common with the age of George Eliot and T.H. Huxley than the 'invigorating strife' of Wagner and Ibsen (*OT* 195). He spent much of his summer with Sidney and Beatrice Webb in Monmouth – having learned to ride a bicycle in April, he now explored the Welsh roads on his 'new toy' with more daring than skill and suffered several accidents (Shaw 1965: 539, 549, 558–60). He was a fanatical proselyte for the new sport, advising William Archer to buy his son a cycle with inflatable rather than solid tyres (540). In mid-August, Thomas Hardy was in Dorchester proof-reading the next instalment of *Hearts Insurgent*, then running in the American *Harper's New Monthly Magazine*, and 'chained [. . .] to the drudgery of misplaced commas & new spellings of my dry old words' (Hardy 1980: 85). Lady Gregory taught herself to type, watched her son Robert play cricket and helped a family friend stuff the 10lb pike he had caught on her estate (Gregory 1996: 79). Having been tormented by a 'blackguard drum and fife band' (Gissing 1994: 5) for months, Gissing needed a holiday, but Sunrise Terrace, Gorleston near Great Yarmouth, turned out to be another circle of hell. After weeks of drought, the Gissings set off on the rainy morning of 19 July. The weather remained poor for the next fortnight. 'In night very heavy rain, and to-day scarcely any sunshine,' Gissing noted on 24 July. 'The boy digging bravely on the sands' (Gissing 1978: 380). Two days later, Gissing's three-year-old son was feverish, and the family were in 'great discomfort here in lodgings; wretched cooking' (381). Although Walter soon recovered, Gissing became embroiled in violent rows with Mrs Bunn, his landlady, when he tried to abort the 'terrible holiday' after a fortnight. Mr and Mrs Bunn locked the Gissings out of their house and threatened to keep their belongings until they paid for the three weeks of their original booking. 'A tragic-ludicrous scene' ensued before they escaped to more pleasant accommodation. Even then the family was plagued by fleas and was glad to return to Epsom on 3 August, though they arrived to find that their servant had left and a thunderstorm had flattened all their sunflowers (381–2).

William Rothenstein's summer also had its disappointments. Visiting

Swinburne and his guardian, the 'absurdly vain' Theodore Watts in Putney on 4 August, the young artist spent the afternoon enjoying their many Pre-Raphaelite treasures, and listening to views on Whistler, Pater and Wilde, whom Watts termed the 'harlequin' who had supplied aestheticism with its '*coup de grâce*'. The following week, Rothenstein was back at The Pines to begin a portrait of Swinburne, but the relationship was cut short when he admitted to Watts that he had once made indiscreet references to Rossetti during a visit to Edmond de Goncourt and that these were quoted in a review of Goncourt's *Journal*. 'This is the kind of thing that gets into the newspapers,' said his host, suggesting that in the circumstances, lunch with Swinburne was inappropriate. Rothenstein left at once, and never saw either man again (Rothenstein 94–6).

For many working class Britons, a holiday took the form of a day's excursion to the sea or countryside, the type of 'spree' depicted in Gissing's *The Nether World* (1889) and Somerset Maugham's *Liza of Lambeth* (1897). One such trip to Hackney's London Fields, 'frequented by the riff-raff of London' (Weinreb 486) ended in a pitched battle between around 140 excursionists and eighty or more gypsies after an argument over hiring horses became violent (*IPN* 17/8/95). Such incidents again showed the aggressive undercurrents of metropolitan life and the thin ice of its decorum; several gypsies, 'part of the horde who infest the vicinity of Epping Forest' received three month prison sentences (*IPN* 23/11/95). However, the *IPN* found the battle of London Fields less fascinating than the continued misadventures of 'toffs' and 'swells', and treated its readers to a lengthy account of a police raid on the Palace Club in London's Jermyn Street. The Palace was a venue for drinking, dancing and sexual assignation; open from midnight until 4 a.m., it soon drew complaints from local people and was closed by the Police – it had only opened on Derby Day.

The Palace's owners appeared in court in early August. The quartet comprised Lily Moore, who had a decade's worth of convictions for running brothels in Nottingham and London, Henry Marshall, Douglas Filgate, who had run the 'Mandoline' and 'New Mandoline' in Baker Street (closed by injunction) and the 'notorious' 'Spooferies' in Maiden Lane, and Raleigh Hyman, who at the age of twenty-three, had already gambled away a £1,000 legacy and was now the personable face of criminal enterprise. When police arrived at the Palace on 18 July, they found a 'Knight of the Garter' party in full swing, with music, dancing, 'lounging', and garters for sale. Many 'disorderly women' were present (*Standard* 10/8/95). The owners were convicted of running a disorderly house, and received heavy fines (Filgate's was £150), as well as being bound over to keep the peace at £100 per head (or £200 in Filgate's case) or risk three months in jail (*RN* 11/8/95; *IPN* 17/8/95). The following week, the *IPN* reported further scrutiny of West End nightclubs, hinting at 'sensational revelations' of 'particularly outrageous [. . .] early morning orgies' (24/8/95), though these did not materialise until a raid on the Umberto Club in Soho made the front page on 21 December. The provinces had a gluttonous appetite for tales of metropolitan depravity, and the scandalous behaviour of the well-to-do remained very much in the public consciousness. The Palace case was reported as far afield as Liverpool, Cardiff, Worcester and York, but whether those drinking and dancing at the Palace really were socially privileged mattered less than the image of them circulated in news coverage. The *IPN*'s sketch of a monocled fellow in evening dress and caddish moustache embodied the music hall stereotype of the 'swell' associated with George 'Champagne Charlie' Leybourne, drinking champagne, smoking cigars and enjoying the attentions of two anatomically-improbable young sirens as the police burst in. It seems unlikely that the Palace was anywhere near as sophisticated as this image suggested, but the misdeeds of their 'social betters' titillated the public, who forgave the *IPN* for blurring reportage and entertainment.

Richard Le Gallienne preferred more discreet sensual abandon and holidayed in Lynemouth with the Danish journalist Julie Norregard. Officially still in mourning for his wife, Mildred, who had died the summer before, Le Gallienne had enjoyed a prolonged flirtation with George Egerton, whom he addressed as 'Sphinx' and 'Dear Little Witch-Woman' despite her 'horrid glasses'. He then turned his attentions to Norregard, whom he had met in December. They quickly became lovers with Le Gallienne judging her 'a *naughty* girl – soft lights, vermouth, and your own white limbs. Fie!' (Whittington-Egan 1960: 275). After several furtive and unsatisfactory nights together in country inns, the couple enjoyed a delightful fortnight in Devon, though the cost of the trip meant Le Gallienne had to borrow money from his father on returning to London. Le Gallienne and Norregard married in February 1897, but the relationship did not last, and they separated six years later.

Marie Corelli was enjoying another form of fulfilment, having at last completed the novel on which she had worked for five hours a day since January. The manuscript was 1,071 pages long, and concluded:

Finished 15th August 1895
Marie Corelli
To thee O God and my Saviour Christ
I commend this work as all work I may do or have done. Amen.
Ave Maria! (Masters 1978: 135)

She at once began negotiations with Methuen over the publication of a 6s edition, and stood poised to profit from the revolution in the literary marketplace that followed the collapse of the library monopoly.

Literary discussion continued throughout the summer. The *Bookman*'s 'New Writers' feature profiled Wells, noting the warm reception accorded *The Time Machine* and looking forward to his new novel, *The Wonderful Visit*. The former had certainly been applauded, with Heinemann's marketing campaign quoting endorsements from the *Westminster Gazette*, the *Referee* and *Black and White* that proclaimed Wells the equal of Poe and superior to Jules Verne. What the *Bookman* did not explore however was the extent to which Wells was praised by journals of compromised objectivity; the *National Observer* would hardly attack a novel it had run as a serial, and the *SR* was unlikely to undermine its own columnists (though it could savage a freelance such as Symons). Its characterisation of Wells as 'a writer of distinct and individual talent' (20/7/95: 87) was borne out by his subsequent career, but it nonetheless showed relationships between authors, critics and publishers were growing increasingly complicated. This was not the simple 'log-rolling' of Le Gallienne praising his stable-mates but the emergence of subtler interconnected interests. When the *PMG* gave the novel extravagant praise the following month, hailing Wells as 'a writer of the highest talent' (10/9/95), cynics could be forgiven for remembering his recent employment as the paper's theatre critic or that he had published a number of articles and stories in it since 1893, collecting them as *Select Conversations with an Uncle (Now Extinct)* (1895) and *Certain Personal Matters* (1897). Indeed, Wells identified the *PMG* as likely to show 'friendly interest' in a letter to Heinemann of 14 May (Wells 1998: 240–1). Such quibbles aside, Wells's novel was bracingly original, both in the economy of its expression, which showed that single volume status did not necessarily lead to inferior literary quality, and in its vision of the future, which gave evolutionists a timely jolt by envisioning a world in which humanity had become extinct, superseded by the brutal subterranean Morlocks and the child-like and helpless Eloi of the planet's surface. Wells did not make the allegorical implications of this division explicit, but those who knew of his socialist sympathies had little difficulty mapping the place that London would become in 802,701 onto the inequalities of the present. Wells sent a copy of his 'very little book' to Huxley, who had taught him at the Royal College of Science (Smith 1986: 48).

Alongside Wells, the *Bookman* interviewed A.L. Humphreys, the manager of Hatchard's. 'The novel is the book of the future,' he said, noting the vogue for Anthony Hope, whose 'brilliant dialogue [. . .]

exactly suit[s] the taste of Mayfair', the lack of interest in Dickens and Thackeray, and a recent visit from Rosebery, freed from the cares of office and mourning that Burney's *Evelina* was not better known (8/95: 141). The Liberal leader, much revived and sleeping better later confessed a fondness for Hope's work, though whether he preferred the frothy romance of *The Dolly Dialogues* to the fantastical political intrigues of *The Prisoner of Zenda* was not revealed (*ILN* 19/10/95: 487). Humphreys also praised W.H. Mallock, who had come to prominence with *The New Republic* in 1878, but the *Athenaeum*, reviewing his three-volume *The Heart of Life*, was less convinced as to his merits. 'Charming and often brilliant,' Mallock was nonetheless repetitive and unsuited to work longer than 'a sketch or a suggestion'. 'Among the writers of fiction to-day he is hardly to be seriously counted' (20/7/95: 92).

Elsewhere in the literary world, writers associated with decadence, however loosely, enjoyed mixed receptions. The *Athenaeum* was unimpressed by Hichens's *An Imaginative Man*, a novel it found 'dreary', 'preposterous' and 'fully justif[ying] the truculent methods of Max Nordau,' not least because of its overblown climax, in which Denison, the 'imaginative man' throws himself off the Sphinx when he discovers his wife is 'normal' instead of mysterious (17/8/95: 219). Both the *SR* and the *World* found the novel an advance on *The Green Carnation* however. 'The decline of Mr Benson continues,' shrugged the *SR*, confronted by E.F. Benson's *The Judgement Books*, a novel explicitly compared to *Dorian Gray* by the *Athenaeum* when judging it 'simply tiresome' (14/9/95: 351). Ernest Dowson's short story collection, *Dilemmas*, was barely noticed. In such a climate, *The Savoy*'s defiance of popular taste seemed at once thrillingly provocative and financially foolhardy.

Summer Gleanings

The Gissings' misfortunes occurred during a rare break in the hot weather, which returned with a vengeance for most of August. Cricketers looked to the heavens, knowing that thundery showers created 'sticky' wickets and allowed bowlers to gain revenge for their toil earlier in the season. Gloucestershire's Charlie Townsend, an eighteen-year-old prodigy from Clifton College, took 122 wickets in the last eleven games of the year with his all-but unplayable leg-breaks. Equally difficult to face was London's main fish market, Billingsgate, which was unbearable in the heat. Many tons of condemned fish had to be dumped in the Thames. Such were the extremes of weather that the Metropolitan Police considered introducing summer and winter uniforms.

As well as tennis, cricket, golf, and impromptu bathing, the heat also encouraged ballooning and parachuting. While some New Women rode bicycles, Alma Beaumont went one better, leaping out of a balloon 800 feet above Leytonstone and parachuting into a suburban garden whose startled occupants 'made her a cup of tea and showed her every kindness' (*IPN* 17/8/95). Other aeronauts were less fortunate. Neil Campbell struck a chimney in Horsham and fell from the basket, breaking his thigh and suffering serious head injuries (*IPN* 20/7/95), while Annie Bassett, who had entertained bank holiday crowds throughout the land in the course of thirty parachute jumps, was killed at Peterborough when her parachute failed and she plummeted over 200 feet. The Peterborough coroner felt 'no useful purpose is served by these senseless exhibitions' and called for them to be made illegal (*Berrow's Worcester Journal* 10/8/95). The growing popularity of ballooning was examined by Baden Baden-Powell, 'Lieutenant, Scots Guards' and brother of Robert, in his 'A Trip Heavenward: Ballooning as a Sport', which appeared in *Blackwood's* in November. Away from the public gaze, Percy Pilcher, a lecturer in Marine Engineering at Glasgow University, experimented with a hang-glider, the *Bat*, which, building on the work of the German aviation pioneer Otto Lillenthal, managed a short downhill glide near Cardross and inspired Pilcher to begin building a superior craft, the *Hawk*, that winter (Frater 2008: 33).

Back in February, *The Importance of Being Earnest* opened in a snowstorm. On 10 August, the first of 'Mr Robert Newman's Promenade Concerts' at London's Queen's Hall had to compete with a thunderstorm of astonishing violence. The meteorologist G.J. Symons told the *Times* that between 9.32 p.m. and 10.05 p.m., he had counted 158 lightning flashes, with twenty-nine between 9.45 p.m. and 9.50 p.m. The rain lasted only eighteen minutes, but was torrential. Against this, Newman's chosen 'lightning' conductor, the popular Henry Wood, led a mixed programme that lasted for three hours. Aimed at broadening the musical knowledge and taste of Londoners, and priced at a shilling per concert or a guinea for the whole season, the first 'Prom' included an orchestrated version of Chopin's Polonaise in A, a pair of Liszt's Hungarian Rhapsodies, excerpts from Bizet's *Carmen*, the overture to Ambroise Thomas's *Mignon*, and, in a British premiere, the 'chromatic concert waltzes' from Cyrill Kistler's opera, *Eulenspielgel*. Encores included 'Father O'Flynn' and 'Every Jolly Jack', but the night was largely ignored by the London press, and only *LWN* covered it in any detail. The *Times* reviewed only one Prom, though by the end of the summer, Newman and Wood's educational mission had impressed the *IPN* which found Wood 'admirable' and fare such as a selection from Verdi's *Il Travatore* 'good and attractive' (7/9/95). The press did however report in some detail on the state of the grouse moors prior to the opening of the shooting season on 12 August.

The summer had its darker side too. While Londoners listened to Wood and his orchestra, Henry Wright (aged thirty-five), a Mansfield labourer, murdered his landlady, Mary Reynolds (aged forty-eight), her two sons and her three-year-old grandson before setting fire to her house, injuring other lodgers. His act was apparently triggered by her scornful rejection of his marriage proposal. The *Derby Mercury* reported Mrs Reynolds had been 'disembowelled' and 'most horribly mutilated' (14/8/95) in a frenzied assault, another example of the increasing (or gratuitous) frankness of news journalism. Indeed, so explicit was the report that the *IPN* included it, verbatim if uncredited, in its own account of the tragedy (17/8/95). Wright attempted suicide but recovered to be tried for murder in December. He was sentenced to death (*T* 5/12/95).

The death of Friedrich Engels from throat cancer on 5 August saw the *Times* offer a brief summary of his life augmented with comment from the *Petite République*. The French newspaper maintained that 'He has seen the grain sown by him burst upward [. . .] It is not as a conquered man doubting his work that he disappears, but as one who has triumphed' (5/8/95). By such a rhetorical move, the *Times* implied Socialism was a largely European phenomenon; the word 'Communist' was conspicuous by its absence throughout the obituary. Considerations of Engels's legacy were lengthier and more insightful in the radical press, with correspondents of *RN* especially animated (18/8/95). The paper printed an obituary (11/8/95) and a detailed account of his funeral at Woking, which was attended by many leading European socialists including Eleanor Marx. It also reported how Engels had specified his ashes were to be scattered over the Channel, thereby preventing 'the manifestations of hero-worship and curiosity which would have prompted his followers to visit any grave or building where the ashes might have been deposited' (18/8/95).

The *Times* may have been eager to underplay the dissemination of Engels's ideas, but the case of Edward Leggatt from West Ham (Keir Hardie's old constituency), who was charged with travelling on the Great Eastern Railway without a ticket suggested radical European politics had gained at least a toe-hold in Britain. Leggatt did not attend his hearing, and a letter from him to the railway company was read out instead. 'I refuse to recognise the right of a section of parasites calling themselves shareholders [to] dictate [to working men] upon what terms they shall travel,' Leggatt said. 'I recognise only one class – namely the working class, who produce all the wealth of the world, and are therefore the only useful class, and the only class entitled to ride.' Politicians and 'sky pilots' should walk, he added, finishing 'I shall be proud to be a "criminal" [. . .] Long Live Anarchy and to ___ with the Government' (*IPN* 13/7/95). Leggatt's well-written letter suggested the educational reforms of the 1870s and 1880s were having a marked effect on working class literacy and that some at least were using their rhetorical powers to hit back at the established order, even if such tactics had yet to make serious alterations to the constitution of Parliament.

Meanwhile, the writer whose provocative essay, 'The Soul of Man Under Socialism' had caused much discussion in February 1891 with its claim 'As one reads history [. . .] one is absolutely sickened, not by the crimes that the wicked have committed, but by the punishments that the good have inflicted' (*WCW* 1182), continued to decline. On 26 August, having served three months of his sentence, he was allowed a visitor. Robert Sherard talked with Wilde through a double row of iron bars for twenty minutes, and observed he was very depressed and unkempt. His hands were sore from oakum-picking. Sherard's visiting order allowed for two visitors but he was unable to find a second. As he wrote later, this was doubtless because it was the holiday season, and 'everybody was unfortunately engaged' (Hyde 1963: 25).

Notes

1. The highest official temperature recorded in the UK remains 38.5°C, logged at Brogdale, near Faversham in Kent, on 10 August 2003.
2. The statue, by Hamo Thorneycroft, was erected in 1899. Rosebery met its £3,000 cost anonymously (McKinstry 377).
3. In the *PMG*'s list of senior political figures' electoral expenditure and its cost per vote, Chamberlain is shown to have spent £2,022.11 for his 19,554 return, an investment of just over 2s a vote (10/8/95).
4. It remains the highest first class score by an Englishman, and was unbeaten in Britain until the West Indian, Brian Lara, scored 501 not out for Warwickshire against Durham in 1994.

Autumn into Winter: 1 September 1895 – 31 December 1895

Football: Football's a manly sport for Titan lads!
Cricket Ball: But spoiled by huckster cliques and noisy cads.
'Bat versus Ball: An Autumn Eclogue', Punch 21 September 1895

Never was there such a season for blackberries as this! The hedgerows are positively weighed down by their embarrassment of rich ripe fruit, and the woods echo at every step to the merry voices of children, gloating over present joy and future jam. Nor can the most fastidious disdain that excellent old-fashioned dish of which it is said her Majesty is specially fond – blackberry and apple tart.
Illustrated Police News, 26 October 1895

The normal state of the present age is emotional; emotional drama should be the rule, passionate drama the exception.
Quarterly Review, October 1895

Let this story be a warning
It's written on that plan
Don't introduce your sweetheart to
A hypnotizing man.
Leopold Jordan, Trilby Re-Versed (1895)

It seems to me in these days, that women cannot be men, but they do all they can to show the people they are not women. And men cannot be women, but a good many of them prove they are not men.
'A MAN, Stapleton-Rd., Bristol' in Reynolds's Newspaper,
3 November 1895

I found that the story was all about the manner in which men amuse themselves with the soiled doves of the highways and byways – and as I was not very well instructed in that sort of thing, I thought I might as well learn. [. . .] Literature is supposed to reflect the time we live in – and that kind of literature being more prevalent than anything else, we are compelled to accept and study it as the mirror of the age.
Sibyl Tempest in Marie Corelli's The Sorrows of Satan, October 1895

'Mr Wilde is wrong,' murmured Constance. Her lips were blanched but her voice was sweet and calm.

Robert W. Chambers, *The King in Yellow*, November 1895

I weigh 9 stone 3 lbs, earnt £40 last month, & am altogether very cheerful.

H.G. Wells to his brother, Fred, late 1895

ॐ

Revolting Ladies

Reflecting on the Conservatives' election victory, *Blackwood's* identified Agriculture, the Poor Law, Education and Labour as urgent priorities for Salisbury's government (8/95: 306). In August however, the Queen's Speech was confined to foreign affairs. Balfour, the Tories' leader in the Commons, hoped for 'a period of calm and peace' (*P* 24/8/95: 91), but it was obvious to informed observers that his party would have to work hard to fulfil their electoral promises. A large majority did not guarantee a common purpose.

Outside Parliament, debate surrounding the 'sex problem' continued. F.A. Atkins's *The Ideal Husband* collected essays on the perfect partnership by eight married women writers without achieving consensus. Eliza Lynn Linton objected to the New Woman, claiming women were happiest when 'nobly mastered', while Mrs Fenwick-Miller, 'going out of her way to sneer at Mrs Lynn Linton', felt the best marriages were between friendly chums (*LWN* 11/8/95). On 22 August, John Lane stoked the controversy by publishing another provocative 'Keynote', Victoria Crosse's *The Woman Who Didn't*.[1] Eurydice Williamson remains faithful to her adulterous husband despite no longer loving him. She also refuses to embark on an affair with an Indian Army officer, described by the *Athenaeum* as 'one of those hopeless cads such as seem only to be conceived by female novelists' (14/9/95: 351). The old-fashioned but insightful *Sir Robert's Fortune* by Margaret Oliphant and Evelyn Sharp's engaging satire of Shaw, *At the Relton Arms* were much more to its taste, while the response to Mary Braddon's final three-decker, *Sons of Fire*, in the same month showed how a once scandalous writer could become an institution while yet managing to remain up-to-date. The book was published on 18 September, and a number of magazines carried a full-page advertisement by Braddon's publishers charting her progress from the sensation fiction of *Lady Audley's Secret* (1862) to the slightly more respectable *Thou Art the Man* (1894) fifty-four novels later. 'The essential of a new story by Miss Braddon is that she should find a fresh setting for a familiar theme,' the *Athenaeum* said. This allowed her 'to display her ingenuity by showing in how many different forms a mystery of homicide can be made attractive.' The novel show-cased Braddon's skills in 'social portraiture', but the reviewer found its heroine, Suzette Vincent, unsympathetic as she 'plays fast and loose with the two men who adore her' (28/9/95: 413). That the two men look alike, and that one turns out to be a jealous and murderous madman, went unsaid. Braddon's novel offered a familiar romantic dilemma – the choice of lovers – spiced with 'modern' psychology and her trademark mystery and violence. Crosse however had no such pedigree and far fewer admirers. Her novel, originally entitled *Consummation*, was neither a convincing rejoinder to Allen nor a success in its own right. Reviewers found it stylistically as well as morally objectionable; the *PMG* saying it was written 'without any adequate knowledge of human-kind' (14/9/95), and the *SR* judging it 'incredibly coarse and tawdry' into the bargain. There was, it felt, a mannish tang in Crosse's writing which 'positively reeks of whiskeys-and-sodas and of physical passion' (21/9/95: 387).

The Woman Who Didn't was reviewed alongside *The Woman Who Wouldn't*, written by Adelina Kingscote under the *Ebbsmith*-derived pseudonym, 'Lucas Cleeve'. Cleeve's preface defended Grant Allen and advocated purity for both sexes in offering the story of the unconven-tional Opalia Woodgate. It began with the bold claim, 'Half the charm to most young girls of early married life is the close acquaintance with the dark stories of immorality which have been kept from them before their marriage,' (Cleeve 1895: ii), and what followed was similarly out-spoken. Even more beautiful than Herminia Barton, Girton-educated Opalia, the daughter of a professor, loves Alan D'Arcy, an artist, but will only marry him if the two can live together platonically. Husband and wife soon find themselves tempted from the path of faithful chas-tity, the erotic tensions of their unconsummated union fascinating the reading public. The first printing sold out in three weeks, but reviewers saw 'Cleeve' as cynical and fraudulent, reinforcing the comments James Noble had made about such writers in April. The *SR* felt the book was 'in no way a contribution to the sexual question' but 'simply an essay in what one might call serious pornography' that showed 'indefinite repetition' of 'the sex-problem' had long since palled (21/9/95: 387). The *Standard* was even less impressed, terming it 'sad and sickening stuff, illiterate and feeble, destitute alike of purity and real passion. We wonder that any woman, even today, could have brought herself to write it' (4/10/95). The following month, W. Pett Ridge's *A Clever Wife* featured a woman writer who agrees to marry the hero on condition that she will be spared becoming 'domesticated and suburban, and interested in back gardens' (Ridge 131). She spends their honeymoon checking the proofs of her first novel, and also suggests they keep separate houses on their return. The *PMG* saw it as a gently comic rewrite of Kipling's *The Light That Failed* (1/1/96), while the *Standard* found it amiable but thought Mrs Halliwell, Ridge's lady novelist, 'conceited' and 'selfish' (1/1/96). A *Punch* cartoon depicted 'The Woman Who Wanted To' as middle-aged, mannish but defiantly flirtatious (26/10/95: 202). In another sketch, a female friend of the author of *The Woman who Durstn't* remarks, 'Now you've had such a Success, I suppose your publishers will take any rubbish you choose to write' (*P* 12/10/95: 174). The magazine even used nursery rhymes as bulwarks against social change:

> There was a New Woman, and what do you think?
> She lived upon nothing but paper and ink,
> Though paper and ink formed her favourite diet,
> This noisy New Woman could never keep quiet! (21/9/95: 136)

Such doggerel cheered reactionaries, but it was no more a nuanced contribution to discussion than Bessie Bellwood's New Woman song, a hit in the halls according to the *IPN* (21/9/95). More sophisticated was the *QR*'s lengthy review of the published plays of Pinero and Henry Arthur Jones and Jones's speeches and essays, *The Renascence of the English Drama*, which examined how the theatre was becoming 'steeped in psychology'. Jones identified the 'four chief qualities' of art as 'beauty, mystery, passion, imagination' (Jones 1930: 17), but the reviewer focused only on the third. At times, he recalled Shaw's response to the disturbances at *Guy Domville*, notably when arguing 'an audience may be, or ought to be, educated by the dramatist, but it can scarcely be transformed'. Elsewhere however, his views were strongly divergent from the Irishman's. The 'New Drama' has 'brought the psychology of the feminine into glaring relief, both in literature and on the stage, so that the modern play and the modern novel are women's plays and women's novels,' he maintained, 'while the study of the masculine degenerates by comparison.' Shaw revered Ibsen, but the *QR* found 'Norwegian psychology [. . .] neurotic and pessimistic' and liable to offend the 'healthful and hopeful' audiences in British theatres. Nevertheless, in pointing out how the New Drama's 'modernity' lay in its 'determination to mirror the contemporary agitations of modern existence', and that 'the doctrines of psychology and physiology are fast affecting our every-day attitude towards sex and sin, towards religion and morals; towards the whole countenance of life,' the critic added his voice to the debate about the possibly corrosive relationship between art, life, and morality (10/95: 399–428). Gosse had addressed 'the decay of literary taste' in the *North American Review*, whining that 'things have come to a pretty pass when the combined prestige of the best poets, historians, critics, and philosophers [. . .] does not weigh in the balance against a single novel by a New Woman' (Miller 1994: 30–1), but others suffered only from *ennui*. 'We know all about and are heartily sick of the woman who would and who wouldn't, who can't, and who did, and all the rest of it [. . .] Do they think there is anything new [in these] nauseous details?' sighed *Blackwood's* weary 'Looker-On' (12/95: 914).

Welling Up

One of the New Woman's (tentative) male supporters, not least because a redrawing of moral boundaries enhanced his own sexual prospects, was H.G. Wells. After publishing *The Time Machine* on 29 May and reviewing James's *Terminations* and Conrad's *Almayer's Folly*, a novel he described as 'exceedingly well imagined and well written' (*SR* 15/6/95: 797), he had done little writing, largely due to his forthcoming marriage, which took place on 27 October, his uncertain health, and, more significantly, the fact that he had a number of works in press already, a legacy of frantic industry since the late 1880s. As David Smith points out, Wells was 'a veritable writing machine' between 1895 and 1914, producing thirty-two books, eight volumes of short fiction and dozens of journalistic articles (Smith 1986: 58). He was therefore perhaps entitled to a short break, learning to ride a bicycle and mourning the death of his old mentor, T.H. Huxley.

On 5 September, his satirical novella *The Wonderful Visit* tested Ruskin's proposition that if an angel arrived in modern England, it would be shot on sight. The scenario allowed Wells to ridicule Nordau, particularly his tendency to use 'scientific diagnosis to stigmatise the inexplicable and to fix abnormal behaviour as a deviant form' (Greenslade 1994: 126), as well as to mock sexual and social hypocrisy. Though it is little read today, eclipsed by the novels Wells wrote either side of it, the attractively packaged tale – it had a cover design by Arthur Rackham – enhanced his reputation considerably. Sidney Low of the *SR* judged it 'a striking fantasia wrought with infinite tact, charm, and wit' (26/10/95: 554), and the *Athenaeum* praised it as a 'very pleasant little *jeu d'esprit*' (26/10/95: 565). The *PMG* was delighted by Wells's 'adorable humour' (25/9/95); the *BDP* found the story 'a delightfully droll conception' (31/10/95). All seemed oblivious to the novel's subversive political content, such as its attacks on the aristocracy and land ownership.

The satirical device of an ornithologically-minded vicar blasting an angel from the sky in the belief it is a flamingo showed the whimsical side of Wells's imagination, but 'The Cone', a story published in the short-lived magazine, *The Unicorn* on 18 September was altogether darker in mood. Published against a background of industrial accidents and unrest – an explosion in Tyldesley colliery near Manchester killed five men on 1 September, there was growing discontent in the mines of the Rhondda Valley and the Belfast and Clyde shipyards, and a five month long strike at Allerton Silkstone Collieries in Leeds showed no sign of resolution – the story was set in a Stoke ironworks. Horrocks, an ironmaster of 'no imagination, no poetry' (Wells 1927: 457) has a theory that 'machinery is beautiful, and everything else in the world ugly' (459). When he discovers his wife is having an affair with Raut, a connoisseur of 'fine effects of moonlight and smoke' (458), he takes the aesthete on a tour of his business before, in a horrific denouement, pushing him into a furnace and throwing coal at him until Raut drops into the roaring fire and is transformed into 'a cindery animal' (468) who is burned alive.

On the surface, 'The Cone' is a nasty *conte cruel*, but it can also be read allegorically. Raut has obviously derived his ideas from Whistler, and appeals to Mrs Horrocks because he is gentler and more poetically-minded than her husband. Horrocks's brutality, motivated by sexual jealousy, sees him mimic Raut's aesthetic language and then dispatch him to fiery perdition; only at the very end of the story does he realise the barbarity of his actions. Wells wrote the tale in 1888, but his publication of it soon after Wilde's downfall makes it possible to see it as dramatising the destruction of qualities popularly associated with Wilde and aestheticism. Raut's 'unmanliness' is no match for the directness of Horrocks's crude but deadly stratagem, and the horror of the story derives from the inevitability of its outcome: once Raut agrees to look over the ironworks, he is doomed, just as Wilde was when instigating libel proceedings. A Procrustean reading of 'The Cone' would be a mistake, but such parallels are nevertheless suggestive, the more so since *The Wonderful Visit*'s prudish Mrs Mendham warns against associating with the strangely-dressed and unconventional angel. 'I've heard the fashion is quite changing,' she says. 'Some of the very best people have decided that genius is not to be encouraged any more' due to 'recent scandals' in the literary world (Wells 2009: 79–80).

Wells reprinted 'The Cone' in *The Plattner Story and Others* (1897), where it won him the friendship of Arnold Bennett, who was impressed by its evocation of industrial Staffordshire. In the autumn of 1895 though, he was more concerned with seeing another collection, *The Stolen Bacillus*, through the press for its publication in November. His stock was rising rapidly, and on 13 October, he was able to tell his mother that four different publishers were vying for his next novel, *The Island of Doctor Moreau*. His literary income had risen from £380 13s 7d in 1893 to £583 17s 7d in 1894 and to £1,056 7s 9d in 1895 (Smith 43). Henry Harland however remained cautious, telling Lane on 22 October:

> On two occasions Wells has offered me scientific stories and neither of them was good – not to be compared to the things of his that I've seen in the *PMG* and the *New Review*. Of course I should be delighted if he'd send up something of his best, but we don't want his or anyone else's *second* best. Let him send his ms. on approval; and if we like it, and if his price is reasonable, we'll take it. (JLA)

The *YB* eventually included 'A Slip Under the Microscope' in its eighth number in January 1896.

Silver and Rubies

On the night of 11 September, thieves smashed their way through the roof of William Shillcock's 'football outfitters' shop in Birmingham's Newtown Row. Their prize was the FA Cup, which had been on display in Shillcock's window for the previous week. Aston Villa's committee had wisely insured the trophy with a movable policy, since the FA made them liable for £200 compensation, far in excess of its material value, should it be stolen while in the club's care. The theft was a blow to Villa's image nonetheless, and notices advertising a £10 reward were immediately posted throughout the city. The theft held little interest for the London papers, but it was reported with breathless excitement in footballing centres such as Liverpool, Leicester, and Sheffield. Blackburn's *Weekly Standard and Express* however was openly sarcastic, perhaps because Villa had ended Blackburn's run of four consecutive victories in the cup in 1887. Describing the robbery as 'appalling sacrilege,' the report asserted:

> The impious hands that coveted the Holy Grail supplied quite a commonplace felony compared with the theft of the English Cup. Colonel Blood's attempt upon the Crown jewels was simply a vulgar piece of housebreaking by the side of the majestic crib-cracking last night. It takes some of our best football teams years to win the English Cup. Some never win it at all; yet it only took Bill Sikes a few minutes with his clever forward play to capture the Cup and put it in his own pocket.

The amusingly hyperbolic account finished with a call for the thief to return the trophy and 'claim the immortality that awaits him. He ought to rise to a proper sense of the importance of his work' (14/9/95). Unfortunately, the thief was an anonymous pragmatist, and the trophy was never recovered. Many believed it was melted down for counterfeit coins, some of which may have been passed in the Salutation, the pub kept by Villa's Dennis Hodgetts (Morris 1974:12) or at the city's race-course. Villa were fined £25 by the FA, money which was spent on a new trophy made by the Birmingham firm, Vaughton's, run by Howard Vaughton, a member of the club's 1887 cup-winning team. As each Villa player was awarded a miniature replica of the cup instead of a winner's medal, it was easy to recreate 'the little tin idol', but the affair caused considerable embarrassment, and it was almost inevitable that Villa would be knocked out of the 1896 competition at the first hurdle, losing 4–2 at Derby County.[2] Their pursuit of the league title got off to a flying start however, and by late October they led the First Division from Bolton and Derby. Almost as gratifying was the fact that their neighbours, Small Heath and WBA, propped up the table after the first ten matches of the campaign.

Villa's reverse was short-lived, but down in London, Oscar Wilde staggered from one ignominy to the next. Haldane's books offered some cheer – September's batch included Pater's *Greek Studies, Appreciations* and *Imaginary Portraits* – but one volume per week was hardly adequate for a culturally-deprived bibliophile. Wilde was now beset by three external considerations as well as the continuing debilitation of life in Wandsworth – by 18 September, his weight was down to 168 pounds. These were the continuation of his bankruptcy proceedings, decisions regarding his future with Constance, and the role of Bosie Douglas in his life.

On 21 September, a frantic Douglas wrote to Sherard, little realis-ing, as McKenna points out, Sherard's true sympathies. 'Tell [Oscar] from me that I love him and am only living to see him again,' Douglas implored. 'If he dies in prison or ceases to love me, I shall kill myself too, for I have nothing else to live for' (McKenna 2004: 559). In the meantime, he consoled himself with the delights of Capri and its young male inhabitants. Constance visited Wandsworth the same day. She was shocked by her husband's dereliction and the conditions of his captivity, but cheered by his remark that he had been 'mad these last three years' and would kill Douglas if he saw him (Hyde 1963: 28). Such comments encouraged her to delay the divorce proceedings urged by her family and friends. A few days later, Sherard engineered an additional visit to the prison, ostensibly on the grounds of encouraging marital reconciliation. However, the real reason seems to have been to inform Wilde about Bosie's proposed *Mercure de France* article. Sherard was granted an hour's stay and managed to hug his friend on departure, but the breach of confidence upset Wilde as well as making him worry as to which letters might be involved. He instructed Sherard to prevent publication.

The bankruptcy proceedings concerned Wilde's outstanding debts of £3,591. He attended a hearing on 24 September, though he was not called and did not therefore make a public appearance, much to the disappointment of a sizeable crowd. Wilde's counsel, J.P. Grain, secured an adjournment for seven weeks, and also suggested that while Wilde presently had no assets, his plays could have royalty value in the future (*PMG* 25/9/95). The financial dealings surrounding Wilde were becoming increasingly complex, but they were less significant for him than incidents that cast new light on his former life. Ross, who had returned to England in late July, stood in the corridor of the court and raised his hat to the manacled prisoner. 'Men have gone to heaven for smaller things than that,' Wilde recalled (*WCL* 722). Such chivalrous action was a marked contrast to Bosie's coded message to Wilde, passed on by a solicitor's clerk: 'Prince Fleur-de-Lys wishes to be remembered to you' (Ellman 1987: 461). This bewildered its recipient, who, when informed that the gentleman in question was abroad, could only laugh. Wilde had once admired Bosie's 'Jonquil and Fleur-de-Lys', a ballad in which a prince and shepherd boy change clothes, but remembering its final verse cannot have helped his morale:

By this the sun was low in the heaven
And Fleur-de-Lys must ride away,
But ere he left, with kisses seven,
He vowed to come another day.

With Wilde feeling abandoned by having had no word from Douglas since his conviction, angry about his family's failure to pay his legal fees, and uneasy about the *Mercure de France* article, this allusion was typically tactless.[3] About ten days after the bankruptcy hearing, Wilde fell over in his cell and bruised his ear. Accused by the doctor of malingering, he fainted in the prison chapel, injuring himself further. He was placed in a cell in the prison infirmary, where he delighted in clean cotton sheets and the first white bread and butter he had eaten since May (Hyde 1963: 31).

After a week, Wilde was moved to the infirmary ward. While he brooded on the loyalty of his friends, his former idol, Lillie Langtry faced troubles of a rather different kind. Before departing for a holiday in Baden-Baden in early August, she deposited jewellery at the Sloane Street branch of the Union Bank. On 18 August, a man arrived at the bank bearing a piece of Langtry's personal stationery on which was instructions in her handwriting to hand over her jewels to him. The letter was a forgery, made possible by the fact that while Langtry's signature was familiar from its reproduction in soap advertisements, her general hand was not. The thief escaped with £40,000's worth of pearls and jewels, among which was purportedly the largest ruby in the world. The crime was not discovered until Langtry's return to London in late September, and despite a significant police investigation, the gems were never found. The uninsured Langtry sued the Union for negligence. The bank argued she had only left a tin box with them and had not informed them of its valuable contents. The stalemate prompted her to engage Sir George Lewis, who secured the services of Herbert Asquith for the prosecution. The bank engaged Edward Carson, but hopes of a courtroom battle royal were dashed when a settlement was reached on the morning the case was due to open, Langtry later regretting she accepted damages of a mere £10,000 when she might have secured at least £25,000 (Langtry 1925: 222–8). *Punch* suggested she sing 'Ti-a-ra Boom-de-ay' instead (5/10/95: 168).

Lewis had a busy Autumn, for on the day *Punch* teased Langtry, the zoologist and degeneration-theorist Edwin Lankester, an Oxford professor, was arrested in Piccadilly after becoming embroiled in an altercation between a group of prostitutes and two policemen. Another prostitute had been arrested earlier, and Lankester told the court (and the *Times*) that, having seen this, he was asking one of the women, who was distressed, what was happening. Arrested for obstruction, Lankester found himself in court defended by Lewis and facing an obviously biased magistrate. Lewis withdrew from the case, complaining that the official had 'interposed at every moment' instead of listening to his argument (*T* 14/10/95), and Lankester was adjudged guilty, though he attempted to set the record straight in a public letter. 'It is time that a departmental enquiry was held, in view of the allegations of violence and concerted perjury which have repeatedly been made against a portion of the police,' he wrote. 'It is a matter of common report that they levy blackmail on the women of the street, and receive bribes from those they have arrested' (*T* 14/10/95). Police witnesses claimed Lankester had been the worse for drink – he was leaving his club in the early hours – and most observers believed he had been the victim of an unfortunate misunderstanding. Few were prepared to consider that elements of the Metropolitan Police may have been as dishonest as his letter suggested.

Trilbymania

The autumn was a busy time for writers and dramatists. 'The Mummer' was excited by Mrs Campbell's forthcoming appearance in *Romeo and Juliet* at the Lyceum and by *Cheer, Boys, Cheer!*, a Drury Lane extravaganza co-written by Augustus Harris, Cecil Raleigh and Henry Hamilton. *Punch* depicted them as *Macbeth*'s witches throwing dramatic ingredients into a cauldron: 'Polo, gold mines, Rotten Row, | Costumes grand, comedian low' (5/10/95: 168). The play lasted over three hours – the *Athenaeum* felt it was ninety minutes too long (28/9/95: 413) – and featured lavish sets, special effects, horses, telephone conversations, machine guns, and Meikstein, 'a rascally [Jewish] City speculator' who promotes a South African goldmine. The most affecting scene depicted a gallant band of British soldiers, out of ammunition and surrounded by their Matabele foe, singing the national anthem and being shot just before their rescuers, led by 'a plucky girl' arrive (*IPN* 21/9/95), a display of courage modelled on the stoicism of those drowned in the sinking of *HMS Birkenhead* in 1852. 'I not only do not understand,' said Shaw, 'but I feel I should go mad if I should try to' (*OT* 205). It was a great success, clocking up 177 performances at Drury Lane and Olympia and running until the end of February.

As a box office phenomenon however, *Cheer, Boys, Cheer!* was overshadowed by Paul Potter's adaptation of Du Maurier's *Trilby*. This had already been highly successful in the US, the *Bookman* claiming it earned Du Maurier $700 a week (7/95: 111) though he had actually sold the dramatic rights to William Terriss for a mere £75. Terriss in turn had sold them to Beerbohm Tree for £100, and it was his production which opened at the Haymarket on 30 October, having first had a brief outing at Manchester's Theatre Royal. Tickets were much in demand, and the box office opened on 23 September. 'It is causing an immense stir, & the advance booking has wiped out all previous records,' noted Arnold Bennett. 'It cannot fail to be awful rot, of course' (Bennett 1968: 24).

The extraordinary success of Potter's *Trilby* is not easily explained. *Blackwood's* felt it had 'taken possession of the public mind by one of those great accidental waves of impression which it is impossible to account for' (12/95: 910). Its source novel was enormously popular, but so was Hall Caine's *The Manxman*, and the stage version of that, which featured Brookfield, managed only thirteen performances in London in late November. Beerbohm Tree was a well-established actor manager, but a big name did not automatically ensure commercial reward. Besides, though she looked uncannily like Du Maurier's illustrations, Dorothea Baird, who played Trilby O'Ferrall, artist's model

Figure 11. The bare-footed Trilby O' Ferrall (Dorothea Baird) serenades Svengali (Herbert Beerbohm Tree) with 'Don't you remember sweet Alice, Ben Bolt?' *Illustrated London News* 21 September.

turned diva, was hitherto unknown on the London stage; she may have been hand-picked by Du Maurier himself but Clement Scott felt Trilby was 'a fine part weakly played', and attributed the show's success to Beerbohm Tree's barnstorming performance as the sinister mesmerist,

Svengali (*ILN* 9/11/95: 573). The play was billed as 'an entertainment in four acts', and perhaps it was the blend of music, melodrama, sentimentality and an eminently hissable villain that endeared it to audiences. John Goode has shown how the sophisticated 'aesthetic philistinism' of the novel distanced the 'bohemian idyll' so that 'what in fact is a lucid portrayal of the conditions of artistic production is presented at once as something belonging to a world richer than the reader's (and author's) tame normality'. The result is 'a classic instance of the best-seller having it both ways', concealing its realities behind a veil of nostalgia (Goode 1979: 121) while tapping into anxieties concerning 'unnatural' art.

Whatever the reasons, *Trilby* was a sensation. An admirer of the novel, Shaw remarked in his assessment of 9 November, 'I know well that there never was any such person as Trilby – that she is a man's dream; but I am a man myself, and delight in her' (*OT* 239). Leonée Ormond claims the play is 'over-dramatic, tasteless and often vulgar' in comparison with the book, and makes 'a great deal of Trilby's modelling and past love-affairs' (Ormond 1969: 493), but Shaw felt the heroine was altogether purer than the woman of the novel. '*Trilby* is the very thing for the English stage at present,' he continued. 'No need to act or create character; nothing to do but make up after Mr Du Maurier's familiar and popular drawings, and be applauded before uttering a word [. . .] Nearly all the favourite pictures and passages from the book are worked in' (240). The result was 'bright and pleasant', a play he was sure 'everyone will enjoy' (241). The first night's audience applauded wildly at the final curtain, and the Prince and Princess of Wales, its most distinguished members, summoned Du Maurier to the Royal Box to congratulate him. His pride was only slightly dampened by the Princess objecting not to vulgarity but to Baird's naked feet (Ormond 1969: 493).

Shaw treated *Trilby* as no more than a harmless distraction from more serious concerns, and Du Maurier himself professed to be mystified by the runaway success of his novel and its adaptation. He told Augusta Gregory he had 'written it "in corners" to amuse himself' and preferred *Peter Ibbetson* (Gregory 1996: 100). Henry James found him depressed by 'the deafening roar of sordid gold flowing in to him,' though this was nothing beside James's own feelings of failure (Edel 1996: 444). That he had encouraged his friend to develop the narrative germ of *Trilby* in March 1889 intensified his ambivalence. Interviewed by Sherard for *McClure's Magazine* in October, a gloomy Du Maurier said that 'a "boom" means nothing as a sign of literary excellence, nothing but money' (Ormond 1969: 480). The novel's success had come too late for him, for his sight was deteriorating daily and he felt overwhelmed by the mass of fan mail, personal letters and patent applications he received from the book's readers. He had also endured a painful rupture with his old friend, Whistler, who took offence at Du Maurier basing the character of Joe Sibley on aspects of himself. On 11 November, Bennett reported that *Trilby*'s manuscript was being exhibited in Bond Street in a glass case, admittance to the holy of holies costing 1s (Bennett 1968: 28); the *ILN* felt it was destined for 'the library of some American millionaire,' though it remains a Du Maurier family heirloom (16/11/95: 610). On 16 November, Lady Gregory found the play a welcome respite from painful dental treatment, its music having charms to sooth a savage toothache (Gregory 1996: 87). Smelling a profit, journalists, songwriters and dramatists cashed in on the craze, if not its palliative properties, with Baird's bare-footed performance sending a *frisson* through their ranks. *Punch* loved her 'naked tootsies exposed to the naked eye' though it felt Svengali's presence was so overpowering his creator should be renamed 'George Jew Maurier' (16/11/95: 232). Owen Hall, Harry Greenbank and Sidney Jones swiftly appended a 'Trilby Waltz' to their musical comedy, *An Artist's Model*, which having opened in February and undergone several alterations was now in its 'second edition' at Daly's Theatre. 'Dull & vulgar & so improper,' was Lady Gregory's verdict (1996: 82). Brookfield and William Yardley collaborated with the composer W. Meyer Lutz on *A Model Trilby; or A Day or Two After Du Maurier*, which ran at the Opera Comique until 1 February 1896. Music hall stars were also quick to exploit the play's portrayal of the bare-footed, cigarette smoking model-cum-singer. Vesta Tilly was soon performing 'I'm Looking for Trilby', and Marie Lloyd sang 'Tricky Little Trilby' in 'toe tights' (*IPN* 26/10/95); the routine allowing an impressive display of her 'terpsichorean abilities' (*IPN* 2/11/95). According to Midge Gillies, when Lloyd performed the song in the East End, her audience was unfamiliar with the play or its source, and 'bewildered at her lack of shoes' (Gillies [1999] 2001: 97), but Lloyd surmounted the obstacle by pretending to be an actress who is ignorant of the character. She reworked Du Maurier with trademark gusto:

'Twasn't in my line I thought because
I had no idea who Trilby was;
But the pay of course, cured my disgust
So I thought I'd play the part or bust,
They said Trilby modest ought to be,
Modest Trilby, what a part for me.
Quiet and prim, me?
Eh, no jolly fear! (Gillies [1999] 2001: 98)

Another performer, Edwin Barwick, offered 'Trilby Mad', a 'dramatic scene' imitating Beerbohm Tree (*IPN* 7/12/95). 'Trilbymania' was all-consuming. 'Socialites performed *tableaux vivants* from the book,' notes Elaine Showalter (Du Maurier [1894] 1998: vii), and it topped many of the *Bookman*'s regional sales lists from October onwards. The *IPN* reported the craze encompassed aprons, blouses, gloves, corsets, tobacco, soap, and boots, as well as hats (7/12/95). Silver scarf-pins, kitchen ranges and even sausages followed. Svengali's notoriety also boosted sales of Guy Boothby's *A Bid For Fortune*, which featured the criminal mastermind and mesmerist Dr Nikola; advertising posters depicting his fiendish black cat were widespread by mid-December, though the *Athenaeum* lamented that 'the hypnotic influences are not very aptly managed' (14/12/95: 831).

Pamela Thurschwell has drawn a suggestive parallel between *Trilby* and Wilde's trials, noting how:

> Fears about influence cluster centrally around the mesmerising potential of transgressive sexualities, but they also emerge through the suggestive potential of linguistic word-play, literature, art and the fluctuations of an expanding marketplace that helps set the term for all these things. (Thurschwell 2001: 63)

Trilby allowed these sometimes unconscious anxieties to be exhibited, performed, and exorcised in the context of exuberant melodrama. As anti-Semitic as *Cheer, Boys, Cheer!*, the novel and play were regarded as harmless in the contexts in which they were consumed, though one can imagine how Carson's forensic and judgemental mind could have (mis) represented them to a jury had he been required to do so. Du Maurier had parodied Wilde and the gospel of aestheticism in *Punch* since the 1880s however, and his associations with reactionary satire outweighed his youthful dabbling in Parisian bohemia. That his son, Gerald, played Dodor in the Haymarket production made the work even more respectable. Yet, at the same time as the Du Mauriers stressed their dynastic bonds, Beerbohm Tree was leading a double life worthy of James Read: seven of his ten children were illegitimate, and as George Taylor writes, 'for over twenty-five years he maintained, not just a regular mistress, but a whole second family' (Taylor 1992: 104).

Ave Satani!

Du Maurier's popularity was inarguable, but his commercial supremacy was about to be challenged by a novel that synthesised and denounced the year's preoccupations with sex, scandal and sinister influence. Marie Corelli's *The Sorrows of Satan* burst upon the literary world on 21 October.

Corelli wrote her novel between January and August, and so had ample opportunity to observe the workings of 'a decadent and ephemeral age' (Corelli 1998: 62): she perhaps did not appreciate the irony of the Prince of Wales requesting the first copy. The book tells how Geoffrey Tempest, a struggling author, inherits five million pounds and is befriended by the suave Prince Lucio Rimânez, the second well dressed philosopher in the history of thought, little knowing his foreign friend is actually the devil (Lucifer Ahrimanes), who is wandering the earth in an attempt to regain his place in heaven. Lucio's ascent requires him to be rejected by humanity, but the fallen men and women of 1890s' London are only too willing to admit him to the highest levels of society. On the final page, Geoffrey sees him arm-in-arm with a Cabinet minister: perhaps Sir Robert Chiltern has once again succumbed to temptation. 'In these days of the "New Woman" and the "New Morality",' said the *Aberdeen Weekly Journal*, 'it is not surprising to find among modern novelties a New Devil', a personage of a decidedly *fin de siècle* kind (23/11/95).

Following Geoffrey from poverty to social triumph and back again, Corelli savages a world that is rotten to the core and denied her literary status – she refused to have the book sent out for review, forcing critics to buy copies for themselves. Peter Keating observes that 'she will turn aside and fulminate against anyone or anything that has annoyed her, often regardless of her diatribe's relevance' (Corelli 1998: xiv), an approach ridiculed by *Punch* (7/12/95: 269). In her eyes, literature has become corrupt and demoralising, helped by unscrupulous publishers who manipulate sales figures and deceive the public, but the commercialisation of art is only part of Corelli's apocalyptic vision. As Lucio says, 'The present time of the world breathes egotism – the taint of Self, the hideous worship of money, corrodes all life, all thought, all feeling' (372). The evidence for this is ubiquitous if unsystematic. London is 'the restless modern Babylon' (172), 'poets teach lewdness, and scientists blasphemy' (372), women unsex themselves by playing tennis, nature is violated (Corelli attacked the building of Scotland's first hydroelectric plant on Loch Ness, which opened in 1896), the Church has lost touch with Christ's teaching, the aristocracy has no sense of tradition and toadies to wealthy Americans, the government is an irrelevance, social division has made the East End a 'lion couchant' (200) and marriage has become no more than a commercial bargain. In a later article in the *Ladies' Realm*, Corelli detached her hatreds from their fictional context, listing 'The "new poet" who curls his hair with tongs and writes his own reviews' – possibly a reference to Le Gallienne – 'the modern marriage market, women bicyclists & he females generally, William Archer & his god Ibsen, *The Woman Who Did*, sneers at faith & aspiration' and 'the "funny man" at a party' (Carr 1901: 74–5). Her unflagging denunciatory rhetoric lacked focus or priorities – she was one of those 'Authors I Cannot Take Seriously' in William Ryan's *Literary London: Its Lights and Comedies* (1898) – and the book is weakened further by the character of Mavis Clare, the saintly novelist who shares Corelli's initials and her low opinion of the literary establishment. A moral paragon, she alone can resist Satan's wiles.

In a generally appreciative twelve page article in October's *Review of Reviews,* W.T. Stead suggested renaming the novel 'The Sorrows of Satan and Marie Corelli' since it was overly preoccupied with settling personal scores in the aftermath of the critical ridicule afforded *Barabbas* (1893). The book's 'shrewish spitefulness' often seemed the 'malice of a disappointed snob, rather than the utterance of a brilliant and distinguished novelist' (Corelli 2008: 379). Similar points were raised by W.L Courtney in the *DT* (25/10/95), but as Corelli had probably hoped, reviewers were powerless in the face of her readers' enthusiasm. 'The great masses of the public in all nations are always led by some instinctive sense of right,' she wrote, 'that moves them to reject the false and unworthy, and select the true' (Corelli 1998: 139). 'I can now understand both her popularity and the critics' contempt,' said Bennett after reading the book, the first of hers he had sampled (1968: 24–5). Using the very promotional tactics the novel itself condemned, Methuen showed they had learned quickly since the failure to promote *Gallia*. They were now handling all of Corelli's work – she had kept the copyrights on earlier novels and transferred them to Methuen in early 1895 (Ransom 1999: 79) – and recognised rich pickings, though full details are no longer extant since Methuen's records were destroyed during the Blitz. On 5 October, a full page advertisement for the novel blared from the pages of the *Athenaeum* (which declined to review it), to be followed up with regular national updates of the book's remarkable sales. On 9 November, another advert was claiming the first edition (more accurately, impression) of 15,000 and the second and third, each of 5,000, were all exhausted, and by 30 November, a seventh edition had been published, suggesting sales had topped 40,000 in a month. Promotional materials selectively excerpted Courtney's review, playing up the cultural legitimacy of a reference to 'Juvenalian' satire but eliminating negative qualifications. Guy and Small note how Wilde's society comedies 'were aimed at an audience who either aspired to that class or (and this is more likely) were fascinated by, perhaps resentful of, the "goings on" of their "betters,"' and 'happy to see representations of them as flawed or immoral individuals' (Guy and Small 2006: 118). The obviously hypocritical *IPN* titillated its readers in recounting the downfall of Wilde or the Palace Club, instilling by default a sense of virtuousness and well-being in those who had enjoyed accounts of misdemeanours. Corelli constructed her audience on similar lines, but the extent of her implication in the world she denounced was harder to judge. It is impossible to doubt the sincerity of Mavis Clare's words, much as Corelli denied the novelist was her fictional mouthpiece, but at the same time, *Sorrows* seemed to linger a little too lovingly over the very sordidness it purported to decry. Add to this Methuen's strongly commercial sensibilities, and the result is a book riven with contradictions, nowhere more so than in its treatment of the 'new fiction', the 'sex novels' which had in some ways blazed the trail for Corelli's. A '*farrago* (Latin) of balderdash and vanity', sneered *Punch*, mocking Corelli's education as much as her story (7/12/95: 269).

Geoffrey Tempest marries the beautiful but dissolute Sibyl Elton, whose immoral sexual attitudes are, she admits, caused by reading literature exalting 'polygamous purity' (Corelli 1998: 297). Sounding rather like the *PMG* reviewing Victoria Cross(e), Geoffrey claims such novels are 'detestable [. . .] in style and morality', with one especially offensive volume 'destitute of grammar as well as decency' (246), a charge often levelled at Corelli's slipshod prose. Sibyl however is addicted to books that go 'into the details of the lives of outcasts – that explain and analyse the secret vices of men – that advocate almost as a sacred duty "free love"' (162). She has no defence against their blandishments, for reading Swinburne's 'Before a Crucifix' (1878) with its depiction of Christ as 'carrion crucified', has shattered her Christian faith. That the most offensive stanzas are quoted in Sibyl's lengthy suicide note, composed after Lucio spurns her, is another instance of the book being drawn to the very things it apparently abominates. Swinburne's lines left a powerful impression on the probably pseudonymous 'John Smith', who wrote to him to say he had read 'Marie Correlli's [sic] book' and had been disgusted by 'the worst, most brutal, and coarsest thing that could be said'. 'You do credit to your name,' Smith finished, 'for your language is of *Swine*' (Swinburne 2004: 84). Smith did not include his address, denying Swinburne the pleasure of vituperative counterblast.

A successful writer could earn a great deal of money in 1895, as Arthur Machen's onetime employer, George Redway realised, publishing *How to Write Fiction*, a practical guide geared to producing short stories for magazines that reprinted Maupassant's 'The Necklace' as a model for would-be writers. As the commercial behemoths Corelli, Du Maurier, Hall Caine and Ian MacLaren dominated the *Bookman*'s lists, the latter with *Days of Auld Lang Syne*, the first edition of which had a 30,000 copy print run, other writers had mixed fortunes. Lord De Tabley had never properly recovered from the influenza he had contracted in the earlier epidemic, and died on 22 November: Theodore Watts promptly offered appropriate memorial anecdotes in the *SR* (30/11/95: 747), though Swinburne told his mother that the poet, 'was what I should call prematurely old' (Swinburne 1962: 92). Bram Stoker's *The Shoulder of Shasta* was praised in some quarters for its evocation of the Californian landscape, but the romance between Esse, a convalescent English heiress, and the bear hunter Grizzly Dick, met with derision. 'The less said about *The Shoulder of Shasta* the better for everyone concerned,' was the *Athenaeum*'s verdict (16/11/95: 677). Violet Hunt was attracting attention with her skilful dialogue in *A Hard Woman*, a successor to *The Maiden's Progress* (1894) which was told almost wholly in dialogue; her experiments influenced Henry James's *The Awkward Age* (1899). George MacDonald's *Lilith* was a 'strange mystical farrago [. . .] neither lucid nor edifying' (*SR* 9/11/95: 639), but the American émigré Robert W. Chambers's collection of supernatural stories, *The King in Yellow* 'succeeds where so many try and fail' said the *Bookman*. 'He makes our flesh creep' (10/95: 29). Chambers's book began with several interlinked tales dealing with a play, *The King in Yellow*, which drives its readers insane. The seventh *YB*, published in October, was a pallid affair, but a yellow book that transmitted madness remained an audacious conception. More startling still was the opening story, 'The Repairer of Reputations', set in the nightmarish America of April and May 1920 where suicide is legal and people gas themselves in public in state-owned execution rooms. As if this were not bizarre enough, the story's narrator believes he has a claim to the American throne and employs Mr Wilde, a man of 'marvellous intelligence and knowledge' (Chambers 2004: 14) to help him pursue it with his 500 strong network of men who repair damaged reputations. Wilde is a deformed dwarf – he has no ears and no fingers on his left hand – 'eccentric' and though 'many called him insane', the narrator knows him 'to be as sane as I was' (14), an unconvincing claim from a character who has himself been in an asylum. From this summary, and from the fact that Mr Wilde dies in May, the story seems a remarkable parallel to the events of the Spring, with Wilde's physical strangeness perhaps a symbolic representation of his sexual difference or the ostracism it prompted, and his network the exact opposite of that muttered about by the London press. However, no reviewer could have drawn such parallels and the *Athenaeum* said instead that the story was an 'almost too realistic expression of the fever-ish dreams and perverted cunning of a lunatic' (23/11/95: 715). While *The King in Yellow* remains admired by connoisseurs of weird fiction, its use of characters called Wilde (and Constance) seems no more than coincidental.

One wonders what Wilde would have thought of Chambers's book or indeed the events of the early morning of 4 November when George Alexander was arrested within twenty yards of his Chelsea home after popping out to post a letter. Solicited by Elizabeth Davis (24), 'a nightly loiterer in the locality', a woman who 'even in the dim light' appeared 'poor, miserable, starved and ill clad,' Alexander gave her a 'the first coin' he pulled from his pocket (*T* 5/11/95), where-upon a passing policeman misinterpreted the exchange and arrested him. The magistrate believed Alexander's explanation, helped by a character testimony from Pinero, then enjoying considerable success with his comedy, *The Benefit of the Doubt,* but the story Alexander told the *Times* following his acquittal hinted, like Lankester's, at an over-zealous police force. He did not go so far as to suggest black-mail and bribery were part of its *modus operandi* but the incident left a nasty taste even if it ultimately enhanced Alexander's popular-ity. When he performed in *Liberty Hall* on 7 November, the audience cheered.

The day of Alexander's hearing saw Lane issue Machen's *The Three Impostors*. Allen's *The British Barbarians* followed on 7 November. Machen's interlinked 'Milesian tales' depicted the sinister activities of a London occultist and his followers and featured a shockingly violent finale in which Joseph Walters, a young man trying to escape the magi-cian's clutches after stealing a priceless coin, is caught, tortured, and nailed to the floor of a deserted house while a fire is lit upon his living body. Less horrific, Allen's story was nonetheless striking, featuring as it did a time traveller from the twenty-fifth century who visits suburban England and becomes embroiled in an at once satirical and melodra-matic relationship with a married woman. Both novels fell on stony ground. The *Lady's Pictorial* thought *The Three Impostors* 'gruesome and *unmanly*', the *GH* found it 'literally sickening' (Machen 1924: 13, 10). Other critics felt it was derivative (especially of Stevenson), repeti-tive, improbable and clumsily constructed. Allen's novel was more obvi-ously antagonistic in its politics, and its depiction of a 'civilised' England governed by social codes that anthropologists would study as taboos if manifested by primitive peoples, offered a deliberately provocative satirical charge. However, with its plot devices linked in the public eye at least with *The Time Machine* and *The Wonderful Visit* – Allen had begun *The British Barbarians* long before either appeared but could not find a publisher for it – and its epigrammatic wit less incisive than Shaw's and less amusing than Wilde's, the book never matched the sales of *The Woman Who Did*. That novel, of course, continued to sell, and did so for the rest of Allen's life. Lane's accounts show that he was easily the Bodley Head's most successful author in 1895, his royalties of £1,047, 15s 1d. leaving him well clear of Watson, Le Gallienne (£250 4s 8d) and Davidson (£224 17s 1d), let alone Machen (£59 16s 7d), Grahame (£45 12s) and Ella D'Arcy (£14 9s 11d) (JLA).

Allen prefaced *The British Barbarians* with a self-righteous defence of his authorial position and a remarkable attack on the 'decadents of the town', their 'sham idyls' [*sic*] and 'tinsel arcadias'. 'We have tired of their stuffy atmosphere, their dazzling jets, their weary ways, their gaudy dresses,' he went on, 'we shun the sunken cheeks, the lacklustre eyes, the heart sick souls of your painted goddesses', not to mention 'strange decadent sins and morbid pleasures' (Allen 1895: xviii-xix). Earlier in the year, Carpenter had signed himself 'Helvellyn'. Now Allen joined him in advocating the clean air of the hill-top as a pulpit from which to issue cultural judgements, a stance *Punch* ridiculed in a poem, 'A Prophet Too Previous' (4/1/96: 6). Rather than being a responsible thinker, it suggested, Allen filled 'the timid with affright' and drove 'advanced young ladies half demented', not least because he portrayed a woman's adultery in a sympathetic manner and mocked the sanctity of marriage.

Despite his respect for Allen's scientific writings, Wells was unforgiving in the *SR*. The novel was 'even farther from the sphere of art than *The Woman Who Did*, which is saying a very great deal' (14/12/95: 785). The *Athenaeum* felt the book lacked subtlety (14/12/95: 830). The *PMG* offered a column's length of summary, before branding it 'as arrant a farrago of nonsense as could conceivably be hurtled [*sic*] into the dustbins of contemporary letters' (12/12/95), while Darlington's *Northern Echo* feared that if 'civilised life' were lived by Allen's 'peculiar code of morals' it would 'soon become chaotic' (23/11/95). Allen's strident preface was an attempt to distance himself from decadence, but his position was complicated by his friendship with Le Gallienne, his publication by Lane, and by the fact that he used epigrammatic strategies seen in Wilde and in earlier Keynotes such as Florence Farr's *The Dancing Faun* (1894) (Freeman 2005: 111–28). Symons felt *London Nights* had been judged on moral rather than artistic grounds, but Machen and Allen were condemned on both counts. Neither published with Lane again; Machen's next novel, *The Hill of Dreams*, did not appear until 1907.

Far From Dear Father

One of *Punch*'s complaints about Allen was that his fiction led astray young women readers. 'A Prophet Too Previous' cited a 'Miss Lanchester' as an example of such unfortunates, an allusion to events in late October, when an outspoken New Woman's domestic disagreements became national news. The daughter of a wealthy architect, twenty-four-year-old Edith Lanchester had studied botany and zoology at what is now Birkbeck, University of London, belonged to the Social Democratic Federation (SDF) and was a friend of Eleanor Marx. 'Intelligent', 'capable', 'self-reliant and independent' according to the *IPN*, which also noted her 'prepossessing' appearance (the *Star* called her 'picturesque'), Lanchester had been dismissed from her teaching post for 'advanced opinions' and was now a secretary and typist for an Australian mining company, doing voluntary advocacy work for the unemployed in her spare time (*IPN* 2/11/95; Bland 159). She had recently inherited £500. Possessing 'dark hair cut short like a boy's', 'a child's face' and 'sparkling eyes' (*LWN* 27/10/95) and fond of walking about whistling with her hands in her jacket pockets, Lanchester looked not unlike a cross-dressed music hall performer, and fascinated the male journalists who reported her story as 'A Socialist Romance' (*LWN*) or 'The London Abduction Case' (*GH*). She lodged with a builder and his wife, Mr and Mrs Gray, fellow members of the SDF in Battersea, and planned to live with her boyfriend, another SDF member, James Sullivan, a twenty-eight-year-old railway clerk (some sources say he worked in a black lead factory). They called each other 'Biddy' and 'Shamus'. Press reports repeatedly termed Edith his fiancée, and Sullivan himself called her this when seeking legal support (*LWN* 27/10/95), but Lanchester had no intention of marrying, and while she denied ever having read *The Woman Who Did*, she shared Herminia's view that the marriage service was cant and left women no better than chattels. Allen's novel was frequently mentioned in the press coverage of the story, its title a handy label for female sexual or political dissidence. 'Grant Allen has not a little to answer for,' said *RN* (3/11/95).

Lanchester told her parents she would be moving in with Sullivan on 26 October. On 25 October, a carriage arrived at her lodgings. In it were her father, her three brothers, and Dr George Blandford, author of the influential textbook, *Insanity and its Treatment* (1871), reprinted as recently as 1892. The Lanchesters were convinced madness was the only conceivable explanation for her behaviour, and when she first refused to return to the family home and then told Blandford marriage was immoral and resisted his attempts to have her committed to an asylum,

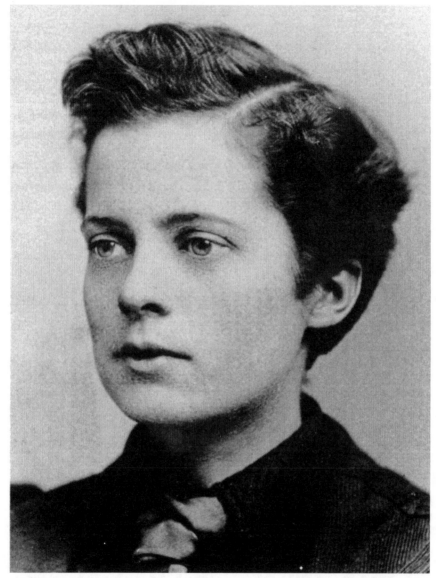

Figure 12. The 'picturesque' but defiant Edith Lanchester. Elsa Lanchester Estate.

they pushed Mrs Gray aside, grabbed Edith, tied her up and dragged her off to the Priory, a private mental institution in Roehampton. She was, it seemed, incapable of appreciating that her behaviour meant, in Blandford's words, 'utter ruin' and 'social suicide' (*Western Mail* 1/11/95).

Edith Lanchester's abduction was an event more suited to *The Woman in White* than *The Woman Who Did*, and even as Sullivan mobilised the Legitimation League (an organisation that campaigned for the rights of illegitimate children), the SDF (which declined to help in an official capacity, fearing the popular equation of socialism with free love) and John Burns, Battersea's radical MP, the press seized on the behaviour of Henry Jones Lanchester and furious controversy ensued. Mr Lanchester wrote to the *Times*, telling the paper's readers Edith was 'not of sound mind' (her grandmother and uncle had suffered from insanity, he claimed) and that her 'naturally impressionable temperament' and 'overstudy' had made her susceptible to dangerous doctrines (31/10/95). Always willing to attack the New Woman, the *DT* supported him, calling Edith a 'wretched girl' (31/10/95), but the letters pages of the *Star* showed such opinions were not confined to the reactionary press. Some correspondents asked what right Lanchester had to make her children bastards, while others pointed out her likely fate when Sullivan abandoned her – the work-house, starvation or whoring (Rubinstein 1986: 61). *RN* pointed out that Lanchester, while headstrong, was a free agent and her abduction was monstrous: it was Blandford, not she, who should be in the asylum (3/11/95). Robert Blatchford's socialist *Clarion* gave her unconditional support, arguing that 'a woman has a perfect right to do what she likes with her own body [. . .] in defiance of priests, laws, customs and cant' (Eley 2002: 14). Even Queensberry got involved, suggesting the couple should go through a marriage ceremony which they could afterwards repudiate. He offered them a wedding present of £100 if they did so, but they did not take up his offer (Rubinstein 1986: 62).

Acquiring a writ of *habeas corpus*, Sullivan and friends from the SDF tracked Edith down and sang 'The People's Flag' outside The Priory on the night of 27 October (Hunt 97). Edith's parents and then three Lunacy Commissioners visited on 28 October, interviewing her at length and deciding she was sane. She was released next day under Section 75 of the Lunacy Act, having been 'detained without sufficient cause' (Rubinstein *ODNB*), leaving the asylum in the company of Sullivan and her MP and giving an interview to the *IPN* (9/11/95). Following her release, she never spoke to her father again, living with Sullivan until his death in 1945. The couple had two children, one of whom, Elsa Lanchester, became a noted actress. Her autobiography paints an unsparing picture of her mother's life as 'a professional avant-gardist' whose unwavering political commitment brought her little happiness (Lanchester 316).

The Lanchester affair was a *cause celebre* which, though it did not lead to immediate reform of the lunacy laws – these went unchanged until 1959 – perhaps prompted their more sensitive interpretation (Rubinstein *ODNB*). The *British Medical Journal* and the *Lancet* both agonised over the implications of Blandford's judgement, but while they were at pains to distinguish between insanity, eccentricity and breaches of social convention, they saw Socialism as a dangerous influence on impressionable women. As Karen Hunt says in her fascinating reading of the case and its repercussions, the SDF and many Socialist politicians, including Keir Hardie, worried about the public's equation of Socialism with sexual immorality, and were still discussing Lanchester's case two years afterwards (K. Hunt 1996: 94–104). The SDF also asked Asquith for legal advice concerning the possibility of Lanchester pursuing damages for her wrongful imprisonment, Blandford's potentially slanderous comments about her insanity, and the bruises suffered by Mrs Gray (98–9), though it eventually decided against taking legal action.

Exit Jabez

Edith Lanchester was abducted on the day Jabez Balfour's long-awaited trial, 'the first prosecution of its kind under the Companies Act' (Marjoribanks [1929] 1989: 87) opened at the Old Bailey. Balfour, his chief lieutenant, George Edward Brock, and two smaller fry faced some of the Crown's most renowned advocates, and while Brock had been so far under Balfour's spell that he had invested £3,500 of his own money mere days before the Liberator's collapse, there was little sympathy for him. Public interest was intense – there were even more journalists in court than there had been for the opening of the Queensberry libel trial – and as David McKie observes, so far had Balfour's tentacles reached, it proved difficult to find jurymen who had not invested something in his many schemes (2005: 213). Balfour's frauds had had tragic repercussions throughout Britain, but the trial itself often lacked human interest because of the complexity of its financial evidence: the Official Receiver spent seven days in the witness box. Balfour and his associates were charged with 'making false entries, publishing false accounts, circulating false balance sheets'; the ringleader faced additional charges concerning his alleged misappropriation of £20,000 in purchasing Whitehall Court in 1886 (214). The deliberately tangled structure of Balfour's affairs soon became obvious, the prosecution demonstrating how 'bogus transactions' (215) shuffled non-existent money between businesses, giving an entirely misleading impression of the Liberator's status. The jury struggled to follow the detail and complained that even when he was in the dock, Balfour could still ruin them by keeping them from their businesses; after the trial, they were spared further jury service for three years. Confused by minutiae, they nevertheless had little doubt of Balfour's guilt. The rules governing fraud cases meant Balfour could not give evidence, but he was permitted to read a statement that attempted to explain and justify his activities. His listeners were unimpressed, the jury retiring for only 35 minutes. The following day, 28 November, Balfour was sentenced to fourteen years with Hard Labour, a punishment that reflected the damage he had done to individual investors as well as to the probity of the British financial sector. Brock, ably defended by Marshall Hall, received only nine months. Balfour's sentence was cheered in pubs and halls nationwide for he was, as the judge said, 'the master mind' behind the fraud who had 'darkened thousands of humble homes' (*IPN* 7/12/95). After a meal of cold beef and pickles, washed down with a bottle of Bass, he was taken first to Holloway and then, on 12 December, to Wormwood Scrubs where, minus his familiar beard and cigars, he sewed mailbags as V460–14. The *IPN* reported that Stockwell Watts's relief fund, established in 1893, had seen 2,629 claims of destitution, and made 7,469 grants to petitioners. It calculated 105 deaths could be laid at Balfour's door, the implication being that many of those he had ruined committed suicide (7/12/95). The fund eventually raised £114,000 (Marjoribanks [1929] 1989: 87). As West Croydon Congregational Chapel wondered whether it should sell its £700 bells, a gift from the disgraced financier when mayor of the town, Charles Smith, a labourer, took the law into his own hands, breaking into the gardens of Balfour's former home and cutting a large quantity of holly to sell as Christmas decorations. As Balfour had robbed the poor, Smith said, 'I am justified in helping myself'. He was fined 8s or seven days in jail (*IPN* 28/12/95).

Jude the Obscene

The publication of Thomas Hardy's *Jude the Obscure* on 1 November was one of the major literary events of the year. Contemporary reviewers looked forward to other books which appeared at the same time, such as Meredith's *The Amazing Marriage* – a new Meredith was 'one of the few really exciting events in literature' said the *Athenaeum* (Williams 1971: 432) – and Watson's *The Father of the Forest and Other Poems*, but neither has endured. Even Meredith's admirers found his new novel challenging, with Gosse noting 'the increasing extravagance of his artificial diction' in the *St James's Gazette*. Meredith was, Gosse said, 'distinguished and original' but 'the Alexandrian extravagance of [his] style has now reached such a pitch that it is difficult to enjoy and sometimes impossible to understand what he writes' (Williams 1971: 429). 'Pertinacious euphuism often painfully clouds the lucidity of his intelligence,' he added in a later piece (R.G. Cox 1970: 263). Watson by contrast was merely dull. 'He seems to be on the point of rising out of rhetoric into absolute poetry,' the *Athenaeum* commented, 'but he never actually makes the ascent' (30/11/95: 747). *Forest* still sold around 5,000 copies, and contributing to an income of £544 for the year.

Hardy began working on *Jude* as far back as 1887, finally finishing it in March 1895. From December 1894 onwards it had appeared in 'mangled and emasculated' instalments in *Harper's New Monthly Magazine*, at first as *The Simpletons* and then as *Hearts Insurgent*, with Hardy bowdlerising his text to make it suitable for 'the most fastidious maiden' (209). This was a painful process, and he was glad of the support of his publishers, Osgood, McIlvaine, whose stock was high following *Trilby*'s success. They issued the 'proper' version as the eighth volume of the collected edition of Hardy's 'Wessex Novels'.

In a letter to Edward Clodd of 10 November, Hardy noted 'the sheaf of purpose-novels we have had lately on the marriage question' (Hardy 1980: 92), pointing out how misleading it was to read *Jude* in such terms. His preface claimed instead that the book dealt with the 'tragedy of unfulfilled aims' and was 'a novel addressed by a man to men and women of full age, which attempts to deal unaffectedly with [. . .] fret and fever, derision and disaster' and dramatise 'without mincing of words, a deadly war waged between flesh and spirit' (Hardy 1985: xxxv). In its depiction of Jude Fawley's doomed attempts to enter university or to resolve the 'deadly war' symbolised by his relationships with Arabella Donn, the 'complete and substantial female animal' (36) whom Margaret Oliphant called 'a human pig' (R.G. Cox 1970: 258), and Sue Bridehead, his Swinburne-reading, highly strung cousin who espouses 'pagan' ideas but shrinks from their sensual enactment as a woman who won't, the novel challenged an array of Victorian shibboleths, as well as offending good taste in its descriptions of drunkenness and animal slaughter.[4] The killing of Sue and Jude's children by 'Little Father Time', the boy Arabella claims is Jude's son, was yet more horrifying than the events so roundly condemned in Egerton's 'Wedlock', dismaying even Hardy's keenest admirers.

Gissing spent the weekend of 14–15 September with Hardy, listening to him complaining how difficult it was 'to describe in decent language' Arabella throwing 'a pig's *pizzle*' at Jude. His visit convinced him that 'Thomas' was 'vastly the intellectual inferior of Meredith' and possessed 'a good deal of coarseness in his nature' (Gissing 1978: 387). Sent a copy of *Jude* by Clarence McIlvaine on 3 November, he felt it was 'likely to make a row' (Gissing 1995: 47). 'Thomas has absolutely lost his saving Humour,' he told his brother on 8 November, and while the 'bitterness' was 'often wonderfully effective,' the overall impression was of 'a sad book' (49). 'Poor Thomas is utterly on the wrong tack,' he told another correspondent. 'At his age a habit of railing at the universe is not overcome' (62). Published reviews shared Gissing's regret at Hardy's humourlessness, with the *Athenaeum* of 23 November finding the novel marred by 'querulous bitterness'. It also misunderstood the book's sexual dynamics, saying Arabella was 'loathsome and repulsive in the highest degree, and she certainly would be to a man enamoured of Sue's comparative grace and refinement' (R.G. Cox 1970: 249–51). Even Swinburne, who was delighted by his presentation copy, hoped for 'another admission into an English paradise "under the greenwood tree"' though he praised Hardy as the finest tragedian since Balzac. On 5 November he told him 'the beauty, the terror, and the truth, are all yours, and yours alone' (Swinburne 1962: 91). Swinburne read Hardy in terms of classical tragedy (he borrowed Aristotle's categorisation of Aeschylus, 'most tragic of poets', to describe him) and reworked Byron's 'The worm, the canker, and the grief, I Are mine alone!' in a way Hardy appreciated, the novelist telling Gosse on 10 November the letter was 'too enthusiastic for me to quote with modesty' (Hardy 1980: 93).

It was Gosse whom Hardy lauded for writing the most 'discriminating' review of the novel to date. If this was the one that appeared in January's *Cosmopolis*, Gosse may have shown Hardy a draft version; that the published piece includes an allusion to 'a sheaf of "purpose" stories on the "marriage question"' (R.G. Cox 1970: 264) suggests either that Hardy was fond of repeating the phrase or that Gosse had seen his letter to Clodd. Either way, Gosse was intimate with Hardy, and this may give the essay the feel of an 'approved' reading despite its criticisms and misinterpretations.

Gosse traced the 'almost rectilinear puzzle of the sexual relations of the four principal characters' (266), played up the novel's consideration of degeneration and heredity, defended Oxford against Hardy's criticisms of 'Christminster' and, like Gissing, observed the 'jarring note of rebellion', asking 'What has Providence done to Mr Hardy that he should rise up in the arable land of Wessex and shake his fist at his Creator?' (269). He also commented that while 'every public bar and village fair knows Arabella', Sue is 'a strange and unwelcome product of exhaustion' whose '*vita sexualis*' is 'the central interest of the book'.

'Enough is told about it to fill the specimen tables of a German special-ist,' Gosse concluded (268), seeing in her not a manifestation of newness but 'a terrible study in pathology' (270). Sue's character was much dis-cussed, with the *Westminster Review* finding her 'nearly as fascinating' as Elfride in *A Pair of Blue Eyes* (273) and the *ILN* 'an intensely vivid personality' despite Hardy's 'too evident effort to focus in her all the restless adventuring of our modern adventurous womanhood' (276). George Egerton was also impressed, judging her 'a marvellously true psychological study of a type less rare than the ordinary male observer supposes' (Hardy 1980: 102). Hardy himself 'liked' Sue, 'depressed' as he was 'at the feebleness of my drawing of her' (98), and he had the effrontery to tell Egerton on 22 December that 'It is extraordinary that a type of woman, comparatively common & getting commoner, should have escaped fiction so long' (Hardy 1980: 102).

Hardy's reputation meant he was generally accorded more respect than New Woman novelists, even by his detractors, but this respect led some to claim it brought with it obligations towards respectability. William Archer chose *Jude* as his book of the year in the *Daily Chronicle* (1/1/96), and Havelock Ellis defended it at length in the *Savoy* as late as October 1896, but the *PMG* called the book 'Jude the Obscene', a work of almost unrelieved gloom. After recounting its plot with distaste, it ended with a plea, 'don't disappoint us again. Give us quickly another and a cleaner book to take the bad taste out of our mouths' (12/11/95). 'We may grant Mr Hardy's right, as a real artist, to be full-blooded,' said the *Standard* 'but we cannot grant his claim to be nasty' (31/12/95). *Punch* retitled it 'Dude the Diffuse' and its author 'Toomuch Too Hardy', chuckling over the hero's ambition to 'fathom the boundless depths of a Meredithian epigram' (14/12/95: 285).

Many (male) critics were beguiled (and irritated) by Sue and shocked by the book's frankness, but Wells struck a different note in arguing the novel's sexual content was less important than its 'tremendous indict-ment' of the university system. He hailed its finale as 'the voice of the educated proletarian, speaking more distinctly than it has ever spoken before in English literature'. No living novelist combined Hardy's 'breadth of sympathy', 'knowledge' or creative power (Wells 1980: 283). In Wells's opinion, *Jude* was a political novel in which Sue was 'the feminine counterpart of Jude's intellectual side' and in which the relationship between sexual desire and social convention was often powerfully antagonistic. 'To have veiled the matter, to have ignored sex altogether in deference to the current fashion, would have gone far to make *Jude the Obscure* into a *John Halifax, Gentleman*,' he said. It was therefore a lamentable reflection on British literary and cultural life that

Hardy's approach should have 'roused the common reviewer to a pitch of malignant hatred' (282–3).

Wells was a young radical whose prospects had been transformed by the educational reforms of the 1870s and indeed, by the mass readership for his work they helped to create. Sexually outspoken, in his own words 'a prodigy of infant Impiety', and educated, after years of privation, at the Normal School of Science (later the Royal College) and finally, at University College, London, Wells may have had the self discipline (and good fortune) that Jude Fawley lacked but he was nonetheless well placed to understand something of Hardy's anger. Older or more conventional reviewers denounced the book, affronted by its 'immoral' message rather than recognising how it addressed the still more iniquitous inequalities of contemporary Britain. Even younger writers were not always impressed; in 1902, Machen dubbed it 'a long pamphlet on secondary education for farm labourers, with agnostic notes' (Machen 1960: 123). The Bishop of Wakefield, W.W. How claimed he had burned the book – 'probably in his despair at not being able to burn me,' Hardy later joked (Hardy 1985: xxxvi) – and it was not stocked by W.H. Smith's lending library. In *Blackwood's* January number, Margaret Oliphant lambasted 'The Anti-Marriage League' she saw represented by Grant Allen and Hardy, condemning *Jude* for 'grossness, indecency, and horror' (R.G. Cox 1970: 257) and sniping at Hardy for publishing even a watered-down version of it in a family magazine. Hardy's laconic disgust at this charge was well illustrated by his letter to Allen of 7 January 1896, which thanked him for a copy of *The British Barbarians* and counter-attacked Oliphant on commercial grounds. 'That a woman who purely for money's sake has for the last 30 years flooded the magazines & starved out scores of better workers, should try to write down novelists whose books sell better than her own, caps all the shamelessness of Arabella,' he observed (Hardy 1980: 196).

While Oliphant pontificated, Hardy showed the difficulty of separating moral from economic questions. *Jude* was not universally condemned, being defended at length by the *Bookman*, which felt Hardy had been accorded no more respect in some quarters than 'some intellectual schoolgirl' (1/96: 121). It was however his final novel; he wrote in 1912 that the controversy 'cur[ed] me of further interest in novel-writing' (Hardy 1985: xxxvii). When he contacted Allen in January, he was taking his mind off the whole business by learning to cycle and accompanying his wife on rides through the Dorset countryside (Pite 2006: 361–2).

An Epidemic of Indecency

The mild autumn weather, which had caused cases of sunstroke in the City in early October, yielded to signs of another cruel winter. In an ominous portent, huge flocks of seagulls appeared on the Thames near Blackfriars Bridge, and a Black-Throated Diver, driven inland by storms, attacked a boy in Ashford Hill, Berkshire (a labourer killed it with a spade) (*IPN* 23/11/95). The 1,400 strong force assembled to establish a military base in Kumasi in defiance of the Ashanti king's wishes, was delayed at Liverpool by heavy seas. When Alexander was arrested in Chelsea, the police implied his rubber galoshes were worn for the sinister purpose of muffling his movements, whereas they were actually a sensible precaution on the muddy streets. Heavy rain swept the country. Birmingham disappeared under a blanket of fog.

In mid-November, Justice Wills ventured out of London to adjudicate at Winchester Assizes. One of his cases involved Richard Stephens, County Magistrate for Bournemouth, who along with Walter Stokes, a policeman, was charged with indecency and related offences under the terms of the CLAA. The pair were lovers, writing long and sexually explicit letters to one another, 'absolutely incredible in their depth of degradation and filth', though it is not clear how the letters came to light or indeed how the men's behaviour came to the attention of the police. They compounded their offence, in Wills's view, by writing such letters on Sundays. One from 7 April 1895 'described in beastly detail what they had done and what they were going to do.' Another of 14 July contained 'filth, piety, gratitude to God for having created opportunities for these persons to misbehave' and then 'lapsed into filth of the most disgusting description'. No stranger to disgust, and finding his duty 'almost intolerable' because it involved 'having habitually to deal with a large mixture of filth,' Wills's conclusions were familiar ones. The country seemed to be 'infested' by 'an epidemic of indecency,' he fumed. 'Whether the present outbreak was due to attention having been drawn to something which had happened in London' he did not know, but he hoped that once sentence was passed, the epidemic would 'die away' as it had following the conclusion of the earlier case. Oblivious to the self-contradictory nature of this summing-up, Wills sentenced Stephens, an Eton and Merton man, to two years Hard Labour and Stokes to five months of the same (*Hampshire Advertiser* 16/11/95). The case was erratically reported, with the *IPN* predictably drawing attention to 'Disgusting Hypocrisy | Sanctity and Vice' (25/11/95) and the Blackburn *Weekly Standard* noting how Wills had described Stokes as Stephens's 'creature', the victim of a prolonged campaign of debauchery

(23/11/95). That Stephens's character was vouched for by a clergyman who had known him for fifty years only worsened his offences in the judge's eyes.

As Wills was denouncing Stephens and Stokes, the 'something which had happened in London' was still in Wandsworth infirmary attempting to resolve three pressing issues: divorce, bankruptcy, and Douglas's planned contribution to the *Mercure de France*. Sherard acted as a go-between for Wilde and Constance, attempting to prevent the initiation of divorce proceedings and trying to persuade Bosie not to reprint Wilde's correspondence. The prospect was abhorrent, Wilde felt, later telling Douglas his letters 'should have been to you things sacred and secret beyond anything in the whole world' (*WCL* 717). When Sherard's arguments foundered, he wrote to the *Mercure*'s editor, telling him of Wilde's objections. The war between Wilde's friends that would continue for the next three decades was now under way.

The Home Office was perturbed by rumours of Wilde's illness and mental decline and ordered an inspection by two Broadmoor doctors, David Nicolson and Richard Brayne, on 22 October. They watched through a spy-hole as Wilde entertained fellow infirmary inmates with his talk, and then interviewed him at length. They recommended he be moved to a country prison, given a larger cell, and put to more varied work than oakum picking or mailbag stitching. He was also to be allowed more books, an increased cocoa allowance and 'such association with other prisoners as may be deemed advisable or desirable or convenient'. They were at pains to point out though that a man of Wilde's 'proclivities and with his avowed love for the society of males' should only be allowed association '*under the continuous supervision of a warder*' (Hyde 1963: 37). The report's initial result was to increase security levels in the infirmary, but it was also decided Wilde would be transferred to Reading once his recovery was complete.

On 12 November, Wilde attended the Bankruptcy Court, where, in the company of A.H. Wildy, the Official Receiver, and watched once more by Ross, he tried to account for his parlous financial state. Never having kept records, his overview of his expenditure was impressionistic but sobering. As Hyde notes, 'an average day's expenses in London' ranged from £12 to £20; the three month rental of a house in Goring-upon-Thames in the summer of 1893 cost £1,340 (Hyde 1963: 39). The sum collected by Wilde's friends was insufficient to cover outstanding debts, and he was declared bankrupt. On 19 November, he was told of his transfer to Reading Gaol, where gardening, bookbinding and library work awaited him. He left Wandsworth the following day.

On 10 November, anniversary of his jailing in the 'Maiden Tribute' controversy of 1885, W.T. Stead went to work in his prison uniform, but for Wilde, the 'livery of shame' could never be worn defiantly. One reason among many for this was an incident that occurred during the transfer from Wandsworth, which Wilde dates as 13 November though it actually occurred a week later. Changing trains at Clapham Junction, Wilde stood on the platform, uniformed and handcuffed, for half an hour while being taunted by what he recalled as 'a jeering mob' (*WCL* 757). In *The Story of an Unhappy Friendship* (1902), Sherard revealed that a man who recognised the playwright called out 'By God, that's Oscar Wilde!' and spat in his face (Hyde 1963: 40). The public humili-ation left Wilde traumatised. 'For a year after that was done to me I wept every day at the same hour and for the same space of time,' he told Douglas in his lengthy prison letter (*WCL* 757), but if he had hoped that life at Reading would be any easier than it had been in London, he was mistaken. On arrival, his hair, which had regained some of its lustre in the infirmary, was again cropped. 'You don't know what this means to me,' he sobbed (Hyde 1963: 52). Under Major Isaacson, a governor who enforced regulations with a strictness tantamount to brutality, Wilde would become C.3.3 and would undergo further privation and bullying until Isaacson was replaced by the altogether more humane James Nelson in the summer of 1896. 'I am not in prison,' Douglas told More Adey on 30 November, 'but I think I suffer as much as Oscar and perhaps more' (Ellmann 464). Adey drafted a petition requesting Wilde's sentence be mitigated, but he won little support. William Holman Hunt offered an especially robust rejection of Adey's approaches, replying that as a 'self-restrained and orderly' member of society, he felt the law had treated Wilde 'with exceeding leniency' (Ellmann1987: 463).

Endings

As the year drew to its close, the tussle for the Football League Championship intensified. Villa almost missed their match at Burnley on 23 November, and were rescued only by their officials chartering a special train from Preston. Arriving shortly before kick-off, they nonetheless managed to overcome a spirited home side reinforced by Scottish signings from Celtic and Motherwell. A 25 yard thunderbolt from Athersmith late in the game secured a 4–3 win, but Villa's form slumped thereafter due to illness and injury. By Christmas, Everton had overcome their indifferent start and topped the table after beating Villa at Goodison on 21 December. Derby County were now second having won all ten of their home games, and Villa third. Small Heath and

WBA were still bottom, while, in the second division, a three-way battle between Liverpool, Manchester City, and Burton Wanderers was in full swing. Attendances continued to rise, and the sport's increasing revenues tempted criminals. Following Everton's home game with Burnley on 30 November, twelve members of the club's staff were arrested. Nine turnstile men, an office boy, a labourer and a groundsman were found to have devised a way to wind back turnstile counters, meaning attendance figures could be falsified and ticket monies pocketed. A total of £35 was recovered after the Burnley game, though the full extent and duration of the fraud remained unknown. Most of those involved received prison sentences of one to three months; the office boy was bound over (*Liverpool Mercury* 3/12/95, BDP 4/12/95).

The death of G.A. Sala, journalist, novelist and pornographer on 8 December was melancholy in itself as well as severing another link between the 1890s and 'High' Victorianism. In the aftermath of the failure of *Sala's Journal* in 1893, he had been in serious financial difficulties that were only partially alleviated by Rosebery awarding him a £100 Civil List pension. A volume of unreliable memoirs, *The Life and Adventures of George Augustus Sala* (1895) had failed to restore his prosperity, and he was forced to sell his library; its 13,000 books included many rare and presentation volumes. He was buried in Hove's Catholic cemetery on 12 December.

Sala may have died in relative poverty, but the publishing industry continued to grow. With Christmas looming, lucrative rewards beckoned once more. The publication of Matthew Arnold's letters caused some disquiet, for he had died only seven years earlier, and many of those about whom he was critical were still alive. Swinburne sulked over his slighting view of *Tristram of Lyonesse* (1882) which criticised a 'fatal habit of using one hundred words where one would suffice' (Arnold 1895: 232), and his mood was not improved by William Michael Rossetti sending him a copy of *Dante Gabriel Rossetti; His Family Letters With a Memoir*, since it brought back unwelcome memories of his one-time publisher, 'that polecat' Charles Howell, 'the vilest wretch I ever came across'. He was sure Howell, who had blackmailed him over his indecent correspondence, was now 'in that particular circle of Malebolge where the coating of eternal excrement makes it impossible to see whether the damned dog's head is or is not tonsured' (Swinburne 1962: 107).

Arthur Conan Doyle, meanwhile, was in Cairo and delighting in Smith Elder having offered him £4,000 for *Rodney Stone*. Serial and American rights meant he had earned in the region of £7,000 from the book (Lellenberg 2007: 365). Kipling was gratified by Macmillan's authorisation of an initial run of 35,000 copies of *The Second Jungle Book* on the strength of advance orders and the success of its predecessor. The Kipling family coffers were boosted further by the *Century* paying $170 per thousand words for 'The Brushwood Boy', a useful return on a 12,000 word story. Arnold Bennett could only dream of such success and was slaving away at reviews for the penny weekly, *Woman*: he wrote thirty-five notices between 11–21 December (1968: 31) though could note that his literary earnings had almost doubled from 1894's, standing at £98 15s 7d (McDonald 1997: 69). Gissing too was hard at work, though he had time to go Christmas shopping in London on 21 December, a 'day of hideous fog'. He bought his son a game of draughts and a copy of Coventry Patmore's *The Children's Garland from the Best Poets* (1884), though does not record what he bought for his wife (Gissing 1978: 397). His Christmas Day was predictably disastrous, with 'a small joint of wretched beef,' 'a plum pudding like lead' and a 'leathery mince tart' (397). He read Huxley's *Lessons in Elementary Physiology* to take his mind off the horror. Richard Le Gallienne's Christmas was more light-hearted, for his two-year-old daughter Hesper received a musical box which played the music hall songs 'The Randy Dandy Dogs' and 'Get Yer 'Air Cut', the latter of which especially amused him (Whittington-Egan 1960: 291).

Children's books continued to offer generous commercial rewards. Longman's issued *The Adventures of Two Dutch Dolls and a 'Golliwogg'*, an illustrated story in rhyme by Bertha and Florence Upton, a mother and daughter partnership who produced a series of successful *Golliwogg* books including *The Golliwogg at the Seaside* (1898), *The Golliwogg's 'Auto-Go-Cart'* (1901) and *The Golliwogg in the African Jungle* (1909). *The Tiger of Mysore*, *Through Russian Snows*, *A Knight of the White Cross* and *A Woman of the Commune* showed G.A. Henty was as industrious as ever. John Lane scored a hit with an attractive reissue of Stevenson's 1885 collection, *A Child's Garden of Verses*, but Le Gallienne's *Robert Louis Stevenson – An Elegy* offended some by seeming to co-opt the death of a great writer to boost the reputation of a mediocre one.

Elsewhere on the adult lists, Sherard's *Jacob Niemand* was dismissed for its clumsy plot, lack of local colour (it was set in the Lake District, but Sherard, Wordsworth's great grandson, had not inherited the poet's eye), and 'ill-compounded elements of realism and romance' (*A* 7/12/95: 787). Ghost stories were again popular seasonal entertainment, with Kipling's aunt, Louisa Baldwin, offering nine in her collection, *The Shadow on the Blind*. J. Meade Falkner's supernatural novella *The Lost Stradivarius* was praised in periodicals as diverse as the *Newcastle*

Journal and the *Court Circular* for the elegance of its style and the compelling nature of its conceit. Published by Blackwood's, its respectability was assured, but were it not for its being set earlier in the century, it might have been read as a response to certain events of 1895. The spectre of Bosie Douglas hovered over its blending of homoeroticism, sinister rites and the corrupting influence of Adrian Temple, a 'very handsome' (Falkner [1895] 2006: 52) and thoroughly dissolute young man who occupies 'the best rooms' in Magdalen College (109), leads 'a notoriously wild life' and feels 'the fascination of pagan Italy' (108). He eventually leaves England for Naples where his 'dark life became still darker' (110).

Hubert Crackanthorpe's bleak vignettes had little appeal as Christmas gifts, and he spent the festive season moving house. Julie Norregard, back from visiting family in Denmark, took over his old flat while he and his wife moved to 96 Cheyne Walk, Whistler's home until 1878. Roger Fry decorated their house early in the New Year, deploying a black-and-white scheme of understated elegance which the householder did his best to disrupt by putting photographs on the plain walls (Crackanthorpe 1977: 122–3). The doyen of black-and-white design, Beardsley, was helping Symons finalise the first edition of *The Savoy*, assisted by Yeats who had moved into Fountain Court with Symons in October, the better to conduct his affair with Olivia Shakespear. 'I think you should clear out of Arthur Symon's [*sic*] vicinity,' AE told his friend, 'and come over here [to Ireland]. It will be much better for you morally, as well as a place to get inspiration' (AE 1961:16). Yeats ignored his advice, even as it was underscored by more mischief from Beardsley, who had amused Smithers but appalled more strait-laced contributors with a prospectus for *The Savoy* featuring a caricature of a visibly aroused John Bull. Smithers mollified the likes of Edgar Jepson by promising to pulp the copies he had – as he had already sent out 80,000 this was a token sacrifice. Matters took a more serious turn with Beardsley's contentious cover design for the first issue, which depicted a cherub urinating on a copy of the *YB*. Smithers was again amused, but his business sense prevailed and the image had to be reworked. Largely as a result of these pranks, *The Savoy* missed the Christmas trade and did not appear until 11 January. It was an inauspicious beginning: the magazine lasted only eight issues (Nelson 2000: 69–70).

Another *Savoy* contributor, Ernest Dowson, was in Paris, where he took hashish with his friend Gabriel de Lautrec and 'worked hankey-pankey [*sic*] with planchette'. 'We got a message from Satan,' he told Conal O'Riordan on 9 December, 'but he appeared to have nothing of the slightest importance to say' (Dowson 1967: 325). A week later, he was accompanying Smithers on a visit to see one of the publisher's friends, probably a fellow pornographer, incarcerated in St Pélagie prison. He was surprised by the relative luxury of the establishment, as the prisoner's 'room' (not 'cell') was 'one for which one would pay 60 francs at the Hotel des Médicis'. Short of money and frequently on the edge of starvation, Dowson asked O'Riordan, 'Why, oh why am I not a prisoner of Saint- Pélagie? I thought of Oscar & marvelled at the quaintness of this adorable country' (332–3).

After a year to forget, Henry James was back in London and embroiled in an intrigue worthy of one of his stories. His friend Paul Harvey, who later became a distinguished civil servant (knighted in 1911) who edited the *Oxford Companions* to English Literature (1932) and Classical Literature (1937), was being drawn towards an unwise marriage with a Miss Gilmore. Augusta Gregory, who acted as an aunt *manqué* to Harvey, begged James to intervene and prevent him from 'drifting' or 'being forced' into an engagement. Harvey himself had little enthusiasm for marriage, disliking Gilmore's family and thinking that 'there are more charming & refined women in the world' even if he had little chance of meeting them (Gregory 1996: 100). Recalling the diplomatic wrangles that ensued, Gregory slipped into Jamesian mode, writing that 'four hands were needed in place of two to draw our nurseling [Harvey was 26] from the slippery slope towards which he was tending, half-willing' (104); James pronounced the rumoured marriage 'too soon – too sudden – & not inevitable enough' on 16 December (103) and using his consummate tact, somehow extracted Harvey from Miss Gilmore's clutches. Her feelings concerning this manoeuvring are unknown. On 27 November, Harvey was made Assistant Private Secretary to the Secretary of State for War, Lord Lansdowne, and his career began in earnest (Bannerjee 2011: 15).

A turbulent year ended in international uncertainty. During 1895, British forces had seen action in Afghanistan, in Chitral in North West India, where a squabble over the Chitrali succession had seen a British fort besieged, and on the Gold Coast, where Anglo-Ashanti relationships were increasingly fractious. All of these were essentially minor affairs, part-and-parcel of the Imperial project, but two other squabbles were potentially far more serious. A dispute with Venezuela over disputed (and gold rich) territory on the Venezuelan-Guianese border caused the Venezuelans to appeal to the USA for help. President Cleveland invoked the Monroe Doctrine as a response to what was seen as the threat of British colonial expansion, and appointed a boundary commission to assess British claims. There was briefly talk of war, one reason why the Kiplings left Vermont, but Salisbury could ill afford conflict and agreed to abide by the commission's ruling. When this was announced in October 1899, it disallowed Britain's recent claims but allowed the retention of other Venezuelan territory, a decision which appeased both powers, though it caused resentment in Venezuela. Yeats followed the affair with great interest, wondering whether 'the magical armageddon [had] begun at last'. Around 19 December, he invited his friend and fellow occultist, Florence Farr to visit him, telling her that the 'inevitable war' would fulfil his 'prophetic vision' but would be 'a dusk of nations' that 'would drag in half the world'. Anxious about the future, he suggested they 'have tea and perhaps divine for armageddon' (Yeats 1954: 260), a blending of the genteel and apocalyptic unlike anything yet seen in Fountain Court. If they did divine the future however, they restricted their knowledge to fellow initiates, and by New Year's Day, Yeats was more interested in the attractive manuscript bands his sister Lily had given him as a Christmas present.

It was in South Africa, rather than South America, that the most serious problems arose. Growing tension between the Transvaal government and the so-called *uitlanders* drawn there by the discovery of gold on the Witwatersrand in 1886 encouraged Cecil Rhodes, the Prime Minister of Cape Colony, to sanction a military excursion into the Transvaal. He hoped this would provoke a *uitlander* uprising against President Kruger. So preoccupied with the Raid that he missed a champagne luncheon in Cape Town with Lord Hawke's touring team of English cricketers (Wilton 1999: 80), Rhodes had invested heavily in toppling Kruger, and many Imperialists supported his schemes, even if the incursion was to be carried out by his British South Africa Company rather than official British forces. Rhodes left much of the planning to his closest friend, Dr Leander Starr Jameson, who assembled a 511 strong mounted force of company police and volunteers including the Middlesex cricketer Cyril Foley (later nicknamed 'The Raider'). This crossed the Transvaal border on 29 December, armed with six Maxim guns and three pieces of light artillery, but the *uitlander* rebellion did not materialise, and Jameson's men, heavily outnumbered, surrendered on 2 January. The Raid was, said Foley, 'a very dark night – beastly ride – rather a bore' (Wilton 475). Jameson and five of his collaborators were sent back to England on the P&O *Victoria* for trial, and arraigned under the Foreign Enlistment Act of 1870.

Salisbury's government was reluctant to punish Jameson too harshly. He was popular in England and had been made a CB in 1894 for his administrative work in Mashonaland, even though his 'chaotic regime' as the administrator of Southern Rhodesia, was 'characterised by ignorance, neglect, irresponsibility, and unscrupulousness' (Lowry *ODNB*).

He received a fifteen-month prison term, but suffering from gallstones and malaria, served only sixteen weeks of it. Rhodes's company was forced to pay compensation of around a million pounds to the Transvaal, and the fiasco badly damaged his authority. More significantly, it reinforced Kruger, who won the 1896 Transvaal presidential election and considerable international prestige in the eyes of Britain's rivals.

Jameson's Raid may not have prompted an *uitlander* rebellion, but it did make conflict between Britain and the Boers increasingly likely. At such a fraught moment, diplomacy and discretion ought to have been paramount, but Imperialists sought revenge for the British defeat at Majuba Hill in the Boer War of 1881 and believed a Boer government in the Transvaal was untenable.

Salisbury's administration ended the year not only by attempting to destabilise Kruger's regime, but also by finally filling the siege perilous of the Laureateship. Rosebery's knighting of Besant and Lewis Morris had exposed public suspicion towards political interference in the arts, but the appointment of Alfred Austin was greeted with derision and disbelief. William Watson, who had felt himself to be a strong contender on the basis of divine recommendation, told his mother that Austin's appointment 'was no surprise'. It was 'far more acceptable' than 'if any *real* rival of mine, like Henley or [Robert] Bridges, men of genius, had been selected.' Sounding a now familiar note, he went on, 'The truth is, Salisbury and Balfour and the rest of this Tory Government and all Tory Governments, are quite ignorant of the best contemporary literature' (J.M. Wilson 1981: 135). Political dissidence debarred Swinburne and William Morris from the Laureateship, and though Davidson was apparently considered, his associations with Lane and his controversial poem 'The Ballad of a Nun' (1894) counted against him. Being a Scot may not have helped either. Kipling was already the Empire's unofficial Laureate, but his unflattering portrayal of British rule in India, the demotic and vulgar content of *Barrack-Room Ballads* (1892), and his residence in the USA did him no favours. Austin, by contrast, could offer political rectitude and a manliness far removed from the Bodley Head's effeminacies. The result was Kiplingesque banality which satisfied no one, and his poem celebrating the Jameson Raid was at best an offensive misreading of the circumstances. That the Laureate's manifestly unapologetic 'Jameson's Ride' appeared in the *Times* on 11 January made it appear the official British response to the crisis, politically provocative as well as poetically maladroit:

Let lawyers and statesmen addle
  Their pates over points of law:

If sound be our sword and saddle,
    And gun-gear, who cares one straw?
When men of our own blood pray us
    To ride to their kinsfolk's aid,
Not heaven itself shall stay us
    Frome the rescue they call a raid.

Ever since "'Omer smote 'is bloomin' lyre', poetry and war had been closely linked, but 'Jameson's Ride' brought both into disrepute. Even those who wrote to the *Times* to point out how Jameson's 'devoted valour' had confounded foreign views of 'the decadence of the old British spirit' (13/1/96) were silent as to the poem's worth. The whole business depressed the elderly and half-blind Edward Burne-Jones. He told his studio assistant, Thomas Rooke, 'Ours is a material empire leaving traces in stout & soda-water bottles, and no material empire can last for ever; it might go in fifty years or even half of that.' Increasingly mystical in outlook, the painter loved 'the immaterial in English achievements' (Fitzgerald [1975] 2003: 269) and shuddered at what the future held.

The Jameson Raid was an ignoble end to the year, but predicting what would happen in 1896 was beyond even the Sibyl of Mortimer Street.

Notes

1. Cross added the 'e' following complaints from winners of the gallantry medal.
2. Vaughton's silversmiths made the medals for the 1908 Olympic Games. On 23 February 1958, seventy-six-year-old Harry Burge, a petty criminal with forty-two previous convictions going back to 1897 confessed to the crime in the *Sunday Pictorial*, posing with a crowbar for photographers. However, his account is inconsistent with reports of the time, and his story is not universally accepted (*Birmingham Mail*, 13/5/2010).
3. Wilde was unfair towards Douglas during and after his imprisonment, as writers such as Croft-Cooke, Hyde, and more recently, Trevor Fisher, Casper Wintermans and Douglas Murray, have shown. Douglas played a significant role in Wilde's downfall, but he should not be charged with the full responsibility for it. He understood aspects of Wilde's character better than anyone else during the final decade of Wilde's life; that he had no understanding whatsoever of other aspects of him makes their relationship all the more tragic.
4. Hardy was strongly opposed to animal cruelty and had found the methods used by slaughtermen 'a great grief' for years. He sent the brutal pig-killing scene in *Jude* to the editor of *The Animals' Friend*, suggesting it 'might be useful in teaching mercy'. The magazine reprinted it in December 1895 (Hardy 1980: 97).

Bibliography

Archives

John Lane Archive, Birmingham City University

Newspapers & Periodicals

Aberdeen Weekly Journal, Academy, Athenaeum, Belfast News-Letter, Birmingham Daily Post, Birmingham Mail, Blackwood's Edinburgh Magazine, Bookman, Daily Chronicle, Daily News, Daily Telegraph, Derby Mercury, Fortnightly Review, Glasgow Herald, Granta, Graphic, Hampshire Advertiser, Illustrated London News, Illustrated Police Budget, Illustrated Police News, Leeds Mercury, Leicester Chronicle & Leicestershire Mercury, Liverpool Mercury, Lloyds Weekly Newspaper, Morning Advertiser, Morning Post, New York Times, Nineteenth Century, Northern Echo (Darlington), *Pall Mall Gazette, Penny Illustrated News, Punch, Quarterly Review, Reynolds's Newspaper, Saturday Review, Sketch, Standard, Star, Times, To-day, Weekly Standard and Express* (Blackburn), *Western Mail, Women's Signal Budget, The Yellow Book*

Books

Adams, E. B. (1971), *Bernard Shaw and the Aesthetes*, Cleveland: Ohio State University Press.

Adlard, J. (1969), *Stenbock, Yeats and the Nineties*, London: Cecil Woolf.

AE. (1961), *Letters from AE*, ed. A. Denson, London: Abelard-Schuman.

Allen, G. [1895] (1995), *The Woman Who Did*, ed. S. Wintle, Oxford: World's Classics.

— [1895] (2004), *The Woman Who Did*, ed. N. Ruddick, Toronto: Broadview.

— (1895), *The British Barbarians*, London: John Lane.

Anon. (1997), *A Ladder for Mr Oscar Wilde*, Reading: Two Rivers Press.

Archer, C. (1931), *William Archer: Life, Work and Friendships*, London: Allen and Unwin.

Ardis, A. (1990), *New Women, New Novels: Feminism and Early Modernism*, New Brunswick, NJ: Rutgers University Press.

Arnold, M. (1895), *Letters of Matthew Arnold 1848–1888*, coll. and arr. G.W.E. Russell, London: Macmillan.

Bannerjee, J. (2011), 'A Good Start: The Making of Paul Harvey', *Times Literary Supplement*, 7 January, 14–15.

Bartlett, N. (1988), *Who Was that Man? A Present for Mr Oscar Wilde*, London: Serpent's Tail.

Beardsley, A. [1970] (1990), *The Letters of Aubrey Beardsley*, ed. H. Maas, J.L. Duncan and W.G. Good, London: Plantin.

Beckson, K. (ed.) (1970), *Oscar Wilde: The Critical Heritage*, London: Routledge and Kegan Paul.

— (1978), *Henry Harland: His Life and Work*, London: The 1890s Society.

— (ed.) (1981), *Aesthetes and Decadents of the 1890s*, Chicago: Chicago Academy.

— (1987), *Arthur Symons: A Life*, Oxford: Clarendon.

— (1992), *London in the 1890s: A Cultural History*, New York: Norton.

—, L.W. Markert, and J. Stokes (eds) (1990), *Arthur Symons: A Bibliography*, Greensboro, NC: ELT Press.

Beerbohm, M. (1894), 'The Green Carnation', *ILN*, 29 September, 406.

— (1895), '1880', *Yellow Book IV*, London: The Bodley Head, 275–83.

Bennett, A. (1968), *The Letters of Arnold Bennett, Volume II: 1889–1915*, ed. J. Hepburn, London: Oxford University Press.

Benson, E.F. [1895] (2001), 'The Recent "Witch Burning" at Clonmel' in *The Collected Ghost Stories of E.F. Benson*, ed. R. Dalby, London: Robinson, 617–24.

Bentley, J. (1983), *The Importance of Being Constance*, London: Robert Hale.

Besant, W. [1882] (1997), *All Sorts and Conditions of Men*, ed. H. Small, Oxford: Oxford University Press.

Bland, L. (1995), *Banishing the Beast: English Feminism and Sexual Morality 1885–1914*, London: Penguin.

Boothby, Guy [1895] (1996), *A Bid for Fortune or Dr Nikola's Vendetta*, ed. J. Sutherland, Oxford: Oxford University Press.

Borges, J.L. (1998), *Collected Fictions*, trans. A. Hurley, London: Penguin.

Bourke, A. (1999), *The Burning of Bridget Cleary*, London: Pimlico.

Bourne Taylor, J. (2007), 'Psychology at the fin de siècle' in Marshall (ed.), 13–30.

Bradbury, M., and J. McFarlane (eds) [1976] (1991), *Modernism: A Guide to European Literature 1890–1930*, London: Penguin.

Brake, L. (1994), *Subjugated Knowledges: Journalism, Gender and Literature in the Nineteenth Century*, Basingstoke: Macmillan.

Brandon, R. [1990] (2000), *The New Women and the Old Men: Love, Sex and the Woman Question*, London: Papermac.

Brennan, G. (1986), 'Yeats, Clodd, Scatological Rites, and the Clonmel Witch Burning', *Yeats Annual* 4, 207–15.

Burdett, O. (1925), *The Beardsley Period: An Essay in Perspective*, London: John Lane.

Cadden, M. and M.A. Jensen (eds) (1995), *Oscar Wilde: A Writer for the Nineties*, Princeton: Princeton University Library.

Cameron, Brooke (2008), 'Grant Allen's *The Woman Who Did*: Spencerian Individualism and Teaching New Women to be Mothers', *English Literature in Transition* 51.3, 281–301.

Carpenter, Edward (ed.) [1902] (1920), *Ioläus: An Anthology of Friendship*, London: George Allen and Unwin.

Carr, K. (1901), *Miss Marie Corelli*, London: H.J. Drane.

Cecil, D. [1964] (1985), *Max: A Biography*, New York: Athenaeum.

Chambers, R.W. (2004), *The Yellow Sign and Other Stories*, Hayward, CA: Chaosium.

Clayton, A. (2005), *Decadent London*, London: Historical Publications.

Cleeve, L. (1895), *The Woman Who Wouldn't*, London: Simpkin, Marshall.

Clodd, E. (1900), *Grant Allen: A Memoir*, London: Grant Richards.

Coates, T. (ed.) (2001), *The Trials of Oscar Wilde, 1895*, London: The Stationery Office.

Colligan, C. (2006), *The Traffic in Obscenity from Byron to Beardsley: Sexuality and Exoticism in Nineteenth-Century Print Culture*, Basingstoke: Palgrave Macmillan.

Colvin, D. (1998), *Aubrey Beardsley: A Slave to Beauty*, London: Orion.

Conrad, J. (1983), *Collected Letters of Joseph Conrad, Volume I 1861–1897*, ed. F.R. Karl and L. Davies, Cambridge: Cambridge University Press.

Cook, M. (2003), *London and the Culture of Homosexuality, 1885–1914*, Cambridge: Cambridge University Press.

Corelli, M., [1895] (1998), *The Sorrows of Satan, or The Strange Experience of one Geoffrey Tempest, Millionaire, A Romance*, ed. P. Keating, Oxford: Oxford University Press.

— [1895] (2008), *The Sorrows of Satan*, ed. J. Kuehn, Kansas City: Valancourt Books.

Cocks, H.G. (2003), *Nameless Offences: Homosexual Desire in the Nineteenth Century*, London: I.B. Tauris.

Cox, R.G. (ed.) (1970), *Thomas Hardy: The Critical Heritage*, London: Routledge and Kegan Paul.

Crackanthorpe, D. (1977), *Hubert Crackanthorpe and English Realism in the 1890s*, Columbia and London: University of Missouri Press.

Croft-Cook, R. (1963), *Bosie: The Story of Lord Alfred Douglas, His Friends and Enemies*, London: W.H. Allen.

Cross, N. (1985), *The Common Writer: Life in Nineteenth-Century Grub Street*, Cambridge: Cambridge University Press.

Cross, V. [1895], 'Theodora, A Fragment', *Yellow Book IV*, London: John Lane, 156–88.

Crosse, V. (1895), *The Woman Who Didn't*, London: John Lane.

Daiches, D. (1969), *Some Late Victorian Attitudes*, London: Andre Deutsch.

Danson, L. (1989), *Max Beerbohm and the Act of Writing*, Oxford: Oxford University Press.

D'Arcy, E. (1895), 'The Pleasure-Pilgrim', *Yellow Book V*, London: John Lane, 34–70.

David, H. (1997), *On Queer Street: A Social History of British Homosexuality 1895–1995*, London: HarperCollins.

Davidson, J. (1895), 'Proem to *The Wonderful Mission of Earl Lavender*', *Yellow Book IV*, London: John Lane, 284–5.

— (1995), *Selected Poems and Prose*, ed. J. Sloane, Oxford: Clarendon.

— [1895] (2008), *The Wonderful Mission of Earl Lavender*, Kansas: Valancourt Books.

Davis, John, (May 2009) Primrose, Archibald Philip, fifth earl of Rosebery and first earl of Midlothian (1847–1929), *Oxford Dictionary of National Biography Online*.

Davis, T.C. (1992), 'Indecency and Vigilance in the Music Halls' in Foulkes (ed.), 111–31.

Dawick, J. (1993), *Pinero: A Theatrical Life*, Niwot, CO: University Press of Colorado.

Denisoff, D. (2001), *Aestheticism and Sexual Parody*, Cambridge: Cambridge University Press.

Desmarais, J.H. (1998), *The Beardsley Industry: The Critical Reception in England and France, 1893–1914*, Aldershot: Ashgate.

Doughty, T. (ed.) (2004), *Selections from* The Girl's Own Paper, *1880–1907*, Peterborough, Ontario: Broadview.

Doré, G., and B. Jerrold (1872), *London: A Pilgrimage*, London: Grant.

Dowie, M.M. [1895] (1995), *Gallia*, ed. H. Small, London: Dent.

Dowson, E. (1967), *The Letters of Ernest Dowson*, ed. D. Flower and H. Maas, London: Cassell.

— (2003), *Collected Shorter Fiction*, ed. M. Borg and R.K.R. Thornton, Birmingham: Birmingham University Press.

Doyle, A.C. (1894), *Round the Red Lamp*, London: Methuen.

Du Maurier, G. [1894] (1998), *Trilby*, ed. E. Showalter, Oxford: Oxford University Press.

Edel, L. (1996), *Henry James: A Life*, London: Flamingo.

Egerton, G. (1894), *Discords*, London: John Lane.

Eley, G. (2002), *Forging Democracy: The History of the Left in Europe, 1850–2000*, Oxford: Oxford University Press.

Ellmann, R. (1987), *Oscar Wilde*, London: Hamish Hamilton.

Evans, I. (1966), *English Poetry in the Later Nineteenth Century*, London: Methuen.

Falkner, J.M. [1895] (2006), *The Lost Stradivarius*, London: Hesperus.

Farr, F. (1894), *The Dancing Faun*, London: Elkin Matthews and John Lane.

Faulk, B.J. (2004), *Music Hall and Modernity: The Late-Victorian Discovery of Popular Culture*, Athens, OH: Ohio University Press.

Fisher, T. (1995), *Scandal: The Sexual Politics of Late Victorian Britain*, Stroud: Sutton

— (1997), *Prostitution and the Victorians*, Stroud: Sutton.

— (2002), *Oscar And Bosie: A Fatal Passion*, Stroud: Sutton.

Fitzgerald, P. [1975] (2003), *Edward Burne-Jones*, Stroud: Alan Sutton.

Fletcher, I. (ed.) (1979), *Decadence and the 1890s*, London: Edward Arnold.

— (1987), *British Poetry and Prose 1870–1905*, Oxford: Oxford University Press.

Fletcher, P.M. (2003), *Narrating Modernity: The British Problem Picture, 1895–1914*, Aldershot: Ashgate.

Flint, K. (1993), *The Woman Reader, 1837–1914*, Oxford: Oxford University Press.

Foldy, M.S. (1997), *The Trials of Oscar Wilde: Deviance, Morality and Late-Victorian* Society, New Haven: Yale University Press.

Foster, R.F. (1997), *W.B. Yeats, A Life I: The Apprentice Mage*, Oxford: Oxford University Press.

Foulkes, R. (1992), *British Theatre in the 1890s: Essays on Drama and the Stage*, Cambridge: Cambridge University Press.

Frater, A. (2008), *The Balloon Factory*, London: Picador.

Frederico, A.R. (2000), *Idol of Suburbia: Marie Corelli and Late-Victorian Literary Culture*, Charlottesville: University Press of Virginia.

Freedman, J. (1990), *Professions of Taste: Henry James, British Aestheticism, and Commodity Culture*, Stanford: Stanford University Press.

Freeman, N. (2005), 'Intentional Rudeness? *The British Barbarians* and the Cultural Politics of 1895' in W. Greenslade and T. Rodgers (eds), *Grant Allen: Literature and Cultural Politics at the Fin de Siècle*, Aldershot: Ashgate, 111–28.

Gagnier, R. (1986), *Idylls of the Marketplace: Oscar Wilde and the Late Victorian Public*, Stanford: Stanford University Press.

Gardiner, J. (ed.) (1993), *The New Woman*, London: Collins and Brown.

Gawsworth, J. (2005), *The Life of Arthur Machen*, ed. R. Dobson, Leyburn: Tartarus Press.

Gillies, M. [1999] (2001), *Marie Lloyd: The One and Only*, London: Orion.

Gissing, G. [1898] (1903), *Charles Dickens: A Critical Study*, London: Gresham.

— (1978), *London and the Life of Literature in Late Victorian England: The Diary of George Gissing, Novelist*, ed. P. Coustillas, Hassocks: Harvester Press.

— (1993), *The Day of Silence and Other Stories*, ed. P. Coustillas, London: Dent.

— (1994), *Collected Letters of George Gissing, Volume V: 1892–1895*, ed. P.F. Mattheisen, A.C. Young, and P. Coustillas, Athens, OH: Ohio University Press.

Goode, J. (1979), 'The Decadent Writer as Producer' in Fletcher (1979), 109–30.

Goodman, J. (1988), *The Oscar Wilde File*, London: Allison & Busby.

Gosse, E. (1917), *The Life of Algernon Charles Swinburne*, London: Macmillan.

Grahame, K. (1983), *The Penguin Kenneth Grahame*, London: Penguin.

Greenslade, W. (1994), *Degeneration, Culture and the Novel, 1880–1940*, Cambridge: Cambridge University Press.

Greer, G. (2003), *The Boy*, London: Thames and Hudson.

Gregory, A. (1996), *Lady Gregory's Diaries 1892–1902*, ed. J. Pethica, Gerrards Cross: Colin Smythe.

Griffin, P. (1991), *Arthur Wing Pinero and Henry Arthur Jones*, Basingstoke: Macmillan.

Gross, J. (1991), *The Rise and Fall of the Man of Letters*, London: Penguin.

Guy, J. and I. Small (2000), *Oscar Wilde's Profession: Writing and the Culture Industry in the Late Nineteenth Century*, Oxford: Oxford University Press.

— (2006), *Studying Oscar Wilde: History, Criticism, and Myth*, Greensboro, NC: ELT Press.

Haggard, H.R. (1926), *The Days of My Life: An Autobiography*, ed. C.J. Longman, London: Longman, Green.

Hall, N.J. (2002), *Max Beerbohm: A Kind of Life*, New Haven: Yale University Press.

Halperin, J. (1982), *Gissing: A Life in Books*, Oxford: Oxford University Press.

Hamer, D. (January 2008), 'Morley, John, Viscount Morley of Blackburn (1838–1923)', *Oxford Dictionary of National Biography Online*.

Hamilton, E. (1986), *The Destruction of Lord Rosebery; From the Diary of Sir Edward Walter Hamilton 1894–1895*, ed. D. Brooks, London: The Historians' Press.

Hammond, J.R. (1979), *An H.G. Wells Companion*, Basingstoke: Macmillan.

— (1999), *An H.G. Wells Chronology*, Basingstoke: Macmillan.

Hardy, T. (1980), *Collected Letters of Thomas Hardy, Volume II: 1893–1901*, ed. R.L. Purdy and M. Millgate, Oxford: Oxford University Press.

— [1895] (1985), *Jude the Obscure*, ed. P. Ingham, Oxford: Oxford University Press.

Harland, H. ['The Yellow Dwarf'] (1895), 'Books: A Letter to the Editor', *Yellow Book VII*, London: John Lane, 125–48.

Harris, F. [1938] (1965), *Oscar Wilde: His Life and Confessions*, London: Panther.

Harrison, F. [1977] (1979), *The Dark Angel: Aspects of Victorian Sexuality*, Glasgow: Fontana.

Henderson, P. (1973), *Swinburne: The Portrait of a Poet*, London: Routledge and Kegan Paul.

Hennegan, A. (1990), 'Personalities and Principles: Aspects of Literature and Life in Fin de Siècle England' in *Fin de Siècle and its Legacy*, ed. M. Teich and R. Porter, Cambridge: Cambridge University Press, 170–215.

Hernon, I. (2003), *Britain's Forgotten Wars: Colonial Campaigns of the Nineteenth Century*, Stroud: Sutton.

Hichens, R. [1894] (1949), *The Green Carnation*, London: Unicorn Press.

Hick, H. (1973), *Henry Hick's Recollections of George Gissing*, ed. P. Coustillas, London: Enitharmon.

Holland, M. (2003), *Irish Peacock and Scarlet Marquess: The Real Trial of Oscar Wilde*, London: Fourth Estate.

Holland, V. [1954] (1999), *Son of Oscar Wilde*, London: Robinson.

Holroyd, M. (1988), *Bernard Shaw, Volume I, 1856–1898: The Search for Love*, London: Faber.

Honeycombe, G. (1993), *More Murders of the Black Museum, 1835–1985*, London: Hutchinson.

Hornung, E.W. [1899] (2003), *Raffles: The Amateur Cracksman*, ed. R. Lancelyn Green, London: Penguin.

Housman, A.E. (1971), *The Letters of A.E. Housman*, ed. H. Maas, London: Rupert Hart-Davis.

Huggins, M. (2004), *The Victorians and Sport*, London: Hambledon.

Hunt, K. (1996), *Equivocal Feminists: The Social Democratic Federation and the Woman Question 1884–1911*, Cambridge: Cambridge University Press.

Hunt, T. (2004), *Building Jerusalem: The Rise and Fall of the Victorian City*, London: Weidenfeld and Nicolson.

Hyde, H. M. (ed.) (1948), *The Trials of Oscar Wilde*, London: William Hodge.

— (1963), *Oscar Wilde: The Aftermath*, London: Methuen.

— (1964), *A History of Pornography*, London: Four Square.

— (1970), *The Other Love*, London: Heinemann.

— (1976), *Oscar Wilde: A Biography*, London: Eyre Methuen.

Innes, C. (ed.) (1998), *The Cambridge Companion to George Bernard Shaw*, Cambridge: Cambridge University Press.

Jackson, H. [1913] (1988), *The 1890s: A Review of Art and Ideas at the Close of the Nineteenth Century*, London: The Cresset Library.

Jackson, R. (1989), *Victorian Theatre*, London: A. and C. Black.

Jalland, P. (1986), *Women, Marriage and Politics 1860–1914*, Oxford: Oxford University Press.

James, H. (1895), 'The Next Time', *Yellow Book* VI, London: John Lane, 11–59.

— (1905), *English Hours*, London: William Heinemann.

— (1934), *The Art of the Novel: Critical Prefaces by Henry James*, intro. R.P. Blackmur, New York: Scriber's.

— (1961), *Guy Domville*, London: Rupert Hart-Davis.

— (1980), *Letters of Henry James, Volume III: 1883–1895*, ed. L. Edel, London: Macmillan.

— (1984), *Letters of Henry James, Volume IV: 1895–1915*, ed. L. Edel, London: Harvard University Press.

— (1987), *Complete Notebooks*, ed. L. Edel and L.H. Powers, Oxford: Oxford University Press.

James, R.R. [1963] (1995), *Rosebery*, London: Phoenix.

— (1975), 'The Earl of Rosebery' in *British Prime Ministers Volume II: Lord John Russell to Edward Heath*, ed. H. van Thal, London: George Allen & Unwin, 145–62.

James, W. (1890), *The Principles of Psychology* I, New York: H. Holt.

Jenkyns, R. (1991), *Dignity and Decadence: Victorian Art and the Classical Inheritance*, London: HarperCollins.

Jones, D.A. (1930), *The Life and Letters of Henry Arthur Jones*, London: Victor Gollancz.

Kaplan, J.H. (1992), 'Pineroticism and the Problem Play: Mrs Tanqueray, Mrs Ebbsmith and "Mrs Pat"', in Foulkes (ed.), 38–58.

Kaplan, M.B. (2005), *Sodom on the Thames: Sex, Love, and Scandal in Wilde Times*, Ithaca: Cornell University Press.

Keating, P. [1989] (1991), *The Haunted Study: A Social History of the English Novel 1875–1914*, Glasgow: Fontana.

Kingston, A. (2008), *Oscar Wilde as a Character in Victorian Fiction*, Basingstoke: Palgrave Macmillan.

Kipling, R. (1990), *The Letters of Rudyard Kipling, Volume II, 1890–99*, ed. T. Pinney, Basingstoke: Macmillan.

Knapp, S.M. (1994), 'Victoria Cross (Annie Sophy Cory)', *Dictionary of Literary Biography 135: British Short Fiction Writers 1880–1914*, ed. W.B. Thesing, Detroit: Gale, 75–84.

Lambert, J.W., and M. Ratcliffe (1987), *The Bodley Head 1887–1987*, London: The Bodley Head.

Lanchester, E. (1983), *Elsa Lanchester – Herself*, London: Michael Joseph.

Langtry, L. (1925), *The Days I Knew*, New York: George Doran.

Lankester, E.R. (1880), *Degeneration: A Chapter in Darwinism*, London: Macmillan.

Ledger, S. (2007), 'Wilde Women and *The Yellow Book*: The Sexual Politics of Aestheticism and Decadence', *English Literature in Transition* 50.1, 5–26.

—, and S. McCracken (eds) (1995), *Cultural Politics at the Fin de Siècle*, Cambridge: Cambridge University Press.

—, and Roger Luckhurst (eds) (2000), *The Fin de Siècle: A Reader in Cultural History c. 1880–1900*, Oxford: Oxford University Press.

Le Gallienne, R. (1895), *Robert Louis Stevenson, An Elegy and Other Poems*, London: The Bodley Head.

— (1926), *The Romantic '90s*, London: Putnam.

Lee, A.J. (1976), *The Origins of the Popular Press in England, 1855–1914*, London: Croom Helm.

Lellenberg, J., D. Stashower and C. Foley (eds) (2007), *Arthur Conan Doyle: A Life in Letters*, London: Harper Press.

Leverson, A. (1895), 'Overheard Fragment of a Dialogue', *Punch*, 12 January, 24.

— (1895), 'From the Queer and Yellow Book', *Punch*, 2 February, 58.

— (1895), 'The Advisability of Not Being Brought Up in a Handbag' *Punch*, 2 March, 107.

— (1895), 'Suggestion', *Yellow Book* V, London: John Lane, 249–57.

Lodge, D. (2004), *Author, Author*, New York: Viking.

Lomax, P. (2004), *The Golden Dream: A Biography of Thomas Cooper Gotch*, Bristol: Sansom.

Lowry, D. (May 2006), 'Jameson, Sir Leander Starr, baronet (1853–1917)', *Oxford Dictionary of National Biography Online*.

McDonald, P.D. (1997), *British Literary Culture and Publishing Practice 1880–1914*, Cambridge: Cambridge University Press.

Machen, A. (1895), *The Three Impostors or The Transmutations*, London: John Lane.

— [1902] (1960), *Hieroglyphics: A Note Upon Ecstasy in Literature*, London: Unicorn Press.

— [1924] (1999), *Precious Balms*, Horam: Tartarus.

McKenna, N. [2003] (2004), *The Secret Life of Oscar Wilde*, London: Arrow.

McKie, D. (2005), *Jabez: The Rise and Fall of a Victorian Rogue*, London: Atlantic.

McKinstry, L. (2005), *Rosebery: Statesman in Turmoil*, London: John Murray.

MacLeod, K. (2006), *Fictions of British Decadence: High Art, Popular Writing, and the Fin de Siècle*, Basingstoke: Palgrave Macmillan.

McWilliam, R. (2007), *The Tichborne Claimant: A Victorian Sensation*, London: Continuum.

Mallet, B. (1913), *British Budgets 1887–88 to 1912–13*, London: Macmillan.

Marjoribanks, E. [1929] (1989), *Famous Trials of Marshall Hall*, London: Penguin.

Marks, P. (1990), *Bicycles, Bangs, and Bloomers: The New Woman in the Popular Press*, Lexington: University Press of Kentucky.

Marshall, G. (ed.) (2007), *The Cambridge Companion to the Fin de Siècle*, Cambridge: Cambridge University Press.

Masters, B. (1978), *Now Barabbas was a Rotter*, London: Hamish Hamilton.

May, J.L. (1936), *John Lane and the Nineties*, London: The Bodley Head.

Mendelssohn, M. (1997), *Henry James, Oscar Wilde and Aesthetic Culture*, Edinburgh: Edinburgh University Press.

Mendes, P. (1993), *Clandestine Erotic Fiction in English 1800–1930: A Bibliographical Study*, Aldershot: Scolar Press.

Meredith, G. (1912), *The Letters of George Meredith II: 1882–1909*, collected and edited by his son, London: Constable.

Mikhail, E.H. (ed.) (1979), *Oscar Wilde: Interviews and Recollections*, 2 vols, London: Macmillan.

Miller, J.E. (1994), *Rebel Women: Feminism, Modernism and the Edwardian Novel*, London: Virago.

Milman, L.M. (1895), 'A Few Notes Upon Mr James', *Yellow Book* VII, London: John Lane, 71–83.

Mix, K.L. (1960), *A Study in Yellow: The Yellow Book and its Contributors*, Lawrence: University of Kansas Press.

Money, T. (1997), *Manly and Muscular Diversions: Public Schools and the Nineteenth Century Sporting Revival*, London: Duckworth.

Moore, H.T. (1974), *Henry James*, London: Thames and Hudson.

Morris, P. (1974), *Aston Villa: The First 100 Years*, Birmingham: Aston Villa Football Club.

Morton, P. (2005), *The Busiest Man in England: Grant Allen and the Writing Trade, 1875–1900*, Basingstoke: Palgrave Macmillan.

Murray, D. (2000), *Bosie: A Biography of Lord Alfred Douglas*, London: Hodder and Stoughton.

Nelson, C.C. (ed.) (2001), *A New Woman Reader*, Peterborough, Ontario: Broadview Press.

Nelson, J.G. (1971), *The Early Nineties: A View from the Bodley Head*, Cambridge, MA: Harvard University Press.

— (2000), *Publisher to the Decadents: Leonard Smithers in the Careers of Beardsley, Wilde, Dowson*, University Park: Pennsylvania State University Press.

Newton, H.C. (1928), *Idols of the Halls: Being My Music Hall Memories*, London: Heath Cranton.

Nordau, M. (1895), *Degeneration*, London: William Heinemann.

Oliver, H. (1983), *The International Anarchist Movement in Late Victorian London*, London: Croom Helm.

Onselen, Charles van (2007), *The Fox and the Flies*, London: Jonathan Cape.

Ormond, L. (1969), *George Du Maurier*, London: Routledge and Kegan Paul.

Overton, R. (1894), *Lights Out!*, London: Jarrold and Sons.

Page, N. (ed.) (2000), *Oxford Reader's Companion to Hardy*, Oxford: Oxford University Press.

Pakenham, T. [1979] (1992), *The Boer War*, London: Abacus.

— (1991), *The Scramble for Africa, 1876–1912*, London: Weidenfeld and Nicolson.

Pater, W. [1893] (1986), *The Renaissance: Studies in Art and Poetry*, ed. Adam Philips, Oxford: Oxford University Press.

Paulin, T. (1984), *Ireland and the England Crisis*, Newcastle-upon-Tyne: Bloodaxe.

Pearson, G. (1983), *Hooligan: A History of Respectable Fears*, Basingstoke: Macmillan.

Pearson, H. [1946] (1985), *The Life of Oscar Wilde*, London: Penguin.

Petrow, S. (1994), *Policing Morals: The Metropolitan Police and the Home Office*, Oxford: Clarendon.

Pick, D. (1989), *Faces of Degeneration; A European Disorder c. 1848–c. 1918*, Cambridge: Cambridge University Press.

Pinero, A.W. (1974), *The Collected Letters of Sir Arthur Wing Pinero*, ed. J.P. Wearing, Minneapolis: University of Minnesota Press.

— (1998), *The Notorious Mrs Ebbsmith* [1895] in *The New Woman and other Emancipated Woman Plays*, ed. J. Chothia, Oxford: Oxford University Press, 61–134.

Piper, L. (1991), *Murder by Gaslight*, London: Michael O'Mara.

Pite, R. (2006), *Thomas Hardy: The Guarded Life*, London: Picador.

Pollard, P. (2004), 'Wilde and the French', *English* 53.1, 19–29.

Powell, K. (1990), *Oscar Wilde and the Theatre of the 1890s*, Cambridge: Cambridge University Press.

Priestley, P. (1985), *Victorian Prison Lives: English Prison Biography, 1830–1914*, London: Methuen.

Pythian, G. (2005), *Colossus: The True Story of William Foulke*, Stroud: History Press.

Raby, P. (ed.) (1997), *The Cambridge Companion to Oscar Wilde*, Cambridge: Cambridge University Press.

Rae, S. (1998), *W.G. Grace*, London: Faber.

Ransom, T. (1999), *The Mysterious Miss Marie Corelli: Queen of Victorian Bestsellers*, Stroud: Sutton.

Rhys, E. (1931), *Everyman Remembers*, London: Dent.

Richards, J. (2005), *Sir Henry Irving: A Victorian Actor and His World*, London: Hambledon Continuum.

Richardson, A. (ed.) (2002), *Women Who Did: Stories By Men and Women, 1890–1914*, London: Penguin.

— (2003), *Love and Eugenics in the Late Nineteenth Century: Rational Reproduction and the New Woman*, Oxford: Oxford University Press.

Ridge, W. (1895), *A Clever Wife*, London: R. Bentley & Son.

Roberts, B. (1981), *The Mad Bad Line: The Family of Lord Alfred Douglas*, London: Hamish Hamilton.

Robbins, R. (2003), *Pater to Forster, 1873–1924*, Basingstoke: Palgrave.

Rodensky, L. (ed.) (2006), *Decadent Poetry from Wilde to Naidu*, London: Penguin.

Rogers, K. (1992), *One Hundred Years of Goodison Glory*, Derby: Breedon Books.

Ross, D. (2001), *W.B. Yeats*, New Lanark: Geddes and Grossart.

Rothenstein, W. (1978), *Men and Memories 1872–1938*, ed. and abridged by M. Lago, London: Chatto and Windus.

Rowbotham, S. (2008), *Edward Carpenter: A Life of Liberty and Love*, London: Verso.

Rowland, P. (1999), *Raffles and His Creator*, London: Nekta.

Rubinstein, D. (1986), *Before the Suffragettes: Women's Emancipation in the 1890s*, Brighton: Harvester Press.

— (2004) 'Lanchester, Edith (1871–1966), socialist and feminist', *Oxford Dictionary of National Biography Online*.

Salmon, R. (1997), *Henry James and the Culture of Publicity*, Cambridge: Cambridge University Press.

Sanders, A. (ed.) (2007), *Great Victorian Lives: An Era in Obituaries*, London: Times Books/HarperCollins.

Sanders, R. (2009), *Beastly Fury: The Strange Birth of British Football*, London: Bantam.

Schaffer, Talia (Summer 1994), 'A Wilde Desire Took Me': The Homoerotic History of *Dracula*', *ELH* 61.2, 381–425.

Schroeder, H. (2002), *Additions and Corrections to Richard Ellmann's* Oscar Wilde, Braunschweig: Privately Printed.

Seaman, O. (1895), *Tillers of the Sand: Being a Fitful Record of the Rosebery Administration from the Triumph of Ladas to the Decline and Fall-Off*, London: Smith, Elder.

— (1896) *The Battle of the Bays*, London: John Lane/The Bodley Head.

Shaw, G.B. [1932] (1954), *Our Theatres in the 'Nineties* I, London: Constable.

— (1965), *Collected Letters 1874–1897*, ed. D.H. Laurence, London: Max Reinhardt.

Shiel, M.P. [1895] (1928), *Prince Zaleski*, London: Martin Secker.

Showalter, E. (1991), *Sexual Anarchy: Gender and Culture at the Fin de Siècle*, London: Bloomsbury.

— (ed.) (1993), *Daughters of Decadence: Women Writers of the Fin-de-Siècle*, London: Virago.

Sinfield, A. (1994), *The Wilde Century: Effeminacy, Oscar Wilde and the Queer Moment*, London: Cassell.

Sloan, J. (1995), *John Davidson, First of the Moderns: A Literary Biography*, Oxford: Clarendon.

Smith, D.C. (1986), *H.G. Wells, Desperately Mortal: A Biography*, New Haven: Yale University Press.

Smith, T. d'Arch (1970), *Love in Earnest: Some Notes on the Lives and Writings of English 'Uranian' Poets from 1889 to 1930*, London: Routledge and Kegan Paul.

Speedie, J. (1993), *Wonderful Sphinx: The Biography of Ada Leverson*, London: Virago.

Spielmann, M.H. (ed.) (1895), *Royal Academy Pictures: Being the Royal Academy Supplement of the 'Magazine of Art' 1895*, London: Cassell.

Springhall, J. (1998), *Youth, Popular Culture and Moral Panics: Penny Gaffs to Gangsta-Rap, 1830–1996*, Basingstoke: Macmillan.

Stetz, M.D., and M.S. Lasner (1994), *The Yellow Book: A Centenary Exhibition*, Cambridge, MA: The Houghton Library.

Stevenson, R.L. (1885), *More New Arabian Nights*, London: Longmans Green.

Stokes, J. (1989), *In the Nineties*, Hemel Hempstead: Harvester Wheatsheaf.

— (1996), *Oscar Wilde: Myths, Miracles, and Imitations*, Cambridge: Cambridge University Press.

Sturgis, M. (1995), *Passionate Attitudes: The English Decadence of the Eighteen Nineties*, London: Macmillan.

— [1998] (1999), *Aubrey Beardsley: A Biography*, London: Flamingo.

Sutherland, J. (2009), *The Longman Companion to Victorian Fiction*, London: Longman.

Swinburne, A.C. (1962), *The Swinburne Letters, Volume VI: 1890–1909*, ed. C.Y. Lang, New Haven: Yale University Press.

— (2004), *Uncollected Letters of Algernon Charles Swinburne, Volume III: 1890–1909*, ed. T.L. Meyers, London: Pickering and Chatto.

Symons, A. [1905] (1966), *Aubrey Beardsley*, London: John Baker.

— (1918), 'Dieppe, 1895' in *Cities and Sea-Coasts and Islands*, London: W. Collins, 227–48.

— (1924), *Poems* I, London: Martin Secker.

— (1977), *The Memoirs of Arthur Symons: Life and art in the 1890s*, ed. K. Beckson, University Park: Pennsylvania State University Press.

— (1989), *Selected Letters 1880–1935*, ed. K. Beckson and J.M. Munro, Basingstoke: Macmillan.

Tanitch, R. (1999), *Oscar Wilde on Stage and Screen*, London: Methuen.

Taylor, G. (1992), 'Svengali: mesmerist and aesthete' in Foulkes (ed.), 93–110.

Thompson, F. (1969), *The Letters of Francis Thompson*, ed. J.E. Walsh, New York: Hawthorn Books.

Thornton, R.K.R., and M. Thain (eds) (1997), *Poetry of the 1890s*, London: Penguin.

Thurschwell, P. (2001), *Literature, Technology and Magical Thinking, 1880–1920*, Cambridge: Cambridge University Press.

Thwaite, A. (1984), *Edmund Gosse: A Literary Landscape*, Oxford: Oxford University Press.

Tóibín, Colm (2005), *The Master*, London: Picador.

Townsend, J.B. (1961), *John Davidson: Poet of Armageddon*, New Haven: Yale University Press.

Turner, E.S. [1950] (1966), *Roads to Ruin: The Shocking History of Social Reform*, London: Penguin.

Vasili, P. (1998), *The First Black Footballer: Arthur Wharton 1865–1930 – An Absence of Memory*, London: Frank Cass.

Waller, P. (2006), *Writers, Readers, and Reputations Literary Life in Britain 1870–1918*, Oxford: Oxford University Press.

Walshe, É. (2005), 'The First Gay Irishman? Ireland and the Wilde Trials', *Eire-Ireland* 40.3 & 40.4, Fómhar/Fall, Geimhreadh/Winter, 38–57.

Waters, C. (1989), 'Progressives, Puritans, and the Cultural Politics of the Council', in A. Saint (ed.), *Politics and the People of London: The London County Council 1889–1965*, London: Hambledon, 49–70.

Wearing, J.P. (1976), *The London Stage 1890–1899: A Calendar of Plays and Players*, 2 vols, Metuchen, NJ: Scarecrow Press.

Weinreb, B. and C. Hibbert (eds) (1995), *The London Encyclopaedia*, Basingstoke: Macmillan.

Weintraub, S. (ed.) (1964), *The Yellow Book: Quintessence of the Nineties*, New York: Anchor Books.

— (1967), *Beardsley: A Biography*, London: W.H. Allen.

Wells, H.G. (1927), *Collected Short Stories*, London: Ernest Benn.

— (1980), *H.G. Wells's Literary Criticism*, ed. P. Parrinder and R. Philmus, Brighton: Harvester.

— (1895), *The Time Machine*, London: William Heinemann.

— [1895], *The Wonderful Visit*, Gloucester: Dodo Press.

— (1998), *The Correspondence of H.G. Wells, Volume I 1880–1903*, ed. D.C. Smith, London: Pickering and Chatto.

White, C. (1999), *Nineteenth-Century Writings on Homosexuality: A Sourcebook*, London: Routledge.

Whittington-Egan, R., and G. Smerdon (1960), *The Quest of the Golden Boy: The Life and Letters of Richard Le Gallienne*, London: Unicorn Press.

Wilde, O. (1994), *Complete Works*, London: HarperCollins.

— (1995), *The Importance of Being Earnest and Other Plays*, ed. P. Raby, Oxford: World's Classics.

— (2000), *Collected Letters*, ed. M. Holland and R. Hart-Davis, London: Fourth Estate.

Wilde, S. [1999] (2005), *Ranji: The Strange Genius of Ranjitsinghji*, London: Aurum.

Williams, I. (ed.) (1971), *George Meredith: The Critical Heritage*, London: Routledge and Kegan Paul.

Wilson, J. (2008), *Inverting the Pyramid: A History of Football Tactics*, London: Orion.

Wilson, J.M. (1981), *I Was An English Poet: A Critical Biography of Sir William Watson*, London: Cecil Woolf.

Wilton, I. (1999), *C.B. Fry: An English Hero*, London: Richard Cohen.

Windholz, A.M. (1994), 'Ella D'Arcy (*circa* 1857 – 2 September 1937)', *Dictionary of Literary Biography 135: British Short-Fiction Writers, 1880–1914: The Realist Tradition*, ed. W.B. Thesing, Detroit: Gale, 85–95.

Winner, D. (2008), *Those Feet: A Sensual History of English Football*, London: Bloomsbury.

Wintermans, C. (2007), *Lord Alfred Douglas: A Poet's Life and His Finest Work*, London: Peter Owen.

Woodruff, D. (1957), *The Tichborne Claimant: A Victorian Mystery*, London: Hollis and Carter.

Wright, T. (2008), *Oscar's Books*, London: Chatto and Windus.

Yeats, W.B. (ed.) (1936), *The Oxford Book of Modern Verse, 1892–1935*, Oxford: Clarendon.

— (1954), *The Letters of W.B. Yeats*, ed. Allan Wade, London: Rupert Hart-Davis.

Index

Abel, Bobby, 155
Acres, Bert, 135
Addleshaw, Percy, 65
Adey, More, 116, 165, 207
'AE' (George Russell), 33, 210
Alexander, George, 48, 51–2, 53, 70, 72, 81, 96, 102, 108, 126, 194, 205
Allen, Grant, 68, 113, 137, 143, 194–5, 196, 204
  The Woman Who Did, 63–6, 69, 88, 89, 143, 191, 195, 198
Anarchism, 52–3, 173–4
Archer, William, 46–7, 90, 91, 92, 126, 127, 167, 191, 203
Ardis, Ann, 40
Arnold, Edwin, 166
Arnold, Matthew, 208
Ashes, The, 77–8
Asquith, Herbert, 8, 9, 46, 53, 60, 102, 135, 184, 199
Aston Villa FC, 6, 42, 44, 59, 74n, 85, 86, 87, 110–12, 181–2, 207–8
Athenaeum, The, 16, 39, 47, 51, 53, 54, 64, 68, 88, 91–2, 93, 96, 120, 124, 142, 145, 158–9, 171, 176, 185, 189, 191, 193–4, 195, 200
Athersmith, Charlie, 44, 74n, 112, 207
Atkins, F. A., 176
Austin, Alfred, 14, 75, 213–14

Baird, Dorothea, 185–9
Baldwin, Louisa, 209
Balfour, A. J., 46, 62, 72, 113, 137, 176, 213
Balfour, Jabez, 125, 137, 148, 199–200
Balloonists, 146, 172
Baron, William, 56–7, 74n
Barrie, J. M., 34, 154
Bartlett, Neil, 117
Bassett, Annie, 172
Bassett, Billy, 111
Bathurst, Benjamin, 151

Battle, Mary, 94–5
Beardsley, Aubrey, 36–8, 46, 65, 70, 74n, 102–4, 106, 122, 132, 135, 142, 145, 163, 164, 165, 210
Beerbohm, Max, 7, 15–16, 18, 31, 38, 41, 46, 47, 97, 105, 117, 118
Beerbohm Tree, Herbert, 8, 92, 108, 185–9
Bellwood, Bessie, 29, 30, 178
Bennett, (Enoch) Arnold, 4, 35, 51, 144, 160, 180, 185, 209
Benson, E. F., 149, 171
Benson, Edward White, 52
Berenson, Bernard, 12
Besant, Walter, 141–2, 144, 213
Bignell, Charles, 29
Birmingham Daily Post, 2, 55, 74n, 89, 110–12, 179
Biron, Chartres, 73n
Biron, Robert, 25
Blackburn Olympic FC, 58
Blackburn Rovers FC, 6, 43, 59, 181
Blackwood's Edinburgh Magazine, 36, 42, 76, 84, 107, 148, 160, 176, 185
Blanche, Jacques-Emile, 166
Blandford, Dr George, 196–7, 199
Blatchford, Robert, 198
Bloxam, John Francis, 18, 19–20, 44, 98, 99
Blyth, Florence, 153
Bolton Wanderers FC, 6, 43, 59, 74n, 87, 182
Bookman, The, 34, 64, 113, 120, 158, 170
Booth, Charles, 10
Boothby, Guy, 108, 189
Borges, Jorge Luis, 1, 6
Boulton, Ernest ('Stella'), 25
Bourke, Angela, 94
Braddon, Mary, 33, 143, 176–7
Bradley, Susan, 74n
Brake, Laurel, 162
Brett, Reginald, 13, 53, 84
Bridge, Sir John, 108, 117, 125
Brock, George Edward, 199–200

Brookfield, Charles, 31, 46, 73–4n, 82, 126, 131, 140, 188
Buchanan, Robert, 109, 125, 136n
Bunbury, Sir Edward, 96, 116
Burdett, Osbert, 105
Burgess, Gilbert, 45, 49
Burnard, Francis, 105
Burne-Jones, Edward, 37, 51, 53, 80, 82, 120, 127, 132, 214
Burne-Jones, Philip, 51–2
Burnley FC, 6, 85, 125, 207–8
Burns MP, John, 148, 198
Burton Wanderers FC, 52, 208
Bury FC, 112
Buss, Frances M., 63
Byron, Lord, 15–16, 109, 202

Caine, Hall, 4, 15, 185, 193
Caird, Mona, 33, 88
Calderon, Philip, 121
Cameron, Brooke, 64
Campbell, Mrs Patrick (Beatrice Stella Tanner), 8, 38, 87, 91, 185
'Captious Critic, The', 72, 91
'Carados' (H. Chance Newton), 71
Carlyle, Thomas, 72, 115
Carpenter, Edward, 103, 114, 132, 195
Carroll, Lewis, 1
Carson, Edward, 81, 82, 93, 95, 96, 98–102, 104, 114, 116, 129, 149–50, 184
Case, Professor Thomas, 162
Cecil, Lord David, 154
Chamberlain, Joseph, 9, 10, 46, 112, 151, 174n
Chambers, Robert W., 176, 193–4
Chameleon, The, 18–20, 49, 158
Chant, Laura Ormiston, 5, 21–4, 40, 73n, 84, 114, 140, 156
Chapman, Herbert (music hall artiste), 73n
Chapman, Herbert (John Lane employee), 103–4
Charles, Mr Justice, 117
Chatt, Bob, 110, 136n
Cheer, Boys, Cheer!, 185, 189
'Cheiro', 95, 136n
Chelford railway accident, 55
Chesney, George, 113–14
Chisholm, Hugh, 160
Churchill, Randolph, 55
Churchill, Winston, 22
Clarke, Sir Edward, 95, 98, 101, 108, 116, 128, 139
Clausen, George, 122
Cleary, Bridget, 94–5, 149–50
'Cleeve, Lucas' (Adelina Kingscote), 177
Cleveland, President Grover, 211–12
Clodd, Edward, 65, 143, 201
Clonmel Witch-Burning *see* Cleary, Bridget
Cocks, H. G., 25
Coldwells, Francis, 148–9

Colligan, Colette, 37
Comyns Carr, J., 30
Comyns Carr, Mrs, 66
Conder, Charles, 38, 164
Conrad, Joseph, 4, 36, 97, 113, 142, 144, 162, 166
Conway, Alfonso, 100
Cook, Matt, 25
Coombes, Harriet, 156–61
Coombes, Nathaniel, 156–61
Coombes, Robert, 27, 156–61
Corelli, Marie, 4, 14, 143
  Sorrows of Satan, The, 169–70, 175, 190–2
Corinthians FC, 44, 86
Coustillas, Pierre, 144
Crackanthorpe, B. A., 41, 80, 88–9
Crackanthorpe, Hubert, 21, 37, 142, 164, 166, 210
Craig, Frank ('The Coffee Cooler'), 116
Crane, Walter, 121
Criminal Law Amendment Act 1885, 18, 24, 108, 139, 140, 205–6
Cross, Nigel, 142
Cross(e), Victoria, 39–42, 176–7, 192, 214n
Custance, Olive, 38
Cycling, 2, 151–3, 156, 167, 204

Daily Telegraph, 4, 21, 68, 107, 191, 198
D'Arch Smith, Timothy, 18
D'Arcy, Ella, 103, 105–6, 124, 195
Daudet, Alphonse, 127
Davidson, John, 33, 39, 67, 109–10, 132, 162, 195, 213
Dawes, Augusta, 25–6
De Tabley, Lord, 62, 193
Degeneration see Nordau, Max
Dennis, Bertha and Florence, 27
Derby, The, 135–6
Derby County FC, 44, 59, 110, 112, 182, 207
Devey, John, 112, 136n
Diglake colliery disaster, 55–7
Dixon, Marion Hepworth, 38, 143
Doig, Ted, 110
Douglas, John Sholto *see* Queensberry, Marquess of
Douglas, Lord Alfred, ('Bosie'), 11, 12, 14, 15, 18, 19, 45, 57, 69–70, 72, 76, 81, 82, 99, 101, 102, 108, 114, 117, 131, 139, 165, 182–3, 206–7, 209, 214n
Douglas, Percy, 72, 81–2, 102, 125, 129, 130
Douglas, Sholto, 116
Dowie, Ménie Muriel, 38, 66–9, 88, 143, 191
Dowson, Ernest, 142, 171, 210–11
Doyle, Arthur Conan, 33, 58, 98, 106, 118, 126, 137, 154, 166–7
Drage, Geoffrey, 150

Drew, Dorothy, 120, 132
Drumlanrig, Viscount, 11, 57, 135
Du Maurier, George, 5, 51, 127, 193
  Trilby, 34, 143, 175, 185–9

Eaton, PC Peter, 153
Ebb-Smith, Joseph and Alice, 92
Edward, Prince of Wales, 46, 118, 155, 187, 190
Edwardes, George, 22
Egerton, George, 32, 33, 40, 64, 66, 88, 105, 142, 163, 169, 201, 203
Elbe, sinking of the, 58
Ellis, Alix, 12–13
Ellmann, Richard, 13, 31
Engels, Friedrich, 173
Eton and Old Etonians, 8, 58–9, 76, 86
Evans, Ifor, 142
Everton FC, 4, 6, 43–4, 74n, 85, 110, 112, 207–8

FA Cup, 58–9, 110–12
  theft of, 181–2, 214n
Falkner, J. Meade, 209–10
Farr, Florence, 195, 212
Faulk, Barry, 22, 73n
Fawcett, Millicent Garrett, 65
Fenwick-Miller, Mrs, 62, 63, 91, 176
'F.H.' (Frederic Harrison?), 96
Fletcher, Alice, 124
Fletcher, Pamela, 120, 124
Foldy, Michael, 107, 131, 134–5
Foley, Cyril ('The Raider'), 212
Football internationals, 85–7
Foulke, William 'Fatty', 86
Fox, John, 157–8
Francis, Westley, 129–30
Frith, W. P., 118–19
Froest, Frank, 125
Fry, C. B., 61, 76, 155
Fry, Roger, 210
Fuller, Ben, 29

Garnett, Edward, 36, 144
Garnett, Richard, 54
Gee, John and Charles, 85
Gilchrist, R. Murray, 160
Gill, C. F., 22, 28, 73n, 116–17, 158
Gillies, Midge, 73n, 188
Gissing, George, 8, 20, 33, 35, 36, 55, 61, 63, 67–8, 80, 97, 124, 143–4, 146, 167, 209
  on Hardy, 201–2
  on Rosebery, 135
  on Wilde, 132–3
Gladstone, William Ewart, 8, 11, 33, 147, 148
Golliwoggs, 209
Goode, John, 187
Gosse, Edmund, 30, 34–5, 48, 51, 103, 104, 132, 143, 178–9, 200–3

Gotch, Thomas Cowper, 120–1, 122
Grace, W. G., 154–6
Grahame, Kenneth, 140, 195
Grainger, Walter, 101
Grand, Sarah, 4, 67, 89, 143
Graves, A. P., and Robert, 93
Gray, Mr and Mrs, 196–9
Green Carnation, The see Hichens, Robert
Greenslade, William, 78
Greenwood, James, 152
Greer, Germaine, 122
Gregory, Lady Augusta, 153, 167, 187–8, 211
Griffin, Penny, 88
Grundy, Sidney, 63
Gully, William, 84
Gunn, Billy, 155
Guy, Josephine, and Ian Small, 191–2

Hacker, Arthur, 121
Haggard, H. Rider, 4, 32, 150
Hake, Edward, 80
Haldane, R. B., 9, 133, 140
Haldane, Richard, 60
Hamerton, P. G., 34, 141
Hamilton, Sir Edward, 46, 60, 84, 132, 134, 135–6, 151
Harcourt, Lewis ('Loulou'), 8, 60, 84
Harcourt, William, 8, 9–10, 60, 84, 133–4, 150
Hardie, Keir, 4, 150, 173, 199
Hardy, Thomas, 33, 63–4, 88
  Jude the Obscure, 2, 167, 200–4, 214n
Harland, Henry, 36, 38, 51, 69, 97, 103–4, 105, 164–5, 166, 181
Harris, Frank, 18, 74n, 117, 126, 127, 138, 139
Harrison, Fraser, 65–6
Harvey, Sir Paul, 211
Hawkins, Mr Justice, 53
Hawtrey, Charles, 31, 74n, 81, 126, 131
Headlam, Stewart, 125, 130
Heart of Midlothian FC, 59
Heinemann, William, 15, 46, 126, 162, 170
Hennegan, Alison, 99
Henty, G. A., 32–3, 74n, 209
Herkomer, Hubert von, 121
Hichens, Robert, 171
  Green Carnation, The, 7, 13–17, 20, 62, 64, 98, 115, 126, 140, 154, 163, 171
Hicks, William, 26
Hicks-Beach, Michael, 133
Hodgetts, Dennis, 182
Holman Hunt, William, 121, 207
Home Rule *see* Irish Issues
Hope, Anthony, 15, 34, 144, 170–1
Horne, Herbert, 166
Hornung, Arthur Oscar, 126, 136n
Hornung, E. W., 126
Housman, A. E., 113, 137

Housman, Lawrence, 145
How, W. W., 204
Howard, Esme, 10–11
Howell, Charles, 208
Howell, 'Raby', 86
Humphreys, Arthur, 70, 126, 170–1
Humphreys, Charles, 81, 95
Hunt, Karen, 199
Hunt, Violet, 143, 193
Huxley, T. H., 62, 147, 170, 179, 209
Huysmans, J.-K., 99, 106, 158
Hyde, Douglas, 93
Hyde, H. Montgomery, 140, 206

Ibsen, Henrik, 38, 54, 79, 88, 89, 178, 191
Illustrated Police News, 2, 4, 7, 22, 24, 26,
    52, 54, 61, 75, 77, 83, 114, 119, 138,
    146, 169, 200
Influenza and its victims, 57, 61–2
Ingram, Percy T., 141
Irish issues, 9, 26, 84, 85, 92–6, 147, 149
Irving, Sir Henry, 30, 53, 80, 141–2, 155
Ives, George, 3, 18, 44–5, 75, 97, 107, 117,
    139–40, 154

'Jack the Ripper', 26
James, Henry, 2, 35, 38, 71, 93, 103, 104,
    105, 127, 142, 145, 147, 167, 187,
    193, 211
    Guy Domville, 30–1, 42, 48–53, 70, 144
James, William, 2, 8, 48, 80
Jameson, Leander Starr, and Jameson Raid,
    121, 212–14
Jerome, Jerome K., 20, 107, 144, 154
Jerrold, Blanchard, 6
Johnson, William, 13, 60, 136n
Jones, Henry Arthur, 66, 126–7, 178
Jones, John, 161–2
Jones, Dr Lamphier Vernon, 69, 72
Jude the Obscure see Hardy, Thomas

Kaplan, Joel, 88, 92
Kaplan, Maurice, 100
Keating, Peter, 190
'Keynotes' series, 63, 92, 194–5
King Arthur (Comyns Carr), 30, 53–4, 65
Kinnaird, Arthur, Lord, 59, 125, 140
Kipling, Rudyard, 1, 30, 32, 33, 34–5, 142,
    178, 208–9, 213
Kortright, Charles, 155
Kruger, President Paul, 212–13

Labouchere, Henry, 18, 37, 60, 139
Lanchester, Edith, 196–9
Lanchester, Elsa, 198
Lane, John, 32, 34, 41, 63–4, 69, 97, 103,
    108, 132, 135, 139, 145, 162–3, 164,
    176, 181, 194, 209
Lang, Andrew, 34, 145, 158
Langdon-Down, Dr and Mrs, 26, 28

Langtry, Lillie, 183–4
Lankester, Professor Edwin, 79, 184, 194
Le Gallienne, Richard ('Logroller'), 33–4,
    88–9, 97, 162, 169, 170, 195, 209
Ledger, Sally, 39
Lee, Vernon, 144
Leeds Mercury, 8, 145, 164
Leggatt, Edward, 173–4
Leighton, Frederick, Lord, 26, 51, 118, 120
Leno, Dan, 29, 139
Leverson, Ada, 14, 18, 19, 41, 46, 49, 57,
    70, 72, 82, 95, 104–5, 106, 108, 127–8,
    131
Leverson, Ernest, 82, 115, 127–8
Lewis, Sir George, 15, 81, 184
Liberator Building Society *see* Balfour, Jabez
Linton, Eliza Lynn, 176
'Little Tich' (Harry Relph), 128
Littlechild, John, 82, 100, 102
Liverpool FC, 6, 44, 59, 86, 112, 208
Lloyd, Marie, 29, 104, 188
Loates, Sam, 135
Locker-Lampson, Frederick, 145
Lockwood, Sir Frank, 27, 102, 118, 128,
    130, 134
Lombroso, Cesare, 79, 143
'Looker-On, The', 36, 161, 179

Macbeth, Robert Walker, 122
MacDonald, George, 193
Macdonald, Leila, 38
Machen, Arthur, 54, 136n, 139, 158, 192,
    194–5, 204
McKenna, Neil, 15, 19, 69, 100
Mackenzie, Alexander Campbell, 54
McKie, David, 199
McKinstry, Leo, 134–5
MacLaren, Archie, 77, 155
MacLaren, Ian, 193
Mallock, W. H., 171
Marks, Patricia, 152
Marsh, Richard, 158–9
Martin, Marius, 28
Marx, Eleanor, 173, 196
Maudsley, Henry, 68, 79
Mayer, Aaron, 56
Meade, L. T., 33, 74n
Medhurst, Anne, 37
Melba, Nellie, 29
Mendelssohn, Michèle, 50
Meredith, Billy, 86
Meredith, George, 53, 55, 141, 142
Meynell, Alice, 103
Meynell, Wilfrid, 103, 107
Millais, John Everett, 62, 118, 120, 146
Millard, Christopher Sclater, 131–2
Millard, Evelyn, 88
Milman, Lena, 142
Mix, Katherine, 107
Moore, George, 33, 88, 158

Morant, Amy, 150
Morley, John, 9, 92, 134, 150
Morris, Lewis, 33, 141–2, 213
Morris, William, 42, 213
Morrison, Arthur, 32, 33, 53
Mudie's Library, 31–2
'Mummer, The', 22, 30, 54, 70, 84, 114, 141, 185

National Vigilance Association, 24, 78, 140, 162
Neilson, Julia, 126
Nelson, James, 207
Nesbit, E., 38
Nethersole, Olga, 92
New Woman, The, 4, 20, 63, 88, 89, 109, 137, 143, 150, 152–3, 172, 178, 190, 196, 198, 203
Newcastle United FC, 6, 43, 59
Newell, John William, 26–7
Newman, Ernest, 139
Newman, Robert, 172
Newnes, Sir George, 54, 150
Nichols, H. S., 163
Nicolson, Dr David, 206
Noble, Edward, 144
Noble, James Ashcroft, 39, 88
Noel, Roden, 34
Nordau, Max, 79–81, 106, 142, 143, 171, 179
Normand, Ernest, 122
Norregard, Julie, 169, 210
Nottingham Forest FC, 44, 59, 85
Notts County FC, 74n, 112

O'Brien, Mr Justice, 149
Old Westminsters FC, 85, 86
Oliphant, Margaret, 176, 201, 204
Olivier, H. A., 122
Onselen, Charles van, 25
O'Riordan, Conal, 210–11
Ormond, Leonée, 187
Oscariana, 20, 70
Osseo, sinking of the, 55
'Our Veteran', 43–4, 59

Palace Club raid, 168–9, 192
Pall Mall Gazette, 10, 14, 24, 37, 40, 64, 71, 134, 143, 144, 164, 170, 177, 179, 192, 195, 203
Park, Frederick, 25
Parker, Charles, 108, 116, 117, 129
Parkinson, Major William, 17–18, 109
Pater, Walter, 14, 16, 34, 40, 76, 113, 140, 158, 160, 182
Patti, Adelina, 29
Paul Pry (Poole), 73n, 84
Paulin, Tom, 96
Payn, James, 128, 156, 161
Pearson, Hesketh, 131

Peel, Arthur, 84
Peel, Bobby, 77
Penny Dreadfuls, 158–62
Pigott, E. F. Smyth, 89
Pilcher, Percy, 172
Pinero, Arthur Wing, 31, 118, 141, 167, 178, 194
    Notorious Mrs Ebbsmith, 30, 51, 87–92
    Second Mrs Tanqueray, 30, 65, 87–8, 92
'Playfair, I.' (James Wilson), 75, 132
Poe, Edgar Allan, 106, 109–10, 160, 170
Pornography, 161–3
Powell, Kerry, 45
Preston North End FC, 44, 59, 86–7
Prinsep, Valentine, 25, 121
Problem plays, 88, 158; *see also* Jones, H. A.; Pinero, Arthur Wing
Promenade Concerts, 172–3
Punch, 4, 7, 10, 16–17, 22–3, 34, 37, 38, 39, 41, 46, 49, 53, 66, 69, 72, 73n, 74n, 78, 88, 92, 103, 109, 110, 113, 118, 121, 134, 135, 143, 149, 150–1, 153, 155, 161, 178, 184, 190, 192, 195, 196, 203

Quarterly Review, The, 50, 158, 178
Queensberry, Marquess of, 11, 74n, 81, 128–9, 198
    libel trial, 98–102
    relations with Rosebery, 11–12, 13, 103, 118
    relations with Wilde, 12–14, 70, 72, 81, 95, 109, 128, 130

Raby, Peter, 46
Rae, Simon, 156
Raffalovich, André, 106, 132
Ranjitsinhji, Kumar Shri, 154–6
Read, Harry, 27
Read, James Canham, 27–8, 156, 189
Reader, Joe, 112
Rebell, Hugues, 165
Redway, George, 192–3
Reed, E. T., 37, 41, 65, 113
Reed, W. W., 154
Reynolds, Mary, 173
Reynolds's Newspaper, 3, 22, 25, 104, 109, 131, 153, 173, 196, 198
Rhodes, Cecil, 54, 121, 212–13
Rhys, Ernest, 33, 116
Richardson, Angelique, 67
Richardson, Tom, 77, 155
Richmond, William Blake, 121
Ridge, W. Pett, 177–8
Ridley, Matthew White, 84, 153, 160–1
Rivez, Henry de, 146
Riviere, Briton, 121
Riviere, H. G., 121
Robbins, Ruth, 71
Roberts, Brian, 12, 109

Robertson, W. Graham, 127
Robins, Elizabeth, 48, 62
Robinson, Mrs ('The Sibyl'), 95, 214
Robson, Sophia ('Madame Minerva'), 95
Rosebery, Harry, 136n
Rosebery, Lord, 1, 2, 4, 8–10, 59, 60, 61, 73n, 84, 118, 133, 151, 171, 174n
  connections with Wilde case, 82, 84, 99–100, 118, 134–5
  Honours Lists, 54–5, 141–3, 147
  resigns as PM, 147–8
  sexuality of, 13, 76, 141
Ross, David, 93
Ross, Robbie, 46, 69, 81, 107, 109, 116, 132, 183, 206
Rossetti, Christina, 35
Rossetti, Dante Gabriel, 43, 80, 109, 168, 208
Rossetti, William Michael, 35, 208
Rothenstein, William, 38, 115, 167–8
Rowbotham, Sheila, 121
Ruskin, John, 80, 179
Russell, Charles, 81
Russell, Countess, 109, 123

Saha, Louis, 136n
Saintsbury, George, 80
Saker, Mrs Edward, 50
Sala, G. A., 208
Salisbury, Lord, 55, 95, 151, 211–12, 213
Salmon, Richard, 50
Sambourne, Linley, 38, 41
Sanders, Richard, 43, 59, 87
Sargent, John Singer, 51, 121, 122
Saturday Review, 10, 14–15, 17, 29, 34, 42, 64, 68, 89, 121, 139, 141, 145, 163, 166, 177
Sardou, Victorien, 47, 92
Saunderson, Reginald, 26–8, 73n
Savoy, The, 165, 171, 203, 210
Schmaltz, Herbert, 25–6, 121
Schroeder, Horst, 136n
Schultz, Walter, 24–5, 29
Schwabe, Maurice, 99, 107, 117, 128
Scott, Clement, 47, 53, 90, 91, 186
Seaman, Owen, 9, 141–2, 147
Sharp, Evelyn, 38, 176
Shaw, George Bernard, 2, 18, 21, 24, 46, 54, 65, 74n, 80, 89–90, 126–7, 136n, 185
  reviews *An Ideal Husband*, 47
  reviews *Guy Domville*, 53, 167, 178
  reviews *Importance of Being Earnest*, 72
  reviews *Notorious Mrs Ebbsmith*, 90–1, 167
  reviews *Trilby*, 187–8
Sheffield United FC, 59, 74n, 86
Shelley, Edward, 103, 130
Sherard, Robert, 58, 108, 144, 174, 182, 206–7, 209
Shiel, M. P., 106, 108

Showalter, Elaine, 39, 189
Sickert, Walter, 37, 38, 104, 122, 164
Silver, Walter Hugh, 73n
Small Heath FC, 44, 59, 86, 182, 207
Smith, Charles, 200
Smith, David, 179
Smithers, Leonard, 163, 166, 210–11
Somerset, Lord Arthur, 19
Somerset, Lord Henry, 18
Sorrows of Satan, The see Corelli, Marie
Southampton St Mary's FC, 59
Southworth, Jack, 44
Spencer, Lord, 134
Spielmann, M. H., 120–1
Spirit Lamp, The, 18, 19
Springhall, John, 160
Sproson, Enoch and William, 56
Stanley, Edward, 12
Star, The, 102, 109, 114, 154, 196, 198
Stead, W. T., 65, 132, 139, 161, 191, 207
Steer, Philip Wilson, 37, 38, 122
Stenbock, Eric, 116
Stephen, Julia, 62, 147
Stephens, Richard, 205–6
Stevenson, Robert Louis, 15, 19, 32, 34–5, 209
Stoddart, Andrew, 6, 77, 136n, 156
Stoke FC, 44, 59, 112, 113
Stoker, Bram, 72, 139, 193
Stokes, John, 132, 166
Stokes, Walter, 205–6
Stott, Edward, 121
Strauss, Andrew, 6
Street, G. S., 34, 91, 127
Sturgis, Matthew, 107, 126
Stutfield, Hugh, 141, 142–3
Sudell, Billy, 87
Sullivan, Arthur, 54
Sullivan, James, 196, 198
Sullivan, Robert, 146
Sumner, Margaret L., 38
Sunderland FC, 6, 43–4, 59, 86, 87, 110
Sutherland, Birdie, 139
Swinburne, Algernon Charles, 33, 35, 109, 141, 168, 192, 193, 201, 202, 208, 213
Symonds, John Addington, 158
Symons, Arthur, 16, 18, 21, 33, 103, 107, 145, 162–6, 195, 210

Tabner, Brian, 43
Taylor, Alfred Waterhouse Somerset, 100–1, 108, 114, 118, 128, 138
Taylor, Frank and Martha, 83–4
Taylor, George, 189
Temperatures, high, 146, 174n
Temperatures, low, 61
Tennis, 153, 156
Terris, William, 185
Terry, Ellen, 53–4, 167
Thomas, Brandon, 29, 102

Thompson, Francis, 33, 137, 145
Thompson, Sir John, 54
Thurschwell, Pamela, 189
Tichborne Claimant, The, 128, 136n, 148
Tilley, Vesta, 29, 188
Times, The, 8, 9, 12, 28, 34, 35, 54, 77–8,
    83, 84, 148, 149, 155, 158, 172, 173,
    194, 198, 213–14
Tomson, Graham R., 38
Townsend, Charlie, 171
Townsend, F. H., 104
Trilby see Du Maurier, George
Trilby homages and borrowings, 188–9
Tucknor, R. J., 129
Tuke, Henry Scott, 122–3
Turner, E. S., 20
Turner, Henry, 73n, 109
Turner, Reggie, 102, 107
Tyrell, Kittie, 29–30

Unwin, T. Fisher, 36, 98, 132

Vaughton, Howard, 182
Verlaine, Paul, 103, 145, 164
Victoria, HRH Queen, 9, 11, 12, 56, 73n,
    84, 147–8, 175
Vincent, Crawford, 116

Wackerbath, Alice, 153
Walkley, A. B., 47, 72
Ward, Albert, 77
Ward, Mrs Humphry, 34, 51, 103
Waterhouse, John William, 43, 120
Waterlow, Ernest, 121
Watson, George S., 122
Watson, William, 33, 103–4, 107, 141,
    143–4, 195, 200–1, 213
Watts, G. F., 51
Watts, J. Stockwell, 125, 200
Watts, Theodore, 168, 193
Webb, Beatrice, 60, 167
Webster, Augusta, 34
Wednesday FC, The, 44, 85, 87, 113
Wells, H. G., 18, 46–7, 50–1, 56, 64, 68,
    71–2, 97, 105–6, 113, 142, 152–3, 176,
    179–81, 195
    Time Machine, The, 36, 52, 135, 170,
        194
    On *Jude the Obscure*, 203–4
West Bromich Albion FC, 6, 59, 85, 86, 87,
    110–12, 182, 208
Weyman, Stanley, 34
Wharton, Arthur, 86
Whistler, James McNeill, 168, 180, 188, 210

Wilde, Constance, 20, 102, 114–15, 132,
    182
Wilde, Cyril and Vyvyan, 32, 115, 132
Wilde, Lady ('Speranza'), 128
Wilde, Oscar, 2, 3–4, 7, 8, 12–13, 18, 32,
    33, 40, 44, 58, 69–70, 76–7, 80, 81, 82,
    95, 106, 120, 154, 156, 163–4, 168,
    180, 189, 214n
    'A Few Maxims for the Instruction of the
        Over-Educated', 16–17, 19
    An Ideal Husband, 19, 30–1, 45–9, 75,
        108
    bankruptcy, 140–1, 183, 206
    first criminal trial, 114, 116–18
    Green Carnation controversy, 13–17
    Importance of Being Earnest, The, 2,
        70–2, 75, 113, 114
    'Phrases and Philosophies for the Use of
        the Young', 18–19, 69, 98, 99, 117
    Picture of Dorian Gray, The, 16, 19, 21,
        49, 98, 99, 117, 126, 136n, 158, 160,
        171
    prison experiences, 108–9, 112–13,
        138–9, 174, 182–3
    Queensberry Libel trial *see* Queensberry
    sale of effects, 114–15
    second criminal trial, 125, 127, 129–33
    transfer to Reading Gaol, 207
Wildy, A. H. (Official Receiver), 199, 206
Wills, Mr Justice, 28, 73n, 109, 128, 130,
    138, 205–6
Wilton, George, 129–30
Windholz, Anne, 105
Wolverhampton Wanderers FC ('Wolves'),
    6, 44, 59, 85, 86
Woman Who Did, The see Allen, Grant
Wood, Henry, 172
Wood, William and Alfred, 108, 117, 129
Woolf, Virginia, 3, 62
Woolwich Arsenal FC, 43, 52, 59
Wright, Henry, 173
Wright, Sydney, 72
Wright, Thomas, 115
Wyndham, Charles, 108
Wyndham, George, 12, 102

Yeames, William Frederick, 123–4
Yeats, W.B., 33, 62, 93–4, 128, 137, 210,
    212
Yellow Book, The, 4, 20, 34, 35, 36–42,
    103–6, 113, 160, 193, 210

Zangwill, Israel, 34, 61
Zola, Émile, 56, 79, 161